Marmalade Days: Winter

Carol Taylor Bond

Edited by Joyce Beecher King

Includes Day-by-Day Activities In All
Subjects, Bulletin Boards, Son
Fingerplays, Games, Poems, Flar
Board Activities, Recipes, Workshee
Patterns, and More!

D1416178

The Patterns, Pictures, Etc. in this book may be reproduced for use only
by the purchaser. Other reproduction of book parts must be with written
permission of the publisher.

Copyright © 1987. Carol Bond

Published by Ɖ PARTNER PRESS
Box 124
Livonia, MI 48152

ISBN 0-933212-36-4

Distributed by:

Gryphon House
3706 Otis Street
Mt. Rainier, Maryland 20822

To my winter baby,

Destin Elizabeth

and

To Brantley,

Her loving father.

Acknowledgements

I wish to thank the following people for their assistance, encouragement, and support: Charlotte Murchison for the endless hours she has devoted to typing, revising, suggesting, and listening; Marilla M. Bond for the time and loving care she has given to my daughter, Destin; my son, Scott, for his "Everyday Errand Service"; and to my former students at Ruby-Wise Elementary, Kolin, Louisiana, for whom my first ideas were created.

Also, thanks to Susan Myrick for her faith in my abilities; my brother, Bill Taylor, for his computer assistance; Donna Deville and Jennifer Kappel for ideas shared; Marion Sullivan for her "librarian's assistance"; Greg Gravel for his friendly legal advice; Cheryl Warner for testing recipes; the kind and helpful staff of the Rapides Parish Public Library, Alexandria, Louisiana; and to my family and friends for their encouragement.

I gratefully acknowledge the authors, publishers, and friends listed below, for granting permission to reprint materials in this book. Every effort has been made to trace the ownership and to acknowledge the use of materials not written by the author. If any error inadvertently occurred, please notify the publisher for corrections in future editions.

Ann Murchison for "Making a Wreath 1."

Boy Scouts of America, National Office, Irving, Texas, for "When I Was a Boy" action game, "Santa's Annual Visit" action story, and "Mr. Washington's Sad Song."

Liz Cromwell and Dixie Hibner for fingerplays from Finger Frolics, published by Partner Press, Livonia, Michigan.

Educational Service, Inc., Stevensville, Michigan, for the song "Teddy Bear" from the Spice Series book, Note.

Table of Contents

Introduction - The Unit Approach

The units in Marmalade Days were developed in my classroom over a period of six years. When I began teaching, I had books of the skills and concepts to be taught, a collection of ideas and methods, and a roomful of eager and very active five-year-olds. I needed a program—one which included these skills and concepts, used a variety of methods and materials, and "fit" the young child with his or her natural enthusiasm and short attention span. I found my answer in the unit approach.

The unit approach is the correlation of learning activities around a central theme. One benefit of using this approach is that high interest is maintained in all subject areas. Learning basic math skills by making a Christmas Number Booklet or counting flannel board holiday symbols is much more stimulating to a child than rote counting or flash cards. Another "super plus" of this program is that many skills can be integrated into one activity, making for effective use of time and an enriched program. Thus, in presenting the "Cherry Tree Legend Puppet Play" in the George Washington Unit, the children not only learn about George Washington, but also develop speaking and listening skills, learn appropriate audience conduct, and experience enjoyment in learning.

Units are not meant to totally replace the class curriculum. You may teach the units as presented or choose different ideas for segregated use. Other programs such as alphabet study or sequential math skills can be taught as usual or can be altered to reflect the unit theme. For example, a math lesson taught during the Valentine's Day Unit becomes adding hearts or Cupids. In addition, the unit activities can be easily adapted to the various levels of your students.

About the Book

Purpose

The purpose of Marmalade Days is to provide the teacher with complete learning units. Included are activities for each subject, step-by-step directions, ready-made worksheets, patterns and pictures of finished projects, words and actions of fingerplays and action songs, tunes or music for songs, recipes, and letters to parents. The teacher, therefore, is free to plan, gather and process materials, and concentrate on the actual teaching and evaluation processes. Due to copyright restrictions, the words to some songs and stories could not be included. In most cases, the titles of the books or records containing these are listed.

Format and Methods Suggestions

Introductory Page - Each unit begins with an introductory page which includes the proposed time of the unit, the unit objectives, and the room environment.

Proposed Time - The time indicated will be extended if the unit is being used in a supplementary manner.

Objectives - The objectives state the purpose of each unit.

Room Environment - The room environment includes bulletin boards, door, table and wall displays, and centers. Most of these are made with childrens assistance, or they are constructed using the children's art projects.

Daily Topics - Each unit is divided into daily topics. For example, the daily topics of the unit Winter are "Introduction," "Winter Weather," "Winter Clothes and Activities," "Animals and Birds in Winter," and "Eskimos."

Subject Headings - Each daily topic includes the following subject headings: Concept Information, the Language Arts - Social Studies - Science block, Art, Math, Music - Movement - Games, Story Time, and Extras.

Concept Information - The concept information provides the teacher with background information on the daily topic. From this, the teacher extracts points of interest to be shared with the children during the discussion. Sample vocabulary words are underlined.

Discussion - Discussions are used to establish and introduce the daily topic. Using the concept information, a foundation is established for the daily activities. Discussions should be more than just lectures. A variety of methods can be used to present the simple discussions in each unit. Have the children role-play or close their eyes and "visualize" the information. Place items relating to the information in a sack and take them out at the appropriate time. Dress up as a character described in the discussion, and let the children interview you. Before or after the discussion, hold a brainstorming session on the daily topic. Read a book or show a film which covers the subject matter. Use questions to check for understanding. Preceding the discussion, hold up pictures or "real" objects. Call on the children to tell what they know about the picture or object. Use the pictures and objects to strengthen understanding as you relate the information. Use your imagination and vary discussion methods. The children will respond with their interest and excitement.

Vocabulary Words - Vocabulary words may be written on the chalkboard and defined before the discussion or defined during the discussion. During the discussion, define a word by offering an alternative word or brief description. Be sure to pick up the discussion at the point before the defined word so that the thought may be completed.

Language Arts - Social Studies - Science Block - In the Language Arts - Social Studies - Science block, a variety of activities are offered which further develop the unit concept. You may substitute appropriate books and films which are available in your area. Reproducible sheets and patterns are found in the Patterns, Pictures, Etc. section following each unit.

Art - On most days, several art activities are offered. This allows you to choose the art activity based on skill levels, time allotment, and the availability of materials. Even when patterns are used in the unit art activities, encourage creativity by offering choices of colors, materials, and design methods. It is also a good idea to set up an art station for small groups at activity time. Include easels and paints, clay, crayons, scrap paper, scissors, glue, and so forth. This practice allows the children to create artwork with few restrictions. Patterns and pictures of art projects are found in the Patterns, Pictures, Etc. section following each unit.

Math - The Math section offers nonsequential activities which teach basic skills such as counting, one-to-one correspondence, number values, spatial concepts, and sets. Ready-made sheets are found in the Patterns, Pictures, Etc. section following each unit.

Music - Movement - Games - Music - Movement - Games contains songs just for singing, action songs, movement activities, and games. Many of the songs are sung to the tune of other popular songs as indicated. When necessary, the music is supplied in the Patterns, Pictures, Etc. section.

Story Time - Story Time is a time set aside each day, preferably before nap time or after lunch, for the children to relax and enjoy a story. You may substitute any books or stories pertaining to the topic theme.

Extras - Extra activities include the Kindergarten Kitchen, field trips, presentations, parties, concept reviews, and the evaluation process.

Kindergarten Kitchen - For cooking activities, assemble ingredients and tools. Write the recipe on an experience chart illustrating each ingredient. At the bottom of the page, draw and label the tools used to prepare the recipe. Spread the ingredients and tools on a covered table. Read the recipe to the class, passing around samples of the ingredients. Encourage the children to describe the appearance, feel, taste, and smell of each ingredient. Present each tool and discuss the appearance, use, and operation of each. Allow the children to do as much of the measuring, mixing, and pouring as possible. A food fund can be set up for expenses.

Field Trips - The most successful field trips are those which are well planned. Make arrangements well in advance with the proper authorities. Explain the points of interest appropriate for the age of your class. Several days before the trip, confirm the arrangements.

Send home letters explaining the trip and requesting chaperones. Permission slips should be included. A chaperone will be needed for every three to six children depending on age. Do not forget name tags.

When you return from the trip, do not forget to send a signed thank-you note. If desired, include the children's pictures of "what they liked best."

<u>Culmination Activities and Concept Review</u> - Culmination activities and concept reviews serve to "wrap up" the unit of study.

<u>Evaluation Process</u> - Along with daily observations, checking of work, and observation during culmination activities and concept reviews, the children may be tested individually for concept understanding. Use a checklist based on the unit objectives and concept information of each daily topic. A space is provided for this at the end of each unit.

<u>Patterns, Pictures, Etc.</u> - This section follows each unit and contains pictures of bulletin boards and displays, patterns, project pictures, ready-made worksheets, and letters to parents. It also contains words and music to some of the songs in the units.

Valuable Junk

Below is a list of valuable junk you will be using with each unit. The corresponding activity title is in parentheses. You may wish to send this list to parents at the beginning of the year or each unit.

Hanukkah

cardboard egg cartons or wooden spools (Dreidel)

Christmas

coat hangers   (Joy mobiles)

old magazines   (Christmas Goodies Discussion)

baby food jars or margarine or frosting tubs (Christmas Smells Jars or Tubs)

plastic utensils, plates, cups   (Manners)

small styrofoam or plastic cups   (Silver Bells)

scrap material   (Patchwork Bells)

plastic milk jugs or plastic container tops   (Stained Glass Bells)

pine cones   (Pine Cone Angels)

toilet paper rolls   (Cardboard Christmas Candle)

shallow boxes or children's shoebox tops   (Shadow Box Candle)

toilet paper rolls   (Shadow Box Candle)

scrap material   (Christmas Pretzel Wreaths)

trimmed branches from Christmas trees   (Making a Wreath 2, Evergreen Balls)

pine cones   (Growing Baby Christmas Trees)

margarine tubs   (Growing Baby Christmas Trees)

tin pie plates   (Tin Punch Trees)

corrugated cardboard dividers   (Tin Punch Trees)

pine cones   (Pine Cone Trees)

mesh vegetable bags   (A Christmas Tree for the Birds)

pickle jars and tops   (Bread Dough Cookie Jars)

macaroni and cheese or similar boxes   (Coupon Holder I)

oatmeal boxes and tops   (Pig String Holder)

strawberry baskets   (Christmas Goody Baskets)

old Christmas cards   (Christmas Card Discussion, Alike and Different Match, Jigsaw Puzzle Cards, Christmas Peepboxes)

shoeboxes   (Christmas Peepboxes)

old magazines   (Christmas Wishes)

old crayons   (Elf Hats)

old muffin tins   (Elf Hats)

New Year's

old calendars   (Calendar Activity)

Winter

styrofoam packing squiggles, scrap batting, white scrap material, white
    fake fur scraps, white buttons   (Winter Scene)

old clothing catalogs   (Dressing Sequence Sheet)

pine cones   (Pine Cone Bird Feeders)

Martin Luther King, Jr.

burlap sacks   (Burlap Sack Race)

Groundhog Day

oatmeal boxes (18 oz.)   (Groundhog Puppets)

Abraham Lincoln

corrugated cardboard box   (Abraham Lincoln Learning Center)

baby food jars   (Lincoln Penny Center)

small box, margarine tubs   (Lincoln Penny Center)

old plastic dishpan   (Plowing the Fields - Demonstration)

old magazines   (Abraham Lincoln Alphabet and Blab School Demonstration)

baby food jars   (Float or Sink Experiment)

coffee can and shoebox   (Over Your Head Drill Game)

orange juice cans   (Stovepipe Hat - Pencil Can)

coat hangers   (Lincoln's Head-Dried Apple)

toilet tissue rolls   (Lincoln Head - Dried Apple)

small jars   (How Many Pennies?)

Valentine's Day

old magazines   (My Favorite Things, bulletin board)

corrugated cardboard box   (Smart Hearts Learning Center)

old wiping cloths   (Smart Hearts Learning Center)

old magazines   (Poem and Stand-Up Collage)

sponge sheets used for packing   (Sponge Heart Prints)

old magazines   (Looking for Mr. Cupid Puppet Skit)

old newspapers   (Drying Flowers)

shoeboxes   (Drying Flowers)

large wooden thread spools   (Hearts and Flowers)

styrofoam egg cartons   (Hearts and Flowers)

old Valentine cards   (Card Mobiles, Valentine Cards Discussion, The C Bag)

shoeboxes   (Valentine Card Holder)

white clothes hangers   (Card Mobiles)

George Washington

corrugated cardboard box   (George Washington Learning Center)

tin cans   (Tin Lanterns)

newspapers   (Tin Lanterns)

large wide-mouth jar   (Cherry Drop)

General

aluminum pie plates   (mixing paint)

corrugated cardboard dividers   (clay boards, etc.)

yarn   (art projects)

HANUKKAH

PROPOSED TIME: 1 day

UNIT OBJECTIVES

To develop understanding and appreciation of Hanukkah
To explain the origins of Hanukkah
To develop understanding of today's celebration of Hanukkah

ROOM ENVIRONMENT - BULLETIN BOARDS

"Lighting the Hanukkah Menorah"

Cover the bulletin board with blue paper and trim with a white border. Staple the title at the top. Make a Hanukkah Menorah, as shown on page 9, from brown kraft paper. Cut nine candles with wicks from white paper. Set aside one candle. This will be the shamos candle which will be placed in the middle cup. Staple the eight candles on the Hanukkah Menorah.

For the flames, cut nine yellow circles and nine blue circles. Glue each yellow circle to a blue circle. Use stick pins to mount eight of the circles, with the blue sides out, behind the eight candles. Glue the top of the ninth (shamos) candle to the bottom (blue side) of the ninth circle. Mount in the center of the Hanukkah Menorah with a stick pin.

To demonstrate lighting the Hanukkah Menorah, remove the shamos candle and "light" by flipping to the yellow side. Let a child use the shamos to touch the first candle. At the same time, remove the stick pin and flip the circle to the yellow side to signify that the candle is lit. Reinsert the stick pin. Repeat the procedure letting different children "light" each candle. (Proceed from right to left.)

ROOM ENVIRONMENT - DISPLAYS

Table Display

On a table, display a 9-branched Hanukkah Menorah, a wooden or clay dreidel, a ceramic oil lamp, a mezuzah (small scroll inside a case hung on a doorpost), and picture books on Hanukkah. Encourage parents and children to contribute to the display.

HANUKKAH

CONCEPT INFORMATION

At the end of November or in December, Jewish people celebrate a holiday called Hanukkah, the Festival of Lights.

Over 2,000 years ago, Jewish people lived in a place called Judea (now Israel). Antiochus, the ruler of Judea, demanded that the Jews stop worshipping God and instead pray to his Greek gods. When the Jews refused to do this, Antiochus sent his soldiers to take over the Jewish Temple in the city of Jerusalem. The soldiers burned the Jewish holy books and put up statues of Greek gods in the Temple.

The Maccabees, a Jewish priest named Mattathias and his five sons, decided to fight back. They were joined by other Jewish people. After three long years, they recaptured Jerusalem and reclaimed their Temple, decorating it with gold crowns and small shields.

When the Temple was completely restored, the Maccabees proclaimed a holiday called Hanukkah which means dedication in Hebrew. The Hanukkah legend says that the priests wished to light the Temple Menorah or candelabrum, but only had enough oil to burn for one day. They used this oil to light the Menorah, and it burned for eight days.

Today, Hanukkah lasts for eight days. Each night families light their Hanukkah Menorahs. The Hanukkah Menorah has nine cups for candles. Eight of the cups symbolize the eight days of the legend. The ninth cup holds the "shamos" (servant) candle which is used to light the other candles. Each night the shamos and another candle are lighted. Some Jewish children receive money or "gelt" on the first night the Menorah is lighted; some receive a small gift on each night of the celebration.

Families share special food and stories during Hanukkah. Some of the special foods are: "latkes," or potato pancakes with applesauce; "couscous," a cracked wheat dish; and "hamentash," a triangular-shaped cookie.

The stories include the Hanukkah legend and tales of the Maccabees' struggle to recapture Jerusalem.

Games are another enjoyable part of the Hanukkah celebration. Jewish children enjoy playing cards, and solving riddles and puzzles. The most well-known game is Dreidels. The children spin a lettered top called a dreidel to win or lose nuts and candy.

For Jewish families, Hanukkah is a time of being together and giving thanks.

LANGUAGE ARTS - SOCIAL STUDIES - SCIENCE

Discussion

Relate the concept information, defining the vocabulary words. Show pictures from Hanukkah by Norma Simon or similar references. Locate Judea, now Israel, on a map. Show pictures of various Jewish symbols such as the Menorah, the Hanukkah Menorah, the Star of David, a pitcher (symbolizes the small container of oil in the Hanukkah legend), a crown, a shield, a dreidel, etc.

Hanukkah Concept Information Review

The star of David is the symbol of Judaism as the cross is the symbol for Christianity. Cut two construction paper triangles per child. Direct the children to glue one triangle on top of the other, as shown, to make the Star of David. Read each statement below. If the statement is true, the children hold up the Star of David. After the children recognize a false statement, ask a volunteer to correct it.

1. Antiochus was the ruler of Judea. (true)
2. Judea is now called Italy. (false)
3. Antiochus' soldiers knocked down the Jewish Temple in Jerusalem. (false)
4. Mattathias and his five sons were called the Maccabees. (true)
5. After three years of fighting, the Maccabees reclaimed their Temple. (true)
6. The Maccabees decorated the front of the Temple with Menorahs. (false)
7. Hanukkah is the Festival of Lights. (true)
8. The Hanukkah legend says the Menorah burned for nine days. (false)
9. The middle candle is called the shamos candle. (true)
10. During Hanukkah, some Jewish children receive a small gift each day. (true)

Hanukkah Alike and Different Sheet

Duplicate and distribute the sheet (page 10). The students look at the Jewish symbols in each row and circle the one that is different. Color the symbols.

Fingerplay - "Nine Little Candles"

Nine little candles all in a row. (Hold up 5 fingers of left hand, thumb and 3 fingers of right hand)

The middle one said, "I'm all aglow." (Lower all fingers, raise thumb of left hand)

The first one said, "My light is bright." (Keep left thumb raised and raise ring finger of right hand)

The second said, "I burn day and night." (Keep others raised, raise middle finger of right hand)

The third one said, "I'm number three." (Others raised, raise pointer of right hand)

The fourth one said, "Oh, don't forget me." (Others raised, raise thumb of right hand)

The fifth one said, "It's now my turn." (Others raised, raise pointer of left hand)

The sixth one said, "I like to burn." (Others raised, raise middle finger of left hand)

The seventh one said, "We're such a sight." (Others raised, raise ring finger of left hand.

The eighth one said, "For the Festival of Lights." (Others raised, raise pinky finger of left hand)

So the little candles burned, and proud were they (Keep 9 fingers up)

To share the spirit of this holiday. (Keep 9 fingers up)

Pass the Gifts - Following Directions Activity

Purchase a lollipop for each child. Individually gift-wrap by gathering small pieces of white tissue paper around the lollipop ends and securing with pieces of blue ribbon or yarn. Leave the sticks exposed. Ask the children to form a circle. Give every child, except one, a Hanukkah gift. Designate a signal to begin and use verbal directions below to keep the gifts "traveling" around the circle. Frequently stop the action with a signal or word. The child without a gift drops out, but gets to take one of the gifts from the circle with him or her. The game continues until there is one child standing. This child receives a sticker award in addition to a lollipop gift. Let everyone open their Hanukkah gifts and enjoy them.

Suggested Verbal Actions -

Pass the gifts to the right
Faster, faster
Now slower, slower

Pass the gifts to the left
Slower, slower
Now faster, faster

Hold the gifts high and pass
Faster, faster

Hold the gifts low and pass

Pass the gifts behind your knees

Pass the gifts with both hands
Slower, slower

Pass the gifts with your right hands

Pass the gifts with your left hands

Pass the gifts behind your necks
Faster, faster
Now slower, slower

Pass the gifts behind your backs
Now slower, slower
Now faster, faster

Note: You may wish to tie a yarn bracelet to the children's right wrists to help with the right and left directions.

ART

Dreidels (Jewish Spinning Tops)

Preparation - Duplicate the Dreidel sheet (page 12). Make a chart of the letters and their meanings for display purposes. Collect cardboard egg cartons or wooden spools and wooden dowels. If using the spools, purchase dowels which will fit snugly within the holes of the spools. If using the egg cartons, cut apart the egg cups. The dowels should be cut approximately 3" long (see note below). Use a pencil sharpener to sharpen one end. Give each child an egg cup or spool and a dowel piece. Set out markers or tempera, paintbrushes, and glue. Display the Dreidel Chart.

Procedure - Use the sharpened dowel to punch a hole in the center of the egg cup. Insert the dowel and push through the hole. The open end of the egg cup will be on top. Dab with glue to secure. Draw or paint a different Hebrew letter (see Chart) on each side of the dreidel. If using spools, draw lines to designate the four sides. Before the dreidel is taken home, attach the Dreidel sheet with tape.

Note: You will need to experiment with different lengths of dowels to see which will spin best with the size egg cups or spools you are using.

Note: The Dreidel game is explained under Music - Movement - Games.

Paper Weave Hanukkah Menorahs

Preparation - Duplicate the Paper Weave Hanukkah Menorah (page 13) on white construction paper. Give each child a copy, a sheet of blue, a sheet of yellow, and a half-sheet of orange construction paper. Set out scissors and glue.

Procedure - Cut out the Menorah. Cut the blue construction paper into ½" x 12" strips. Beginning at the bottom of the menorah and working upward, weave the first blue strip over and under, over and under the branches of the Menorah. The next strip will be woven under and over, under and over. Continue weaving in this manner, stopping an inch below the top. Dab glue to secure the ends of the strips to the Menorah. Dry.

Trim excess. Glue the Menorah to the sheet of yellow construction paper.
Cut out orange flames and glue above each candle.

Note: Because cutting the Menorah is somewhat difficult, you may wish to
cut out each child's duplicated Menorah beforehand.

MATH

Hanakkah Flannel Board Symbols

From felt or pellon, cut out ten each of the following shapes: six-pointed
stars, candles, dreidels, pitchers, crowns, and shields (see Patterns,
Pictures, Etc., page 14). Place the symbols near the flannel board. Call
on a child to place three different symbols on the flannel board. Lead the
class in counting the three symbols. Repeat the procedure using different
children and numbers. To emphasize the concept of sets, make a yarn
circle on the flannel board. Call on a child to make a set of nine
dreidels, four crowns, and so forth. To include addition and subtraction,
ask a child to place six symbols on the flannel board; then add or remove
two symbols. Count the total or remainder.

MUSIC - MOVEMENT - GAMES

Song - "Dreidel, Dreidel, Little Top"
Tune: "Twinkle, Twinkle, Little Star"

Dreidel, dreidel, little top,

Spinning, spinning 'til you drop,

Landing on the side you choose,

Will I win or will I lose?

Dreidel, dreidel, little top,

Spinning, spinning 'til you drop.

Game - Spinning the Dreidel

Preparation - Purchase plenty of penny candy and nuts, and place in a
bowl for each group. Teach the meaning of the Hebrew letters on each
side of the dreidel. Display the Dreidel Chart (see Art) so that it is
visible to all groups. Divide the class into small groups so that the
children don't lose interest waiting for their turns. Give each group a
dreidel (see Art) and a bowl of goodies. Decide on a "forfeit" amount of
candy and nuts (e.g., two pieces).

Procedure - The candy and nuts are divided equally among the players in a
group. Direct the players to contribute so many nuts or pieces of candy
to the "kitty." These are placed in the bowl. The players keep their

remaining portions nearby. The players take turns spinning the dreidel and reading the letter on top after the dreidel falls. If the letter is "he," the player gets one half of the kitty. If the letter is "shin," the player puts the forfeit amount (in this case, 2) into the kitty. If the letter is "nun," nothing happens; and the next child spins. If the letter is "gimel," the player gets all that is in the kitty. When this happens, all players must again contribute to restock the "kitty." The game is over when one player wins all the candy and nuts, or when time runs out.

Note: As the dreidel spins, the children may repeat this traditional chant:

> I have a little dreidel, I made it out of clay,
>
> And when it's dry and ready, then with it I will play.

KINDERGARTEN KITCHEN

Latkes (Potato Pancakes)

5 medium potatoes	1/8 teaspoon pepper
1 medium onion	1/2 teaspoon baking powder
2 eggs, slightly beaten	Salad oil
2 tablespoons flour	Prepared applesauce
1 teaspoon salt	

Wash the potatoes thoroughly. Do not peel. Coarsely grate the potatoes, add ice water, and set aside. Using another bowl, finely grate the onions. Stir in the eggs, flour, salt, pepper, and baking powder. Drain the grated potatoes and add to the mixture. Mix thoroughly.

Pour ¼" layer of salad oil into a large skillet and heat over medium heat. When the oil is hot, drop the potato mixture, by heaping tablespoonfuls, into the skillet. Flatten with a slotted spatula. When the edges and underside are brown, turn and brown the other side. Drain on paper towels. Serve warm with prepared applesauce. Yield: approximately 16

CONCEPT EVALUATION

Dear Parents,

On _____, our class will learn about Hanukkah. We
will learn the origins and customs of Hanukkah through games, discussions,
songs, fingerplays, and other activities. Below are ways you can help.

Things To Send: _____

_____

_____

Volunteers Needed To: _____

_____

_____

Follow-Up: At the end of the unit, ask your child to share the following
Hanukkah information and activities:

_____

_____

_____

Thank you for your cooperation.

Sincerely,

Bulletin Board

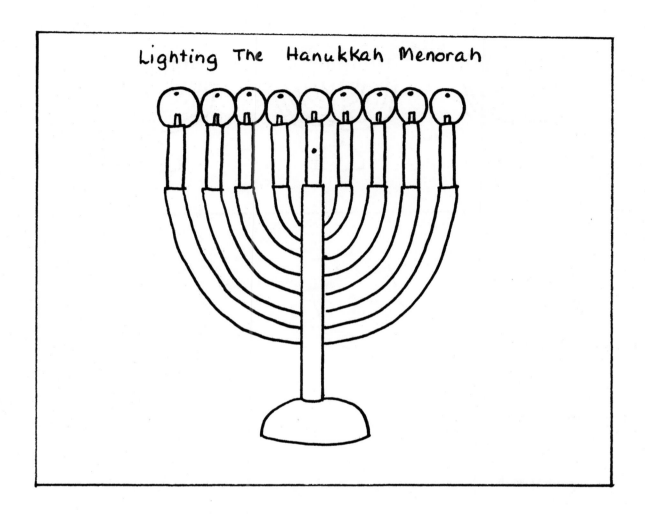

Lighting The Hanukkah Menorah

Hanukkah Alike and Different Sheet
Look at the symbols on each row. Two are alike and one is different. Circle the one that is different. Color the symbols.

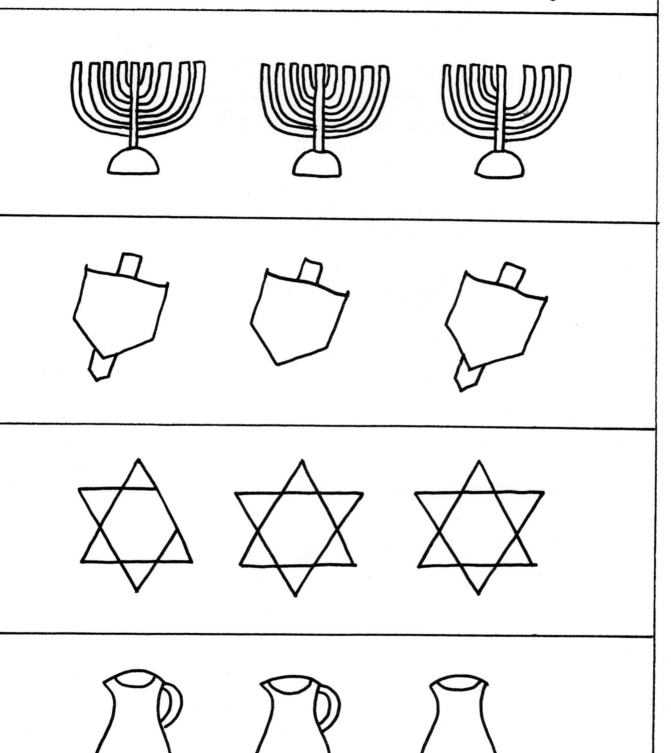

Name:

Examples

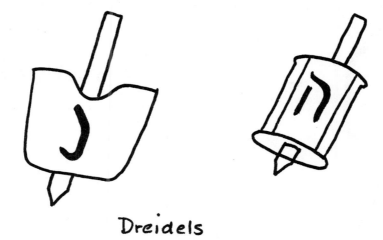

Dreidels

Paper Weave Hanukkah Menorahs

Dreidel Sheet

Hebrew Letter - Yiddish Word - Game Meaning

נ   –   nun   –   nothing

ג   –   gimel   –   get

ה   –   he   –   half

ש   –   shin   –   share

Paper Weave Hanukkah Menorah's

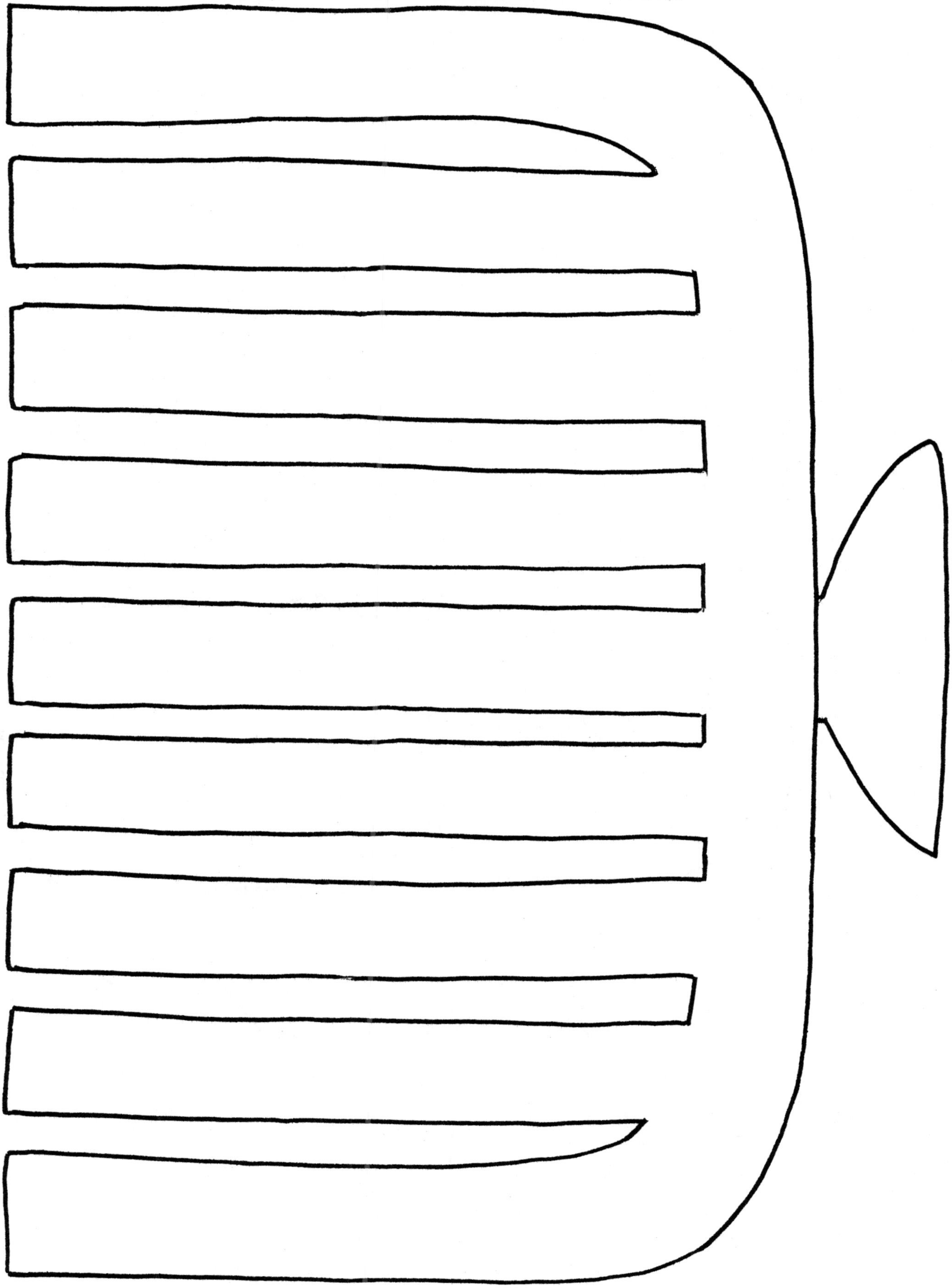

Hanukkah
Flannel Board Symbols
Math

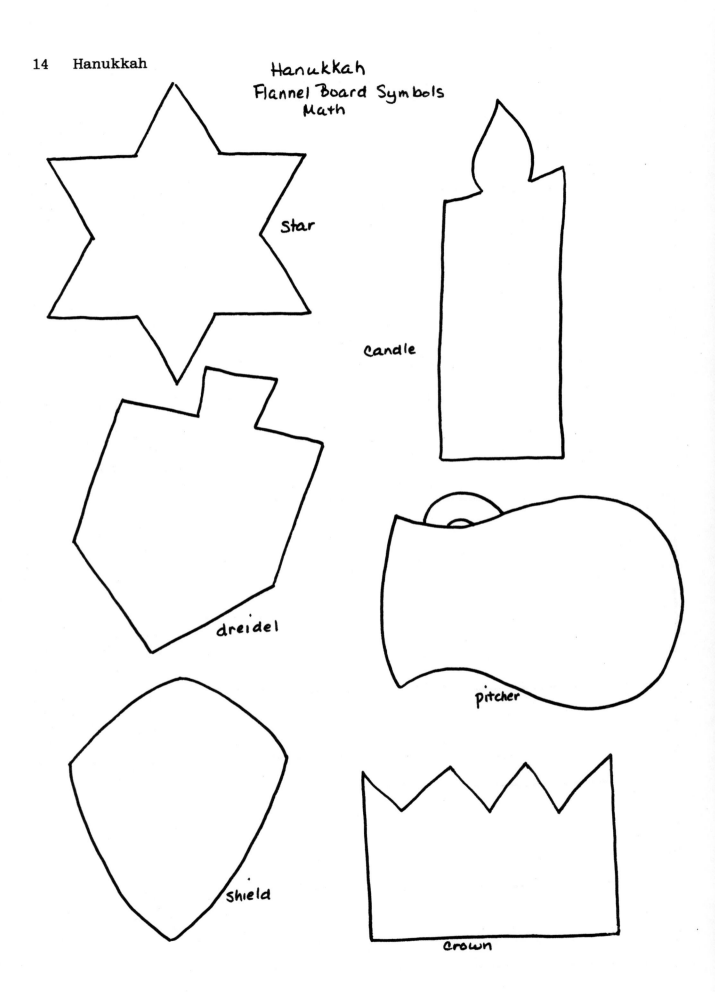

Star

Candle

dreidel

pitcher

shield

crown

SIGNS OF CHRISTMAS

PROPOSED TIME: 17 days

UNIT OBJECTIVES

To develop understanding of Christmas and Christmas symbols
To instill the true spirit of Christmas
To emphasize the meaning of giving
To encourage enjoyment of the holiday season

ROOM ENVIRONMENT - BULLETIN BOARDS

"Visions of Sugarplums"

Cover the top two-thirds of the bulletin board with white paper. Next, cover the bottom one-third with green paper, stapling only the sides and bottom. Using the "Christmas Night Children" (see Art - Day 1), slip each "head," with eyes showing, halfway under the top of the green bulletin board paper. Staple. Mount the "hands" on either side of each head. On the white portion, staple the candy canes and gingerbread men (see Art-Day 2). (See example, page 107.)

Note: Make two rows of sleeping children by covering the top half of the bulletin board with white paper and placing two strips of green paper on the bottom.

"Signs of Christmas"

Make the bulletin board a large Christmas gift by covering it with Christmas wrapping paper, preferably a light color or white with a small design. Use Christmas ribbon or material cut into strips with pinking shears to represent ribbon. Staple one strip vertically and one horizontally so that they cross in the middle of the bulletin board. Make a large bow and staple at the top. Cut a "gift card" from poster paper. Punch a hole at one end and label "Signs of Christmas." Lace a piece of yarn through the hole and staple the yarn under the bow. Use the four sections of the "gift" to display the Christmas symbols made by the children in art. Be sure to include artwork for each child. (See example, page 107.)

ROOM ENVIRONMENT - DISPLAYS

"Hand Tree"

Have the children trace around each hand on green paper. Cut out the paper hands. Decorate with glitter. Once the glitter dries, arrange in a tree shape to determine the size of the triangular backing needed. Cut this triangle from green poster paper or stiff paper. Arrange and glue the hands to cover the triangle. The fingers will be the leaves. Glue a brown strip of construction paper at the bottom to represent the trunk. Cut and glue a container to the trunk and label "Our Hand Tree." (See example, page 108.)

"Paper Chain Tree"

Note: This project requires the cooperative efforts of several classes.

Obtain a cardboard carpet roll and place it in a Christmas tree stand. Have the children make green paper chains. Join all together to make one long chain. Tack and staple one end to the top and wrap around and around and around the roll, forming a Christmas tree shape. While waiting for additional lengths to attach to the chain, clothespin the end of the paper chain to the tree. After the tree is completed, use ornament hooks or paper clips to decorate with paper ornaments from Art.

"Christmas Tree Learning Center"

Cut a tree shape approximately four feet tall from corrugated cardboard. Cover with green felt or bulletin board paper. Cut off the tops of twenty-seven half-pint milk cartons. Spray-paint. Use an ice pick and metal fasteners to attach the cartons in rows on the tree. Label the cartons with each letter of the alphabet. Cut twenty-six strips of paper and write an alphabet letter at the top of each. When placed in the boxes, the letters should be visible. Put all the letter strips in the twenty-seventh box. The children sort the strips into the correct boxes. (See example, page 108.)

Variations: The learning center can be used for different matching activities such as numerals and numeral dots, colors and color words. For interchangeable activities, punch a hole at the front of each milk carton and insert a paper clip; and punch holes in all labels. Different labels can be hung on the cartons. Make additional strips for each activity.

DAY 1 - INTRODUCTION

CONCEPT INFORMATION

On December 25th of each year, we <u>celebrate</u> a very special <u>holiday</u> called Christmas. Christmas is the day when people remember the birth of Jesus Christ who was born in a <u>manger</u> in <u>Bethlehem</u> many years ago. The name Christmas comes from the words "Christ" and "Mass," a church service.

Christmas is an exciting time for everyone. Children make lists to send to Santa Claus. Families buy and <u>decorate</u> Christmas trees, shop for gifts to <u>exchange</u>, and cook wonderful things to eat. Houses and stores are decorated, Christmas <u>carols</u> are sung, and people shout "Merry Christmas" to each other.

There are many Christmas <u>customs</u> and symbols or signs of Christmas. In the next few weeks, we will be learning about these customs and symbols and why we use them at Christmas.

LANGUAGE ARTS - SOCIAL STUDIES - SCIENCE

Discussion

Relate the concept information and define the vocabulary words. Show a calendar of December with a mark or symbol indicating the 25th. Direct the children to count the days until Christmas. Show pictures of Christmas gatherings and decorated houses and stores. Ask the children to describe decorations they have seen.

Note: This year take snapshots and save newspaper and magazine pictures of Christmas scenes for next year's discussion.

Book

Read <u>Let's Find Out About Christmas</u> by Franklin Watts.

Flannel Board Activity and Song

Make the flannel board symbols as shown (see Patterns, Pictures, Etc., pages 109-113). Use pellon or flannel. Each day, to the tune of "Twinkle Twinkle Little Star," sing the following:

"Now I know it's Christmas time

Since I saw this Christmas sign, (name sign)."

Following the song, place the symbol on the flannel board. Repeat this procedure for each symbol. Then remove all symbols except the one to be discussed that day. For Day 1 only, leave all of the symbols on the flannel board.

Poem - "Alphabet of Christmas" - (Anonymous) (Adapted)

A is for the Animals out in the stable

B is for the Baby in a manger cradle

C is for Carols so happy and gay

D is for December, the 25th day

E is for Eve when we're all so excited

F is for Fire when the Yule log is lighted

G is for the Goose, golden brown and fat

H is for the Holly you stick in your hat

I is for Ivy that decorates the wall

J is for Jesus, the cause of it all

K is for Kindness shared at the feast

L is the Light which shone in the East

M is for Mistletoe - we like to hang

N is for Noel that the angels sang

O is for Oxen, the first to adore Him

P is for Presents the Wise Men laid before Him

Q is for the Quiet on Christmas Eve

  As the children dream of what Santa will leave

R is for Raisins to eat and enjoy

S is for Stockings for each girl and boy

T is for Toys that Santa will bring

U is for Us - as we laugh and sing

V is for Visitors we're happy to see

W is the Warmth of friends and family

X is for Xylophone to ring and chime

Y is for the Yule log at Christmas time

Z is for Zip - the sound of Santa's sleigh

  As it visits our houses and flies away

We've run out of letters as you can see

So have a Merry Christmas wherever you may be.

Procedure - Read the poem. Then read the poem again, allowing the children to recall what each alphabet letter represents.

Holiday Sounds

Use a tape recorder to tape holiday sounds such as jingle bells, toy drum rolls, Santa's "ho-ho-ho," Christmas music, the rustling of paper, scissors cutting; and cooking sounds such as the sounds of a blender, chopping sounds, and a spoon on a metal pot. Play the tape and have the children identify the sounds.

Poem - "Clap Your Hands"

Oh clap, clap your hands, and sing out with glee, (clap)

For Christmas is coming, and merry are we,

Now over the snow come Santa's reindeer,

They scamper and scamper to bring Santa here.

We'll hang up our stockings and when we're asleep

Down into our houses old Santa will creep.

He'll fill all our stockings with presents and then

Santa Clause and his reindeer will scamper again.

So clap, clap your hands, and sing out with glee, (clap)

For Christmas is coming and merry are we.

ART

Christmas Calendar

Preparation - Duplicate one calendar on heavy white paper for each child (page 114). Provide crayons or markers. You will also need one small cellophane-wrapped candy cane or piece of hard candy for each child and a stapler.

Procedure - Distribute the calendars. Demonstrate drawing simple Christmas symbols on the board. Direct the children to color the word "December" and decorate the border with symbols as desired. Explain the calendar instructions, and staple the candy on December 25.

Christmas Night Children

Preparation - Use paper plates or, if displaying on a bulletin board, cut circles of white paper according to the size of the class and the bulletin board. Cut two paper ovals for each child. Provide scraps of paper, curling ribbon, yarn, markers, glue, and scissors. Demonstrate how to draw "sleeping eyes" and lines on ovals to represent fingers (see page 115).

Procedure - Each child makes his or her sleeping face using scrap paper and/or markers for features and ribbon or yarn for hair. Draw lines on ovals. See "Visions of Sugarplums" bulletin board (page 107).

Joy Mobiles

Preparation - For each child provide: one white coat hanger, four pieces of curling ribbon (36", 14", 13", and 12"), one sheet of red, one sheet of white, and one sheet of green construction paper, pencils, markers, scissors, and hole punchers. Label each coat hanger with a masking tape name tag. Make several patterns of "JOY" (see Patterns, Pictures, Etc., pages 116-118). On the board, demonstrate simple Christmas symbols and designs to use in decorating the one white letter.

Procedure - Assist the children in tying a bow (36" ribbon) at the neck of the hanger. Tie the three remaining ribbons (12", 14", then 13") at the base of the hanger. Set aside.

Distribute the pencils, construction paper, markers, scissors, hole punchers, and the patterns which should be shared. Direct the children to trace one letter on each piece of construction paper and cut out. Markers are used to decorate both sides of the one white letter. Punch a hole in the top of each letter and tie to the mobile ribbons. Using one blade of a pair of scissors, demonstrate how to curl the loose ends of the ribbon. (See example, page 115.)

Note: This activity can be extended for two art periods. By taping a yardstick to a table and marking the yardstick with four different colors for each length of ribbon, the children can measure and cut their own ribbon with minimum supervision.

Merry Christmas Sign

Preparation - On fourteen sheets of white construction paper, make each of the letters in "Merry Christmas" (see Patterns, Pictures, Etc., page 119). Provide markers, colors (or tempera of different Christmas colors), and scissors.

Procedure - Distribute each letter to one or two children. Review ways to decorate the letters such as solid, stripes, dots, and symbols. The children cut out their letter and decorate as desired. Using strong tape, mount the letters on the wall in the room or hall. You may wish to tuck holly sprigs in and around the letters.

Note: A long piece of butcher paper can be used in place of the sheets of construction paper. Draw or trace the letters on the paper and assign the children to outline and decorate. No scissors will be needed.

MATH

Christmas Number Booklet

Duplicate the sheets (pages 120-131). Assemble a booklet for each child, stapling together at one corner. Distribute and read the poem. Reread the poem as the children trace each numeral with crayons. Note: The covers will be added later.

Christmas Scene

Duplicate and distribute the sheet (page 132). Provide crayons. Direct the children to:

1. Draw a ball under the tree.
2. Draw a star at the top of the tree.
3. Draw a present on the couch.
4. Draw a stocking on the fireplace.
5. Draw another stocking next to that stocking.
6. Draw some ornaments on the tree.
7. Put a candle on the table.
8. Draw a wreath beside the tree.
9. Draw some shoes below the table.

Note: Colors can be included. Example: Draw a red ball under the tree.

MUSIC - MOVEMENT - GAMES

Song - "We Wish You a Merry Christmas" (Traditional)

Source: Take Joy by Tasha Tudor

Procedure - Form a circle and join hands. To the beat, raise joined hands and step forward on one foot; then lower hands and step back on the other foot. When singing the "Good Tidings" line, the children shake hands with their neighbors; then join hands and repeat the above actions.

Action Chant - "Santa's Sleigh"

Preparation - The children sit on the floor in a large circle. The middle is designated as Santa's Sleigh. Have the children choose a toy "to be" and practice acting it out. Practice rhythmic clapping with hands together, then hands on thighs. (Clapping will proceed throughout the activity.) Now add the clapping to the chant:

> There's one Christmas toy
>
> In Santa's Sleigh
>
> Make room, little toy,
>
> Make room!

Note: After the first toy, substitute the word "another" for "one" or integrate counting by substituting the proper number for "one." Using this method, you may wish to hold up number cards.

Procedure - Explain the procedure. The children clap and recite the chant. One child is chosen to enter the sleigh and act out his or her chosen toy. He or she then makes room for the next toy and sits quietly. When all the toys are in the sleigh, the teacher claps and says:

"There's no more room in Santa's Sleigh.
Let me see all the toys before you go away!"

The children act out their toys once more.

STORY TIME

Book - <u>The Cowboy's Christmas</u> - Joan Walsh Anglund
Book - <u>Merry Christmas Mom and Dad</u> - Mercer Mayer

KINDERGARTEN KITCHEN

Kid-in-a-Blanket Pies

Prepared apple pie filling, or 1 apple per 3 or 4 children
Cinnamon
Sugar
Butter
Premixed pie crust, or 2 cups all-purpose flour, sifted
1/2 teaspoon salt
3/4 cup shortening
2 1/2 teaspoons water

Mix salt and flour. Cut in shortening with two knives until it is the consistency of cornmeal. Sprinkle on water, one tablespoon at a time, adding to the driest parts of the mixture. Form into a ball and roll out on a floured surface.

Purchase prepared pie shells, or prepare pie crust as above. Cut into rectangles. On each rectangle, put a spoonful of prepared filling or apples which have been cut, chopped, and sprinkled with cinnamon and sugar. Roll up strips and pinch edges. Pierce the tops with a fork and baste with butter. Bake in a preheated oven 350° until golden, about 30 to 35 minutes. Yield: 20-25

Christmas Punch

4 cups cranberry juice cocktail
1 1/4 cups granulated sugar
2 packages raspberry drink mix
3 quarts water and ice cubes, mixed

Combine all ingredients, mixing well to dissolve sugar. Makes 32 4-oz. servings.

Note: Freeze sprigs of mint, maraschino cherries, small candy canes, and/or cranberries in the ice cubes. Place a peppermint stick in each cup for stirring.

EXTRA

Organize a Door Decorating Contest including the whole school or classrooms in your wing.

DAY 2 - CHRISTMAS GOODIES

CONCEPT INFORMATION

Since <u>ancient</u> times, great <u>feasts</u> were held to celebrate special days. Families and friends ate roast goose, pig, beef, <u>peacocks</u>, and even roast <u>swan</u>. Christmas pies were made of flour, eggs, and butter; and were filled with goose, <u>pigeon</u>, or blackbird meat. They were <u>oblong</u> in shape in <u>memory</u> of the manger of Jesus and were eaten for good luck. For dessert, the people of long ago enjoyed plum pudding and wassail (a drink made of ale, sugar, eggs, cream, and spices). Years later, <u>bakers</u> baked bread which was formed to look like Baby Jesus and Mary. They began making gingerbread, cookies, and sweet cakes.

In America, for Christmas dinner, we eat ham or turkey and dressing with cranberry sauce, potatoes, vegetables, bread, and salads. Our desserts are cakes, cookies, puddings, and pies. Gingerbread men are a Christmas favorite.

Almost everyone likes sweet things to eat. Many years ago, candy was made with fruits and honey. When it was <u>discovered</u> that sugar could be made from <u>sugar cane</u>, candymakers began making all kinds of candy. Now there are more than 2,000 <u>varieties</u> of candy. Candy can be hard, soft, creamy, or chewy and can come in many different <u>flavors</u> such as cherry, cinnamon, chocolate, and vanilla. One popular Christmas candy is the red and white striped candy cane. Other favorites are fudge and chocolate kisses. Making and eating Christmas sweets or "goodies" is a special part of the holiday.

LANGUAGE ARTS - SOCIAL STUDIES - SCIENCE

Discussion

Repeat the Flannel Board Symbols Activity and Song from Day 1. Relate the concept information and define the vocabulary words. Show food cards or food pictures from magazines, encyclopedias, or cookbooks. Ahead of time, collect baby food jars or margarine or frosting tubs. The baby food jars should be spray-painted or covered with contact paper. Punch holes in the tops.

In each jar or tub, place one of the following: vanilla flavoring, banana extract, orange peels, a sprig of evergreen, pieces of peppermint, pieces of a cinnamon stick, cloves, popcorn, a spoonful of strained turkey (baby food), plums, peas and carrots, cranberry juice or sauce, apple juice or apples, a piece of uncooked (Brown 'N Serve) roll, and so forth.

After the discussion, pass around one of the "Christmas Smells" jars or tubs. After each child has smelled it, call on one to guess the contents. Repeat.

Note: Food cards can be purchased or found in some reading or language kits.

Film

Show a film or home movie of Christmas customs and feasting.

Making Sentences Activity

Seat the children in a circle. Distribute one food card or food picture to each child. The cards should be held so that they are visible to all. The first child looks at his or her card and says, "I am going to eat turkey on Christmas Day." The next child repeats this sentence (naming the child) and makes his or her own sentence. Example: "Tom is going to eat turkey on Christmas Day. I am going to eat mashed potatoes." The activity is continued in this manner around the circle.

The next round adds a descriptive sentence to the first sentence. Example: Tom says, "I am going to eat turkey on Christmas Day. Turkey is light brown and juicy." According to group ability, the next child may repeat both of Tom's sentences, his first sentence only, or simply state his or her own two sentences. If the children are enthusiastic, switch cards and repeat the activity.

Matching Sheet - "You're the Cook"

Duplicate and distribute the sheet (page 133). The children draw lines from the food to the correct cooking pan.

Cooking Demonstration

Ask a parent to demonstrate a favorite Christmas recipe.

Fingerplay - "I Ate"

I ate one bite of apple. ("Bite" and hold up thumb)

I ate one chunk of cake. ("Bite" and hold up index finger)

I ate one piece of chocolate. ("Bite" and hold up middle finger)

And one cookie Grandma baked. ("Bite" and hold up ring finger)

Then I took one lick of my peppermint stick. (Lick and hold up pinky)

Everything tasted yum-yummy. (Lick lips)

I had a smile across my face (Smile)

But now there's a frown in my tummy. (Frown and rub stomach)

Manners

Preparation - Obtain four or more table settings of plastic plates, serving pieces, cups, napkins, and utensils.

Procedure - The children stand around the table and chairs. Include the children in demonstrating how to set a table. Choose children to sit at each place. Narrate the meal as the children act out eating, drinking, asking for food, passing and serving themselves food, etc. Use positive comments to reinforce good manners, such as saying "please," "thank you," chewing slowly with mouths closed, and using napkins and correct utensils. Repeat with other children until all have participated. Everyone helps with "clean up."

Note: Place a rubber band or tie a piece of yarn to each child's right hand to help with table-setting directions.

Puppet Show - "Missing Manners"

Preparation - You will need two puppets that have mouths which open and "hands" for your thumbs and fingers; plastic tea set plates, cups, and utensils; and a napkin tablecloth. Make food and napkins from cut and/or crumpled colored paper. Use a puppet theater; cut-away box or table tipped on its side for a stage.

"Wrong Way" Howie:

>Hello friends out there! Oooh, oooh, I'm so excited! Joe is coming for Christmas dinner. Let me set the table. I can't remember—what do I need to set the table? (Encourage the children to answer.) Oh yes, plates, forks, spoons, knives, cups, tablecloth, and napkins. (Howie throws utensils and napkins on plates, puts cups upside down, then throws tablecloth over it all.) Oh, something is wrong! Can you help poor Howie, poor me? (The children help. He straightens it out.)

(Knock, Knock)

Howie: Ooh, that must be Joe! Let me go to the window and let him in. What, no Joe? (Knock, knock) Where could he be? (The children answer, "The door!") Oh, the door! Hi, Joe, come in! (Joe comes in.)

Joe: Merry Christmas, Howie! That food smells good.

Howie: Merry Christmas to you! Let's eat! (Howie and Joe put the serving plates on the table.)

Howie: Now let's dig in! (starts cramming food into mouth with hands)

Joe: Howie, I think we forgot something. (turns to audience) Do you know what? (The children answer, "The blessing.") (Howie and Joe bow their heads.)

Howie: Now let's eat. (He grabs the food in front of Joe.)

Joe: Howie, have you forgotten your manners?

Howie: Manners—what's that?—a new dessert?

Joe: No, manners—polite ways to act.   You should say, "Pass the potatoes, please," instead of reaching for them.

Howie: But the potatoes are in my mouth! (chews loudly and paper food falls out)

Joe: Another nice manner is eating with your mouth closed.   I don't like see-food.

Howie: See-food?   (food still falling from mouth)

Joe: Yes, I don't like to see the food you're chewing in your mouth!

Howie: Pretty yukky, huh?

Joe: Yeah, yukky! And you should use your fork, spoon, and knife to eat—not your hands—except for drumsticks or French fries or bread.

Howie: So I have to chew with my mouth closed?

Joe: Right.

Howie: And say "please" and "thank you" and use utensils to eat, and don't reach?

Joe: Yes

Howie: And I do all these things so I won't make others feel yukky?

Joe: You've got it!

Howie: It's kind of like rules, huh, Joe—like in baseball?

Joe: That's right—eating rules, like baseball rules.

Howie: Well, you know the rule in baseball.

Joe: What rule, Howie?

Howie: 1-2-3 strikes you're out! (Howie swings Joe around three times, then tosses him out the door.) Baah, rules! Now I'll be yukky all I like.   (Plates drop and food flies as he crams food into his mouth.   He waves tablecloth to audience with mouth overflowing and says:) Hope you have a yukky Christmas too! Ha! Ha! Ha!

ART

Pipe Cleaner Candy Canes

Preparation - Provide one red and one white large pipe cleaner and one 22" piece of green ribbon per child.

Procedure - Hold the ends of the two pipe cleaners with one hand and twist with the other.   Curve the top and tie a bow in the middle with the green ribbon. (See example, page 134.)

Paper Gingerbread Men

<u>Preparation</u> - Make and distribute several patterns of the Gingerbread Man (see Patterns, Pictures, Etc., page 135) to be shared. Provide brown construction paper, markers or tempera of different colors, scissors, glue, construction paper scraps, scraps of ric-rac and other trims, and buttons or small hard candy.

<u>Procedure</u> - Trace around the pattern and cut out the gingerbread man. Decorate as desired. (See example, page 134.)

Note: If the gingerbread man is to be used as an ornament, punch a hole and insert a ribbon or string loop.

Plum Pies

<u>Preparation</u> - Make several of the 8" oblong patterns. (See Patterns, Pictures, Etc., page 136.) Mix reddish-purple tempera paint. Distribute the patterns, three pieces of manilla paper, scissors, and glue. Set out shallow pans of the purple tempera.

<u>Procedure</u> - The children use the pattern to trace an oblong on one sheet of manilla paper. Plums are made by dipping a thumb in the purple paint and covering the oblong with purple thumbprints. While this paint is drying, direct the students to cut the remaining two manilla sheets into (approximately) $\frac{1}{2}$" wide strips. They should cut "the long way" so that the strips are 12" long. Demonstrate making lattice tops on the pies by placing strips about 1" apart in one direction, then "crossing" them in the same manner. The children repeat the procedure, gluing the strips in place. When the glue has dried, turn the pies over and trim excess lattice by cutting around the oblong. The leftover pieces can be glued around the outside of the pie to represent the edge of the crust. (See example, page 134.)

MATH

Christmas Number Booklet

Read the lines. Discuss the numeral one, then color the candy cane.

Christmas Clothesline

<u>Preparation</u> - Purchase stickers of Christmas symbols. Cut out ten six-inch squares of tagboard. Use the stickers to make sets containing 1 through 10 objects on each of the ten squares. For example, mount a wreath sticker on the first square, two candy cane stickers on the second square, three angel stickers on the third square, etc. You will also need one to ten numeral cards and twenty clothespins. If you do not have a clothesline, mount two stick-on hangers on either side of the chalkboard low enough for the children to reach. Tie heavy cord to one hanger and,

at the other end, tie a loop in the cord to fit on the hanger. This allows you to remove the clothesline when necessary.

Procedure - Line the numeral cards in order on the chalkboard ledge. Hang the symbols squares at random on the right side of the clothesline. Hold up the numeral 1 card. Choose a child to clothespin the card to the clothesline, and then find the symbol square which has one object. This should be hung beside the numeral 1 card. Continue until all numbers are used; then repeat choosing other children. (See example, page 137.)

MUSIC - MOVEMENT - GAMES

Song - "Christmas Day Is Coming"

Tune: "My Bonnie (Lies Over the Ocean)"

Oh Christmas Day is coming,

Oh Christmas Day is near,

The wonderful smells from the kitchen,

Say it is that time of the year.

Christmas, Christmas, it is that time of the year again,

Christmas, Christmas, my favorite time of the year.

Action Song - "Alice's Restaurant" from Learning Basic Skills Through Music - Health and Safety by Hap Palmer

Distribute food cards and follow directions.

Game - Christmas Treasure Hunt

Preparation - Purchase a candy cane for each child. Duplicate the Treasure Hunt symbols (see Patterns, Pictures, Etc., page 138) and cut into squares. In the classroom, hide the symbol squares and one candy cane.

Procedure - The children search for the treasures. The child who finds the candy cane wins the game and keeps the candy cane. Call on each child to show and name how many symbols he or she found. Give candy cane prizes for the most found, the most of certain symbols found, the hardest searcher, the quietest searcher, and so forth, so that each child gets a candy cane prize.

STORY TIME

Book - The Christmas Cookie Sprinkle Snitcher - Robert Kraus
Book - Fudge Dream Supreme - Graham Tether
Book - Arthur's Christmas Cookies - Lillian Hoban
Book - Candy Canes - Marty Links

KINDERGARTEN KITCHEN

Gingerbread Men

1 cup butter	1 1/2 teaspoons baking soda
1 cup sugar	1 1/2 teaspoons cinnamon
5 cups flour (sifted)	1 1/2 teaspoons ginger
1/2 cup water	1/4 teaspoon allspice
1 cup light molasses	1/2 teaspoon nutmeg
1 teaspoon salt	1 teaspoon ground cloves

Preheat oven to 375°. In a large bowl, cream the butter and sugar. Add remaining ingredients and blend. Chill the dough for several hours. Roll on lightly-floured surface. Use gingerbread men cookie cutters to cut the shapes. Bake at 375° for 10 to 12 minutes. Yield: approximately 30

Decorations

2 cans ready-to-spread white frosting
Food coloring or decorating icing in different colors
Raisins
Sprinkles

Divide one container of white frosting among several small bowls. Set out. For different colors, divide the other containers among several small bowls and add food coloring. Mix well and set out. Use toothpicks or popsicle sticks to decorate the cooled gingerbread men. If using the decorating icing, the students gently squirt on the gingerbread men.

Note: For each child's gingerbread man, cut a piece of aluminum foil. After cutting, place the gingerbread man on the foil for baking and decorating.

Candy Cane Cookies

1 cup soft margarine
1 cup confectioners sugar
2 eggs
1 teaspoon vanilla
1 teaspoon almond extract
3 cups flour
1 teaspoon salt
1 teaspoon baking soda
Red food coloring
Granulated sugar

Preheat oven to 375°. In one bowl, cream butter and sugar; then add eggs, vanilla, and flavorings. Mix well. In a separate bowl, mix flour, salt, and soda. Blend into first mixture. Divide the dough in half. Use red food coloring to color one mixture.

On a floured surface, roll a heaping tablespoonful of the red mixture into a 4" rope. Repeat with the white mixture. Place the two ropes side by side and twist; then curve the top. Sprinkle with granulated sugar. Repeat, using all the dough. Place on ungreased cookie sheet and bake for 7 to 9 minutes.

EXTRA

Contact organizations which distribute to the needy at Christmas. Organize a canned food drive and present the contributions to one of these organizations.

DAY 3 - BELLS

CONCEPT INFORMATION

Long ago, <u>African tribes</u> and <u>North American Indians</u> shook <u>rattles</u> filled with seeds in their <u>religious ceremonies</u>. Later, bells were <u>invented</u>. Bells come in many sizes and shapes. Usually a bell is shaped like a cup, made of <u>metal</u> or other hard materials, and rings when it is <u>struck</u>. The clapper or tongue of the bell is that part which <u>strikes</u> against the bell to make it ring. The size of bells and what they are made of <u>determine</u> the sound they make. Big bells and small bells ring differently. Glass bells and metal bells do not sound the same.

Long ago, people thought that ringing bells would drive away <u>fiends</u>, <u>goblins</u>, and other <u>evil spirits</u>. Churches began using bells and rung them when it was time for church or on Christmas Day to <u>announce</u> the birthday of Jesus. At Christmas time we also use bells as decorations. We hear bells at <u>shopping centers</u> and in Christmas songs. Bells are a sign of Christmas.

LANGUAGE ARTS - SOCIAL STUDIES - SCIENCE

Discussion

Repeat the Flannel Board Symbols Activity and Song from Day 1. Display a variety of bells. Share the concept information and define the vocabulary words. Allow the children to ring the bells. Discuss the appearance and sound of each bell. Have the children close their eyes and guess which bell is being rung. Discuss bells the students have heard.

The Science of Bells Activity

Materials: a rubber band for each child, a tuning fork, a bell, and an old-fashioned alarm clock with bells exposed.

Discussion: Sound is vibrations. A vibration is when something moves back and forth very quickly like this rubber band when I pluck it, or this tuning fork when I strike it against the table. The vibrations travel through the air and into our ears.

Distribute rubber bands for the children to pluck. Pass around the tuning fork to strike. Hold up a bell and ask the children, "What makes a bell vibrate?" (The clapper hits the bell.) Ring the alarm clock and ask, "How does this bell ring?" Tell the children to find bells at home and see what makes them ring.

Fingerplay - "Five Little Bells"

5 little bells hanging in a row   (Hold up hand)

The first one said, "Ring me slow." (Point to thumb)

The second one said, "Ring me fast."   (Point to index finger)

The third one said, "Ring me last."   (Point to middle finger)

The fourth one said, "I'm like a chime."   (Point to ring finger)

The fifth one said, "Ring me at Christmas time."   (Point to little finger)

Bells of Many Colors - Booklet

Preparation - For each child, duplicate the two cover sheets (pages 139-140) on construction paper and the bell pages (pages 141-145) on regular ditto paper. Provide the booklet pages, crayons, scissors, and a stapler.

Procedure - Cut out the bell-shaped covers and pages. Color each bell as directed and staple the pages between the covers.

Bells Pathtracer Sheet

Duplicate and distribute the sheet (page 146). Ask the students to identify where each bell should be. Use a crayon to trace the path from the bell to its proper "home."

ART

Silver Bells

Preparation - For each child you will need two plastic styrofoam or paper cups, one 36-inch piece of curling ribbon, two small jingle bells, and two sheets of aluminum foil large enough to cover each cup. Provide pencils.

Procedure - Invert each cup and use the pencil to punch a hole in the bottom. Put the aluminum foil sheets on the table, dull side up. Place the cup, right side up, in the middle of the aluminum foil sheet. Bring the sides of the foil up and fold into the mouth of the cup. Gently squeeze the foil to mold it to the cup. Use the pencil to punch through the aluminum foil in the hole of each cup. Tie a bow in the middle of the 36-inch ribbon. Double-knot the bow. Work each end of the ribbon through the two cup holes, then through each jingle bell and knot. Another knot may be placed four or five inches above the bell so that the jingle bells will be exposed. A Christmas sticker or decal may be used to decorate each bell. (See example, page 147.)

Note: The double-knotted bows can be tied beforehand or assign those who can tie well to assist others.

Variations:

Patchwork Bells - With pinking shears, cut strips of Christmas-colored material in different designs.   The children use fabric glue to cover the cups with the strips.

Tiny Bells - Use four medicine cups per child, two ribbons, and various colors of aluminum foil to make a cluster of four bells.   Tie a double bow with the two pieces of ribbon.

Stained Glass Bells

Preparation - Collect plastic milk cartons and/or plastic tops from coffee cans, margarine containers, etc.   Using the pattern (page 147), trace and cut one bell per child from plastic.   Punch a hole in the top of the bell with a hole puncher or ice pick.   Distribute bells, permanent markers of various colors, and ribbon for hanging (string or yarn cut into eight-inch pieces).   Demonstrate the procedure.

Procedure - Use the black markers to color inside the edges of the bell and to make the "divisions" as in stained glass.   Use the colored markers to completely color the remaining areas.   Insert the hanger (ribbon) through the hole.

Note: Wear paint smocks and protect tables when using permanent markers.

Crayon Relief Bells

Preparation - Make several bell patterns (page 148).   For each child, provide a sheet of white construction paper.   Set out crayons, scissors, thinned red and green tempera, and paintbrushes.   Distribute patterns.

Procedure - Trace around the pattern on the construction paper and cut out.   Using the crayons, color designs or a scene on the bell.   Use the tempera to paint over the entire bell.   The design or scene will stand out "in relief."

MATH

Christmas Number Booklet - Cover

Duplicate the cover sheets (page 149).   Distribute along with a sheet for the back cover.   Direct the students to use crayons to color over the dotted numerals on the bell page.   Cut out each bell, then glue on the corresponding "dot bell" on the cover.   The booklet title should be traced over with crayons and the child's name added at the bottom.

Ringing Bells

Distribute rhythm bells, triangles, or jingle bells strung on pipe cleaner bracelets. Hold up a numeral card and call on a child to ring the bell as many times as the card indicates. Repeat.

MUSIC - MOVEMENT - GAMES

Song - "Christmas Bells"

Tune: "Frère Jacques"

Are you listening?

Are you listening?

Girls and boys,

Girls and boys,

Christmas Bells are ringing,

Can you hear them ringing?

Ding - Dong - Ding,

Ding - Dong - Ding.

Note: Distribute bells and triangles. Sing the song again. The children ring the bells on the last two lines.

Game - Where's My Bell?

Divide the children into groups of three with one child remaining. In each group, two children are the "bell." They face each other with arms extended upward and hands clasped together. The third child is the "clapper" and stands between the two children underneath the "peak." The extra child, a "clapper," stands nearby. The teacher continuously rings a bell or plays a record of bells ringing. With the ringing, the "clapper" in each "bell" gently steps from side to side as if ringing the bell. When the teacher stops the record or stops ringing the bell, the "clappers" have to find another bell. The extra "clapper" joins in. One clapper will be left and will wait for the next chance to find a bell. After a time, alternate bells and clappers.

STORY TIME

Book - <u>Twelve Bells for Santa</u> - Crosby Bonsall
Book - <u>The Haunted Churchbell</u> - Barbara Ninde Byfield

KINDERGARTEN KITCHEN

Stained Glass Bells

1 cup butter or margarine
1 cup shortening
2 cups sugar
1 teaspoon vanilla
1 teaspoon almond flavoring
2 eggs
5 cups all-purpose flour, sifted
1 teaspoon baking soda
1 teaspoon salt
Clear lifesavers - 2 or 3 per child

Preheat oven to 350°. Mix together the first six ingredients. Add flour, soda, and salt. Mix well. Chill for 3 to 4 hours.

Give a portion to each child. On a floured surface or waxed paper, each child rolls his or her dough into "snake shapes," reserving a small amount for the center section (of the bell). Have each child make a bell shape with the snake piece, pressing the ends together. Roll the reserved dough into short "snakes." Use these pieces to divide the inside of the bell into two or three sections similar to stained glass windows. (See Stained Glass Bell - Art for example.) Be sure to press ends together well. Place on a cookie sheet and put a lifesaver in each space. Bake for 8 to 9 minutes. Makes about 2½ - 3 dozen cookies.

Note: It is best to give each child a piece of aluminum foil on which to form and bake his or her cookies. Place aluminum foil pieces on the cookie sheet. "Write" students' names on aluminum foil with a pencil or an ice pick.

Baked Bells

1/2 pear per child
toothpicks
Sugar
Cinnamon
Hot water
Cherries

Preheat oven to 400°. Peel pears, cut in half, and core. Place pears, rounded side down, in baking pan. Sprinkle with cinnamon and sugar. Pull the stems out of the cherries and use toothpicks to attach the cherries to the ends of the pears to represent the clappers. Cover the bottom of the pan with hot water. Bake for 30 to 45 minutes or until tender. Every 10 minutes or so, spoon some of the liquid over the pears.

Other pear stuffings: raisins, honey, brown sugar, pineapples, cinnamon candy.

DAY 4 - ANGELS

CONCEPT INFORMATION

An angel is believed to be a <u>messenger</u> of God. Angels are usually pictured in white <u>robes</u>, with wings and a <u>halo</u>.

In the story of the birth of Jesus, angels told the <u>shepherds</u> that Jesus had been born. Angels also told of God's wish for <u>peace on earth</u>. At Christmas, we remember this by using angels as decorations. Angels are also mentioned in Christmas songs and stories. Angels are a sign of Christmas.

LANGUAGE ARTS - SOCIAL STUDIES - SCIENCE

Discussion

Repeat the Flannel Board Symbols Activity and Song from Day 1. Share the concept information and define the vocabulary words. Display pictures to show the various ways angels are depicted.

Film - "The Littlest Angel"

Show "The Littlest Angel." Then ask the children to recall the story in sequence.

The A-Angel

Procedure - Trace the A-Angel patterns (see Patterns, Pictures, Etc., pages 151-153) on pellon, color, and cut out. Place on the flannel board as you tell the story.

(Story) - All the little angels were sent down to earth to find words. The Big Angel told Amanda, "You are to bring back all the things that start with the letter A. Then you can share them with the other angels." Amanda was unhappy. She was scared of going to earth, and she did not know any of the things that started with A. But she put on her angel backpack and flew to earth. The first thing she saw was a ball. "Are you an A word?" she asked. "No," said the ball, "I am a ball. I start with B," and the ball rolled away.

Amanda saw a car. "Are you an A word?" she asked.

"No, I am a car. I start with a C," and away drove the car.

Amanda saw a door. "This must be an A word," she thought. But when she asked, the door said, "What? Are you kidding? I am a door and start with the letter D." And then the door closed and said no more.

Amanda flew and flew and was very tired. She had not found one **A** word to share with the other angels. Then she saw something that looked soft and white.

"This is a good place to rest," she said as she sat down on the pillow.

"What? Who's there?" said a voice.

"I am Amanda Angel. I am looking for **A** words. Who are you?"

"I am an Ear. I start with an E. I also hear many sounds. I know the sounds **A** makes," said the Ear.

"Oh! Oh! What are they?" asked Amanda.

"In some words an **A** makes an **a** sound, just like its name - **A**. In other words, **A** makes an aah sound—like aah-choo," said the Ear.

"So an **A** makes two sounds!" said Amanda. "It says its name, **a**, and it says aah—like sneezing—aah choo!"

"Right," said the Ear. "Amanda is an **A** word—the aah sound. Angel is also an **A** word—the **a** sound."

Then I am an **A** word?" asked Amanda.

"Yes, and here are some more. . . ."

The Ear told Amanda many **A** words which Amanda found and put in her backpack, and then took back to share.

You can help her remember what they are and which **A** sound they make.

Remove the **A** words from Amanda's backpack (colored lunch sack), place on the flannel board, and call on children to name and determine which **A** sound it makes.

Follow-Up - "A-Angel Sheet"

Duplicate and distribute the sheet (page 154). Provide crayons. Ask the children to name the **A** objects on the clouds. Color the objects, the angel, and the **Aa** letters.

Wearing My Halo

Preparation - Make a halo for each child by cutting out the center of paper plates. Make a halo for a hand puppet by rolling up a piece of aluminum foil and squeezing together the ends to form a circle. Let the puppet talk for you. Distribute the halos.

Procedure - Tell the children: When you do something nice and you are behaving well, your mother might call you an angel. She doesn't call you an angel when you are not minding her or you are being impolite. I am going to read some pretend sentences about you. When you are being good, put the halo on your head. When you are not being good, hold the halo in your lap and frown.

  1.   You picked up all of your toys without being told.
  2.   You slammed the door because you were mad.

3. You pulled your sister's pigtail and made her cry.
4. You fed the dog for your mother.
5. You washed your hands before dinner.
6. You looked at your vegetables and yelled "Yuk!"
7. You said "please" and "thank you" at the table.
8. You broke your brother's toy because he wouldn't let you play with it.
9. You wore your good shoes to play in the mud.
10. You looked both ways before you crossed the street.

Angel Maze

Duplicate and distribute the sheet (page 155). The children complete as directed.

ART

Angel Paper Bag Puppets

Preparation - Duplicate the boy angel for the boys and the girl angel for the girls. (See Patterns, Pictures, Etc., pages 157-158.) Distribute the patterns and provide lunch-sized sacks, scissors, crayons, glue, and glitter.

Procedure - Cut out the two sections of the angel's face. Color as desired. Dab glue on the halo and sprinkle on glitter. When this has dried, glue the top part of the face on the bottom of the bag. Lift the "lip" of this section and glue the other part of the face in position. (See example, page 156.)

Pine Cone Angels

Preparation - For each child provide: a pine cone, two leaves, a walnut, one half of a yellow pipe cleaner, one long pipe cleaner, and a cotton ball. Set out black fine point permanent markers and glue.

Procedure - Use the markers to draw a face on the walnut. Pull off a piece of cotton from the cotton ball and glue on the walnut for hair. Glue the walnut to the top of the pine cone. If the pine cone has a point, remove this so the walnut "rests" in the glue on the pine cone.

While this dries, make a circle with the yellow pipe cleaner to represent a halo. Glue on top of the angel's hair. Holding it horizontally, work the long pipe cleaner into the front of the pine cone, bring around to the back and twist. Then bring the ends back around to represent the arms. Glue or tape the leaves to the back of the arms for the wings, or punch through each leaf in two places and thread the pipe cleaner arms through the holes. (See example, page 156.)

Flying Angels

Preparation - Duplicate and distribute the sheet (page 159). Provide crayons or markers, scissors, glue, and a paper drinking straw per child. Set out staplers.

Procedure - Color the parts of the angel and cut out. Flatten the top of the straw and glue to the back of the angel's face. Fold the robe and wings section on the dotted line. Dab glue and lay the straw on the dotted line. Staple to secure. When dry, wave the straw to make the wings flap. (See example, page 156.)

MATH

Christmas Number Booklet

Read the lines. Discuss the numeral "2"; then color the two angels.

Angel Shapes Puzzle

Duplicate the two sheets and distribute (pages 160-161). The children identify and cut out the shapes and then glue in the corresponding spaces. Color when dry.

MUSIC - MOVEMENT - GAMES

Songs

Teach the Christmas carols "Hark the Herald Angels Sing" by Charles Wesley and "It Came Upon a Midnight Clear" by Edmund H. Sears.

Sources: Sing for Christmas by Opal Wheeler and Take Joy by Tasha Tudor.

Movement Activity - "Angel Turn Around"

Procedure - For each child you will need a hoop, a beanbag, and a rhythm stick. To begin, recite the first two lines as the children find a "cloud" (hoop). Also use these lines between activities to allow the children to move to a new hoop. When each of the students is standing in a hoop, and to begin a new set of activities, recite the second two lines. At the end of the activity, recite the last two lines.

What do angels do all day?
Fly to a cloud to dance and play!

Angel jump, now turn around two, (turn around two times)
Angel stop, and do what I do.

Angel jump, now turn around two,
Angel, rest, for now we're through.

<u>Set 1 - Movement Activities</u>

Angels:

1. Stand on one foot.
2. Stand on other foot.
3. March in place.
4. Stand on tiptoes.
5. March on tiptoes.
6. Walk around inside your cloud.
7. Turn and walk the other way.
8. Jump up and down two times.
9. Run in place.
10. Sit down and rest
11. Stand and run in place, lifting your knees as high as possible.
12. Waddle like a duck on your cloud.
13. Bend your knees and crouch low.
14. Stand and stretch as high as you can.
15. Jump forward, then backward.

<u>Set 2 - Beanbag Activities</u>

Angels:

1. Hold the beanbag in one hand.
2. Toss it to the other hand.
3. Balance the beanbag on your head.
4. Hold the beanbag with your wrists, then your elbows.
5. Hold the beanbag between your knees.
6. Throw the beanbag upward and catch it with both hands.
7. Throw the beanbag upward and catch it on the back of your hands.
8. Balance the beanbag on top of your foot.
9. Now kick the beanbag upward and try to catch it.
10. Sit down and rest.
11. Stand and balance the beanbag on your nose.
12. Toss the beanbag above your head and clap before you catch it.
13. Place the beanbag in the middle of the cloud. Jump forward over the beanbag.
14. Leave the beanbag in the middle of your cloud. Place one hand on it and move quickly around it (like a crank on an ice cream freezer).
15. Hop over the beanbag on one foot, then the other.

Set 3 - Stick Activity

1. Hold the stick (vertically) in one hand.
2. Move the stick in a circle.
3. Move the stick in a circle the other way.
4. Toss the stick and catch it with your other hand.
5. Hold the stick in your right hand.
6. Hold the stick above your head.
7. Hold the stick in your left hand.
8. Touch the floor with the end of the stick.
9. Pass the stick around and behind your knees to your other hand.
10. Sit down and rest.
11. Stand and balance the stick on four fingers, three, two, then one finger.
12. Repeat #11 with the other hand.
13. Balance the stick on one palm, then on the other.
14. Sit down. Tap the floor three times with the stick. Switch hands and repeat.
15. Balance the stick on different parts of your body.

STORY TIME

Book - The Doll's Christmas - Tasha Tudor

KINDERGARTEN KITCHEN

Halo Cookies

Butter cookies with holes in the center
Lemon Ready-to-Spread Frosting
Silver Cookie Sprinkles

Give each child several cookies and a wooden popsicle stick for spreading frosting. In small bowls, set out frosting and sprinkles. The children spread the frosting on the top of the cookies and decorate with silver sprinkles.

Note: If you wish to make your own cookies, use the recipe for Candy Cane Cookies. Omit separating and coloring the dough. Cut with donut-shaped cookie cutters.

Angel Food Cake

Purchase Angel Food Cake Mix and Frosting Mix. Prepare according to package directions.

Variations: Instead of frosting, sprinkle the cake with powdered sugar; or glaze by mixing 1 cup sifted confectioners sugar with 2-3 tablespoons warm milk and ½ teaspoon vanilla or almond extract.

DAY 5 - CANDLES

CONCEPT INFORMATION

For <u>thousands</u> of years, fire has been used for special days. <u>Bonfires</u> were built for <u>celebrations</u>, and later candles were used.

A candle is made of wax or tallow (cow or sheep fat) with a wick or string running through the middle. When lit with a match, the wick burns and the candle gives off light.

Before we had electric lights, families made their own candles. Candles became a symbol of Jesus Christ and were used to light Christmas trees. Today we use candles to <u>decorate</u> our homes and churches at Christmas. In many places, candles are placed in windows on Christmas Eve to "light the way for the Christ Child." Candles are beautiful symbols of Christmas.

LANGUAGE ARTS - SOCIAL STUDIES - SCIENCE

Discussion

Repeat the Flannel Board Symbols Activity and Song from Day 1. Several days beforehand, send notes home asking parents to send a candle of any kind to share. Bring a block of candle wax, a piece of wicking, candles of any kind including holiday candles and candleholders from home. You may use baby food jars, jar lids and/or ashtrays to hold the candles. Drop a small amount of melted wax in each to secure the candle. Follow safety precautions.

Define vocabulary words and relate the concept information. Show the wax and wicking and a candle which has been cut lengthwise to reveal the wick. Turn off the lights and light the candles. Remind the children that, before electricity, homes were lit with candles. Discuss the different candles and flames.

Candlemaking Demonstration

Preparation - Materials needed are a hot plate, medium-sized pot, a tall narrow coffee can, 15"-20" of candle wicking, a block of candle wax, candle coloring or crayons, a dull knife, an old spoon, hot pad, trivet, newspaper, and a coat hanger.

Procedure - Cover the work area with newspapers. Turn the hot plate on low. Fill half the pot with water. Use the dull knife to break the wax into chunks. Place these in the can until it is three-fourths full. Put the can in the pot of water. Add coloring or crayons to color the wax. Use the spoon to blend. When the wax has melted, turn off the hot plate. Remove the can and place on the trivet. Bend the wick in the middle. Hold at the middle and dip both ends into the wax. Pull it out, wait a few minutes for it to dry; then repeat. Keep the wicks straight as you dip. Continue until the candles are the desired size. Hang the candles on the clothes hanger to harden. Then cut apart and light.

Note: Candle scent can also be purchased and added.

SEATWORK - "Initial Sounds Sheet"

Duplicate and distribute the sheet (page 162). The students circle the candle; then circle any other object that begins with the same "c" sound.

<u>Poem</u> - "Jack Be Nimble"

Jack Be Nimble

Jack Be Quick

Jack Jumped Over

The Candlestick

Show a picture of "Jack Be Nimble" from a Mother Goose book and read the rhyme. Ask the children to repeat. Place a short candle in a plastic candleholder or a tall block on the floor. The children form a line. While chanting the rhyme, the students jump over the candlestick and circle around to again form a line. For the next rounds, direct the children to hop on one foot, jump backwards, sideways, and so forth, over the candlestick.

<u>**Candle Colors**</u>

<u>Preparation</u> - For the candles, cut about twenty 6" strips of different colors of construction paper. For the flames, cut 2" strips of yellow construction paper and glue to the back so that 1" (of yellow) shows at the top of the candle.

<u>Procedure</u> - Place the candles in a pile. Choose one; then say, "Red, green, yellow, purple, blue (insert any color words you use). Candle, candle, which are you?"

Call on a child to name the color of the candle and find a matching one in the pile. Assist when necessary. Next, that child chooses a different colored candle, leads the class in the rhyme, and calls on another child to answer and match. Repeat, as necessary, for all children to participate.

ART

<u>**Cardboard Christmas Candles**</u>

<u>Preparation</u> - Cut a 7" x 7" square of red (or color of your choice) tissue paper and a 1" x 1-3/4" piece of cardboard for each child. You will also need a cardboard toilet tissue roll and a jar lid or small paper plate per

child. Provide scrap yellow paper, scissors, and glue. Evergreen sprigs, tiny pine cones, and bows can also be used to decorate around the candle base.

Procedure - Dab glue on one edge of the red tissue paper. Place the tissue roll on this edge; roll and glue. Tuck the excess tissue paper into the top and bottom holes of the roll. Insert the small piece of cardboard in the top of the roll to fit. Cut a small piece (about 2") of yellow scrap paper to represent the flame. Glue to the inserted piece of cardboard. Make a puddle of glue in the middle of the jar lid or paper plate. Set the candle in this puddle to dry. Later, glue sprigs, bows and/or pine cones around the candle. (See example, page 163.)

Shadow Box Candles

Preparation - Collect small, shallow boxes or box tops from children's shoeboxes, toilet tissue rolls, dried red beans, shell macaroni, popcorn seeds, and small sprigs of evergreen. Cut the tissue rolls in half lengthwise. Give each one half to each child, along with the box and a paper clip. Set out red and green tempera, paintbrushes, glue, and dried beans, macaroni, etc.

Procedure - Paint the box and tissue roll with the tempera. When dry, glue the tissue roll "candle" inside the box at the bottom. Use the dried beans, macaroni, and so forth, to form: a flame, a candleholder, and the background of your choice. Glue in place. Glue evergreen sprigs around the base of the candle. When dry, glue the paper clip to the back as a hanger. (See example, page 163.)

Jack Be Nimble Sheet

Preparation - Each child will need one sheet of colored construction paper and one-half sheet of construction paper of a different color, scissors, glue, and crayons. Demonstrate drawing a stick figure.

Procedure - Cut a strip of the one-half sheet to represent a candle. Place the whole sheet the "long way" in front of you. Glue the candle to the bottom of this sheet. Color a flame with an orange or yellow crayon. Draw Jack jumping over the candlestick. (See example, page 163.)

MATH

Christmas Number Booklet

Read the lines, discuss the numeral "3"; then color the candles.

One-to-One Correspondence Sheet

Duplicate and distribute the sheet (page 164). The students color the candles and then draw a flame on each one.

MUSIC - MOVEMENT - GAMES

Song - "Ten Little Candles"

Tune: "Ten Little Indians"

One little, two little, three little candles,
Four little, five little, six little candles,
Seven little, eight little, nine little candles,
Ten Christmas candles burning.
Ten little, nine little, eight little candles,
Seven little, six little, five little candles,
Four little, three little, two little candles,
One Christmas candle burning.

Procedure - The children hold up, then put down a finger for each candle.

Game - Light the Candle Relay

Preparation - Provide a straw or "matchstick" made from thin cardboard strips for each player. Mark a starting and finish line with tape or rope. Place two chairs several yards apart behind the finish line. Lay the matchsticks on the chairs. Divide the class into two even teams of "candles." Each team forms a line behind the starting line.

Procedure - At the signal, the first two members of each team race to the finish line, pick up a "match," race back, and light the next "candles" by tapping the next players' heads with the "matches." After lighting the "candles," these players go to the end of the line. The race continues in this manner until the last runners of each team complete the relay. The first team to have all "candles" lit wins the game.

STORY TIME

Book - The Grouchy Santa - Lillie Patterson
Book - Something for Christmas - Palmer Brown

KINDERGARTEN KITCHEN

<u>Fruit Salad Candles</u>

Per Child: 1/2 banana   1 cherry
            1 slice pineapple   1 toothpick
            1 slice peach   1 spoonful peanut butter
            1 lettuce leaf   1 paper bowl

Set out all ingredients. The children line the bowl with the lettuce leaf,
lay the pineapple slice on the lettuce, and stand the banana half in the
center of the pineapple slice (as shown below). Then they "stick" half of
the peanut butter on top of the banana candle, stick the cherry on one
end of the toothpick, and insert the other end through the peanut butter
and into the banana. The remaining peanut butter is used to stick the
peach slice, curved side up, at the base of the banana.

DAY 6 - STOCKINGS

CONCEPT INFORMATION

At Christmas, children hang stockings for Santa Claus to fill with goodies. Stocking is another name for sock. It is believed that switches and ashes are left in the stockings of children who have been bad.

In Turkey, a country across the ocean, the children call their Santa Claus by another name, St. Nicholas. Legend says that long ago, St. Nicholas dropped bags of gold down the chimney for three poor sisters. The gold fell into their stockings which were hanging by the fire to dry. After that, children began hanging stockings at Christmas. Stockings are also hung on doors and trees as decorations because they are a sign of Christmas.

LANGUAGE ARTS - SOCIAL STUDIES - SCIENCE

Discussion

Repeat the Flannel Board Symbols Activity and Song from Day 1. Several days beforehand, send letters home telling parents that today will be "Crazy Socks Day" (see page 165). The children should wear their brightest and "craziest" socks, preferably a different one on each foot.

Share the concept information, defining vocabulary words. Then ask the students to take off their shoes and, if necessary, roll up their pants to display their socks. Discuss the colors, textures, and designs of each sock.

Books

Read and discuss Baby Socks by Anne Baird and/or Socks for Supper by Jack Kent.

Crazy Socks Game

The children sit in a circle, leaning back on both arms. Explain; then give the following directions:

"Red socks up; green socks up; yellow socks up." (Children with these
    colored socks lift one leg and point sock in air.)
"Now wave bye, bye." (wave with foot)
(Repeat with different colors or designs.)

"All right socks up; all left socks up; now both socks up." (Children point
    right foot, left foot, then both feet.)
"And wave bye, bye." (wave with foot)

"All blue socks make a circle; all black socks make a circle; all purple socks make a circle." (circular motion with foot)
"Now wave bye, bye." (wave with foot)

Continue with various directions. The children can stand and continue the activity with certain colors; hopping, jumping, etc.

Note: During the day, use the children's socks for identification purposes. For example, "Will the child with the pink and purple striped socks lead the song?" "All students with polka dot socks line up," and so forth.

Stocking Dot-to-Dot

Reproduce and distribute the sheet (page 166). The children complete the stockings by drawing lines from one alphabet letter dot to the next. Color.

Little Stocking

Preparation - Copy the room pages (see Patterns, Pictures, Etc., pages 167-168), cut away the margins, tape together, and color. Make the "Little Stocking." Tape the room pages to a file cabinet and stick a piece of magnetic tape on the back of the Little Stocking; or use tacks on a bulletin board or flannel board. The children verbally fill in the blanks as you tell the story and place the stocking in the appropriate locations.

(**Story**) - Once there was a very tiny stocking named Little Stocking. Little Stocking had waited all year for his first Christmas. He was so happy that Christmas was here!

Little Stocking watched with wonder as the other decorations were hung and placed around the room. He just couldn't wait until it was his turn, so he hopped on the _____ (mantel) beside the other stockings. "You don't belong here," said one of the big stockings. "You are too little. You belong on the Christmas tree."

Little Stocking hopped down. He did not know what a tree was. So he jumped on the_____ (door) beside the _____ (wreath).

"This must be a tree," Little Stocking said.

"Hhrump," said the door. "I am no tree. Go away. You're crowding my wreath!"

Down came Little Stocking. He landed on the nice, soft _____ (rug).

"This is a pretty tree," said Little Stocking. "It is soft and warm. I will like it here!"

"Little Stocking," said the rug, "I am a rug. If you stay here, you will get stepped on. You need to be on the Christmas tree!"

Little Stocking looked around the room. That must be the tree," he said. And up he jumped on the big _____ (clock).

"Tick Tock," said the clock. "I'm no, Tick Tock, tree. Hop down, Tick Tock, little one, Tick Tock."

So Little Stocking hopped down and fell into the _____ (chair).

"Don't tell me," said Little Stocking. "You aren't a tree either."

"Right you are!" said the chair.

The little stocking jumped to the _____ (floor) and began to cry.

"Boo hoo, my first Christmas and I can't find where I belong! Boo hoo."

"Why don't you ask?" said a soft voice.

"What?" said Little Stocking, looking around.

"When you don't know something, it is always better to ask," said the voice.

"Okay," said Little Stocking, "Can someone please tell me where the Christmas tree is?"

"I am the tree," said the same soft voice, "over here in the corner."

"Little Stocking looked in the corner and saw the tall _____ (tree) decorated with beautiful ornaments.

"Is there room for me?" Little Stocking asked.

"Of course," said the tree. "I have saved a special place for you."

So Little Stocking found his place on the _____ (tree), and proud he was! For he was hung under the beautiful shining _____ (star).

And each year, if you wish to find him, that is where he will be.

Fingerplay - "Five Skinny Stockings"

Five skinny stockings on Christmas night (Hold up 5 fingers slightly bent, right hand)

Hanging in a row by the soft firelight.

Along came Santa (Make index finger of left hand walk to right hand)

And quick as that (Snap fingers of "Santa hand")

The five skinny stockings were big and fat. (Straighten and spread five fingers)

ART

Construction Paper Stockings

Preparation - Duplicate pattern (page 170) on different colors of construction paper. Provide five or six cotton balls per child, glue, glitter, scissors, ornament hooks, and a hole puncher.

Procedure - The children choose a stocking and cut it out. Apply glue at the top of the stocking, pull the cotton balls to spread apart, and fill in the glued area. The students dip one finger in the glue and use to write his or her first name initial on the stocking. Sprinkle this with glitter and shake off the excess. Punch a hole in the corner and insert an ornament hook. (See example, page 169.)

Sewing Burlap Stockings

Preparation - Purchase white burlap, large blunt needles, small candy canes, and red or green yarn. Double the burlap. Using the pattern (see Patterns, Pictures, Etc., page 171), trace around the stocking with a red permanent marker. This will be the child's stitching line; therefore, cut about ½" out from this line through both thicknesses of burlap. Staple once in the middle of the two stocking pieces to secure. Repeat for each child. Cut 20" of yarn for each child. Make a 1" loop, and knot. Use the marker to put each child's name on the back and an X at the beginning point (see pattern).

Procedure - Working with small groups, distribute the stockings, needles, and yarn. The children insert the needle at the beginning X and sew around the line, leaving the top open. Assist with the finishing knot. (The end loop will be the hanger.) Remove the staple and insert a candy cane prize for a job well done. (See example, page 169.)

Note: I have found that it is easier for the child to sew using this method: Place the burlap on the table, anchor with one hand, then use the other to sew. Push the needle in, push for about ½", push out the needle, then "pull" the length of the yarn. Some children will be able to make two or three stitches before pulling the length of yarn.

MATH

Christmas Number Booklet

Read the lines and discuss the numeral "4". Color the stockings.

Wallpaper Stockings

Preparation - Make several of the patterns (see Patterns, Pictures, Etc., page 172). Give each child a piece of wallpaper from a sample book, a pencil, scissors, and glue. Have old magazines available.

Procedure - The students trace and cut out the wallpaper stockings. As each child finishes, the teacher writes a numeral on the stocking. The children find and cut out that many toys from old magazines and glue them around the numerals on the stockings.

MUSIC - MOVEMENT - GAMES

Song - "Three Red Stockings"

Tune: "Three Blind Mice"

Three red stockings,

Three red stockings,

All in a row,

All in a row,

They all hang next to the Christmas tree,

So Santa will fill them as full as can be,

The children are peeking so they can see,

Three red stockings.

Game - Bed Check!

This is a variation of "Red Light." One child is chosen to be "Santa" and stands at one end of the room or at the finish line. The "children" stand behind the starting line. Santa will try to catch any of the children moving. To begin the game, "Santa" stands with his back to the "children" and yells "Asleep." At this time, the children try to sneak forward. When Santa yells "Bed Check" and turns around, the children freeze. If Santa sees anyone moving, he or she must go back to the start. The first person to touch Santa is the new Santa.

STORY TIME

Book - Holly Hobbie's The Night Before Christmas - Clement C. Moore, Illustrated by Holly Hobbie

KINDERGARTEN KITCHEN

Pimento Cheese Stockings

1 lb. mild Cheddar cheese, grated
1 7-oz. jar chopped pimentos
Mayonnaise
Grated carrots
Bread

Mix cheese, pimentos, and enough mayonnaise to proper consistency.

Refrigerate. Cut bread, as shown, to resemble stockings. The children spread pimento and cheese on bread stockings using popsicle sticks. Grated carrots are sprinkled at the top of each stocking.

DAY 7 - CHRISTMAS CAROLS

CONCEPT INFORMATION

Even in <u>ancient times</u> people sang songs to <u>celebrate</u> special days. Singing songs, or carols, at Christmas started <u>thousands</u> of years ago, but a man named St. Francis of Assisi encouraged singing at the Christmas <u>season</u>. <u>Groups</u> of people began going from house to house singing Christmas songs. Sometimes they were <u>rewarded</u> with small gifts or <u>refreshments</u>. Today "<u>carolers</u>" still sing at homes, town <u>gatherings</u>, or hospitals.

There are many different Christmas carols. Some are new, and some are very old. The words usually tell about the birth of Christ, our feelings at Christmas, and the joy of the season. Some of the popular carols are "Silent Night! Holy Night!" "O Come, All Ye Faithful," and "Away in a Manger." Everyone enjoys hearing Christmas carols at Christmas.

LANGUAGE ARTS - SOCIAL STUDIES - SCIENCE

Discussion

Repeat the Flannel Board Symbols Activity and Song from Day 1. Relate the concept information and define the vocabulary words. On a record player, play the first parts of several familiar carols. Ask if the children know the names of the carols. Show a picture of carolers singing. Ask if the students have seen carolers.

Book

Read <u>We Wish You a Merry Christmas</u> by Tracey Campbell Pearson.

Choral Reading - "Christmas Carol" - (Author unknown)

Read the poem and define the words. Teach the students to recite their lines on cue.

Teacher:	God bless the master of this house,
Teacher:	The mistress also.
Class:	And all the little children,
Class:	That round the table go,
Teacher:	And all your kin and kinsmen
Teacher:	That dwell both far and near;
Class:	I wish you a Merry Christmas
Class:	And a Happy New Year.

Maze - "The Lost Caroler"

Reproduce and distribute the sheet (page 173). The children use a crayon to draw the path as directed.

Christmas Rhyme Board

Color, cut out, and then paste the Christmas Rhyme Board pictures (page 174) on poster paper. Call on the children to name each picture. Then ask:

1. Which picture rhymes with **barrel?**
2. Which picture rhymes with **bunch?**
3. Which picture rhymes with **tell?**

Have the children:

4. Find the picture that rhymes with **car.**
5. Find the picture that rhymes with **knee.**

Continue in this manner, using other rhyming words such as tar, bar, crunch, lunch, bee, see, well, and sell.

ART

Booklet - "The Twelve Days of Christmas" - (Adaptation)

Duplicate and assemble the booklet pages (pages 175-181). Give each child a booklet and crayons or markers. Sing the song as you show a finished booklet.

On the first day of Christmas, my best friend gave to me -
   A star for the top of my tree.

    2. Teddy bears
    3. Candy canes
    4. Christmas cards
    5. Holly wreaths
    6. Candles burning
    7. Stockings-a-hanging
    8. Reindeer-a-prancing
    9. Cakes-a-baking
   10. Angels-a-flying
   11. Bells-a-ringing
   12. Santa's sleighing

Stand-Up Caroler

Preparation - Duplicate the pattern (see Patterns, Pictures, Etc., page 182) on white construction paper. Provide a sheet for each child, scissors, crayons or markers, glue, staplers, and pieces of yarn for hair.

Procedure - Cut out the caroler, color, and add facial features. Glue on yarn for hair. Staple the cone-shaped body at the back.

MATH

Christmas Number Booklet

Read the lines and discuss the numeral "5". Then color the carolers.

"Count the Notes" Sheet

Duplicate and distribute the sheet (page 183). The students count the notes in each block and circle the corresponding number.

MUSIC - MOVEMENT - GAMES

Song - "Here We Come A Caroling"

Source: <u>Take Joy</u> by Tasha Tudor

Game - Christmas Carolers

Preparation - With chalk, draw the hopscotch "snail" on pavement. Mark off enough spaces for each child in the class. The center is marked "home." Review different Christmas carols.

Procedure - Each child hops on one foot to the center without touching any lines. When the child reaches home, he must sing one line of a Christmas carol, and then return in the same manner. If successful, the child is a "Christmas caroler" and gets to write his name in any square. If a child touches a line, he is out until his next turn.

Note: Add more spirals to the snail for a larger class.

Caroling

Teach the children several Christmas carols. Arrange for the children to carol outside the lunchroom or other classrooms. Return to the room and serve Wassail Punch (see Kindergarten Kitchen on next page).

Note: Ask parents to send flashlights (labeled with names). Cover the ends of the flashlights with cellophane of different colors. The children hold the flashlights as they carol.

STORY TIME

Book - <u>On Christmas Eve</u> - Margaret Wise Brown
Book - <u>The Christmas Mouse</u> - Elisabeth Wenning (Read in installments.)

KINDERGARTEN KITCHEN

Wassail Punch

1/2 gallon apple cider
6 oz. frozen orange juice concentrate
6 oz. frozen lemonade
3 cups water
1 1/4 cups sugar
15-20 cloves
2 oranges
2 cinnamon sticks

Insert cloves into oranges. In a small baking pan, bake for 20 minutes at
350°. Meanwhile, mix remaining ingredients in a large pot. Simmer on
low heat for 1½ hours. (Add oranges as soon as they are baked.)
Refrigerate overnight, or for several hours. Remove oranges and cloves.
Reheat to serve.

DAY 8 - CHRISTMAS GREENERY

CONCEPT INFORMATION

Evergreens are plants or trees which stay green all year long, even in winter. Because of this, ancient people thought that evergreens were magic. They hung branches of evergreens on doors and windows to keep away evil and the bring good luck.

Evergreens seemed to show people that "life goes on forever." Since Jesus also believed this, evergreens became a symbol for Christmas. Holly is a popular evergreen. It has waxy green leaves and red berries. Many people believe that the Christmas colors, red and green, came from the holly plant, and that the holly stands for peace and joy. Holly and other evergreens are used to make decorations for our homes at Christmas. One of these is the wreath. People used to decorate and hang their wagon wheels on their doors. That is why today wreaths are round.

Long ago, mistletoe was believed to be a plant of healing and friendship. When people met under mistletoe, they were supposed to kiss. Today mistletoe is still the "kissing plant," adding fun to our Christmas season.

Poinsettia is a red star-shaped Christmas flower. The legend is that a poor Mexican boy had no gift to take the Christ Child so he knelt to pray outside the church. When he stood, he saw that a beautiful plant with red leaves had grown in the spot where he had knelt. He picked the plant and took it to the Christ Child as his gift. Mexicans call this plant "Flower of the Holy Night." In 1828, Dr. Joel Roberts Poinsett brought the plant to this country, so it was renamed after him.

LANGUAGE ARTS - SOCIAL STUDIES - SCIENCE

Discussion

Repeat the Flannel Board Symbols Activity and Song from Day 1. Show examples or pictures of the Christmas greenery as you relate the concept information and define the vocabulary words. Encourage the children to touch and smell each example.

Science Act - Why Are Leaves Green?

For this discussion, show pictures from Childcraft How and Why Library, Volume 6, "The Green Kingdom." Before the discussion, prepare the following experiments:

1. Pour rubbing alcohol in a jar. Then place several green leaves in the jar. Cover. The alcohol will drain the chlorophyll from the leaves.

2.   Use one of the classroom plants for this experiment. Cut two 1"
squares from black construction paper. Pin one square above and
one below one leaf of the plant. Set the plant in a window.
Remove the squares after a few days.

Discussion - Plants need water, sunlight, and air to live. The leaves of
plants are green because inside they hold a green coloring called
chlorophyll (show Experiment #1). Leaves are like the kitchen of a plant.
Chlorophyll is like the cook in the kitchen. Chlorophyll takes sunlight,
water, and air, and makes it into food for the plant. If the chlorophyll
doesn't have sunlight or water or air, it cannot make the food.

We will place the plant (Experiment #2) in the window. A part of one
leaf is under the paper and cannot get sunshine. We will see what
happens. (Later observe the spot which was covered.)

In fall, many leaves turn brown, orange, or red, and fall to the ground.
They die because the stems of the leaves seal up and no water can get
into the leaf. Without water, the chlorophyll disappears.

Evergreen trees or plants stay green all year. The leaves of evergreens
are very tough. They do not seal up, so the water can get to the
cholorphyll. They also do not freeze.

Making a Wreath and Experience Story

Making a Wreath 1

Preparation - Purchase a large styrofoam ring and ribbon for the bow.
Collect pittosporum leaves. You will need quite a few.

Procedure - Allow the children to take turns pushing the stems of the
pittosporum leaves into the styrofoam ring. Be sure that none of the
styrofoam shows through. Tie a big bow and secure on the finished
wreath (with a wire pin). Hang on the classroom door.

Note: Cedar leaves can be used instead of pittosporum leaves.

Making a Wreath 2

Preparation - Purchase a large straw wreath base, wire pins, and ribbon
for the bow. Obtain permission and collect pieces of greenery from a
place which sells Christmas trees. Explain the process to the class and
demonstrate the careful way to insert pins and greenery in the base.

Procedure - Assist the children as they take turns pinning the greenery in
overlapping rows in the base. Tie a big bow and secure it on the finished
wreath. Hang it on the classroom door.

Experience Story - As the children dictate, write the steps of making the
wreath on large experience chart paper. Leave spaces after each step. In
these spaces, the students illustrate the steps.

Poem - The Wreath Is Hanging on Our Door

The wreath is hanging on our door;
Ornaments are piled upon the floor;
Cinnamon and raisins fill the air;
Christmas, Christmas, everywhere!

The wreath is hanging on our door;
Gifts are piled upon the floor;
Friends and family gathered there;
Christmas, Christmas, everywhere!

The wreath is hanging on our door;
Paper is piled upon the floor;
With my new bike and teddy bear,
Christmas, Christmas, everywhere!

The wreath is hanging on our door;
Soon we'll take it down once more;
But then I'll say again next year,
"Christmas, Christmas, everywhere!"

ART

Paper Plate Wreaths

Preparation - Cut the center out of a paper plate for each child. Punch two holes ½" apart at the top of each. Mix green tempera. Provide a 12" piece of red yarn and a small square of red construction paper for each child. Set out hole punchers, glue, and paintbrushes.

Procedure - Paint the back rounded side of the paper plate with the green tempera. While this dries, punch "red berries" from the red construction paper. Glue these on the wreath. Thread the yarn through the holes and tie in a bow. (See example, page 184.)

Variation: Cut green and red (for berries) tissue paper into 2" squares. Crumple and glue to cover one side of the paper plate wreath.

Christmas Pretzel Wreaths

Preparation - Each child will need sixteen small heart-shaped pretzel twists, one 3/8" x 24" strip of red gingham or any Christmas material cut with pinking shears, a 6" piece of gold thread, and a piece of aluminum foil. Set out bottles of strong craft glue. Provide clear acrylic sealer and paintbrushes.

Procedure - On the aluminum foil, glue two pretzels together with parts matching. Use a generous amount of glue. Repeat with the remaining pretzels. You will have 8 double-decker pretzels. Allow to dry. Form a circle with the 8 double pretzels' sides touching and "double-humps" outward. Glue where the sides touch. Dry. "Paint" with sealer. When it is dry, weave material strip in and out of the pretzel holes. Tie a bow with the ends. Tie on a loop of gold thread as a hanger.

Note: The teacher should check each wreath before the glue dries to make sure all pretzel sides are touching. Be certain sealer is very dry before weaving strips. (See example, page 184.)

Bread Dough Picture Wreaths

<u>Preparation</u> - You will need a small school picture or snapshot of each child. Mix green tempera paint. For each child, cut a 10" piece of red yarn, a circle of green construction paper, and a circle of green felt, both ¼" smaller than the cookie cutter. Provide donut-shaped cookie cutters, an ice pick, acrylic sealer spray, and fine permanent red markers. Mix the bread dough recipe as follows:

4 cups flour
2 cups salt
1 cup water

<u>Procedure</u> - Mix well and knead on a floured surface. Roll out to ¼" thickness. Cut with donut-shaped cookie cutters. With the ice pick, make a larger hole than necessary for the yarn hanger. Bake at 325° for 30 minutes or until light brown. After the wreaths dry, paint with green tempera. Spray with several coats of sealer. Use permanent markers to make dots for berries and, if desired, a name and the date on each wreath. Thread yarn through the hole and tie a loop with a double bow at the top. Glue the two green circles together. Cut school pictures to fit and glue on the construction paper side. Center the picture and glue to the back of the wreath. (See example, page 185.)

Variation: Use wooden curtain rings, instead of bread dough, for wreaths.

Evergreen Balls

<u>Preparation</u> - Collect a large supply of evergreen sprigs (not holly). Each child will need: an apple, enough sprigs to cover it, two florist pins or hairpins, and a piece of ribbon long enough to tie around the apple and into a bow.

<u>Procedure</u> - Tie the ribbon around the apple and into a bow so that it can be hung up. Insert pins through the ribbon and into the apple to secure. Push the sprigs into the apple to cover. Hang in a window or a doorway. (See example, page 185.)

MATH

Christmas Number Booklet

Read the lines and discuss the numeral "6".   Color the wreaths.

Set of Holly Leaves

Duplicate and distribute the sheet (page 187).   The students cut the sheet in half on the dotted line; color and cut out the leaves; then glue the leaves on the remaining half page.

MUSIC - MOVEMENT - GAMES

Song - "Deck the Halls" - (Old Welsh)

Sources: <u>Take Joy</u> by Tasha Tudor and <u>Sing for Christmas</u> by Opal Wheeler

Game - Beanbag in the Wreath Toss

<u>Preparation</u> - Paint a wreath on the side of a large box.   Cut out the center hole.   Supply beanbags.

<u>Procedure</u> - Divide the class into two teams.   Each child has three chances to toss the beanbag through the hole for two points.   The team with the most points wins the game.

Game - Drop the Mistletoe

Like "Drop the Handkerchief," the children are standing or sitting in a circle.   One child is "It."   "It" walks around the circle and drops a piece of mistletoe behind one player.   That player picks up the mistletoe and chases "It" who tries to make it around the circle back to that player's spot.   If "It" is caught, he must hug the person who caught him and then sit in the "Love Seat" (center of the circle).   The person who caught him is the new "It."   If "It" is not caught, he remains "It" for another turn. The other player returns to his spot.

STORY TIME

Book - <u>Richard Scarry's The Animals Merry Christmas</u> - Kathryn Jackson (21 short stories)

KINDERGARTEN KITCHEN

Donut Wreaths

Purchase donuts or make your own, using canned biscuits. (Cut holes in the middle with a small plastic medicine vial. Coat with flour and fry in deep fat until light brown. Roll in powdered sugar.)

Topping: Mix 3/4 cup sifted confectioners sugar with 2 tablespoons milk. Add green food coloring and mix well. Spread the frosting on the donuts; then decorate with red sprinkles or cinnamon candy.

DAY 9 - CHRISTMAS TREES

CONCEPT INFORMATION

At Christmas we bring an evergreen tree into the house and decorate it. This is called a Christmas tree, and it is a special part of Christmas. Whether you buy your tree or cut it down yourself, whether it is real or artificial, whether it is tall or short, fat or skinny, Christmas trees are enjoyed by all. The most popular Christmas trees are fir, spruce, and pine trees.

There are many stories about the very first Christmas tree. Many people believe that a German preacher named Martin Luther was the first to have a Christmas tree. On Christmas Eve, as he walked home, he looked at the trees and twinkling stars and thought of the night Jesus was born in Bethlehem. He wanted his family to share his feelings, so he cut down a small evergreen tree, brought it home, and decorated it with small candles to look like stars.

Each year, the President lights the tall Christmas tree at the nation's capital. The decorations for this tree come from every state. In California, we have the "Nation's Christmas Tree," which is a giant sequoia, 267 feet high and 107 feet wide. Another huge tree, which is put up at Rockefeller Center in New York, is visited by many, many people each year.

Christmas trees are a favorite Christmas symbol.

LANGUAGE ARTS - SOCIAL STUDIES - SCIENCE

Discussion

Repeat the Flannel Board Symbols Activity and Song from Day 1. Set up the classroom Christmas tree. Display a cross section of a tree trunk, cones and needles, seeds, and pictures of different evergreen varieties. Discuss the concept information and define the vocabulary words.

Book - Christmas Trees and How They Grow - by Glenn O. Blough

Since this book is long, you may wish to summarize each page and show the pictures.

Evergreen Trees - Stages of Growth

Duplicate and distribute the "Stages of Growth" sheet (page 187). Divide the chalkboard into six sections. Explain and illustrate the stages of growth (see example, page 188). The children illustrate each section of their sheets.

Stages of Growth:

1. Seed falls from cone on tree.
2. Breeze blows seed.
3. Rain, wind, or animals bury seeds.
4. Seed splits.
5. Roots push down into the ground.
6. Leaves and trunk push out of ground.

Fingerplay - "Christmas Tree"

I'm a Christmas tree, (Arms extended slightly)

High or low, (Raise up and down)

If I'm on my knees (On knees)

Or on my toes. (Up on toes)

Action Story - "Christmas Tree Day"

Seat the children on the floor. Read the story. The children perform the actions as directed.

(**Story**) - Jessica and David jumped out of bed (jump up), got dressed (dress), and ran downstairs (run in place). They quickly ate their breakfast (eat) and brushed their teeth (brush). Then they shouted "Ready!" (shout "Ready!") They were going to the tree farm to pick out a Christmas tree and could hardly wait. Dad got in the car (act out). Jessica and David got in the back (act out). They all put on their seat belts (act out). Soon they were there. David and Jessica ran to see the trees (run in place). David saw a tall, skinny tree (stretch arms high) that he liked. Jessica saw a short, fat tree (stretch arms wide) that she liked.

Dad said, "Have you found a tree?"

Jessica said, "This one, this one!" (point)

David said, "No, this one, this one!" (point higher)

Dad saw another tree. It was as tall as David's (stretch arms high) and as fat as Jessica's (stretch arms wide).

"Do you like this one?" asked Dad. (point)

"Yes, yes," shouted Jessica and David. (shout "yes, yes" and nod heads)

The tree farm man picked up his big axe (pick up) and chopped down the tree (chopping motion). The tree fell (fall gently on floor). The man took the tree to the car (carry tree and walk in place). Dad, David, and Jessica got into the car (act out). They couldn't wait to get home and decorate their tall (stretch arms high), fat (stretch arms wide) Christmas tree (make point with hands together over head).

Growing Baby Christmas Trees

Preparation - For each child, provide one pine cone, one margarine tub, potting soil, and grass seed. Pour ½" of water into each margarine tub. Fill a large bowl with water. Soak each pine cone in water for a few minutes; then place in margarine tub. Sprinkle potting soil, then grass seed evenly over each cone. Place the pine cones in a sunny location. Make sure the water level remains the same. The grass will grow within two weeks. Use scissors to trim in the shape of a tree. (See example, page 189.)

ART

Cellophane Trees

Preparation - Duplicate the cellophane trees (see Patterns, Pictures, Etc., page 190) on green construction paper. Cut small squares of different colored cellophane. Provide glue, scissors, hole punchers, and ornament hangers. Distribute trees and cellophane strips.

Procedure - Punch holes in the tree. If necessary, fold the tree to punch the middle holes. Apply glue to the edges of the cellophane squares. On the back of the tree, glue the squares over the holes. Vary the colors. Attach ornament hangers at the top. Hang on the class tree or in a window. (See example, page 189.)

Tin Punch Trees

Preparation - Collect tin pie plates and corrugated cardboard squares. Trace tree pattern (see Patterns, Pictures, Etc., page 191) on plates and cut out with strong scissors. Cover the edges with silver-colored vinyl tape. Give each child a tree and a cardboard square. Provide hammers and nails, and yarn or string for hanging.

Procedure - Using the cardboard for padding, punch holes as desired in the tin tree. Punch a hole in the top and insert the hanger. Tie in a knot. (See example, page 189.)

Stand-Up Trees

Preparation - On green construction paper, duplicate two stand-up trees (see Patterns, Pictures, Etc., page 192) for each child. Provide glue, glitter, scissors, and two gold sticker stars for each child. Have staplers available.

Procedure - Cut out both trees. Dab with glue, and sprinkle with glitter on both sides. Dry. Fold each tree in half lengthwise on the dotted lines. Staple together on this line. Stick the two stars together on either side of the top of the stand-up tree. (See example, page 189.)

MATH

Christmas Number Booklet

Read the lines and discuss the numeral "7". Color the trees.

Tree Number Puzzle

Preparation - Duplicate and distribute the puzzle outline and puzzle pieces (see Patterns, Pictures, Etc., pages 193-194). Provide scissors, glue, and crayons.

Procedure - Cut out and color the puzzle pieces. Count the objects and glue in the correct numeral spaces.

MUSIC - MOVEMENT - GAMES

Song - "O Christmas Tree"

Source: A Musical Christmas with Peter Duchin

Listening

Sesame Street A Merry Christmas (LP or tape), "A Christmas Pageant"

Movement - Growing Trees

Read once and explain the actions. Read again as the children act out the story.

Tiny seeds sleeping in the ground,   (Lie on floor in curled position with eyes closed)

The rain and the sun wake you up. (Open eyes)

You begin to grow and grow. (Slowly rise)

You reach and reach for the sun. (Stretch, stretch, then form a ball with arms)

The gentle wind blows you from side to side. (Sway from side to side)

You catch the rain on your leaves. (Cup hands and catch the rain)

You have grown tall. (Tiptoe and stretch arms above head)

Birds light on your branches. (Hold out arms)

The sun goes down (Form ball with arms and lower)

It is time for sleep. (Fold hands beside cheek, close eyes)

STORY TIME

Book - <u>ABC Christmas</u> - Ida DeLage

Story - "Happy Christmas Tree" - Frances Ann Brown (from the book <u>Told Under the Magic Umbrella</u> selected by Literature Committee of the Association for Childhood Education)

KINDERGARTEN KITCHEN

Merry Krispie Trees

1/4 cup margarine
4 cups miniature marshmallows
5 cups Rice Krispies cereal
Sprinkles

Over low heat, melt margarine in a large saucepan. Add and stir marshmallows until completely melted. Cook for three more minutes, stirring constantly. Remove from heat and add cereal. Stir until well-coated. Use waxed paper to press warm mixture into a 9" x 13" x 2" buttered pan. Depth should be approximately $\frac{1}{2}$". With cookie cutters, cut into tree shapes and decorate with sprinkles. Yield: approximately 12 trees.

EXTRAS

Field Trip

Arrange for the class to visit a Christmas tree farm. Before the trip, list questions and points to observe. When you return, list on the board or an experience chart the trees you saw and information learned. Ask the children to draw and color "what they liked best." Send their pictures along with a thank-you note to the Christmas tree farm.

DAY 10 - DECORATING THE TREE

CONCEPT INFORMATION

Everyone enjoys <u>decorating</u> the Christmas tree. Long ago, Christmas trees were decorated with real fruit, gingerbread cookies, <u>sugarplums</u>, flowers, and lighted candles. <u>Paper chains</u>, <u>tin soldiers</u>, paper stars, cotton ball angels, and long strips of popcorn and <u>cranberries</u> were also used. Then <u>glassblowers</u> in Germany started making glass balls to use as <u>ornaments</u>. These were pretty and not as heavy as fruit and nuts. Many people still make ornaments from <u>cloth</u> and paper and glitter and wood because it is so much fun. Today in stores we can buy ornaments for our trees.

Angels, bells, reindeer, and Santas are all symbols of Christmas that we hang on our trees. Many people believe we use <u>tinsel</u> because long ago some little spiders decided to <u>explore</u> a Christmas tree. As they crawled, they left <u>spider webs</u> all over the tree. When the Christ child saw the tree, he touched the webs and turned them to <u>silver</u>. Ever since then, we use shining silver tinsel to decorate our trees. Another story is about a little pine tree that had no gift for the Christ Child. Seeing how sad he was, God sent some stars to <u>rest</u> on the pine tree's little branches. Later, candles were put on Christmas trees—to look like these stars. In the year 1895, a man named Ralph E. Morris thought of putting <u>electric light bulbs</u> on his family's Christmas tree. Now we put more colorful electric lights, which are safer to use, on our trees, houses, and stores at Christmas.

LANGUAGE ARTS - SOCIAL STUDIES - SCIENCE

Discussion

Repeat the Flannel Board Symbols Activity and Song from Day 1. Display pictures of the decorated trees of long ago, ornaments resembling those used long ago, and "modern" ornaments. Share the concept information, defining the vocabulary words. Encourage the children to examine and compare the ornaments.

Class Christmas Tree

Begin decorating the class tree. Ornaments made in art can be added each day.

Decorating the Learning Tree

Using colored chalk, draw a large Christmas tree on the chalkboard. Draw twenty-six (or as many as needed) ornaments on the tree. Call on one child at a time to write an alphabet letter in each ornament. Once this is completed, let the students add their own decorations with colored chalk.

Variation: Substitute numerals or names for the alphabet.

Classification Activity

<u>Preparation</u> - Draw and/or cut out magazine pictures of ornaments, food, and clothing. Glue on paper squares. Duplicate a Symbols sheet (see Patterns, Pictures, Etc., page 195) for each child. Direct the children to cut out the three symbols.

<u>Procedure</u> - Hold up one picture at a time. The students decide if the picture is an ornament, food, or clothing, and hold up the proper symbol.

Rebus Story - "The Best Tree"

Place the rebus story sheet (see Patterns, Pictures, Etc., page 196) on the opaque projector. Read the story, letting the children supply the words for the pictures. If necessary, enlarge the story before using.

Fingerplay - "Here's a Ball"

Here's a red ball for Tina. (Form ball with thumb and index finger)

Here's a blue ball for me. (Repeat with other hand)

Here's a candy cane for Thomas. (Hold up arm, curve hand downward)

Let's decorate the tree! (Arms up, elbows out, fingertips form point)

ART

Toothpick Ornaments

<u>Preparation</u> - Purchase colored toothpicks, 15-20 per child; pipe cleaners, one per child; and aluminum foil. Tear a 7" sheet of foil for each child. Roll one-third of each pipe cleaner into a small circle. Supply glue.

<u>Procedure</u> - Place the circle end of the pipe cleaner in the center of the aluminum foil. Crumple the foil into a tight ball around the circle. Curve the top of the pipe cleaner to form a hanger. Dip the ends of the toothpicks in glue and insert into the foil ball.

Note: Make small name tags of paper and punch holes in the tops. Place on the pipe cleaner hanger. (See example, page 197.)

Decorated Trees

<u>Preparation</u> - Duplicate the tree pattern (see Patterns, Pictures, Etc., page 198) on green construction paper. Give one tree and paper scraps of different colors to each child. Provide scissors, glue, and hole punchers.

<u>Procedure</u> - Cut out the tree. Punch holes in the scraps to make "ornaments." Glue these scrap dots to the tree. (See example, page 197.)

Pine Cone Trees

<u>Preparation</u> - One pine cone per child, glue, and glitter are needed.

<u>Procedure</u> - Dab glue on the scales of the pine cone. Sprinkle on glitter. Dry. (See example, page 197.)

Variation: Spray-paint the cones green. Glue on tiny ornaments or beads.

MATH

Color Patterns - Paper Chains

<u>Preparation</u> - Give each student a different color of construction paper. Provide scissors and glue.

<u>Procedure</u> - The children cut the sheets of construction paper into 1" x 9" strips, then exchange strips with others so that each person has different colors. Call out the first color. Each child finds this color and glues the top of one end to the bottom of the other end, and holds for a count of ten or until the glue bonds. Call out the second color. The child puts this strip through the first circle and glues as before. Repeat until all strips are used. Call on children to name the different colors of their paper chains. (See example, page 197.)

Note: These short paper chains may be hung on the tree like ornaments. If you want one long chain, use extra strips to join all of them together.

Ornament Shapes Sheet

Duplicate and distribute the sheet (page 199). The children trace with crayons: all of the circles with red, the squares with blue, the rectangles with green, the triangles with orange, the ellipses with purple, the diamonds with brown, and the stars with yellow. Call out one step at a time.

MUSIC - MOVEMENT - GAMES

Movement - "O Christmas Tree"

Form a circle around the class Christmas tree. Sing "O Christmas Tree" (see Music - Movement - Games, Day 9) while performing the following movements:

    Line 1 - Circle moves to the right.
    Line 2 - Stop, swing clasped hands up and down.
    Line 3 - Circle moves to the left.
    Line 4 - Stop, swing clasped hands up and down.

Line 5 - Hands remain clasped; step back five mini-steps.
Line 6 - Hands remain clasped; step forward five mini-steps.
Line 7 - Sliding feet, circle moves right.
Line 8 - Sliding feet, circles moves left.

Game -"Ornament Relay"

Preparation - Obtain unbreakable ornaments and two soup spoons. Mark a starting and finish line. Divide the class into even two teams. Line up the teams behind the starting line. Give the first player in each line an ornament and a spoon.

Procedure - The first two players run to and from the finish line balancing the ornament in the bowl of the spoon. The second two players take the ornaments and spoons and repeat the procedure. If the ornament drops, the player picks it up and proceeds from the point where it dropped. The team whose last player finishes first wins.

STORY TIME

Book - The Beautiful Christmas Tree - Charlotte Zolotow
Book - The Christmas Tree Book - Carol North

KINDERGARTEN KITCHEN

Paintbrush Cookies

Cream together:	3/4 cup butter or margarine 1 cup sugar
Add and blend:	2 eggs 1 teaspoon vanilla
Add and mix with a fork:	2-1/2 cups all-purpose flour 1 teaspoon baking powder 1 teaspoon salt

Chill for at least one hour. Roll out on floured surface. Cut with cookie cutters into shapes. Place on greased cookie sheet. Use paintbrushes and cookie paint (see recipe below) to paint designs on the cookies. Bake at 375° for 8-10 minutes. Yield: 3 dozen 2-3" cookies

Cookie Paint

Blend 3 egg yolks with 3/4 teaspoon water. Divide into small cups and add food coloring to each. Mix well. If the mixture thickens too much, add a few drops of water.

EXTRAS

A Christmas Tree for the Birds

Select a nearby tree to hang bird food ornaments (see below) for the birds. Use string or strips of mesh vegetable bags (from the supermarket) for hanging.

Bird Food Ornaments

Mix two large jars of peanut butter with raisins, dry breakfast cereal, and oatmeal. Form into small balls. Place in refrigerator until hard. Tie with string or the vegetable bag strips and hang in tree.

DAY 11 - STARS

CONCEPT INFORMATION

Most of our Christmas ornaments are symbols, which means they stand for something. Stars are placed at the top of Christmas trees to remind us of the star of Bethlehem. This star guided the Wise Men to the manger where Jesus was born.

Stars used on Christmas trees are made of paper, glass, metal, or plastic. They come in all sizes and colors. Some have a place in the center for a light. Stars are one of the most favorite of all Christmas symbols.

LANGUAGE ARTS - SOCIAL STUDIES - SCIENCE

Discussion

Repeat the Flannel Board Symbols Activity and Song from Day 1. Show examples or pictures of star ornaments as you share the concept information. Define vocabulary words.

Science Activity - "What is a Star?"

Send Homes:

Duplicate the Follow-up sheets and Parents' Letter (see Patterns, Pictures, Etc., pages 200-204) to send home.

Star Box

Find a box which is a little smaller than 9" x 12" and is 4" or 5" deep. Remove the top. Cut a hole in the bottom of the box large enough to insert a flashlight or light bulb. Reproduce the Constellation sheets (see Patterns, Pictures, Etc. pages 205-207). Place black construction paper under the Constellation sheets and use a needle or an ice pick to punch holes, designating the stars, through both thicknesses. Stand the box on its side. Tape or tack the black sheet only over the top. Share the following discussion information and book. Then turn on the flashlight or lamp. Name and view the constellations. Repeat with the other sheets.

Note: If you cannot find a box of the correct dimensions, enlarge or reduce the Constellation sheets to fit the box you use.

Discussion

How many of you have seen stars in the sky at night? Did you ever wonder what a star is? A star is really a sun. It is a cluster of hot gases.

The gases of stars blaze and make light. The light travels through the air. Since air is always moving, the lights of the stars move also. This is why they "twinkle."

Stars also shine during the day, but we cannot see them. This is because the sun, which is also a star, is closest to us. It shines so brightly that we cannot see the other stars. We see them after the sun goes down.

Thousands of years ago, people noticed that groups of stars seem to form pictures. They gave these constellations names that we still use today such as the Big Dipper, the Little Dipper, the Lion, Hercules, the Crab, and the Twins.

Book

Read The Big Dipper by Franklyn M. Branley.

Fingerplay - "Stars"

The tiny stars you see at night   (Point upward, count stars)

Are like our sun, so warm and bright.   (Shade eyes)

But far away, they look so small.   (Separate thumb and index finger by small amount)

They barely give us light at all.   (Open eyes wide, strain to see)

Fingerplay - "The Falling Star"

I looked up at the dark night sky   (Look up, shade eyes)

And saw a falling star pass by.   (Smile, point, allow arm to descend)

It died before it hit the ground

And to this day it can't be found.   (Search floor)

Star Name Game

Preparation - Duplicate and distribute the Star sheet (see Patterns, Pictures, Etc., page 208) for each child. Provide crayons and scissors.

Procedure - The students color, cut out, and write their names on the stars. Assist if necessary. Collect the stars and seat the children in a circle. Spread out the stars on the floor. Call on each child to find his or her name star and pick it up. Spread out the stars once more. Call on children to pick out others' name stars.

ART

Popsicle Stick Stars

Preparation - You will need four wooden popsicle sticks and one paper clip per child, yellow fluorescent paint, paintbrushes, and strong craft glue.

Procedure - Paint both sides of the sticks with fluorescent paint. Dry. Glue two sticks in the middle to form a cross. Repeat with the other two sticks. Dry. Glue both sets together to form an eight-point star. Place the paper clip hanger in a "puddle of glue" on the back of the star at the top of one of the sticks. An ornament hook may be inserted through this hanger. (See example, page 209.)

Shiny Stars

Preparation - Make several Shiny Star patterns (see Patterns, Pictures, Etc., page 209). Provide tagboard, pencils, scissors, hole punchers, paintbrushes, and ornament hooks. Mix "Shiny Star Paint" as follows: one part white liquid glue and one part yellow tempera. Stir thoroughly. Store in an air-tight container.

Procedure - Trace the pattern on tagboard and cut out. Punch a hole in the top of one point. Paint. Hang with an ornament hook or yarn.

Star Shapes

Preparation - Duplicate the Star Shape (see Patterns, Pictures, Etc., page 210) on white construction paper. Provide star-shaped cereal and glue.

Procedure - Cover the star with a generous amount of glue. Fill in with star-shaped cereal. (See example, page 209.)

MATH

Stars in the Sky Sheet

Preparation - Give each child: a sheet of black and a sheet of yellow construction paper, a square of corrugated cardboard, a pencil, and a yellow or white crayon. Provide a stapler.

Procedure - Direct the children to fold the black sheet in half lengthwise, then in half widthwise. Using the yellow or white crayon, draw lines on the folds dividing the sheet into fourths. Call out four different numerals for the children to write at the bottom of each block. The sheet is then placed on the cardboard. The students use their pencils to punch the correct number of holes, or "stars," in each block. Staple the yellow sheet behind the black sheet.

Note: The pencil should be punched through the paper and "wiggled" to make sure the hole stays open.

One-to-One Correspondence Sheet

Preparation - Duplicate the sheet (page 211). Hand out the sheet, four sticker stars, and crayons.

Procedure - Color the trees. Put a star at the top of each tree.

MUSIC - MOVEMENT - GAMES

Song - "There's a Star"

Tune: "There's a Hole in the Bottom of the Sea"

There's a star at the top of the tree.

There's a star at the top of the tree.

There's a star, there's a star,

There's a star, there's a star,

There's a star at the top of the tree.

Verses:

2.   There's a light in the star at the top of the tree . . .

3.   There's a shine from the light in the star at the top of the tree . . .

Song - "Twinkle, Twinkle, Little Star"

Sing the song. Turn off the lights, hold up the fluorescent Popsicle Stick Stars (see Art), and sing the song again.

Song - "Stars Are the Windows of Heaven"

From There's a Hippo in My Tub (LP) - Anne Murray

Game - Catch a Falling Star

Preparation - Blow up a yellow balloon. Draw a star on the balloon with a permanent marker. Give each child a number card strung on yarn to wear as a necklace or a numbered contact paper square to stick on his or her hand. Make sure each child knows his or her number. Seat the children in a circle. Have star candy or stickers available.

Procedure - The teacher stands in the center of the circle, calls out a number, and drops the balloon. The child with that number tries to catch the balloon before it hits the floor.   Repeat until all participate.   Pass out rewards.

STORY TIME

Book - <u>Tiny Shiny</u> - Lloyd Funchess, Jr.
Book - <u>A Star for Hansi</u> - Marguerite Vance

KINDERGARTEN KITCHEN

No-Cook Fudge

1 lb. confectioners sugar, sifted
2 eggs, well beaten
1 1/2 teaspoons vanilla
1 6-oz package semi-sweet chocolate chips
2 tablespoons butter
1 cup chopped nuts (optional)

Mix sugar and eggs until smooth.   Add vanilla and nuts, if desired.   Set aside.   Over low heat, melt chocolate chips in a double boiler.   Stir constantly.   Blend butter with chocolate.   Combine chocolate mixture with sugar mixture. Mix well. Pour into greased 9" x 9" pan. When the fudge has hardened, cut into pieces.   Yield: approximately 36 1" pieces

DAY 12 - GIVING

CONCEPT INFORMATION

The first Christmas <u>gifts</u> were brought to Baby Jesus by the three Wise Men long ago. Today at Christmas, we <u>exchange</u> gifts with our families and friends. It is a wonderful feeling to give a <u>present</u> to someone you love. It is also <u>exciting</u> to open gifts and see what is inside. What is a gift? A gift is something given to someone else. A gift can be big, like a bicycle; or small, like a watch. A gift can make noise if it's a puppy; or rattle if it's a game. A gift can come in all colors and <u>shapes</u>. But a gift is really another way of saying "I love you," "I care about you," and "I'm thinking about you." It is <u>important</u> to remember this! Whether Grandmother gives you a bicycle or a book, both gifts mean the same thing—that Grandmother loves you. There are other gifts besides wrapped presents. A hug or a kiss is a wonderful gift. It is also something given to someone else that shows you care. Doing something nice for someone, like taking out the trash or setting the table, or <u>complimenting</u> others, is also a gift. We can give gifts like these all year long.

LANGUAGE ARTS - SOCIAL STUDIES - SCIENCE

Discussion

Share the concept information and define the vocabulary words. Explain and demonstrate giving sincere compliments. Ask the students to exchange kind words. Discuss the feelings involved. Encourage the children to follow this practice each day.

Story - "A Christmas Story"

From <u>Sesame Street Merry Christmas</u> (LP or tape)

Play the story which is similar to "The Gift of the Magi." Ernie trades his rubber duckie to get Bert a cigar box for his paper clip collection. Bert trades his paper clip collection to get Ernie a soap dish for his rubber duckie.

Poem - "The Joy of Giving" by John Greenleaf Whittier

Read and discuss the meaning of the poem. Reread.

Somehow, not only for Christmas
 But all the long year through,
The joy that you give to others
 Is the joy that comes back to you:

And the more you spend in blessing

    The poor and lonely and sad,

The more of your heart's possessing

    Returns to make you glad.

Book or Play - "The Elves and the Shoemaker" - by the Brothers Grimm

One source is <u>Favorite Fairy Tales Told in Germany</u>, retold by Virginia Haviland.

Read and enjoy the story. To present this story as a play, appoint the following characters: Shoemaker, Shoemaker's Wife, seven Customers, and two Elves. Props include: a table and chair, brown paper for leather, seven pairs of shoes, play money, a candle and a candleholder, play tools, shoes, suits and caps for elves. Read the story as the children act it out.

ART - Gift Ideas

Picture Wreaths

See Bread Dough Picture Wreaths (Art, Day 8).

Bread Dough Cookie Jars

Collect pickle jars and tops. Mix bread dough recipe (see Bread Dough Picture Wreaths - Art, Day 8). Roll dough to ½" thick. Place a lid on the dough. Use plastic knives to cut a circle 1½" wider than the lid. Use a spatula to move the dough and lid to a piece of aluminum foil. Gently mold the dough around the sides of the lid. Turn over. Use a cookie cutter and cut a shape from the extra dough. Moisten and place on the top of the bread dough lid. Bake at 325° to 350° on a foil-covered cookie sheet for one hour, or until lightly brown. (See example, page 212.)

Finish: If desired, baste with a beaten egg after baking for 15 minutes. Return to oven. Or (after baking) paint with tempera, dry, then varnish.

Bread Dough Candleholders

Purchase candles. Mix bread dough recipe (see Bread Dough Picture Wreaths - Art, Day 8). Roll into a 2" or 3" ball. Flatten the bottom. Press the bottom of the candle into the ball. Add cookie cutter or hand-formed shapes to base. Moisten to stick. Remove candle and bake, as above; or air dry.

Finish: Same as Cookie Jar, above. (See example, page 212.)

Recipe Booklets

Each child dictates his or her favorite recipe, just as he or she would prepare it, as you write it on half of a ditto master. Duplicate and assemble the booklet. Use construction paper decorated by the children for the cover.

Handprint Placemats

Preparation - Purchase burlap in the color desired. Cut each placemat approximately 13" x 16". Mix tempera and pour a thin layer into a tin pie plate. Furnish paintbrushes, a bucket of water, and towels for cleanup.

Procedure - Unravel 1" of burlap on all sides. Dip each hand in the tempera and print on the placemat. Use the paintbrush to write your name under the print, or the names of family members on the placemat. Dry. (See example, page 212.)

Coupon Holder I

Preparation - Collect small boxes, such as macaroni and cheese boxes. Cut in half across the middle, making two short boxes. Spray both halves with enamel paint. Give each child: the two halves of one box, a large pipe cleaner, scrap paper, and glue or scraps of contact paper. Provide permanent markers, hole punchers, scissors, and staplers. Write "Coupons" on the board. Duplicate the Coupon sheets (see Patterns, Pictures, Etc., pages 214-215).

Procedure - Staple the boxes together back to back with the openings at the top. Punch a hole on each side of the center piece and insert a pipe cleaner handle. With permanent markers, write "Coupons" on either side of the holder. Decorate with scraps. Cut out, sign, and insert the coupons in the holder. (See example, page 213.)

Coupon Holder II

Preparation - Cut colored tagboard into pieces 11" wide by 10½" tall, one per child. Furnish two 6" pieces of yarn or ribbon per child, crayons or markers, glue, and a stapler. Duplicate the Coupon sheets (see Patterns, Pictures, Etc., pages 214-215).

Procedure - Fold up 3" of the bottom of the tagboard piece, forming a 3" pocket. Crease. (The pocket will measure 3" x 11".) Bring the right and left sides together and crease in the middle. Glue the pockets at the edges. Staple the pocket on the middle crease. Punch a hole midway at both sides. Tie yarn pieces to holes. Decorate the holder with crayons or markers. Cut out, sign, and insert the coupons in the holder pockets. Close the coupon holder and tie the yarn pieces into a bow. (See example, page 213.)

Pig String Holders

Preparation - For each child, provide: an oatmeal box and top, two 2½" pieces of drinking straw, a 1" x 2" piece of cardboard, two 1½" cardboard circles, and one pink pipe cleaner. Set out pink tempera paint, paintbrushes, pink scrap paper, brown fine point markers, pencils, and scissors. Purchase several balls of string. Remove the top of each oatmeal box, cut the box to measure 4" tall, and replace the top. Give each child an ample length of string.

Procedure - Paint the box and top pink. Use the pencil to punch two holes side by side in the middle of the bottom of the box. With the brown marker, draw a circle around the two holes to represent the pig's snout, and then draw two eyes. Insert the straw pieces halfway into each hole. Dab with a small amount of glue to secure. For the tail, curl the pipe cleaner around a finger and remove. With a pencil, punch a small hole in the middle of the box top. Dip the pipe cleaner tail in glue and glue in the pencil hole. Cut two ears from the scrap paper and glue to the box. To anchor the pig, spread glue on the middle portion of the 1½" circles and glue to the underside of the pig, 1" apart. Wrap the length of string around and around the piece of cardboard. Place inside the pig, threading one end through one of the straws. (See example, page 213.)

Bunch of Grapes - Refrigerator Magnets

Preparation - Cut several patterns (page 213). Give each child: 13 purple pipe cleaners, a piece of white tagboard, and a strip of magnetic tape. Provide the patterns, glue, pencils, and scissors.

Procedure - Trace the pattern on tagboard. Cut out. On the back, mount the strip of magnetic tape. Wrap each pipe cleaner around and around a finger to resemble a spring. Arrange all pipe cleaners on the tagboard. Glue in place.

Christmas Goody Baskets

Make baskets by weaving Christmas ribbon through the spaces of strawberry baskets. Attach four pieces to the corners, and tie together to form a hanger. Or, cut a circle, 6" to 8", from heavy wrapping paper. Cut a slit from the edges and staple to form a cone. Punch holes and insert a pipe cleaner handle. Fill the baskets with candy or cookies. (See example, page 213.)

ART

Wrapping Paper

Preparation - Purchase white shelf, tissue, or wrapping paper. Cut in lengths to cover parents' gift. Cut candy cane shapes from corrugated cardboard with the wavy part exposed on one side, and/or Christmas shapes from sponges. Mix tempera. Pour thin layers into aluminum pie plates.

Procedure - Dip wavy side of candy canes and either side of sponge shapes in tempera. Print on paper. Dry.

Note: Clothespins can be attached to one side of the sponge shapes as handles.

MATH

Christmas Number Booklet

Read the lines and discuss the numeral "8". Color the gifts.

Counting Bows

Purchase several packages of Christmas bows. Seat the children in a circle on the floor. Place the bows in the center in a pile. Lay numeral cards 1 to 10 across the area. Call on children to read the numeral card, count and pick up that many bows, and place them under the card. Change the procedure by asking a child to pick up a handful of bows, count them, and find the correct numeral card. (You may also wish to designate certain colors.)

MUSIC - MOVEMENT - GAMES

Song - "What a World We'd Have if Christmas Lasted All Year Long"

From Holiday Songs and Rhythms (LP) by Hap Palmer

Song - "All I Want for Christmas Is My Two Front Teeth"

Source: Children's Christmas Party (LP), Halo Records

Game - What?

This game is played like "Gossip." Seat the children in a circle. Ask one child, "What would you like to give your mother (father, sister, brother, etc.) for Christmas?" That child whispers the answer in the ear of the child next to him or her who, in turn, whispers the answer in the ear of the next child. This is repeated until the last child hears the answer. Ask that child to repeat the answer he or she heard. Compare with the original answer. Repeat, starting with another child each time.

STORY TIME

Book - <u>The Twelve Days of Christmas</u> - Hilary Knight
Book - <u>Paul's Christmas Birthday</u> - Carol Carrick
Book - <u>The Christmas Camel</u> - Nancy Winslow Parker

KINDERGARTEN KITCHEN

Humdingers

1 stick butter
3/4 cup granulated sugar
1 8-oz. package of dates
1 teaspoon vanilla
2 cups Rice Krispies cereal
1 cup chopped nuts
Powdered sugar

In a saucepan over low heat, melt butter. Add sugar and chopped dates.
Stir all together. Cook for 5 minutes. Remove from stove. Mix in
vanilla, Rice Krispies, and nuts. Form into small balls, then roll in
powdered sugar.

EXTRAS

Care Trip

Make Christmas Goody Baskets and fill with Humdingers, cookies, or candy.
Make arrangements to visit a nursing home or hospital and present the
favors. Sing carols and perform Christmas fingerplays.

DAY 13 - CHRISTMAS CARDS

CONCEPT INFORMATION

Another way we show people we care about them is to send Christmas cards. A Christmas card is a heavy piece of paper which is folded much like a book. Different Christmas symbols of scenes are printed on the outside with a message such as "Merry Christmas" or "Season's Greetings" on the inside. Under this message, we sign our names. The card is put in an envelope, addressed, and mailed. Christmas cards can be bought at the store or made at home.

The first Christmas cards were made by schoolboys in England for their parents. They were called "Christmas pieces." The oldest known printed Christmas card is in the state of Massachusetts. It was made in 1839. In 1875, a man called Louis Prang began printing Christmas cards, and they became popular. Today, Christmas cards of all kinds are found in many stores.

LANGUAGE ARTS - SOCIAL STUDIES - SCIENCE

Discussion

Repeat the Flannel Board Symbols Activity and Song from Day 1. Share the concept information and define the vocabulary words. Display Christmas cards. Discuss the scenes and messages of each.

Christmas Card - Alike and Different Match

Preparation - Collect Christmas cards, two of each kind.

Procedure - Display two "alike" cards at a time. Call on a child to determine if the two cards are alike or different. Display two "different" cards and ask the same question. Repeat. After each answer, ask the children to point out the similarities or differences of the two cards.

Christmas Card Completion Sheet

Duplicate and distribute the sheet (page 216). Provide crayons. The children draw lines to complete the scene. Color.

Class Christmas Card

Fold a piece of tagboard in half. Decide on Christmas symbols to decorate the front. Draw symbols on the board and choose volunteers for each. Set out construction paper, glue, crayons, and scissors. After the symbols are completed, arrange and glue on the front of the card. Decide on a message.   Write it on the board, calling out each letter.   Different children write each letter on the card.   Everyone signs the card.

Stand the card on the chalkboard ledge.   Ask the children to find the symbols that start with certain letters.   Then ask the children to name the symbols that are green, red, etc., that make sounds, that have smells, and so forth.   Hang the card on the classroom door or in the hall.

Jigsaw Puzzle Cards

For each child, cut an old Christmas card into a simple puzzle and place it in an envelope.   Pass out the puzzles.   The students put them together. Puzzles may be exchanged.

Note: To prevent pieces being mixed up, code each puzzle.   To code, write a letter, number, or symbol on the back of each puzzle piece.

ART

Christmas Peepboxes

Preparation - Collect a shoebox for each child.   Cut a square in the top a few inches from one end for light.   Cut a peephole in the front end of the box.   Distribute boxes, old Christmas cards, scissors, and glue.   Show the children how to leave an extra ½" as a tab when cutting the bottom of each object.

Procedure - Cut objects or figures from the cards to make a scene inside the box.   Fold the tabs and glue in the box at the end opposite the peephole.   Some objects or a scene can be glued to the inside back of the box as a background.   Tape the top.   Look through the peephole at the scene.   (See example, page 217.)

Printed Pop-Up Cards for Mom and Dad

Preparation - Distribute sheets of white construction paper a 3" x 4½" piece of white construction paper, and crayons.   Mix red tempera and pour thin layers in tin pie plates.   For each child, cut two ½" x 1" strips of paper and fold accordion-style.

Procedure - Fold the sheet of white construction paper in half to form a card.   Hold up your hand with fingers straight.   Now slightly curl your fingers.   Keep you hand in this position.   With thumb pointing upward, dip the side of your palm and curled little finger into the paint and print on the front of the card.   The shape should be that of a candy cane.   Repeat as desired.   Use crayons to write "Merry Christmas" or "I love you" on the 3" x 4½" piece of paper.   Turn it over.   Glue the bottom of each accordion strip to the back of this piece.   Dab glue on the tops of the two accordion strips.   Open the card and glue these inside.   This part will pop up when the card is opened. Sign the card and attach to the parents' gift. (See example, page 217.)

Santa Claus Christmas Card Bags

Preparation - Purchase small lunch-sized red paper bags and plastic "wiggle" eyes. Make several 5" circle and 5" triangle patterns (page 218) from cardboard. Give each child: a bag, two eyes, two gummed reinforcements, 10 or 12 cotton balls, an 18" piece of ribbon, and a half-sheet of red and a half-sheet of pink construction paper. Provide glue, scissors, pencils, and hole punchers.

Procedure - On the pink paper, trace a circle and cut out. On the red paper, trace the triangle and cut out. For a face, glue the circle at the top of the bag. Glue the triangle hat on top of the circle. Glue on the plastic eyes. Glue one cotton ball to the top of the hat. Use the other cotton balls for the eyebrows, the hair, and the mustache and beard. Punch holes on either side of the bag, stick on the reinforcements, and string the ribbon for hanging. (See example, page 217.)

MATH

Christmas Number Booklet

Read the lines and discuss the numeral "9". Color the cards.

MUSIC - MOVEMENT - GAMES

Song - "Jingle Bells" by J. S. Pierpont, 1857

Dashing through the snow in a one-horse open sleigh:

O'er the fields we go, laughing all the way;

Bells on bob-tail ring, making spirits bright;

Oh, what fun it is to ride and sing a sleighing song tonight!

Refrain:

Jingle bells, jingle bells, jingle all the way!

Oh, what fun it is to ride in a one-horse open sleigh!

Jingle bells, jingle bells, jingle all the way!

Oh, what fun it is to ride in a one-horse open sleigh!

Game - Snatch the Card

Preparation - Divide the class into two teams. The teams line up facing each other about 15' to 20' apart. Assign a different number or color to each child on the first team. Use the same numbers or colors for the members of the second team.   Place a Christmas card on the floor in the center of the area.

Procedure - Call out one of the numbers or colors.   The two children with this number or color race to the card.   The object is for one of them to snatch the card and return to his place without being tagged by the other player.   If successful, he scores two points for his team.   If he is tagged, the other team scores one point.

STORY TIME

Book - <u>The Christmas Cat</u> - Efner Tudor Holmes
Book - <u>Looking for Santa</u> - Henrik Drescher

KINDERGARTEN KITCHEN

Graham Cracker Christmas Cards

Graham crackers, one whole cracker per child
Decorations: cans of decorating icing (or see icing recipe below), gumdrops, peppermints, tiny candy canes, cinnamon drops, cookie sprinkles
Fishing line

Snow White Icing

1 egg, separated
2 cups confectioners sugar
1/8 teaspoon lemon juice

Using an electric mixer at high speed, beat the egg white until frothy and white.   Reduce to medium speed and gradually add sugar.   Beat until thick and smooth.   Add the lemon juice and mix for 5 minutes.   Spread immediately.

String a 5" piece of fishing line through the corner hole of the graham cracker.   Widen the hole with a large needle if neccessary.   Tie in a knot. Use a plastic knife to cover the front of each graham cracker with icing. Decorate with candy, etc.   Allow to dry; then hang on the tree.

DAY 14 - TOYS

CONCEPT INFORMATION

Children have always <u>enjoyed</u> playing with toys. Even the children of long ago had toys. Then, there were no stores and no <u>manufacturers</u> to make toys, so toys were <u>homemade</u>. Children played with sticks, balls, <u>hoops</u>, rag dolls, stick dolls, and <u>carts</u>.

Today there are many <u>companies</u> which make toys. Four or five thousand new toys are <u>invented</u> each year. All toys belong to certain toy groups or families. Some of these families are: (1) vehicles, like cars, trucks, and bicycles, (2) balls, (3) dolls, (4) games, board-type or computer, and (5) stuffed toys.

It is fun to use toys to <u>pretend</u>. When you pretend, a doll can be a real baby and a toy car can be a real car. Even a plain stick can become a <u>sword</u>. The children of long ago pretended just like you do, so they enjoyed their homemade toys just like you enjoy your toys. It is <u>exciting</u> at Christmas to go to the toy store and see the new toys. Then you can make a list and send it to Santa.

LANGUAGE ARTS - SOCIAL STUDIES - SCIENCE

Discussion

Repeat the Flannel Board Symbols Activity and Song from Day 1. A few days beforehand, send home the parents' letter for the day. Display a variety of modern toys and examples or pictures of toys of long ago. Relate the concept information, defining vocabulary words. List the toy families on the board. Call on the children to point out a toy for each family.

Peek-a-Boo Activity

Seat the students in a circle, facing outward with eyes closed. Place three or four toys on the floor in the center of the circle. Cover with a towel or small blanket. Ask the children to turn around and open their eyes. Remove the cover for a few seconds, allowing the children to look at the toys. Cover. Call on a child to name the toys he or she saw. Repeat the procedure substituting different toys.

Teddy Bear Day

As explained in the Parents' Letter, each child brings a teddy bear to school. Prepare a yarn and paper name tag necklace for each bear. On each tag, designate the owner and the bear's names.

Seat the children with their bears in a circle.   Each child displays and discusses his or her bear.   Discuss the appearances, similarities, and differences of the bears.

Teddy Bear Information

The first teddy bear was made by a man named Morris Mitchum and his wife.   They named the bear "Teddy" after Teddy Roosevelt who was then the President of the United States.   President Roosevelt loved to hunt. Once when he was hunting, he saw a bear.   The President wouldn't shoot it though because it was too small.   This is why Mr. Mitchum named stuffed bears after the President.

So many people love teddy bears that they have rallies and festivals for them.   Both adults and children bring their teddy bears to show off.   They have food, games, and teddy bear contests.   The National Bear Rally is held at the Philadelphia Zoo.

There are also teddy bear clubs and many books about teddy bears, such as Paddington Bear and Winnie the Pooh.

Contest

Duplicate the contest awards (see Patterns, Pictures, Etc., page 220), one for each bear.   Tape two pieces of blue ribbon to the back.   Punch a hole in the top and insert a paper clip.   Label awards, "Biggest Bear," Smallest Bear," "Best Dressed Bear," "Most Loved Bear," and so forth.   Judge the bears and attach the other end of the paper clip to the yarn name tag necklace.   Be sure all bears get a prize.

Teddy Bears' Picnic

Prepare the recipes (see Kindergarten Kitchen).   Set the tables and place a teddy bear in each seat.   Serve the food.   Each child sits with his or her bear and eats the refreshments.   Play the song "Teddy Bears' Picnic" from "There's a Hippo in My Tub" (LP) by Anne Murray.

Teddy Bear Alphabet Match

Preparation - Before duplicating the sheet (see Patterns, Pictures, Etc., page 242), write a different upper-case alphabet letter on the sweaters of the bears on the top row.   Write the matching lower-case alphabet letter on the remaining bears.   Duplicate and distribute the sheets.

Procedure - The children draw lines to match the bears, and color.

ART

Name Your Bear

Preparation - Purchase alphabet noodles. Duplicate the bear pattern (see Patterns, Pictures, Etc., page 222) on heavy white paper. Provide crayons, markers or tempera, scissors, glue, and noodle letters.

Procedure - As a reference, help each child write the name of his or her bear on the paper outside the bear pattern. The students cut out and color the bear, and then glue on the bear's name using the noodle letters. (See example, page 222.)

Bear and the Bee Game

Preparation - Collect half-pint milk cartons. Cover with contact paper, spray-paint or leave as is. Punch a hole $\frac{1}{2}$" from the top of one side. Purchase a yellow bead for each child. Cut 8" lengths of string. Transfer the bear face pattern to a ditto master, duplicate, and distribute (see Patterns, Pictures, Etc., page 222). Provide colors or markers, fine point black markers, glue, and scissors.

Procedure - Cut out the bear face, and color. Glue to the side of the milk carton under the punched hole. With the permanent marker, draw black stripes on the yellow bead. Tie one end of the string in the hole of the milk carton and one end to the bead. The game is played by swinging the bead and catching it in the box. (See example, page 222.)

Note: This is a nice gift for a brother or sister.

MATH

Christmas Number Booklet

Read the lines and discuss the numeral "10". Color the toys.

Toys and Boxes Match

Preparation - Collect five or six toys and find boxes into which they just fit. Set out the boxes and the toys.

Procedure - Discuss the sizes of the toys and boxes. Call on students to find and place the toy in the correct box.

MUSIC - MOVEMENT - GAMES

Action Song - "Teddy Bear"

Sing the song (see Patterns, Pictures, Etc., page 224) and perform the actions.

Bear Tag

Choose one child to be the Bear. The others stand side by side in a line 20' to 25' away. Tap four or five children on the shoulder. Call out "Bear! Bear! There's a bear!" The children tapped run to the Bear. The first to touch the Bear's hand trades places with him or her for the next round. Tap different children for each round. When you call out "Bear! Bear! A gigantic bear!" everyone runs to tag the Bear.

When I Was a Boy - (Courtesy of the Boy Scouts of America)

Take a seated position in front of the audience so they can all see you. Tell them to imitate your actions as you tell this story:

When I was a boy, my dad used to bring me presents. Once he brought me a rocking chair. (Rock back and forth.) Another time he brought me a fan. (Wave hand fan-fashion while continuing to rock.) I remember when he gave me a pair of scissors (move two fingers of the other hand scissors-fashion while continuing the first two actions) and a toy airplane that he hung from the ceiling; it went round and round. (Rotate your head.) Finally, he brought me a bicycle. (Peddle with your feet. At this point, jump up and yell, "Wow!")

STORY TIME

Book - The Nutcracker - Adapted by Warren Chappel (Read in installments.)
Book - Paddington Bear (books) - Michael Bond
Book - Winnie the Pooh (books) - A. A. Milne
Book - The Berenstain Bears (books) - Stan and Jan Berenstain
Book - Little Bear (books) - Else Holmelund Menarik
Book - Bedtime for Frances - Russell Hoban
Book - A Bargain for Frances - Russell Hoban

KINDERGARTEN KITCHEN

Banana Cooler

1 1/2 cups cold milk
1 large banana, sliced
1/4 teaspoon cinnamon
1 tablespoon molasses

Pour into blender. Mix to desired consistency. Serve chilled.
Yield: 2 servings

Teddy Bear's Granola

2 1/2 cups raw rolled oats
3/4 cup chopped nuts
1/4 cup sunflower seeds (already shelled)
1 cup shredded coconut
1/4 cup sesame seeds
1/2 cup raw wheat germ
3/4 cup honey
1/4 cup vegetable oil
1 cup raisins

Mix together all ingredients except raisins. Spread in shallow pans. Bake
at 275°, turning every 10 minutes or so until lightly browned. Add raisins.
Cooking time - approximately 30 minutes. Serve in cups.

No-Bake Honey Balls

3/4 cup peanut butter, crunchy
1 cup nonfat dry milk
1 cup Corn Flakes cereal
6 tablespoons honey

Crush the Corn Flakes to a fine consistency. Mix together the peanut
butter and honey. Gradually add nonfat dry milk. Grease hands. Form
mixture into balls and roll in crushed cereal.

DAY 15 - REINDEER

CONCEPT INFORMATION

A reindeer is a <u>deer</u> which lives in the <u>northern</u> <u>areas</u> of the world. Reindeer are about 3½ feet high and weigh about 300 pounds. Reindeer can be <u>tamed</u> and are used to pull <u>sleds</u> for people. The most famous reindeer are Santa's eight reindeer which pull his sleigh each year. They are named Dasher, Dancer, Prancer, Vixen, Comet, Cupid, Donner, and Blitzen. When it is storming or foggy on Christmas Eve, Santa uses Rudolph the Red-Nosed Reindeer to guide the way.

LANGUAGE ARTS - SOCIAL STUDIES - SCIENCE

Discussion

Repeat the Flannel Board Symbols Activity and Song from Day 1. Share the concept information, defining the vocabulary words. Show pictures from an encyclopedia or similar reference book.

Books - <u>Rudolph the Red-Nosed Reindeer</u> and <u>Rudolph Shines Again</u> by Robert L. May

Science Experiment - Fog

Rudolph guided Santa's sleigh on a foggy Christmas Eve. Have you ever seen fog? Do you know what fog is? Clouds that are closer to the ground are called fog. Fog is made when warm air is cooled. Then little drops of water are formed. These droplets are close together and form a cloud or fog. Today we will make our own fog.

Preparation - You will need a large-mouth bottle, crushed ice, hot water, a rubber band, and a thin cloth.

Procedure - Fill the bottle with hot water. When the bottle feels hot, pour out all but 1" to 1½" of water. Place a handful of crushed ice on the cloth. Stretch across the mouth of the bottle and secure with the rubber band. Explain that the warm air is being cooled by the ice. Ask, "What is happening?"

Fingerplay - "Nine Little Reindeer"

Nine little reindeer playing in the snow   (Hold up 9 fingers)

Nine little reindeer at the North Pole   (Hold up 9 fingers)

All of them waiting for Christmas Day   (Hold up 9 fingers)

Waiting and listening for Santa to say   (Cup hands around mouth)

"Come, Dancer, Prancer, Dasher, and Vixen. (Raise first, second, third, fourth fingers)

Come, Comet, Cupid, Donner, and Blitzen." (Raise first, second, third, fourth fingers, other hand)

And Rudolph, of course, guides the sleigh   (Raise one thumb)

Bringing toys and goodies for your Christmas Day. (Hug imaginary toy and rub stomach)

Rudolph Puppet Play

Preparation - Duplicate, color, and cut out the puppets (see Patterns, Pictures, Etc., pages 225-226). Glue to tongue depressors or corrugated cardboard strips. The puppet theater can be a covered table or open-ended box placed on a table. Choose a child for each puppet.

Procedure - As the teacher reads Rudolph the Red-Nosed Reindeer, the students use the puppets to dramatize the story. Repeat, allowing other children to participate.

Rudolph's Feelings Sheet

Duplicate and distribute the sheet (page 227). On the chalkboard, illustrate simple facial expressions. Read each sentence. Ask the children to show how Rudolph feels by drawing his facial expressions.

ART

Reindeer Baskets

Preparation - Duplicate the Eyes and Nose sheet (see Patterns, Pictures, Etc., page 229). Give each child: a sheet of brown construction paper, a sheet of tan or yellow construction paper, two eyes, a nose, a pencil, a red marker and a black marker, scissors, glue, and a 12" piece of plaid Christmas ribbon. Provide a stapler.

Procedure - Roll up the brown construction paper to form a 9" cone. Staple at the back. Cut out the eyes and nose. Color the bottom half of the eyes black and the nose red. Trace each hand, including the wrist, on the tan or yellow construction paper. Cut out. Glue the hand antlers to the top of the cone. (The bottom of the antlers will be inside the cone, or "basket.") Glue the eyes in the middle and the nose on the point of the cone. Staple the ribbon to the top corners. Use it to carry home gifts and/or goodies. It can also be hung on a door. (See example, page 228.)

Note: A red pom-pom can be used for the nose.

Reindeer Paper Bag Puppets

Preparation - Give each student a lunch-sized paper bag. Make eyes, nose and antlers of the Reindeer Basket (on the previous page). Provide staplers and glue.

Procedure - Fold under and staple the two bottom corners of the flap to make the reindeer's face. Glue the nose at the center bottom of the flap, the eyes in the middle, and the antlers at the top. (See example, page 228.)

Reindeer Candy Canes

Preparation - Purchase 5½" cellophane covered candy canes, green pipe cleaners, small red pom-poms, and "wiggle" eyes (approximately ½" in size). Give each child a candy cane, two pipe cleaners, one pom-pom, and two eyes. Set out glue.

Procedure - Glue the pom-pom nose to the end of the curved portion of the candy cane. Glue the eyes above the nose. Fold both pipe cleaners in half. Place the middle crease of one pipe cleaner on the candy cane above the eyes. Twist the ends of the pipe cleaner around the candy cane to secure; then pull in opposite directions to form the "antlers." Cut the other pipe cleaner in half at the crease. Fold each half in the middle. Wrap one pipe cleaner near the end of each antler as shown in the example. (See page 228.)

MATH

Reindeer Shapes Puzzle

Preparation - Duplicate the puzzle pieces and puzzle outline sheets (see Patterns, Pictures, Etc., pages 230-231). Hand out the sheets, scissors, crayons, and glue.

Procedure - Ask the children to cut out all the puzzle pieces. Then direct them to find the following shapes and glue in the puzzle outline: the large triangle, the small triangle, the ellipse, the biggest circle, the two rectangles, the four squares, and the two small circles for eyes. When the glue has dried, the children color the reindeer.

MUSIC - MOVEMENT - GAMES

Songs - "Rudolph the Red-Nosed Reindeer" and "Up On the Rooftop" from Children's Christmas Party (LP), Halo Records

Game - Poor Rudolph

(Adaptation of "Poor Kitty")

Seat the children in a circle and choose one to be Rudolph. Rudolph crawls around the circle. When he stops in front of someone, that player must look Rudolph in the eyes, pat his head, and say "Poor Rudolph" three times without smiling. Rudolph can make faces or "deer" actions to try to make that player smile or laugh. If Rudolph is successful, that player becomes Rudolph. If Rudolph fails, he must try again with another player.

Game - Where Are My Reindeer?

This game is a Christmas version of "Hide 'n Seek." One child is Santa. Santa covers his eyes or leaves the room. The rest of the children, the reindeer, hide as the teacher counts to twenty. The teacher then says, "Santa, it's Christmas Eve and time to leave!" Santa opens his eyes or returns to the room and shouts, "Where are my reindeer?" The hidden reindeer "paw the ground" two or three times while Santa searches for them. When Santa needs more help, he again shouts, "Where are my reindeer?"; and the hidden reindeer "paw the ground" again. The last reindeer found is the new Santa.

STORY TIME

Book - Jan and the Reindeer - Tony Palazzo
Book - The Reindeer Book - Aurelius Battaglia
Book - Santa's Moose - Syd Hoff

KINDERGARTEN KITCHEN

Rudolph Sandwiches

Rye Bread
Peanut butter
Pretzel Sticks
Pitted dates or raisins
Cherries

Cut each slice of bread into four triangles by cutting from corner to corner. Cut dates and cherries in half. Spread peanut butter on the triangular face. Use dates or raisins for the eyes and the cherry for the nose. Insert two pretzels at the top for antlers.

DAY 16 - SANTA

CONCEPT INFORMATION

Santa Claus is the chubby, rosy-cheeked man who brings toys to children on Christmas Eve. It is believed that Santa lives at the North Pole at the top of the world, where he and his elves work all year making toys for good girls and boys. On Christmas Eve, Santa brings the toys in a sleigh pulled by reindeer.

In other countries, Santa is called St. Nicholas or Father Christmas or Befana. Whatever he is called, Santa is the spirit of Christmas, bringing gifts to honor the birthday of Jesus.

LANGUAGE ARTS - SOCIAL STUDIES - SCIENCE

Discussion

Repeat the Flannel Board Symbols Activity and Song from Day 1. Relate the concept information and define the vocabulary words.

Book - 'Twas the Night Before Christmas

Read 'Twas the Night Before Christmas by Clement C. Moore. Reread the book omitting the last rhyming word of every second line. Example:

"'Twas the night before Christmas and all through the house

    Not a creature was stirring, not even a _____."

The children supply the missing word.

Santa's Sack - Sorting Activity

Fill a burlap potato sack or large pillowcase with items that belong to certain groups. For example: canned goods and boxed items of food, a variety of toys, items of clothing, tools for cooking, and so forth. Empty Santa's sack and direct the students to sort into various groups.

Action Story - "Santa's Annual Visit" - (Courtesy of the Boy Scouts of America)

Ask everyone to join in this group stunt and see how Santa goes on his annual trip around the world. Tell them to follow you and repeat what you say or do:

Mrs. Claus waved to her husband from the window (wave). Santa walks across the hard-packed snow (say, "crunch, crunch, crunch, crunch") to the barn where his sleigh is waiting with the reindeer (slap hands rapidly on knees) all hitched up and raring to go. He walks (stamp feet on floor) across the barn floor and enters his sleigh. He calls, "Ho and away," and they're off with a swish (rub hands together in one upward swishing motion).

It begins to snow (rub palms together with circular motion). Soon millions of sparkling snowflakes fill the air. He calls to his dashing reindeer (slap hands on knees) and says, "Down, my fine fellows, we make a stop here."

They descend to a snow-covered roof. Santa gets out and walks to the chimney (beat fists against chest). He's down the chimney with one big swish (make downward swish with the hand). He fills the stockings (fill stockings) and swish (use upward motion), he's up on the roof. Then away he goes with his reindeer (slap hands on knees).

Sounds from the earth reach him as he glides across the sky. (Half of the group says, "Merry Christmas, Merry Christmas, Merry Christmas," and the other half of the group answers in deep voices, "to you, to you, to you.")

Christmas Wishes - Silhouette Activity

For each child, tape a large sheet of white paper to the wall. Place a stool and a light source next to the wall. Seat each child on the stool so his or her shadow appears on the paper. Outline each child's profile and head. Label "Christmas Wishes." Set out old magazines, scissors, and glue. The students find and cut out pictures of things they would like for Christmas. The pictures are glued inside the head.

Poem - "When Santa Claus Comes" - (Author unknown)

A good time is coming, I wish it were here.

The very best time in the whole of the year;

I'm counting each day on my fingers and thumbs—

The weeks that must pass before Santa Claus comes.

Then when the first snowflakes begin to come down,

And the wind whistles sharp and the branches are brown,

I'll not mind the cold, though my fingers it numbs,

For it brings the time nearer when Santa Claus comes.

ART

Star Santas

Preparation - Duplicate the Star Santa (see Patterns, Pictures, Etc., page 233) on white construction paper. Give each child: a Santa, a red and black marker, three or four cotton balls, scissors, glue, and an ornament hook.

Procedure - Color Santa's suit and hat red. Color the belt and boots black. Leave hands and face white. Spread glue on the tip and the bottom of the hat, the beard, at the top of the hands, and the top of the boots. Tear the cotton balls into "wisps" and glue. Punch a hole in the hat with the ornament hook; insert and hang. (See example, page 232.)

Santas

Preparation - Give each child: two sheets of scratch paper, a sheet of pink construction paper and a sheet of red construction paper, white scrap paper, a pencil, crayons, and glue. Provide cotton balls.

Procedure - Practice drawing a large circle and a large triangle on the scratch paper. Draw a large circle on the pink paper and tear on the lines. Draw a large triangle on the red paper and tear as before. Glue the triangle on the circle to represent Santa's face and hat. Tear eyes and the pom-pom for the hat from scrap paper. Color the eyes. Glue all in place. Draw a nose, a mouth, and red circles for cheeks. Spread out each cotton ball and glue at the bottom of the triangle, on the pom-pom, and on the face for the beard and mustache. (See example, page 232.)

Elf Hats

Preparation - On white construction paper, reproduce the hat patterns (see Patterns, Pictures, Etc., page 234); and cut strips 2" x 24", one per child. Place old crayons, separated by color, in muffin tins. On a hot plate, heat slowly until melted. When the muffin tin has cooled, place on the table. Provide scissors, cotton swabs, and a stapler.

Procedure - Cut out the hats. Dip swabs in melted crayons and decorate the hats as desired. At the bottom of the hat, staple the strip to one side, fit on head, and staple to the other side. (See example, page 232.)

Note: Elf hats may be worn to lunch, at the party, or on outings.

MATH

Christmas Number Booklet

Read the lines; then color Santa and his reindeer.

Cookies for Santa

Preparation - Write different numerals on paper plates. Total the numerals and duplicate as many cookies (see Patterns, Pictures, Etc., page 235) as needed. Cut the cookie pages into sections so each child has a few to cut out. Give each child a section of cookies, a numbered paper plate, crayons, scissors, and glue.

Procedure - Cut out the cookies and place them in the middle of the table. Read the numeral on the plate. Pick up that many cookies from the stack; color and glue around the numeral on the plate.

MUSIC - MOVEMENT - GAMES

Songs - "Santa Claus Is Coming to Town" and "Here Comes Santa Claus"

Source: Children's Christmas Party (LP), Halo Records

Song - "Santa"

Tune: "Bingo"

I know a chubby jolly man

And Santa is his name - ho!

S-a-n-t-a, S-a-n-t-a, S-a-n-t-a,

And Santa is his name - ho!

He comes to visit once a year

Late on Christmas Evening

When I'm fast asleep,

When I'm fast asleep,

When I'm fast asleep,

He makes his Christmas visit.

Game - In My Sack

Seat the students in a circle. They should pretend to be Santa filling his sack. The first player says, "I'm putting a _____ in my sack," naming one thing. The next player repeats what the first player said, then adds another item for the sack. The game proceeds around the circle with each player repeating in order what the other players said, then adding someting new.

Optional: A player is out when he leaves something out or mixes up the order.

Note: For younger children, form a small circle and play the game. The others observe until it is their turn to play. This way, the players have to remember fewer items.

STORY TIME

Book - <u>The Santa Claus Book</u> - Aurelius Battaglia
Book - <u>How Santa Had a Long and Difficult Journey Delivering His Presents</u> - Fernando Krahm
Book - <u>Here Comes Santa Claus</u> - M. Hover

KINDERGARTEN KITCHEN

Santa Sugar Cookies

Slice and Bake Sugar Cookies
White ready-to-spread frosting
Red food coloring
Chocolate chips or raisins

Slice the cookies $\frac{1}{4}$" thick. Two slices will make a Santa face. The first slice is the face. Cut the second slice as shown above. Place the triangle at the top of the circle for the hat. The two remaining pieces are placed on the face, curved sides down for the mustache.

Bake as directed. With food coloring, color half of the frosting red for the hats, noses, and mouths. Use the white frosting for the mustache and hat trim. The chocolate chips or raisins are the eyes.

Note: Use toothpicks to apply the frosting noses and mouths.

DAY 17 - CULMINATION

LANGUAGE ARTS - SOCIAL STUDIES - SCIENCE

Flannel Board Activity

Review the symbols by singing the song and placing all symbols on the flannel board (see Language Arts, Etc., Day 1).

Book - ABC Santa

Read ABC Santa by Ida Delage.

Symbols Game

Use pictures or cards of Christmas symbols, foods, or toys from previous lessons. Call on a child to stand in front of the class. Secretly show the child his or her symbol, food, or toys; then pin or clothespin to the back of his or her shirt. The child gives clues or actions to help the class guess the correct answer. After someone guesses or everyone gives up, the child turns around and displays the symbol, food, or toy.

Variation: Divide the class into two teams and keep score.

Tongue Twister

Teach the students the following tongue twister: "Soft snow slows Santa's sleigh." After practicing, volunteers recite the tongue twister for the class.

Letters to Santa

Each child dictates a letter to Santa, then illustrates it. Mail all of the letters to the local Santa show.

Variation: Write one large letter on experience chart paper, including one item for each child. Illustrate and mail.

ART

Mural

Provide a very long sheet of butcher, shelf, or bulletin board paper and markers. The students find a space and fill it with Christmas scenes or symbols. Hang in the hall or cafeteria.

MATH

Christmas Number Booklet

Remove the staple from each booklet.   Assemble pages and covers; staple.

MUSIC - MOVEMENT - GAMES

Christmas Party

Suggested activities for the Christmas party include singing Christmas carols, performing fingerplays, a visit from a volunteer Santa, refreshments, games, and exchanging gifts. A simple method of exchanging gifts is for the boys to bring a boy's gift and the girls to bring a girl's gift.   Each gift is labeled with "boy" or "girl," and the giver's name. Number the boys' gifts; then number the girls' gifts; then draw numbers for boys, then girls.   Set a price limit, such as $1.00 or $1.50.

Game - Pin the Nose on Rudolph

With colored chalk, draw Rudolph's face on the board. A simple triangle with eyes and antlers will do. Put an X for the nose. Cut out red circles and label with each child's name. Ahead of time, roll loops of transparent tape and place on a piece of aluminum foil. Use these to stick the noses in place. Use a blindfold and play just like "Pin the Tail on the Donkey." The child who gets closest to the X wins.

EXTRAS

Door Contest

Ask members of the school staff to judge the classroom doors (see Extras, Day 1).   Make award ribbons from 6" circles of paper with ribbon streamers attached to the backs. The class presents the awards.

CONCEPT EVALUATION

Dear Parents,

On _____, our class will begin our unit on Christmas. Each day we will learn about a different sign or symbol of Christmas such as angels, bells, stockings, toys, and Santa Claus. The activities for each day will center around these topics. Please read below to see how you can help.

Things To Send: _____
_____
_____

Volunteers Needed To: _____
_____
_____

Follow-Up: At the end of the unit, ask your child to share the following songs, fingerplays, or stories we have learned:
_____
_____
_____

Activities Scheduled For Christmas: _____
_____
_____
_____

Thank you for your cooperation.

Sincerely,

Bulletin Boards

Visions of Sugarplums

Signs of Christmas

Displays

Hand Tree

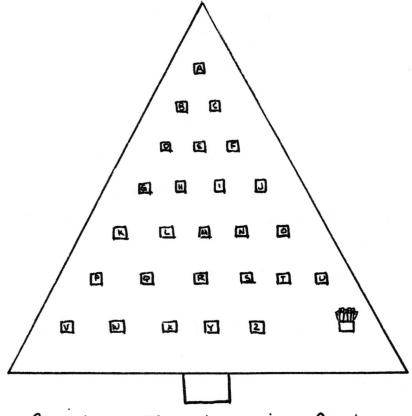

Christmas Tree Learning Center

Signs of Christmas Flannel Board Activity

Signs of Christmas Flannel Board Activity

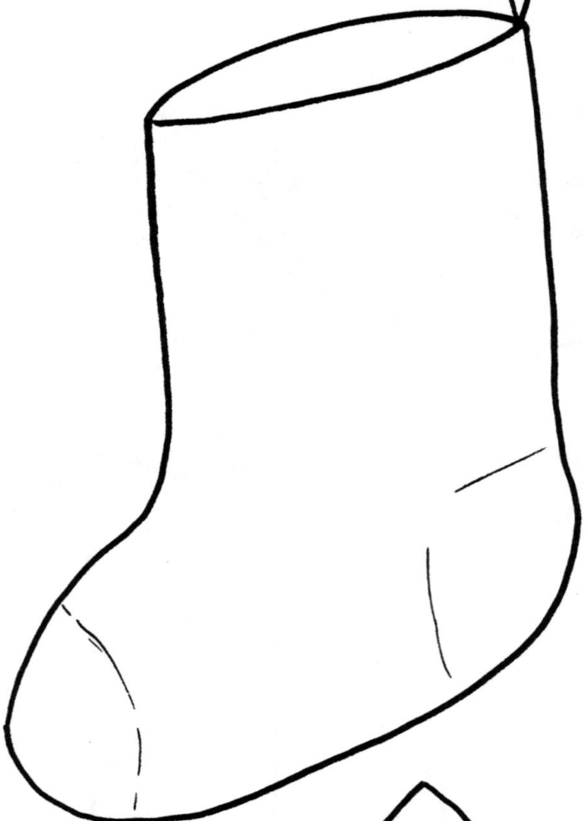

A Christmas Song

American

A Christmas Song, A Christmas Song

We love to sing a Christmas Song

Christmas is a time for song!

Verses

2. It's Christmas Time, it's Christmas Time..

3. A Christmas Carol, a Christmas Carol..

4. Join hands and sing, join hands & sing .....

Signs of Christmas Flannel Board
Activity

Signs of Christmas Flannel Board Activity

Signs of Christmas Flannel Board Activity

Merry Christmas

Christmas

DECEMBER

Calendar

Sunday	Monday	Tuesday	Wednesday	Thursday	Friday	Saturday

Number the days of the month. Each day draw and color a different Christmas symbol in the correct square. On December 25th, remove the candy and write "Christmas" in the square. Enjoy the candy!

Christmas Night Children

Example

Joy Mobiles
Example

Joy Mobiles

pattern -

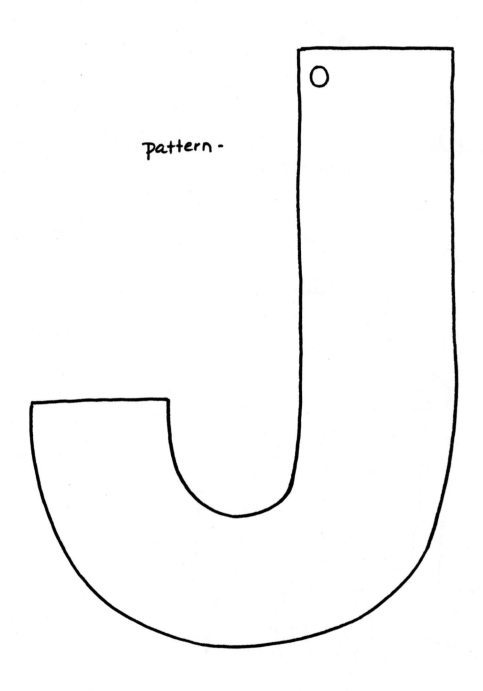

Joy Mobiles

Pattern -

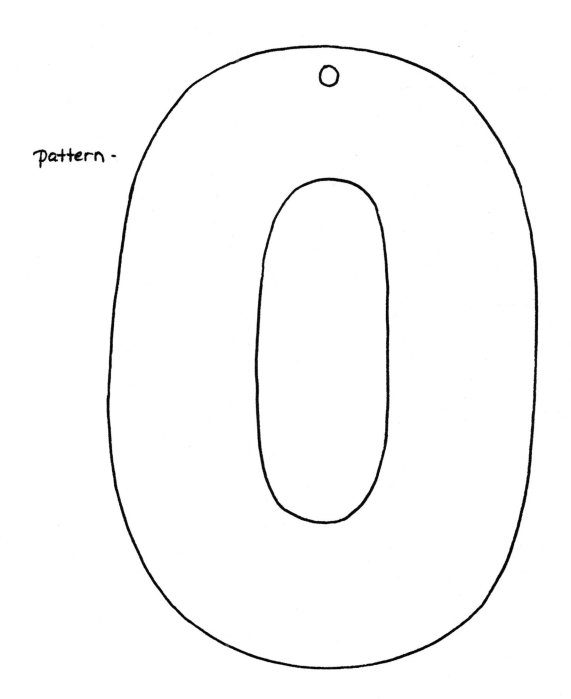

Joy Mobiles

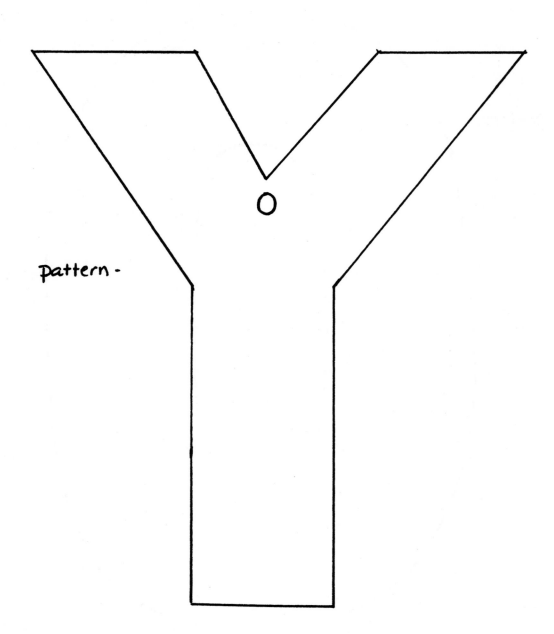

pattern -

Merry Christmas Sign

MERRY

CHRISTMAS

example

Christmas Number Booklet

Come to the Christmas Parade,
Everyone's ready to go,
Come to the Christmas Parade,
Sit down and watch the show!

First in line is 1 Peppermint Stick,
Dressed in red and white and ready to lick.

Then 2 Angels with halo's glowing,
Fluttering wings and soft robes flowing.

Look, 3 Candles marching in a row,
Standing tall with flames aglow.

Next 4 Stockings are such a sight,
Ready to be filled on Christmas night.

See 5 Carolers singing a song,
Of peace on earth all year long.

And 6 Christmas Wreaths roll down the street,
Tipping their bows to all they meet.

7 Christmas Trees march side by side,
Which is the prettiest? You decide.

Then 8 beautiful Gifts of every size and shape,
Wrapped with Christmas paper, shiny ribbons, bows, and tape.

Next are 9 pretty Christmas Cards to send,
Near and far to every special friend.

And last in line are 10 wonderful Toys,
From Santa's workshop for all the girls and boys.

So that's it—no wait, is that sleigh bells I hear?
Yes, it's Santa, Jolly Santa and his 8 reindeer.

He waves and shouts Merry Christmas to you,
Now he is gone, and our parade is through.

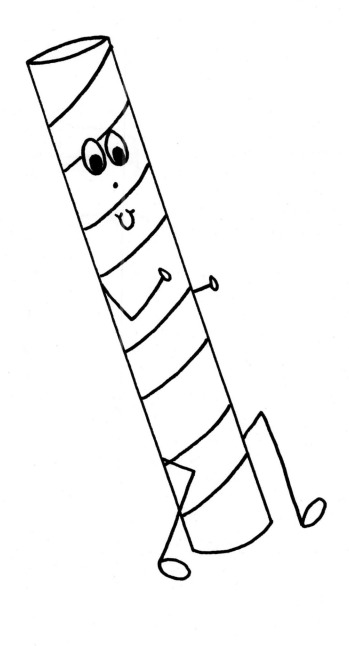

First in line is 1 peppermint stick,
Dressed all in red and white · and ready to lick.

2

Then 2 angels with halos glowing,
Fluttering wings and soft robes flowing.

Look, 3 candles marching in a row,
Standing tall with flames aglow.

Next, 4 stockings are such a sight,
Ready to be filled on Christmas Night.

5

See 5 Carolers singing a song,
Of peace on earth all year long.

And 6 Christmas wreaths roll down the street,
Tipping their bows to all they meet.

7 Christmas trees march side by side,
Which is the prettiest? You decide!

Then 8 beautiful gifts of every size and shape,
Wrapped with Christmas paper, ribbons, bows, and tape.

Next, 9 pretty Christmas cards to send,
Near and far to every special friend.

And last in line are 10 wonderful toys,
From Santa's Workshop for all the girls and boys.

So, that's it - no wait, is that sleigh bells I hear?
Yes, it's Santa, Jolly Santa and his 8 reindeer!

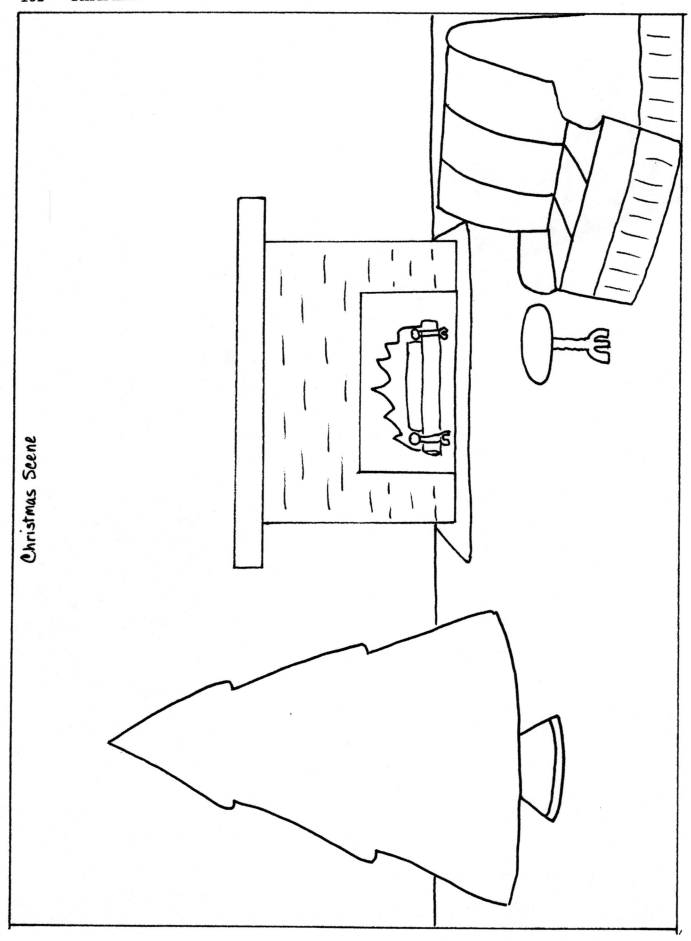

Christmas Scene

You're the Cook

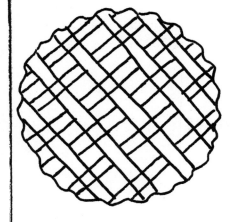

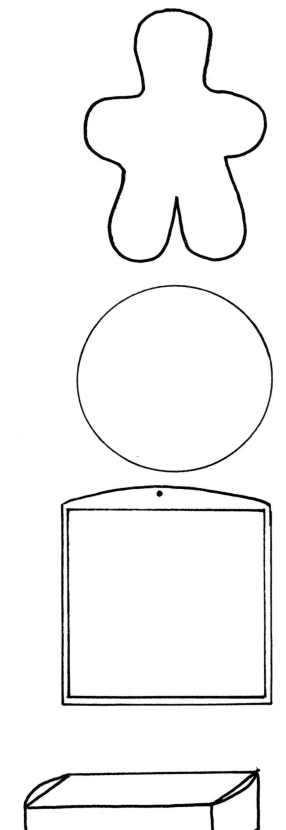

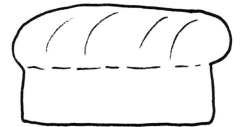

Examples

 - Pipe Cleaner Candy Canes

Plum Pies -

 - Paper Gingerbread Men

Paper
Gingerbread Men

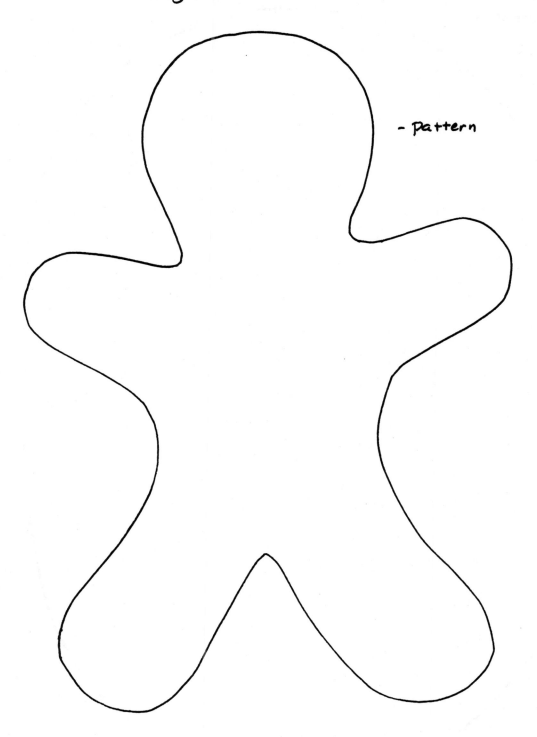

- Pattern

Plum Pies

Pattern -

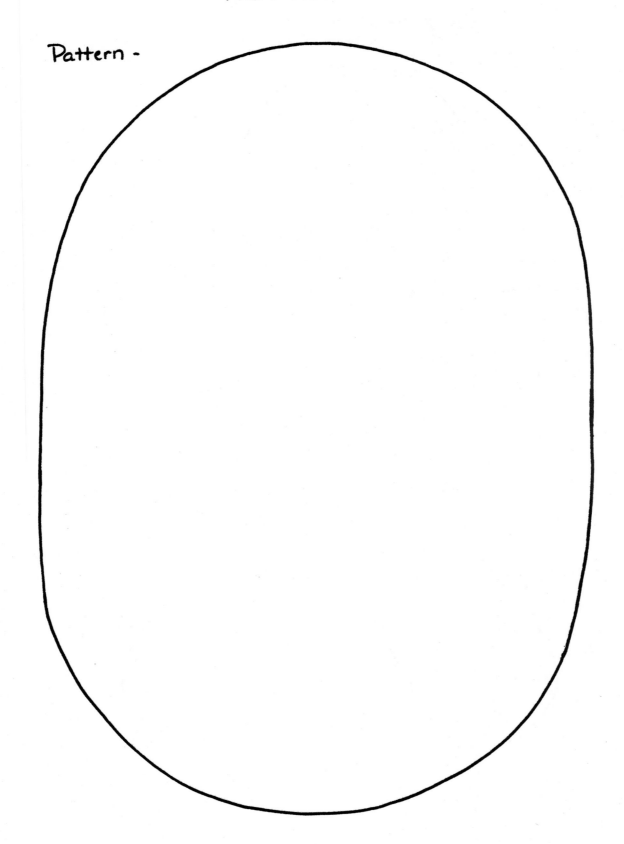

Christmas Clothesline

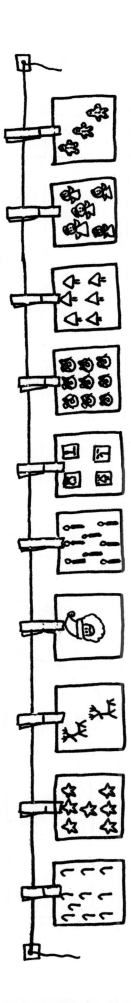

Christmas Treasure Hunt

Front Cover

Bells of Many Colors

I'm a little Christmas bell,
I like to sing a Christmas song,
When I sing,
You hear me ring
Ding dong, ding dong.

Name _____

Bells of Many Colors. Cover

Back Cover.

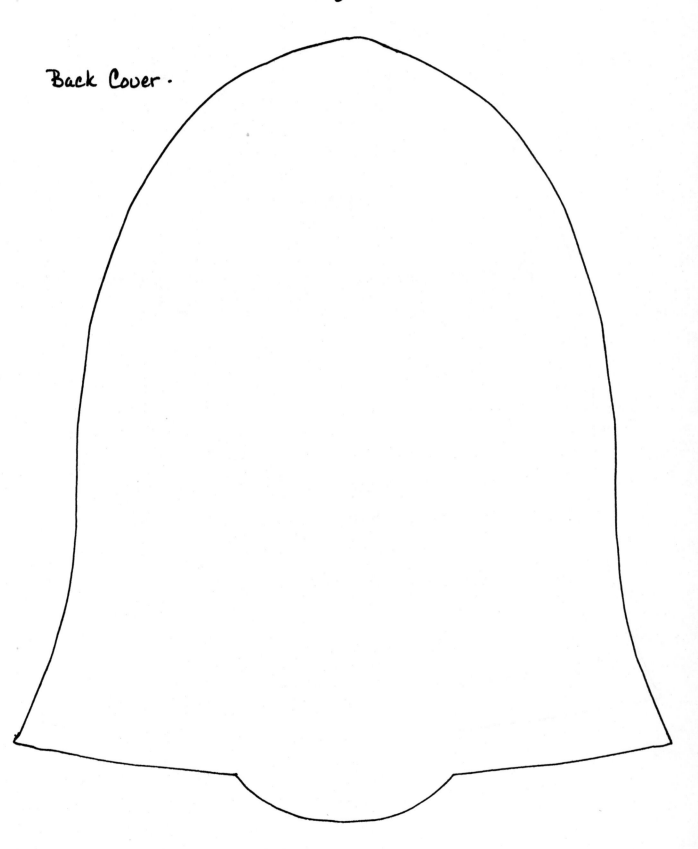

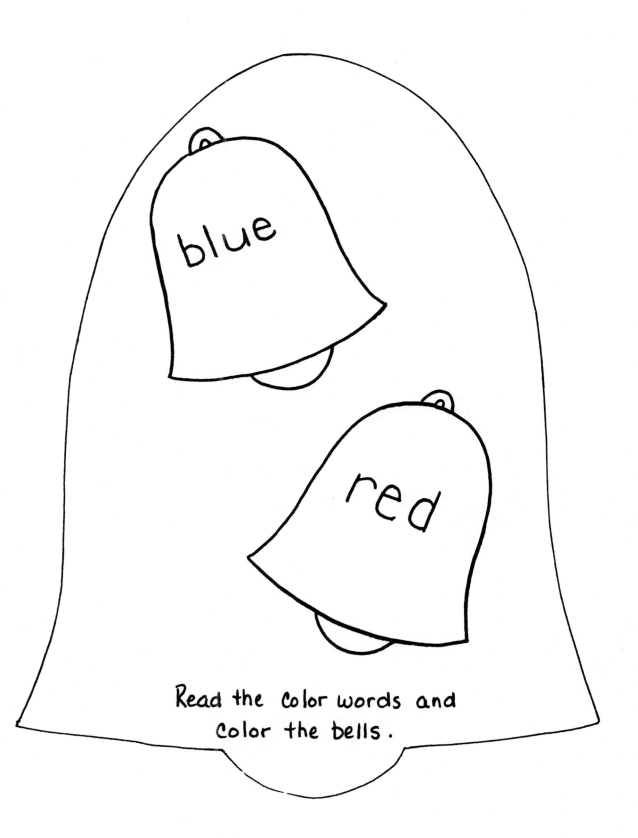

blue

red

Read the color words and
color the bells.

Bells of Many Colors - Pages

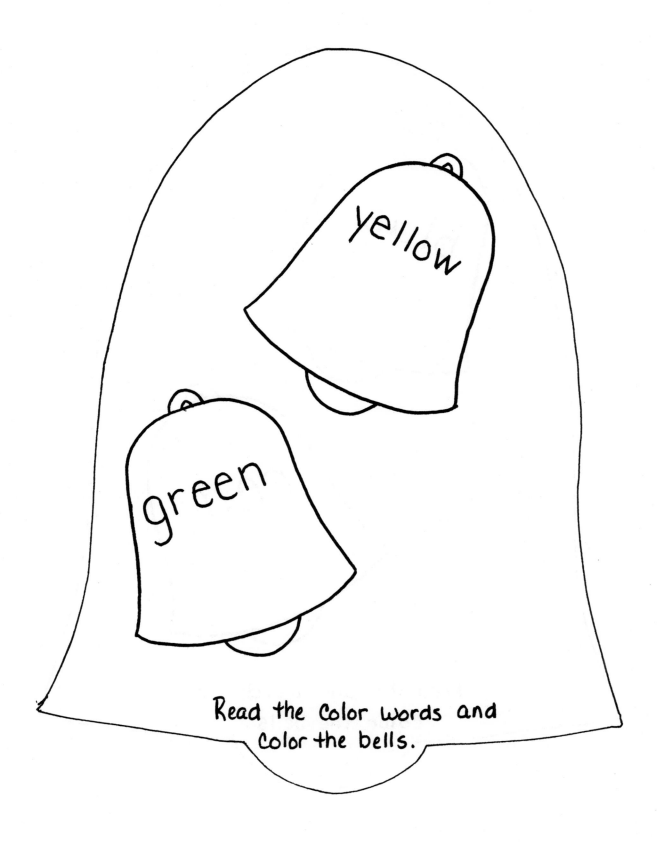

yellow

green

Read the color words and
color the bells.

Bells of Many Colors - Pages

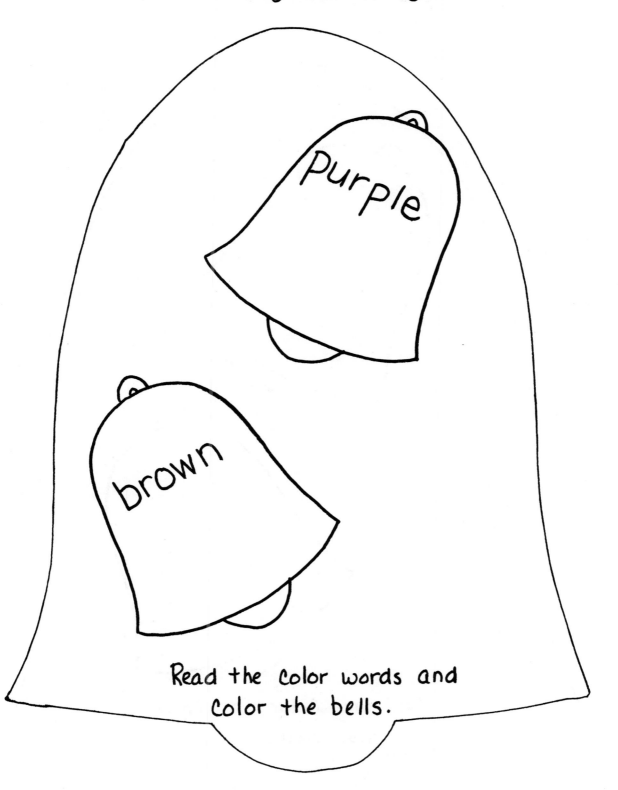

Read the color words and
color the bells.

Bells of Many Colors- Pages

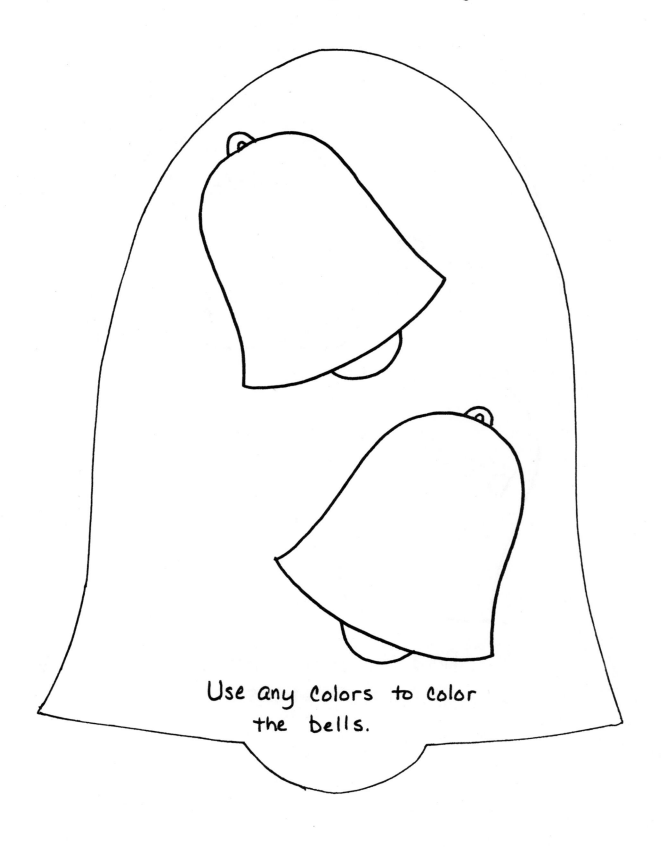

Use any Colors to Color
the bells.

Bells of Many Colors - Pages

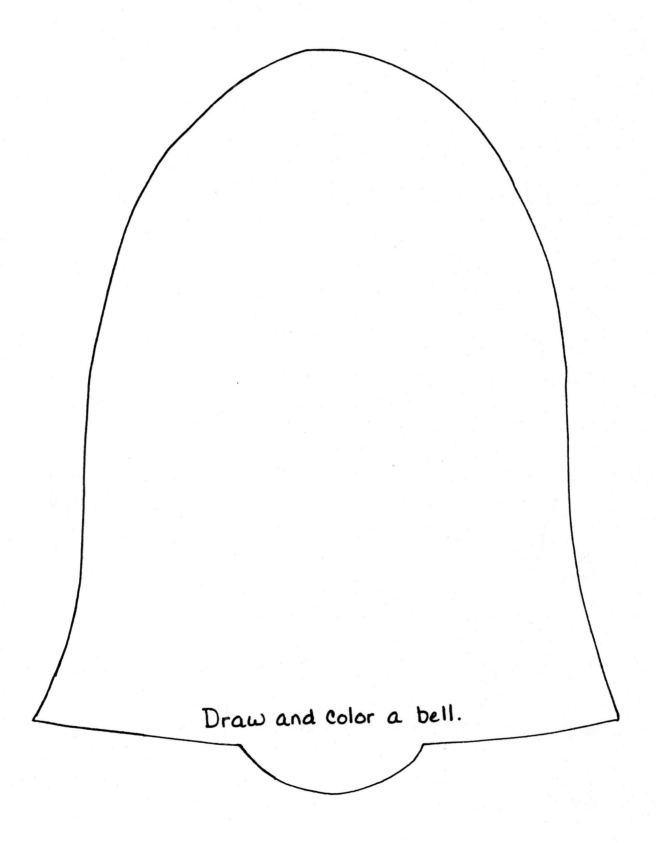

Draw and color a bell.

Bells Pathtracer Sheet

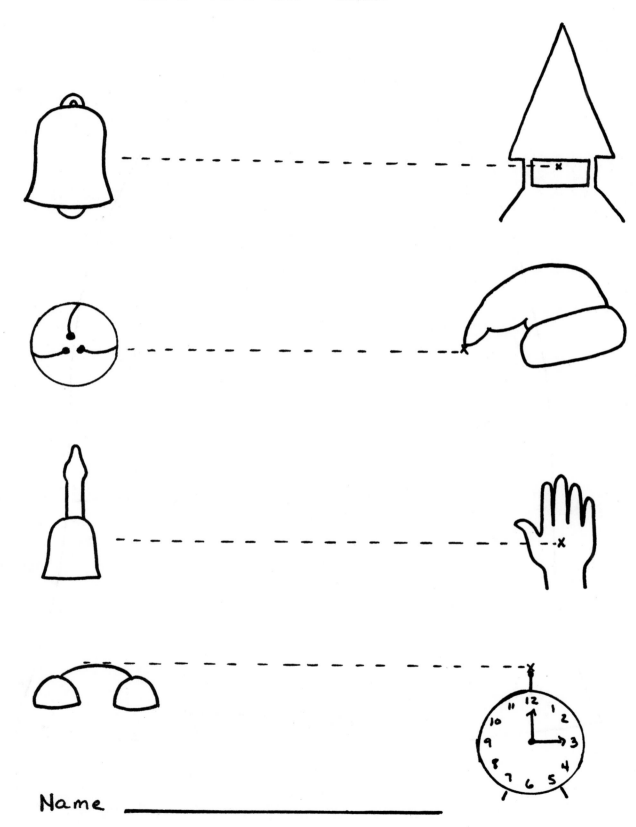

Name _____

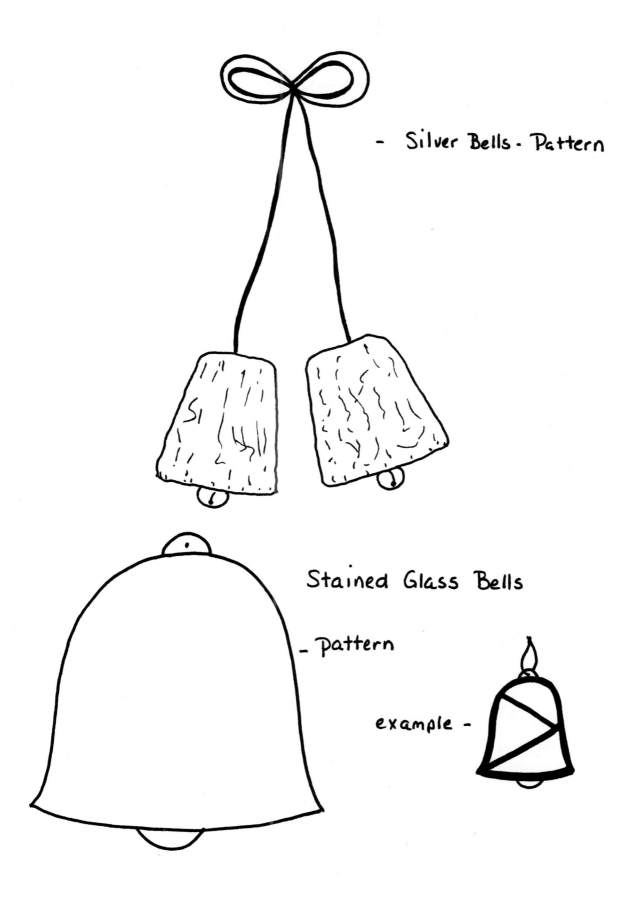

- Silver Bells - Pattern

Stained Glass Bells

- Pattern

example -

Crayon Relief Bells

pattern -

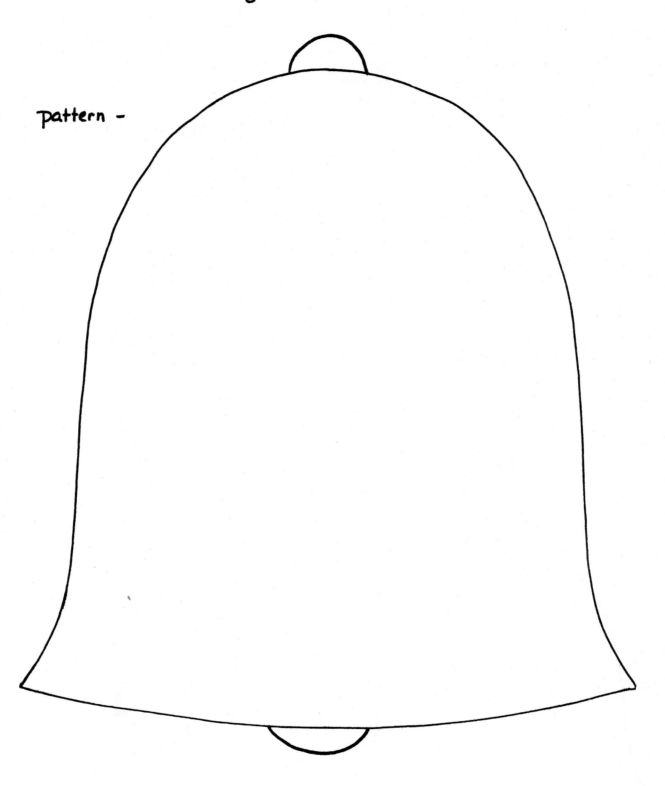

Christmas
Number Booklet

Christmas Number Booklet · Bell Page

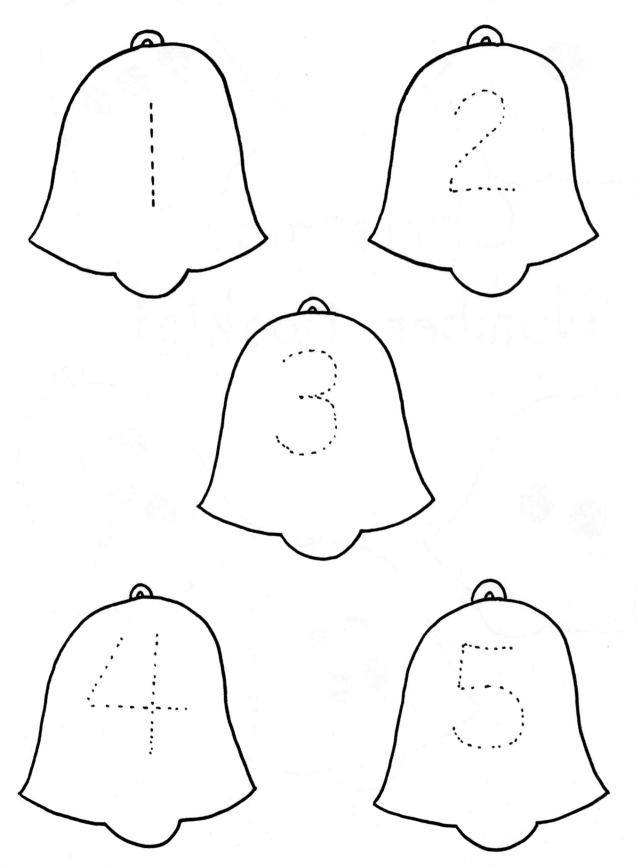

The A-Angel
Patterns

Aa

ball

car

door

pillow

The A-Angel
Patterns

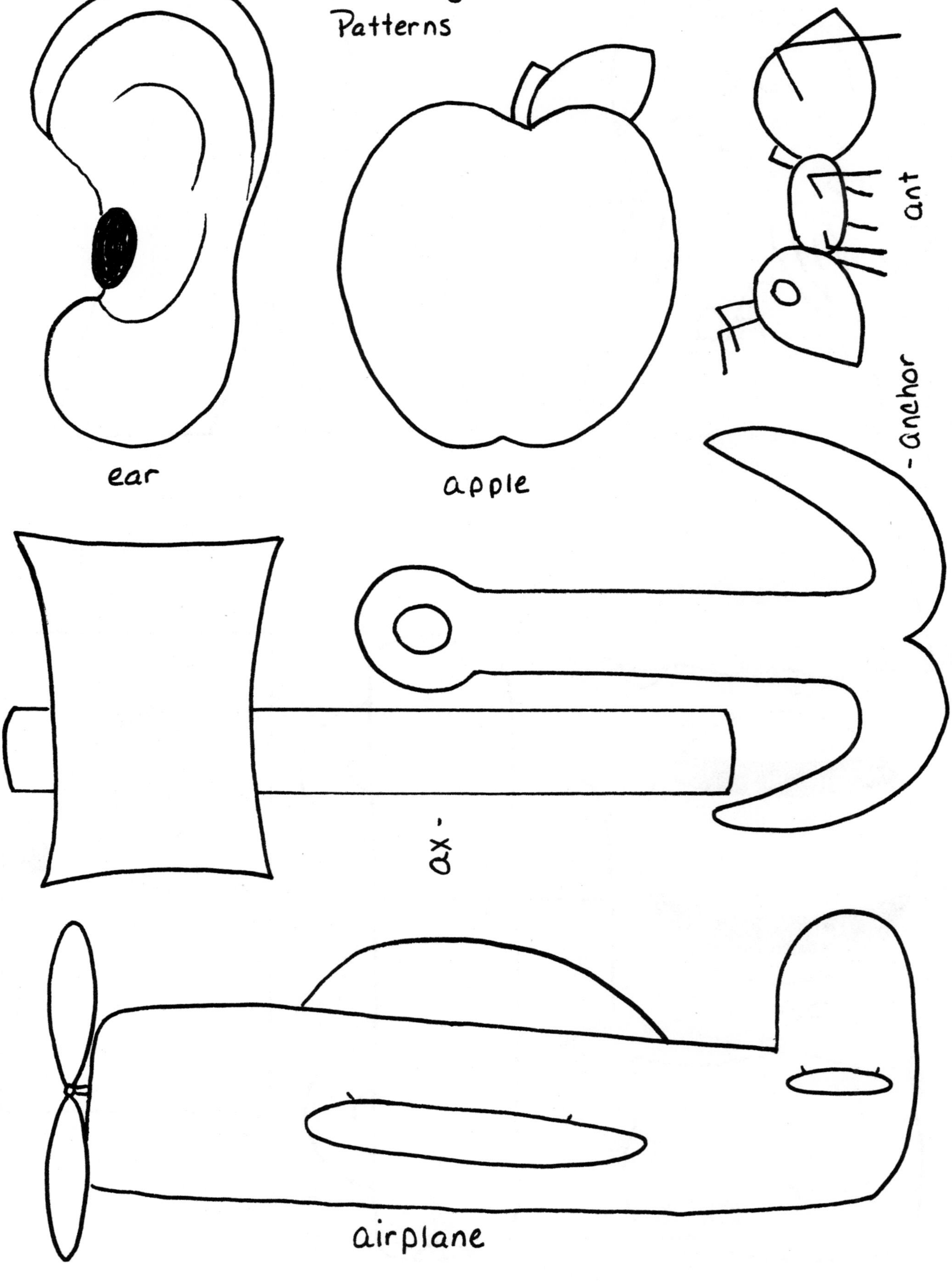

ear

apple

ant

-anchor

ax-

airplane

The A- Angel
Patterns

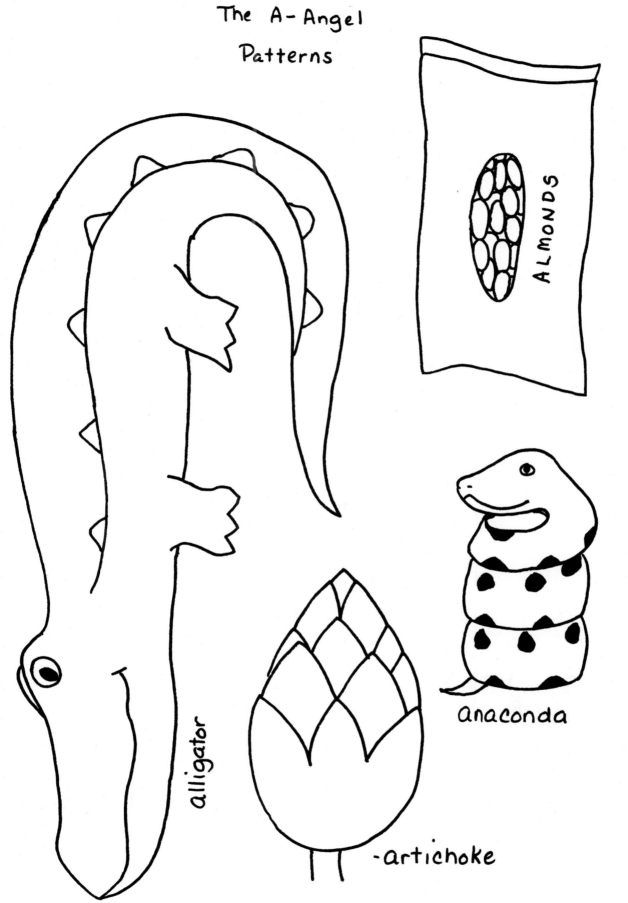

ALMONDS

alligator

-artichoke

anaconda

A-Angel Sheet   Name _____

Angel Maze

Name _____

Help the angel find its cloud by drawing
a line on the path. Color the angel.

Examples

- Angel Paper Bag Puppets

Pine Cone Angels -

- Flying Angels

Angel Paper Bag Puppets

- girl

Angel Paper Bag Puppets

- boy

Flying Angels

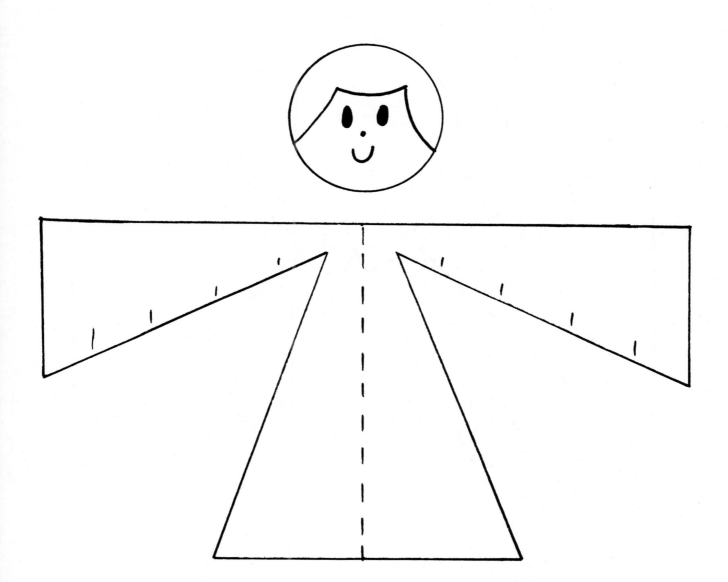

Angel Shapes Puzzle

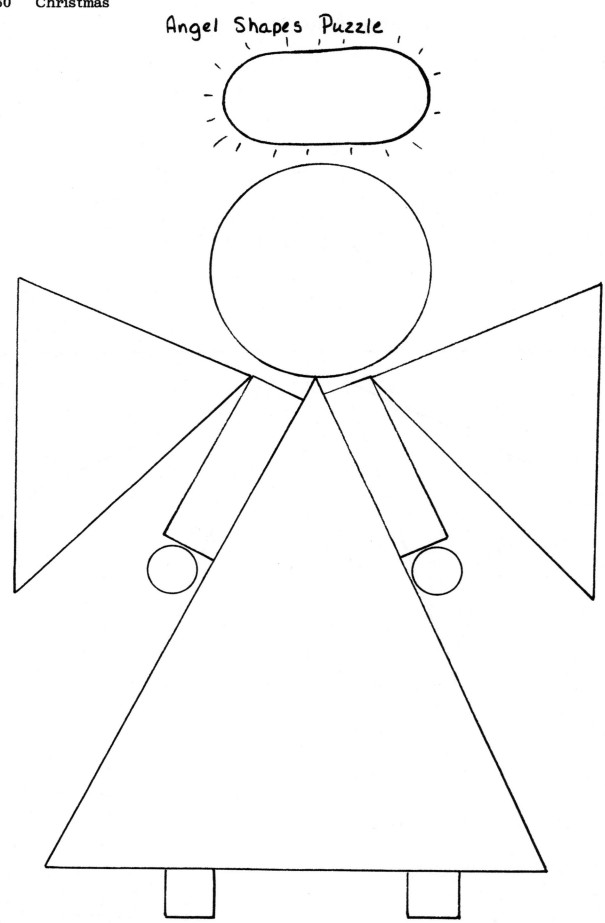

Angel Shapes Puzzle

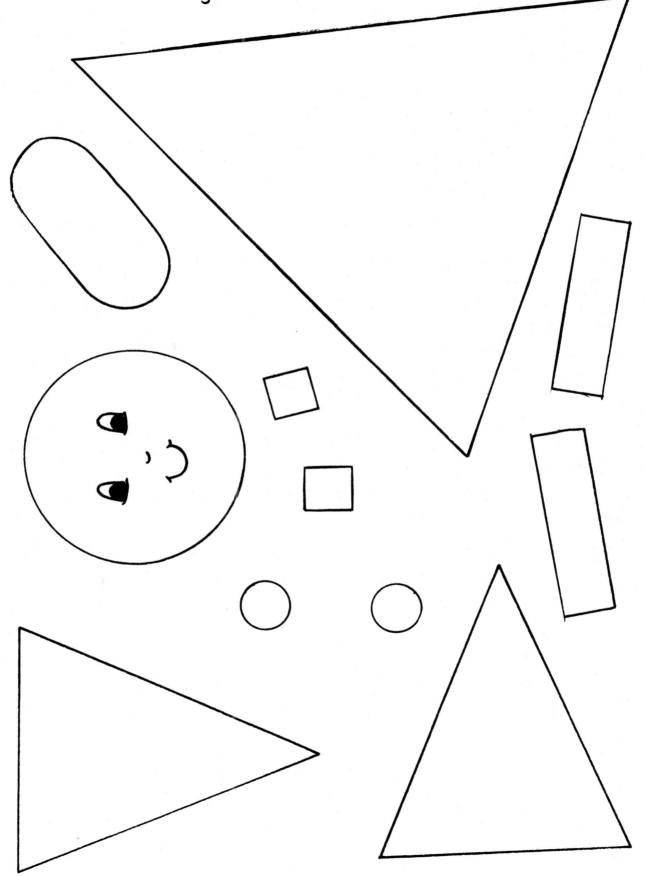

Initial Sounds Sheet

Circle the C sounds, then
color the objects.

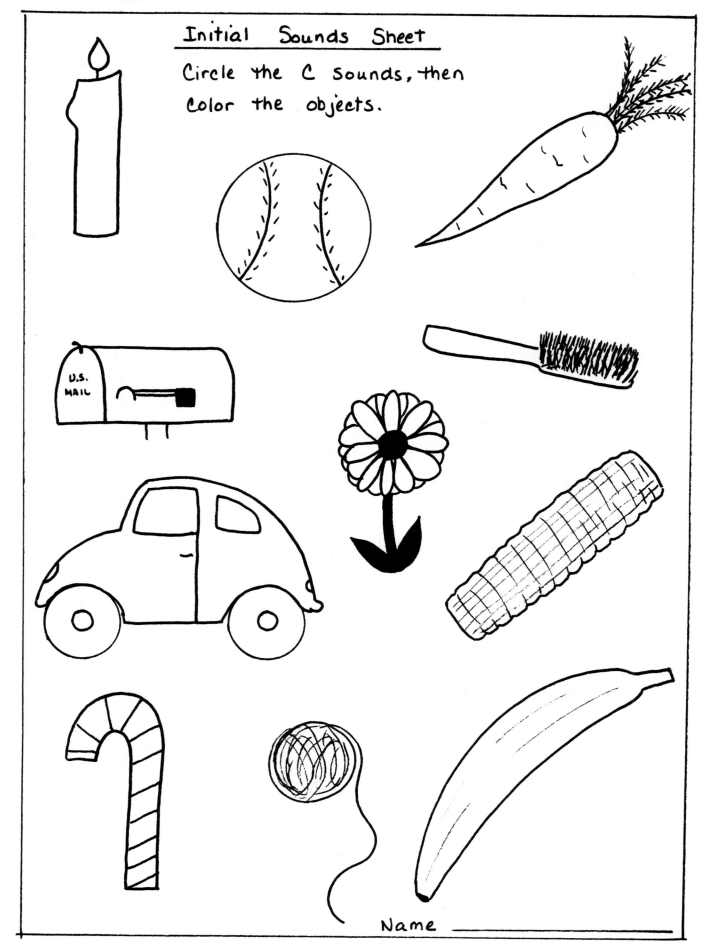

Name _____

Examples

– Jack Be Nimble Sheet

– Shadow Box Candles

Cardboard Christmas
Candles –

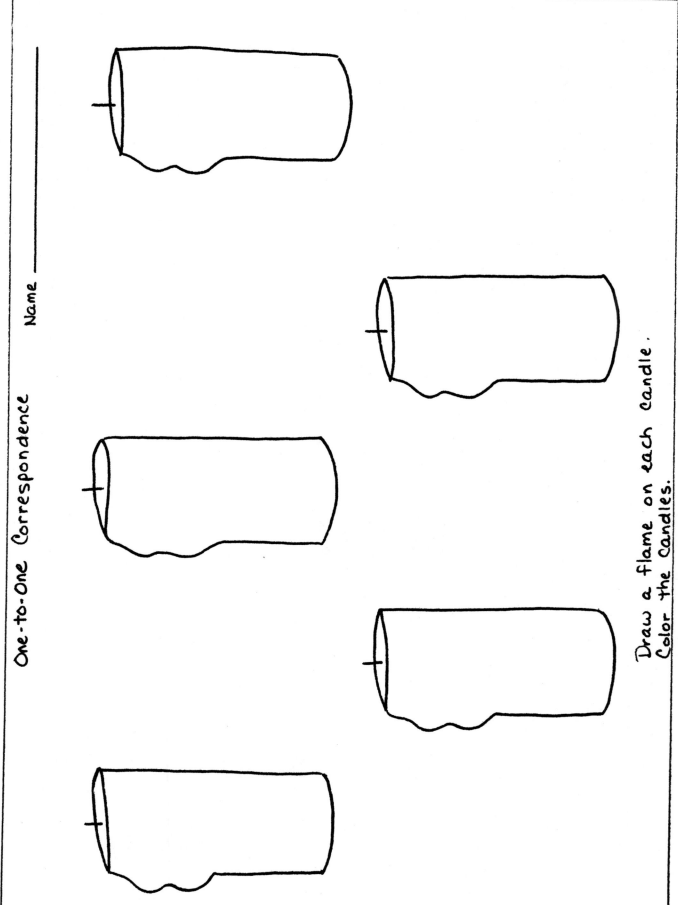

One-to-One Correspondence

Name

Draw a flame on each candle. Color the candles.

Dear Parents,

On _____, as part of our Christmas unit, we will have "Crazy Socks Day." Please let your child wear his/her brightest and "craziest" socks (and shoes as usual), preferably a different sock on each foot. We will use our "Crazy Socks" to add fun to the daily topic, Christmas Stockings.

Thank you.

Sincerely,

Dear Parents,

Just a reminder that tomorrow is "Crazy Socks Day." Please let your child wear his/her craziest socks (and shoes as usual) to school. Thank you.

Sincerely,

Stocking Dot-to-Dot

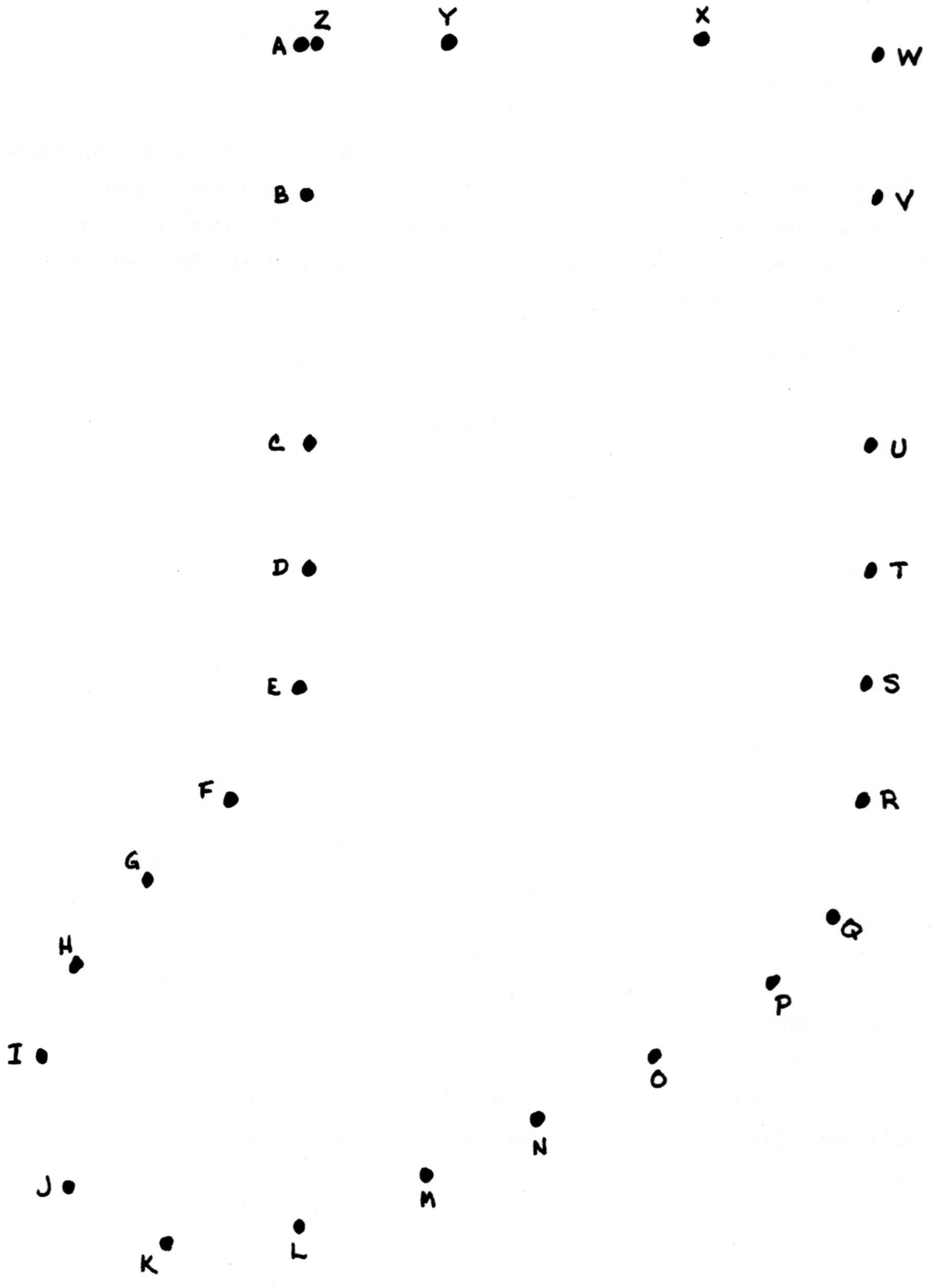

Z Y X
A W

B V

C U

D T

E S

F R

G Q

H P

I O

N

J M

K L

Little Stocking

Little Stocking

Examples

 - Little Stocking

Construction Paper
    Stockings -

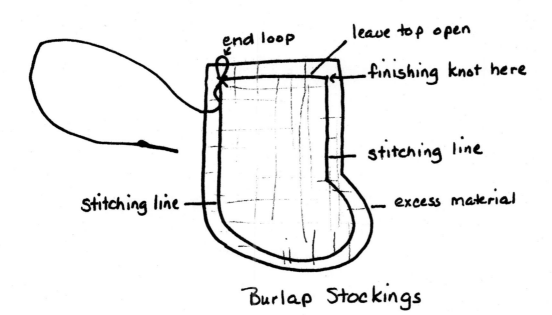

end loop

leave top open

finishing knot here

stitching line

excess material

stitching line

Burlap Stockings

Construction Paper Stocking

Pattern -

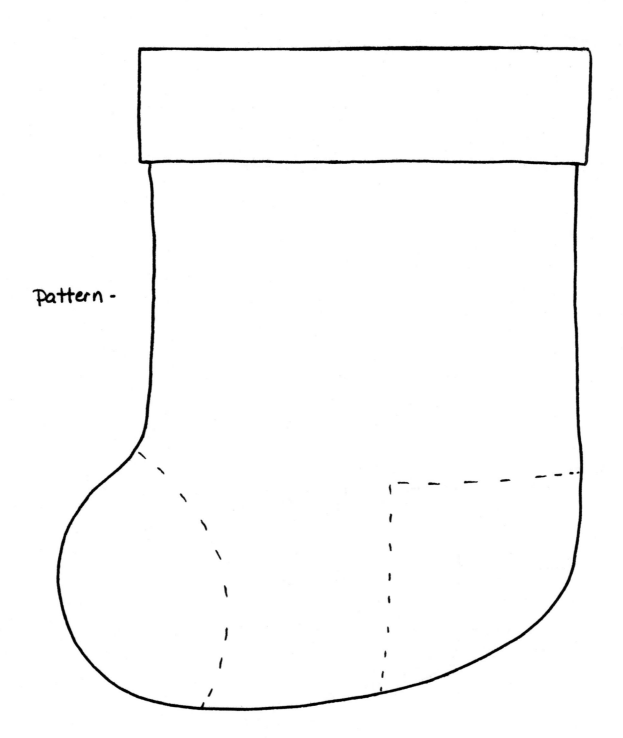

Burlap Stockings

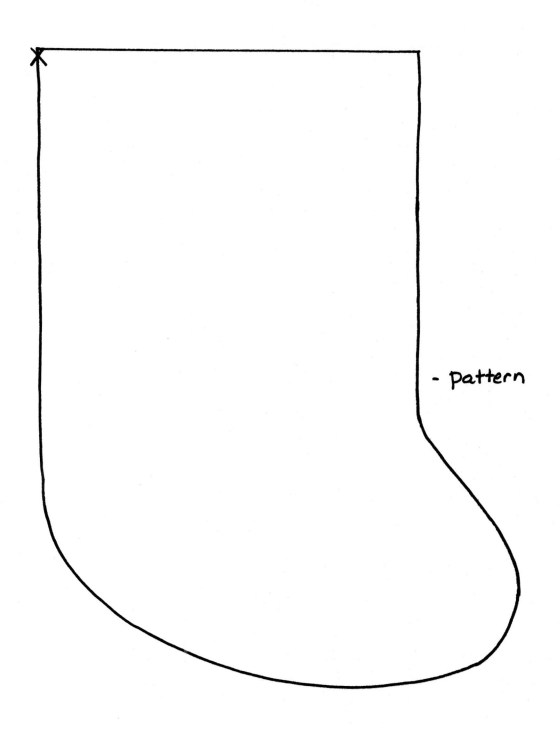

- pattern

Wallpaper Stockings

pattern,

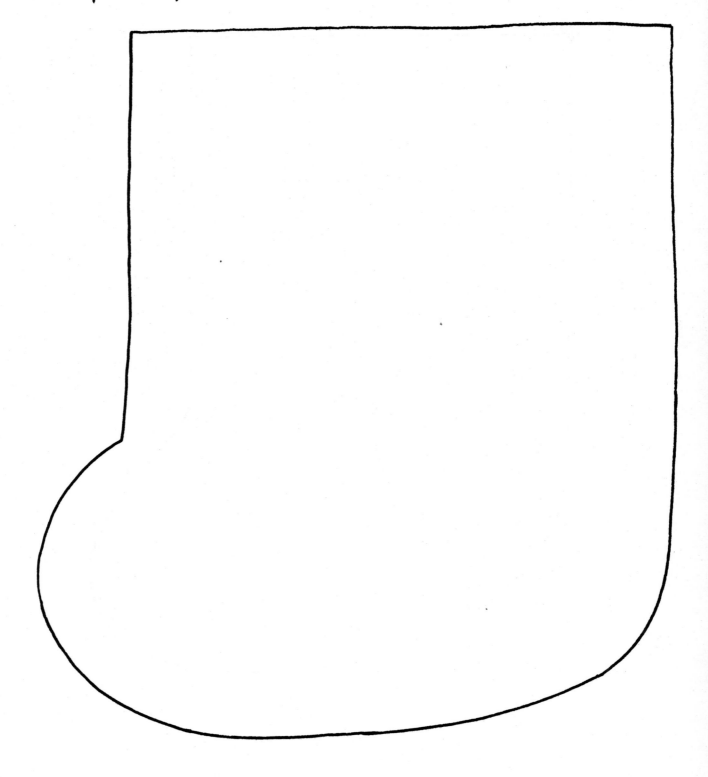

The Lost Caroler

Sherman is lost! Help him by drawing a
path to the other Carolers. Color the
Carolers.

Christmas Rhyme Board

The 12 Days of Christmas Booklet

The 12 Days of Christmas

Cut apart the pages on the dotted lines.

The 12 Days of Christmas Booklet

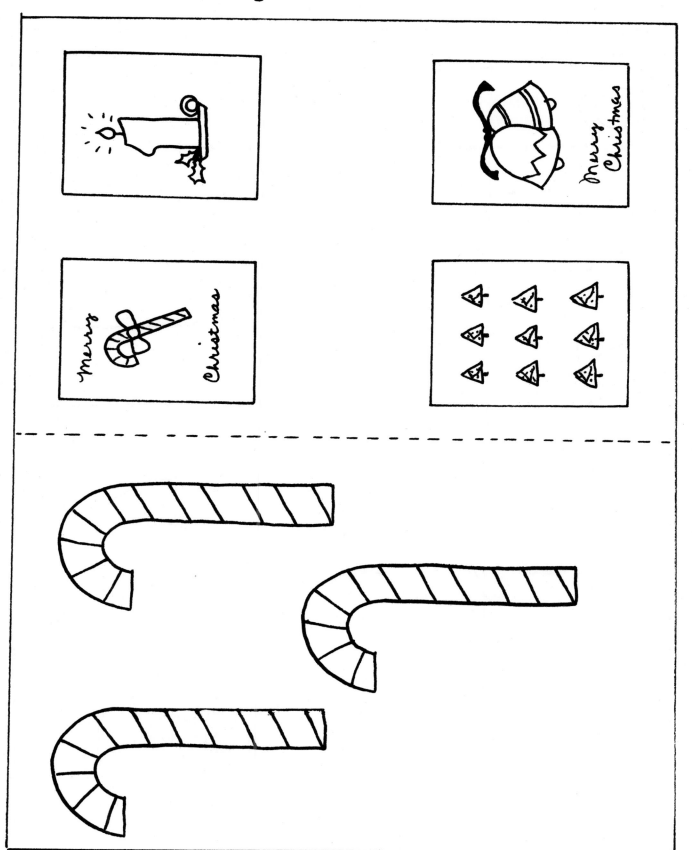

The 12 Days of Christmas Booklet

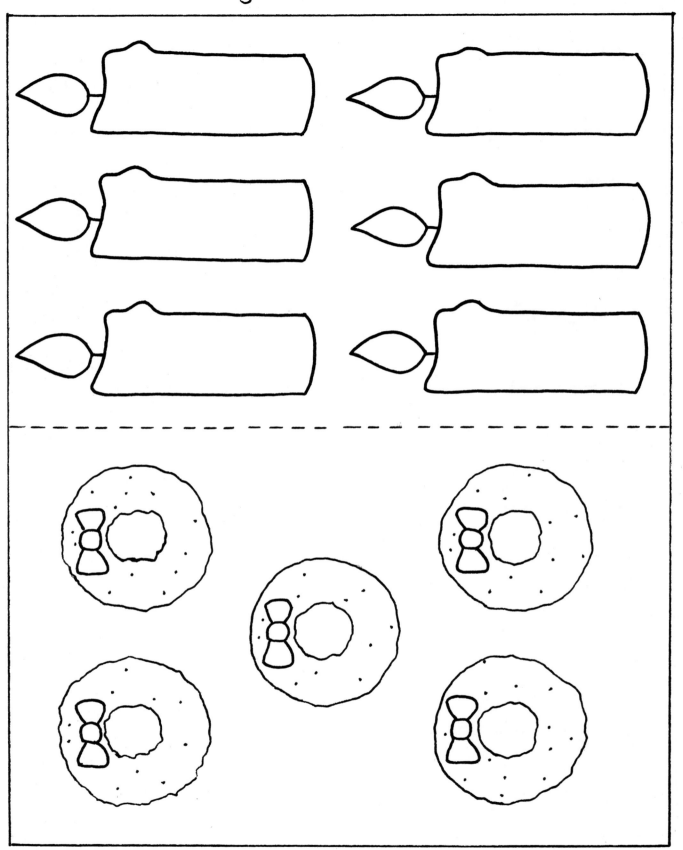

The 12 Days of Christmas Booklet

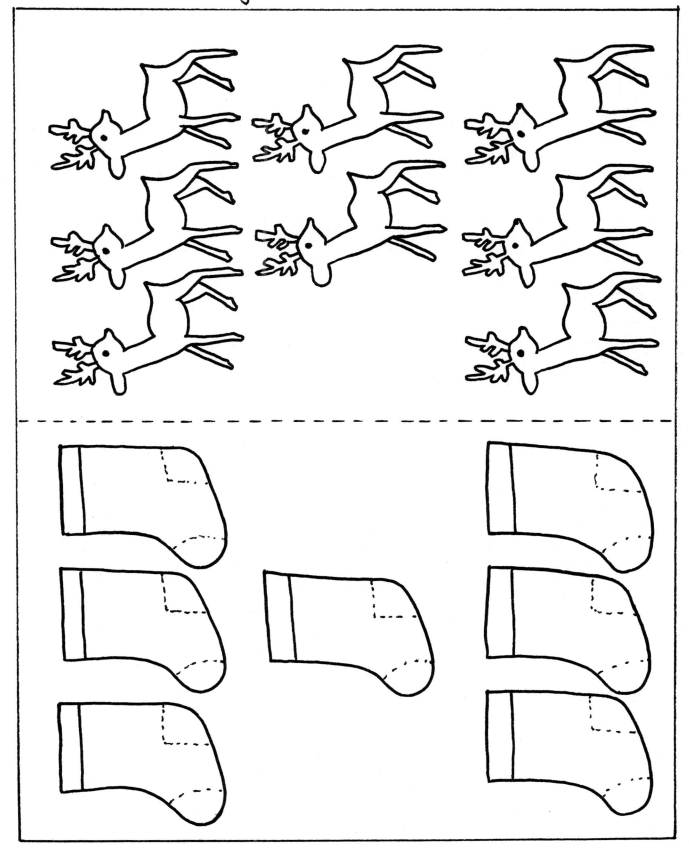

The 12 Days of Christmas Booklet

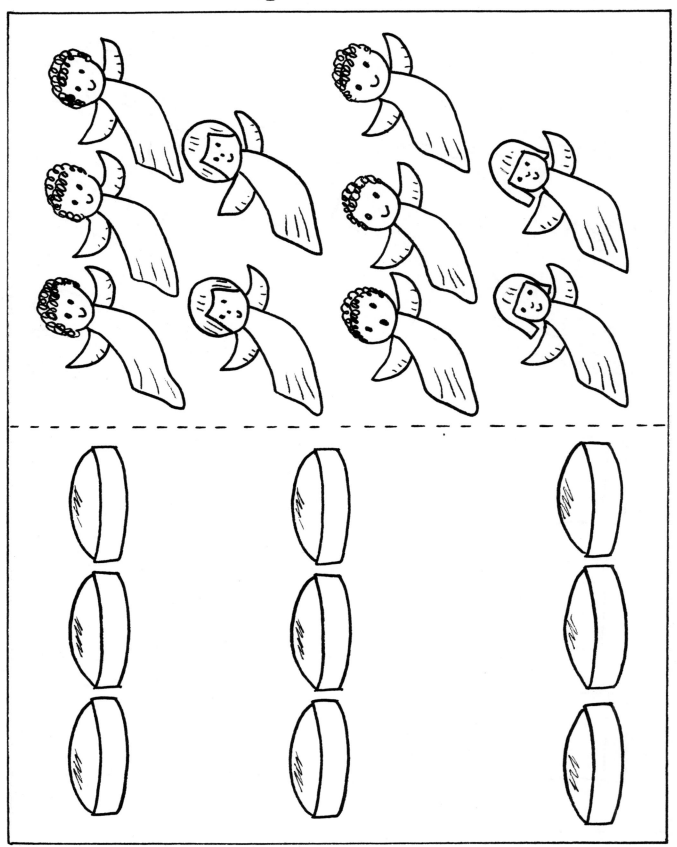

The 12 Days of Christmas Booklet

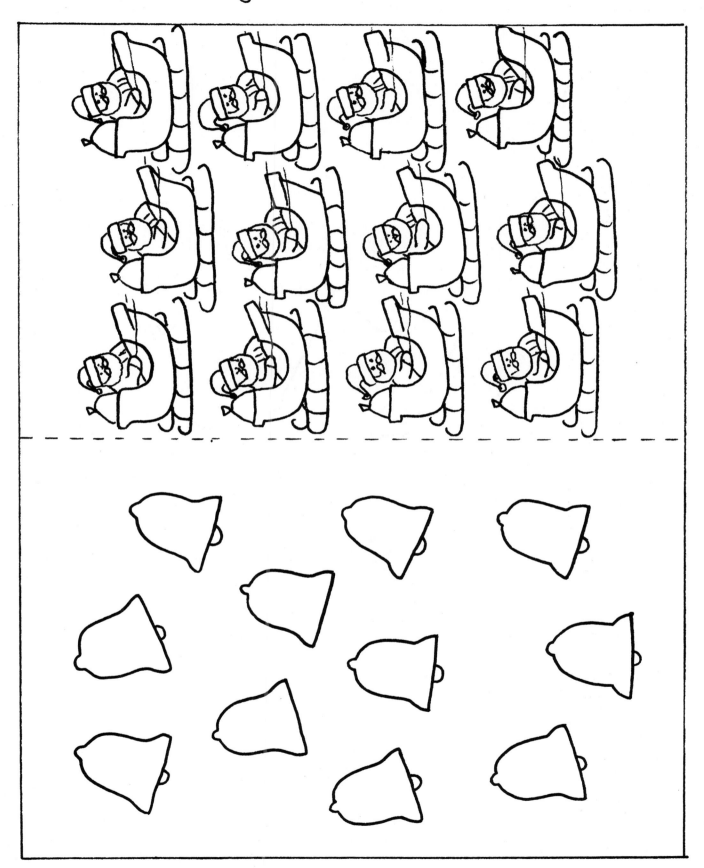

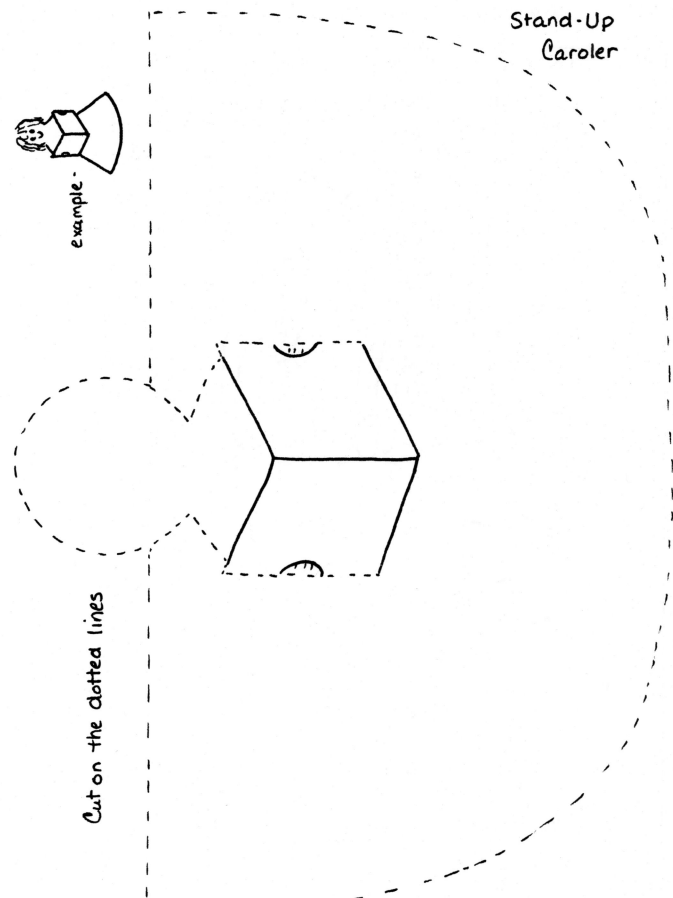

Stand-Up
Caroler

example-

Cut on the dotted lines

183

Count the Notes

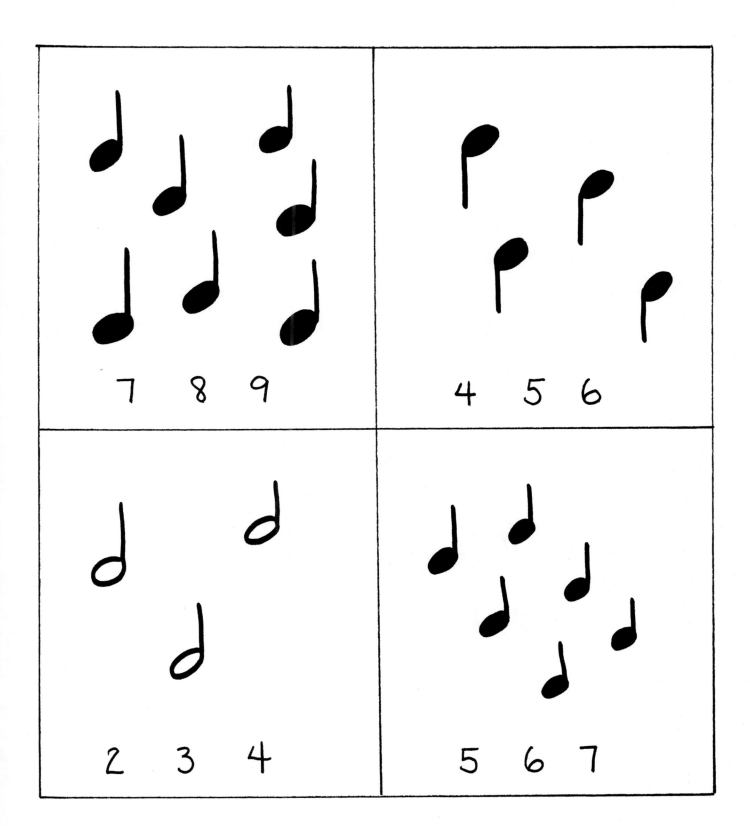

Examples

Paper Plate Wreaths

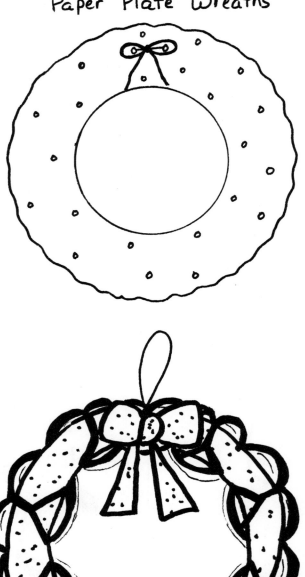

Christmas Pretzel Wreaths

Examples

Bread Dough Picture Wreaths

Evergreen Balls

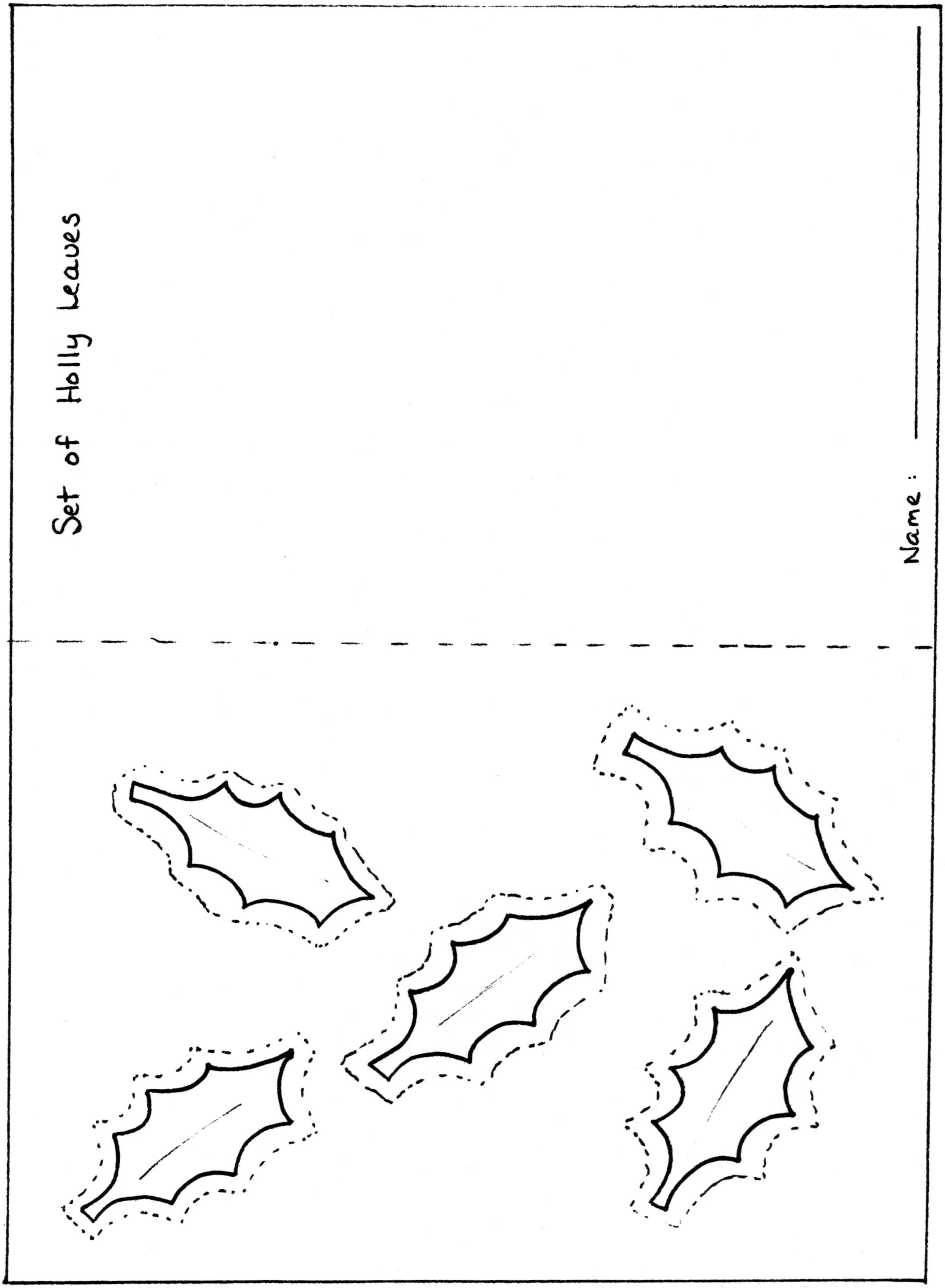

Set of Holly Leaves

Name : _____

Evergreen Tree - Stages of Growth

1

2

3

4

5

6

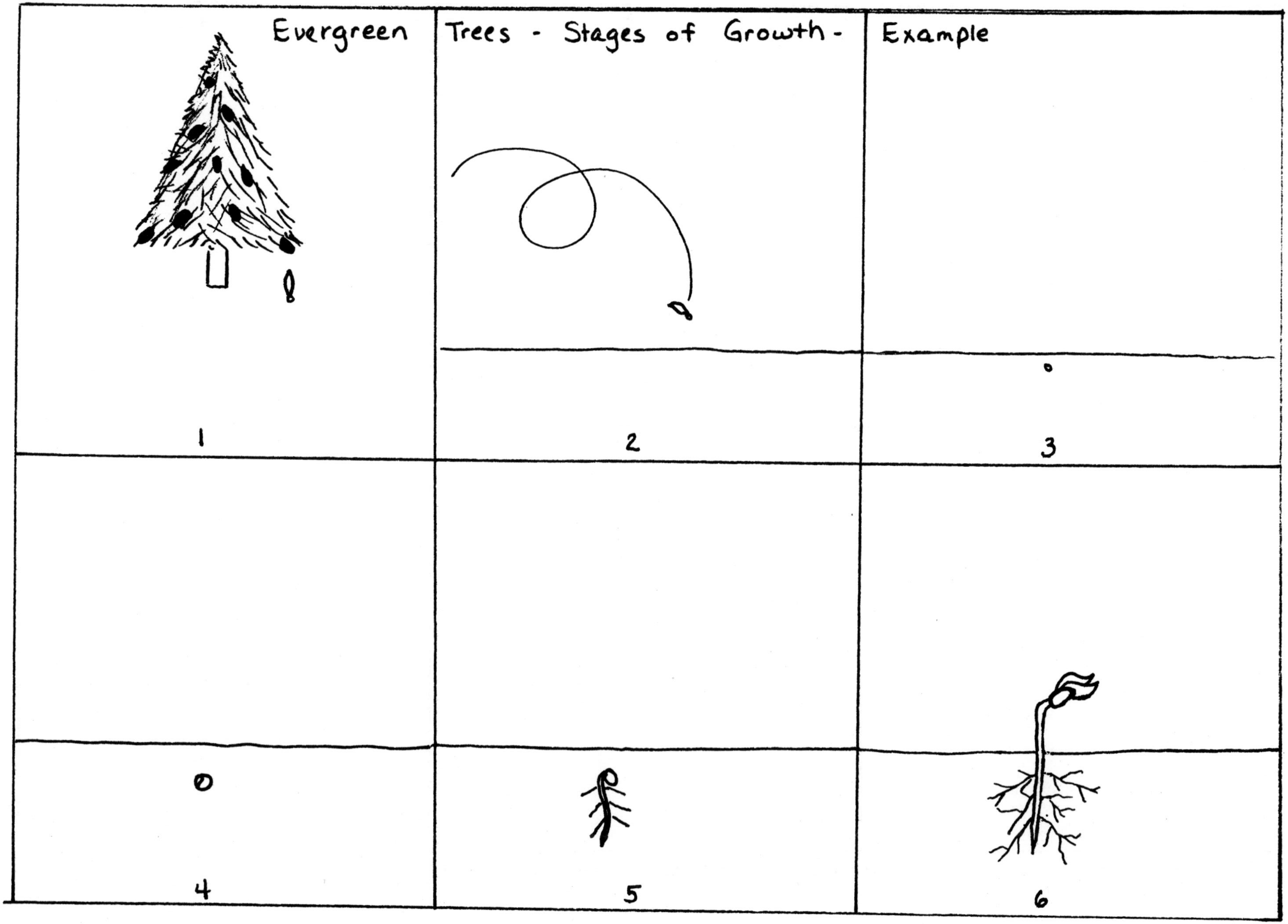

Evergreen Trees - Stages of Growth - Example

0

1

2

3

4

5

6

Examples

Baby Christmas Trees

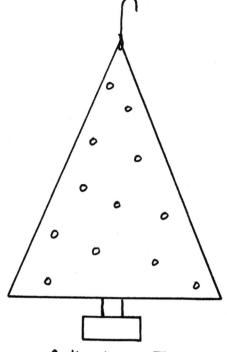

Cellophane Trees

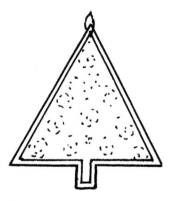

Tin Punch Trees

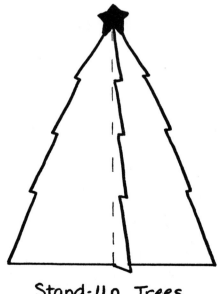

Stand-Up Trees

Cellophane Trees

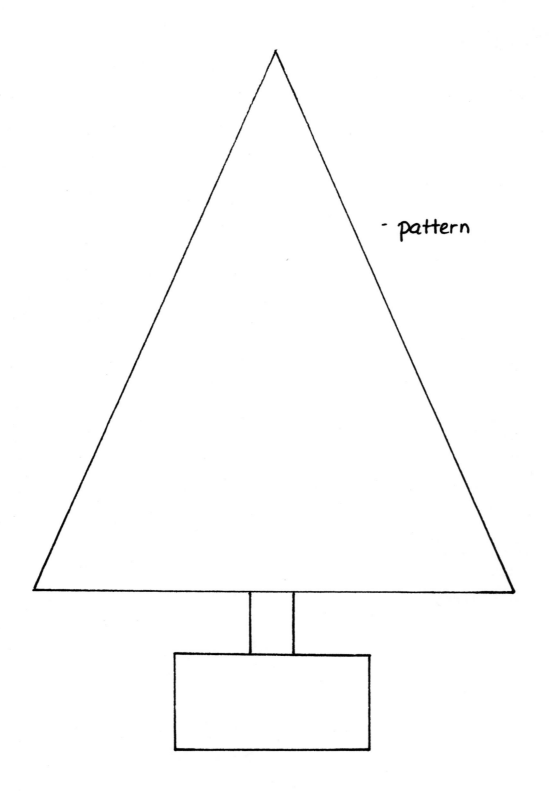

- pattern

Tin Punch Trees

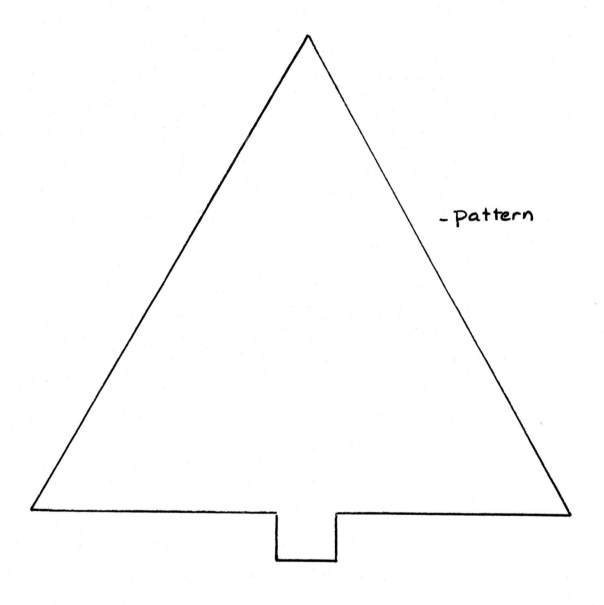

- pattern

Stand-Up Trees

patterns

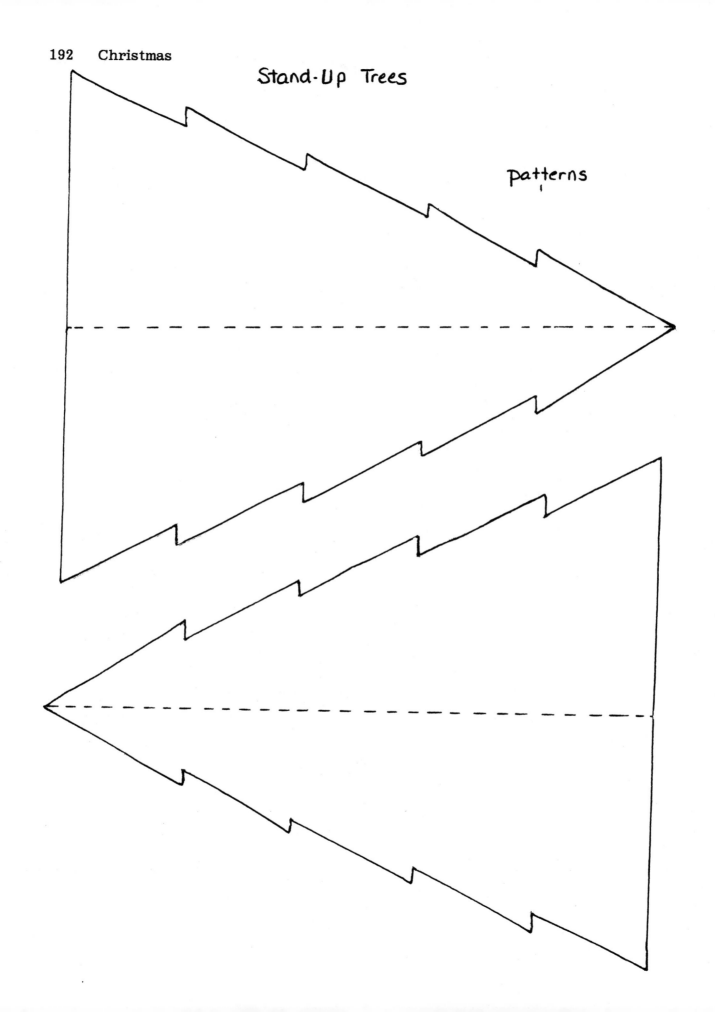

Tree Number Puzzle

Outline

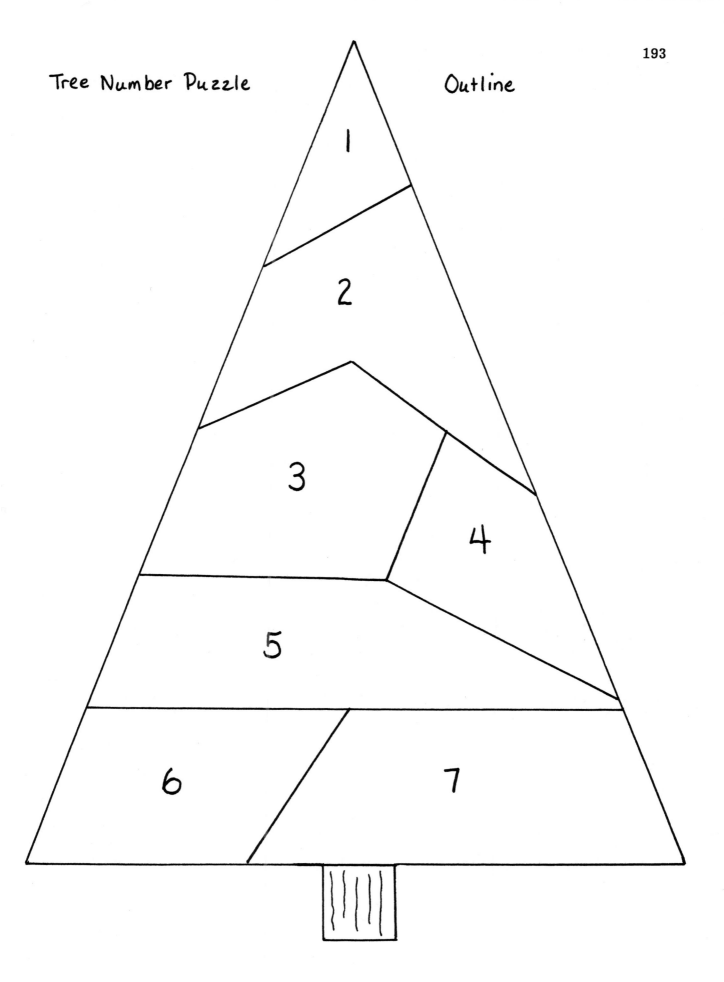

Tree Number Puzzle - Pieces

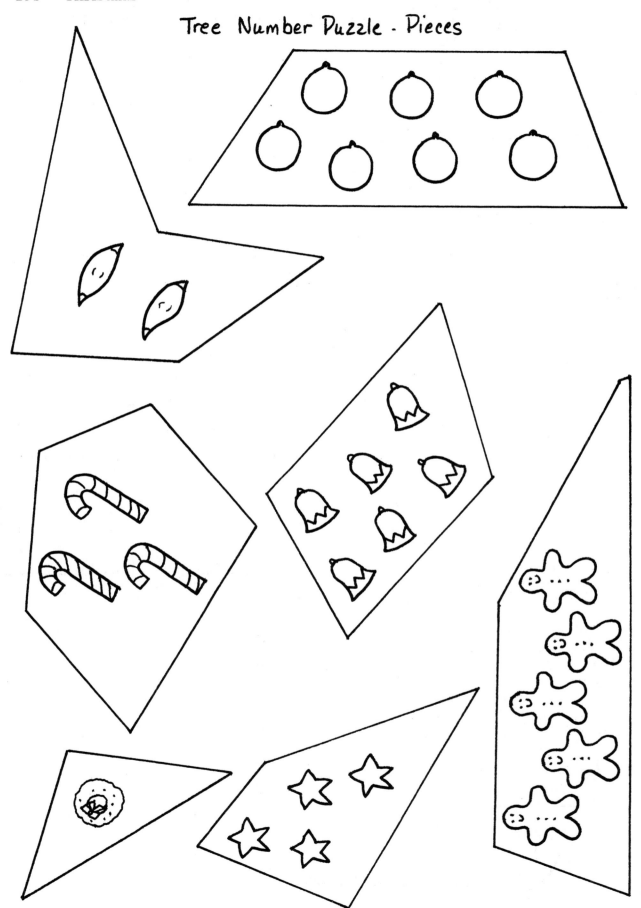

Classification Activity - Symbols

Rebus Story

The Best Tree

Corky 🦌 and Rolly 🦌 looked around the big empty barn. 🏠 How empty it was since the Hanleys moved away! "What we need is a Christmas tree 🎄," said Corky. "The Hanleys always had a beautiful tree," said Rolly. 🦌 "Follow me," said Corky. 🦌 "Look in this box," 📦 said Corky. 🦌 He scampered up a ladder 🪜 and Rolly 🦌 followed. Rolly 🦌 looked and saw some old Christmas ornaments. 🔔🎁🕯️

"Oh, Rolly, 🦌 put on a smile," 🙂 said Corky. 🦌 "They are kind of old," he said. "We will put them on the little evergreen tree 🎄." Corky 🦌 stood near the barn. 🏠 The evergreen tree 🎄 stood near the barn. Corky 🦌 hung a candy cane 🍬 ornament 🎄 on the tree. 🎄 Rolly 🦌 hung a silver ball. 🔔 A friendly bird 🐦 attached the star. ⭐ Soon all the ornaments 🔔🎁🕯️ were hung. Animals 🐾 and birds 🐦 came to see the little tree. 🎄 It glistened on the tree's branches. 🌲 Everyone sang Christmas songs and agreed it was the best tree 🎄 ever.

Snow ❄️ began to fall.

Examples

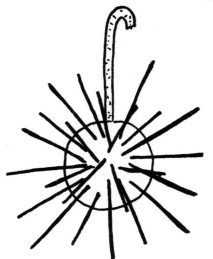

Toothpick Ornaments

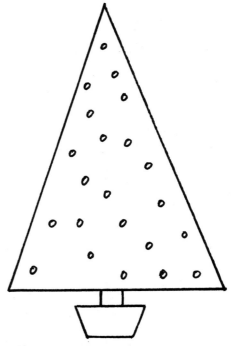

Decorated Trees

Pine Cone Trees

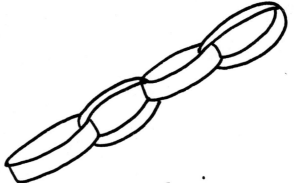

Paper Chains

Decorated Trees

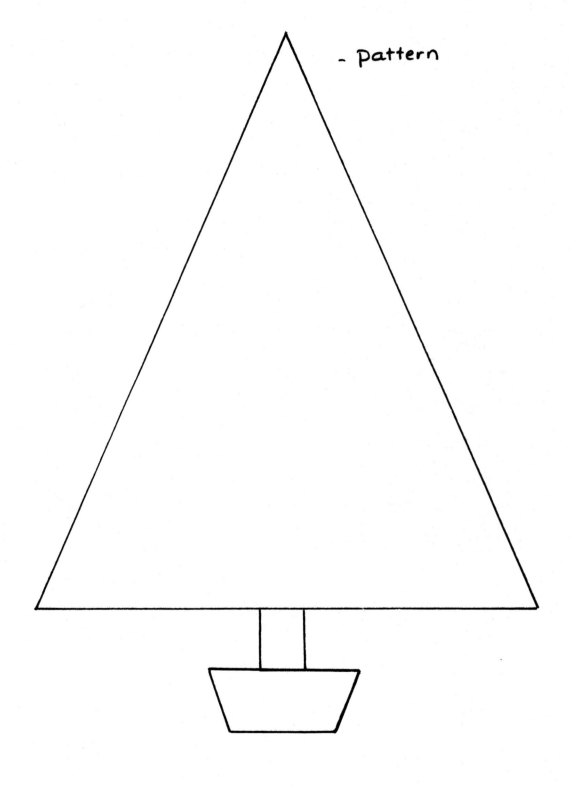

- pattern

Ornament Shapes

What Is a Star? — Follow-up Sheet

Follow the numbered dots to draw the constellations.

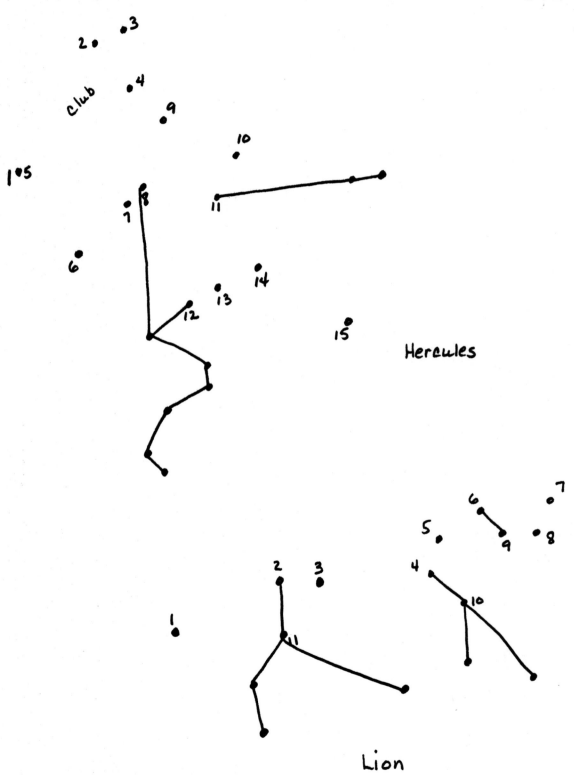

Club

Hercules

Lion

What Is a Star? – Follow-up Sheet
Follow the numbered dots to draw the constellations.

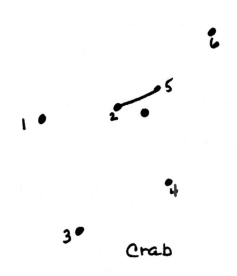

Crab

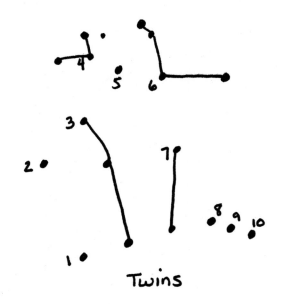

Twins

What Is a Star?- Follow-up Sheet

Follow the numbered dots to draw the constellations.

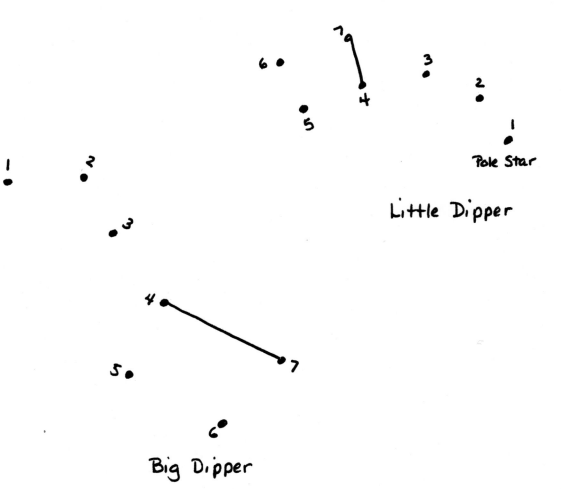

Little Dipper

Big Dipper

What Is a Star? - Follow-up

Wish Sheet

Would you like to wish on a star? Go outside on a clear night. Recite the following rhyme to the first star that you see. Draw and color what you wished for in the space below.

Star light, Star bright
First star I see tonight,
I wish I may, I wish I might,
Have the wish I wish tonight.

Dear Parents,

Today we learned that a star is really a sun and is a cluster of hot gases. We also learned that thousands of years ago, people noticed that groups of stars seemed to form pictures. They gave these constellations names which we still use today.

The constellations which we studied are the Big Dipper, Little Dipper, Lion, Hercules, Crab, and Twins. On a clear night, perhaps you and your child can locate these constellations.

Please assist your child with the attached follow-up sheets.

Thank you for your cooperation.

Sincerely,

Constellation Sheet

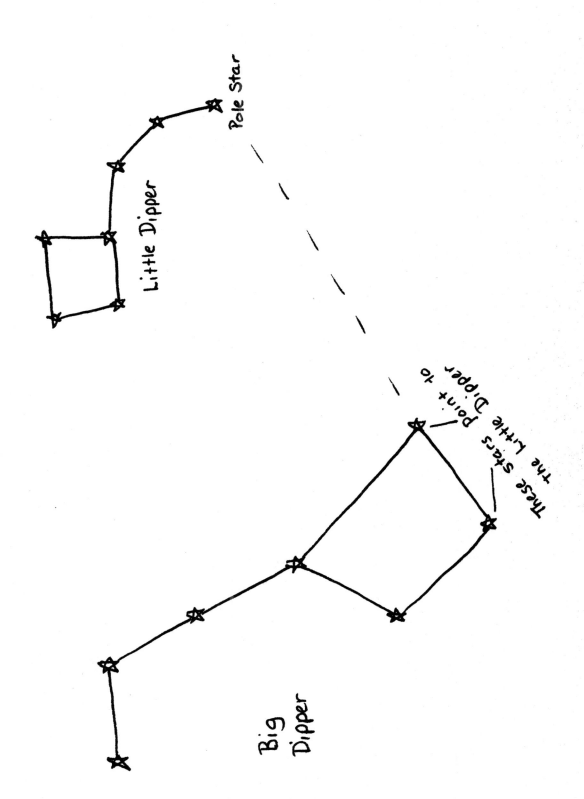

Constellation Sheet

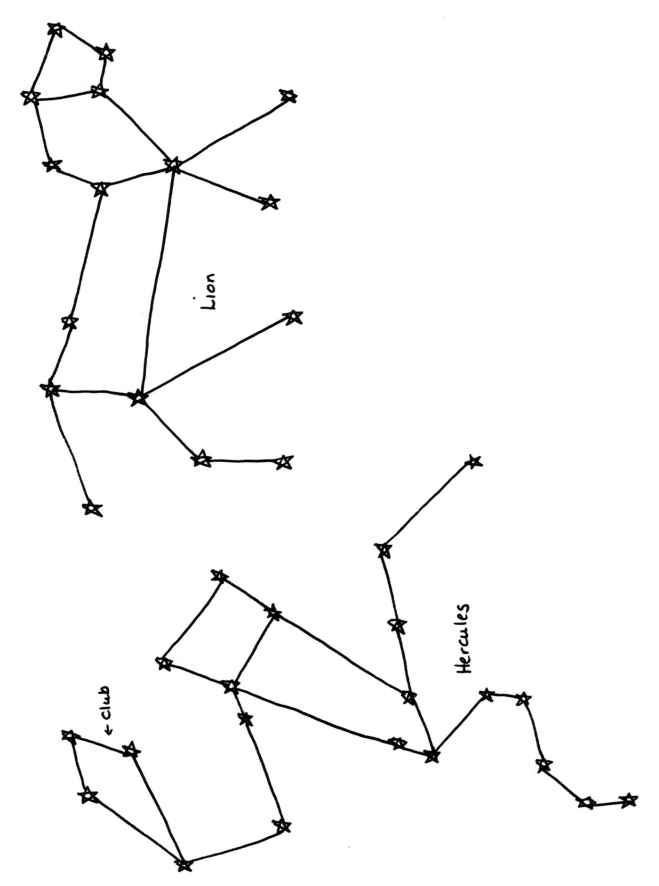

Constellation Sheet

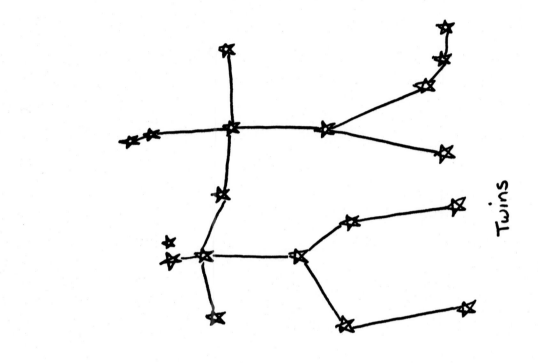

Twins

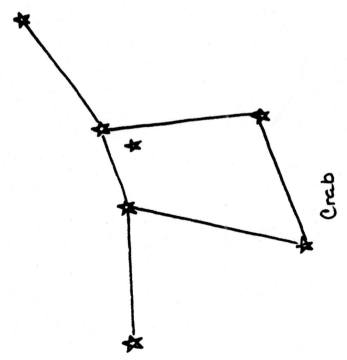

Crab

Star Name Game

Examples, Pattern

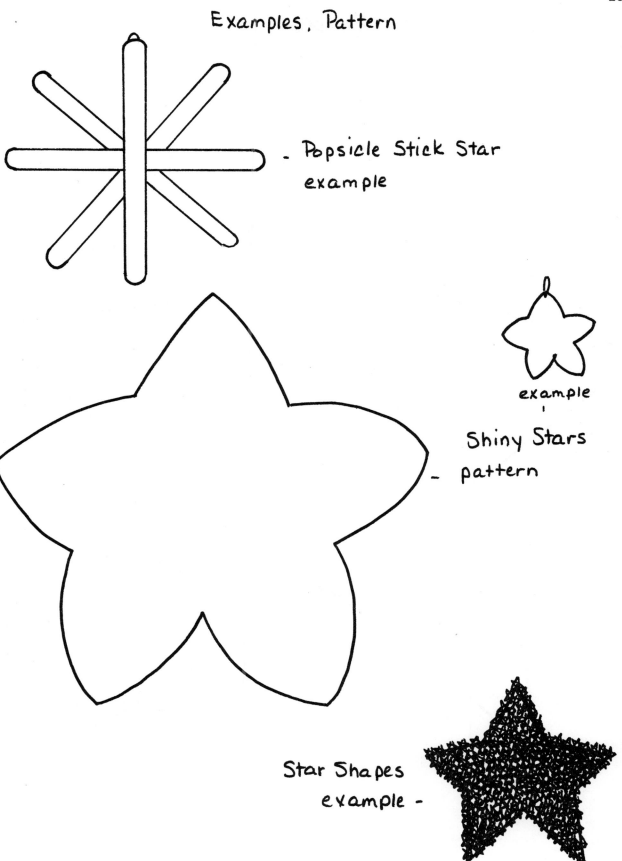

- Popsicle Stick Star
example

example
|
Shiny Stars
- pattern

Star Shapes
example -

Star Shapes

One-to-One Correspondence
Put a sticker star at the top of each Christmas tree.

Name _____

Examples

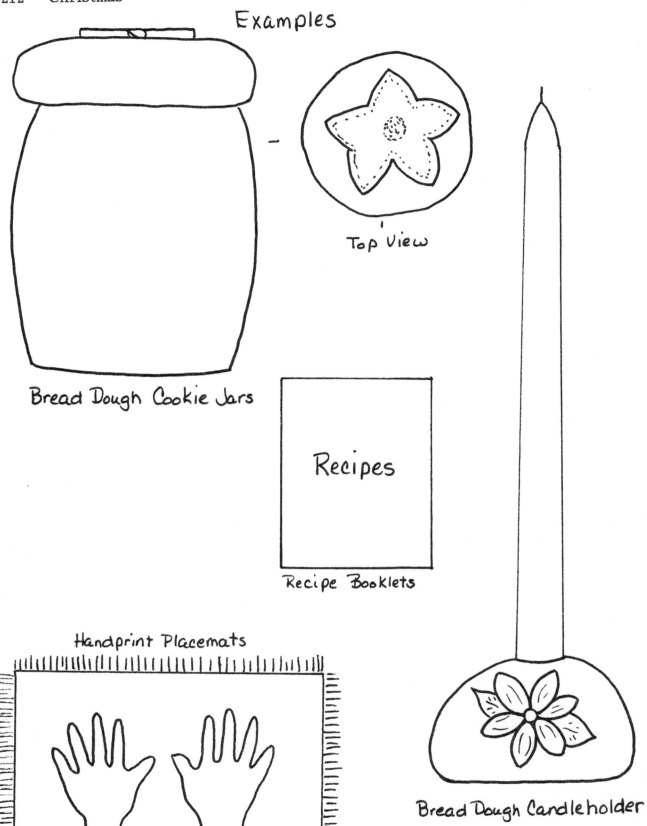

Top View

Bread Dough Cookie Jars

Recipes

Recipe Booklets

Handprint Placemats

Susan

Bread Dough Candleholder

Examples, Pattern

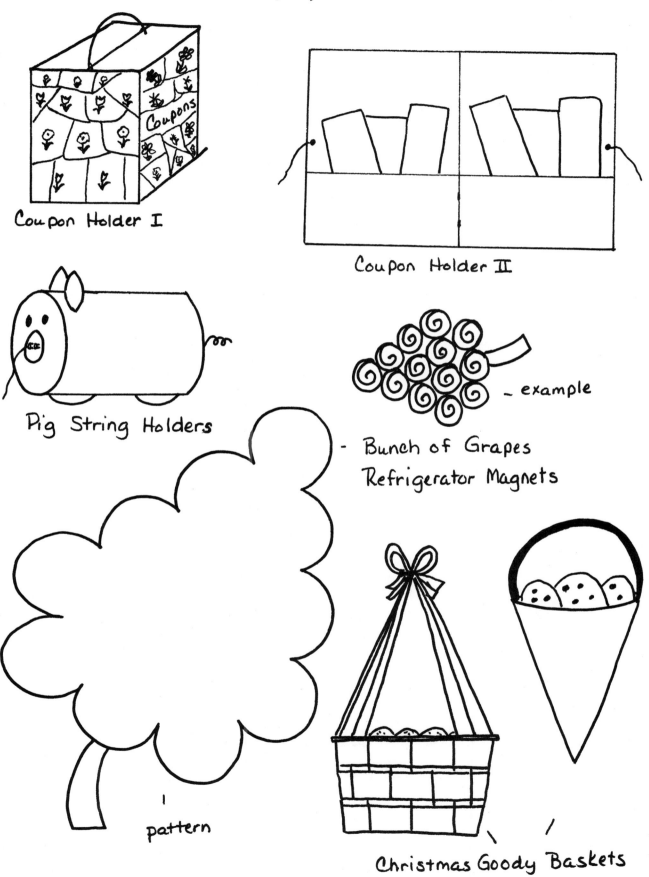

Coupon Holder I

Coupon Holder II

Pig String Holders

— example

— Bunch of Grapes
Refrigerator Magnets

pattern

Christmas Goody Baskets

(COUPON)

This Coupon entitles you
to one
Breakfast in Bed

Courtesy of

_____

(COUPON)

This coupon entitles you to
have the
Trash Emptied

Courtesy of

_____

(COUPON)

This Coupon entitles you to
have the
Bed Made

Courtesy of

_____

(COUPON)

This Coupon entitles you to
have the
Dishes Washed

Courtesy of

_____

(COUPON)

This Coupon entitles you to
have the
Mail Collected

Courtesy of

_____

(COUPON)

This Coupon entitles you to
have the
Table Set

Courtesy of

_____

(COUPON)

This Coupon entitles you to
have the
Furniture Dusted

Courtesy of

_____

(COUPON)

This Coupon entitles you to

One Free Chore

Courtesy of

_____

Christmas Card Completion Sheet

Merry Christmas

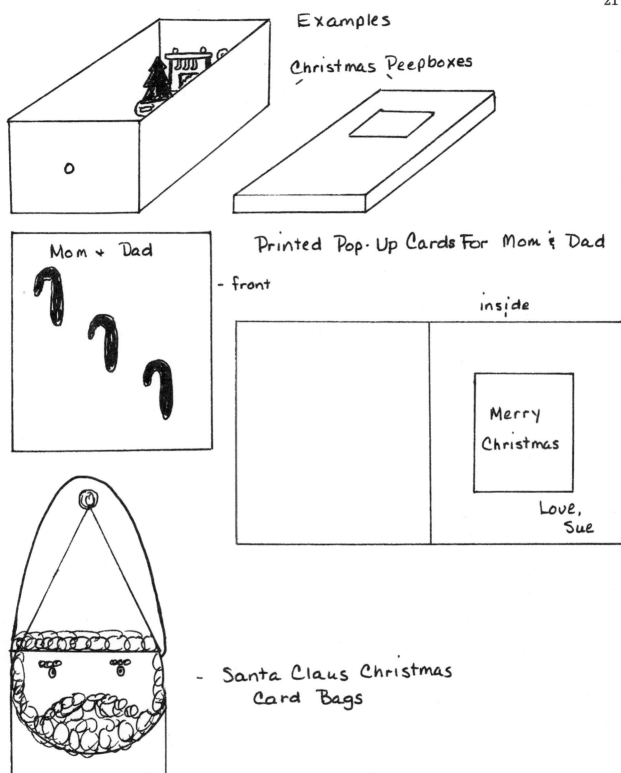

Examples

Christmas Peepboxes

Printed Pop-Up Cards For Mom & Dad

Mom + Dad

- front

inside

Merry
Christmas

Love,
Sue

- Santa Claus Christmas
  Card Bags

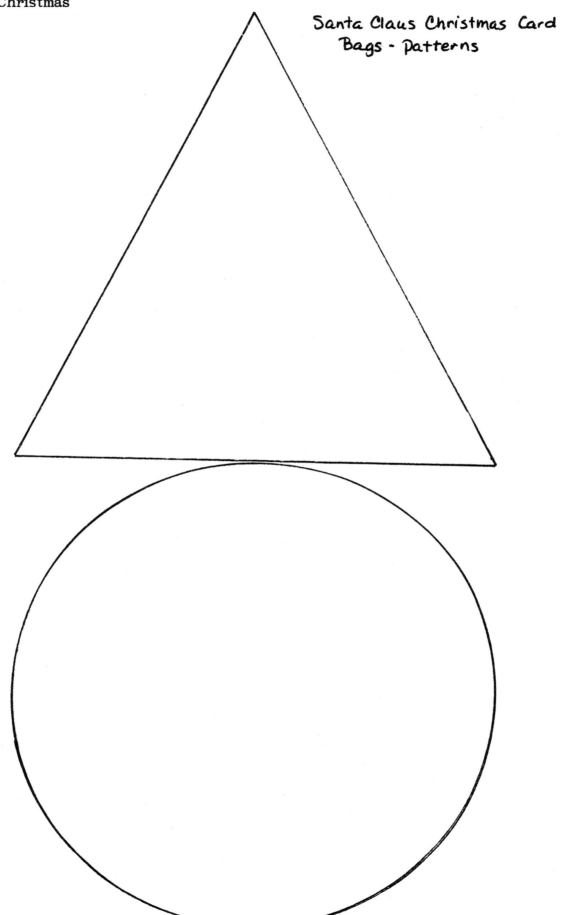

Santa Claus Christmas Card
Bags - Patterns

Dear Parents,

On _____, our class will have a "Teddy Bear Day." I am asking that each child bring a teddy bear to school to participate in the "Teddy Bear Day" activities. We will discuss the origins of the teddy bear, teddy bear clubs, festivals, and books. A "Teddy Bear Contest" will be held, then we will prepare the refreshments for the "Teddy Bear's Picnic."

Please send the teddy bear in a sack with your child's name on it. If your child does not have a teddy bear, please let me know. I will make arrangements for a "temporary adoption."

Thank you very much for your help.

Sincerely,

Dear Parents,

Just a reminder that tomorrow is "Teddy Bear Day." Please send a teddy bear with your child. Don't forget to put it in a sack with your child's name on it. Thank you.

Sincerely,

Teddy Bear Contest Awards

patterns

Biggest
Bear

example

Name: _____

Teddy Bear Alphabet Match

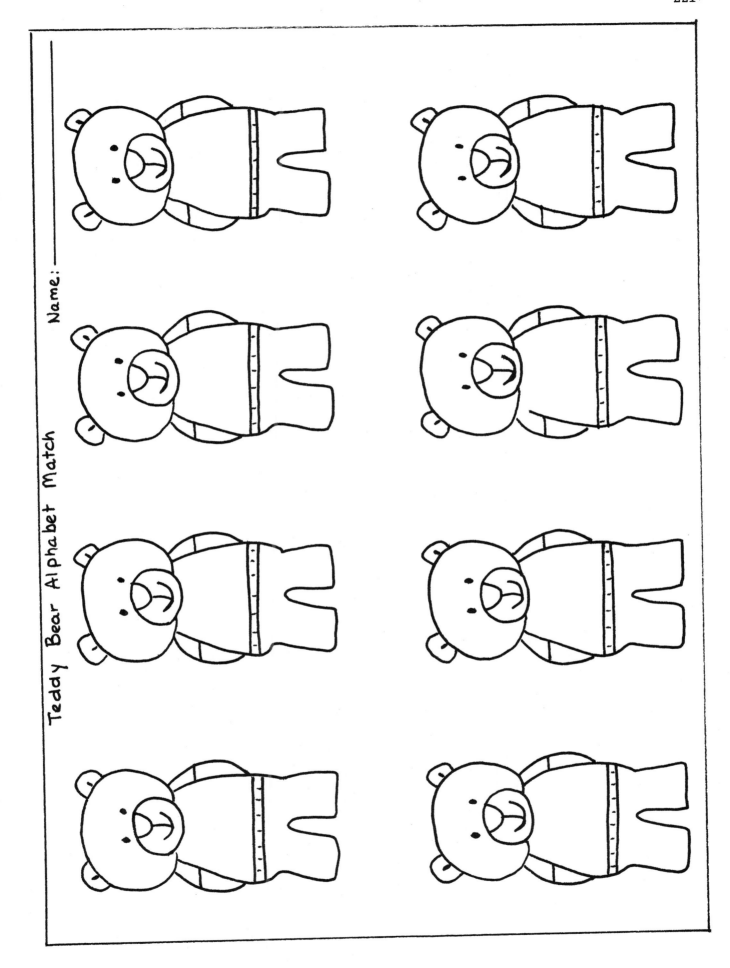

Examples, Pattern

TEDDY, JR.

- example

Name Your Bear

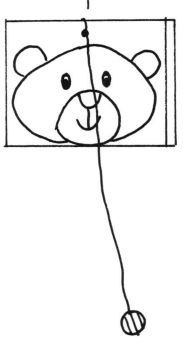

Bear and the Bee Game - Example

Pattern - Bear Face

Bear and the Bee Game

Name Your Bear

Teddy Bear

Children's Singing Game

Teddy Bear, Teddy Bear, turn around. Teddy Bear, Teddy Bear

touch the ground.   Teddy Bear, Teddy Bear,   show your shoe.

Teddy Bear,   Teddy Bear,   that will do.

2. Teddy Bear, Teddy Bear, go upstairs,
   Teddy Bear, Teddy Bear, say your prayers.
   Teddy Bear, Teddy Bear, switch off the light,
   Teddy Bear, Teddy Bear, say "Good-night."

Courtesy of Educational Services, Inc.

Rudolph
Puppet Play

Rudolph
Puppet Play

Duplicate to total 8 or more.

Rudolph's Feelings Sheet

Rudolph isn't included in
the reindeer games.

Santa asks Rudolph
to guide his sleigh.

Another reindeer played
a mean trick on Rudolph.

Rudolph hears a creepy
sound in the night.

Examples

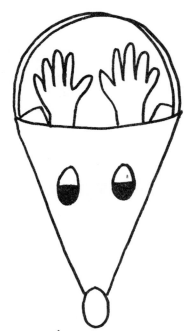

Reindeer Baskets

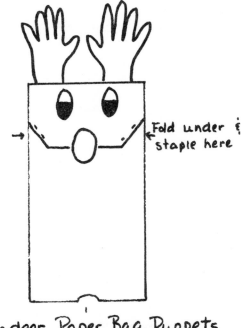

Fold under & staple here

Reindeer Paper Bag Puppets

- Reindeer Candy Canes

Reindeer Basket, Reindeer Paper Bag Puppet
Eyes and Nose Sheet

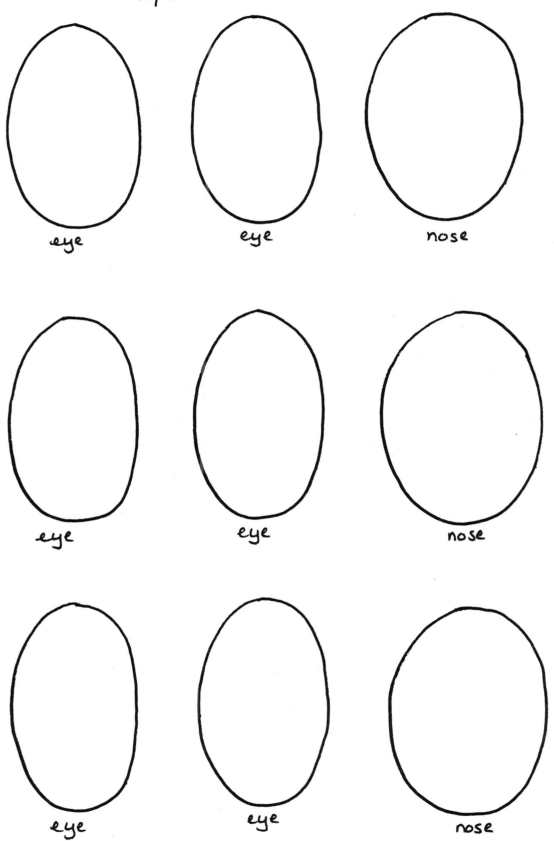

eye   eye   nose

eye   eye   nose

eye   eye   nose

Reindeer Shapes Puzzle
Outline Sheet

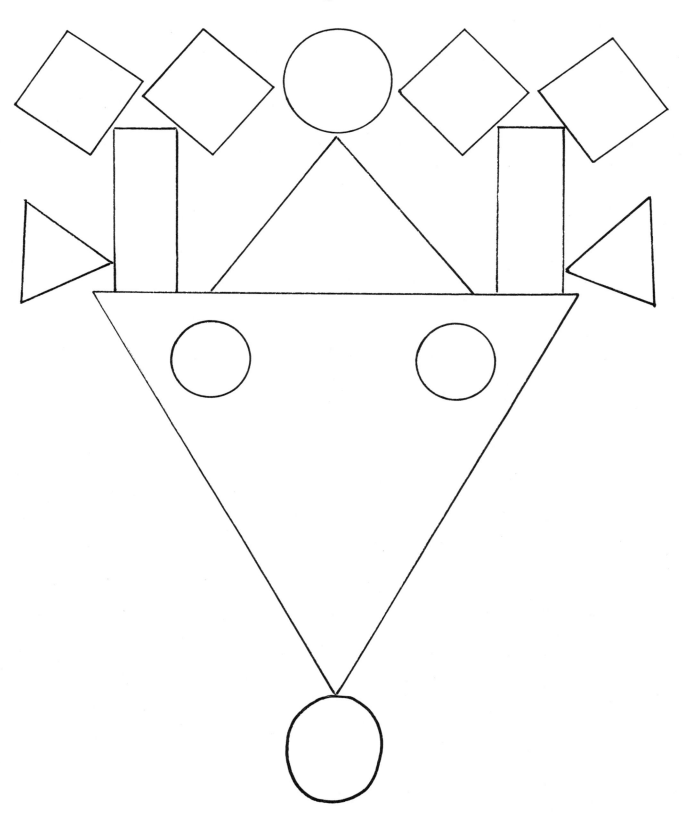

Reindeer Shapes Puzzle
Pieces Sheet

Examples

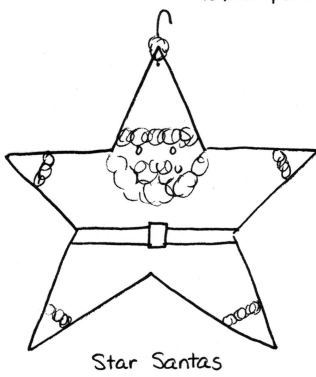

Star Santas

Santas

Elf Hats

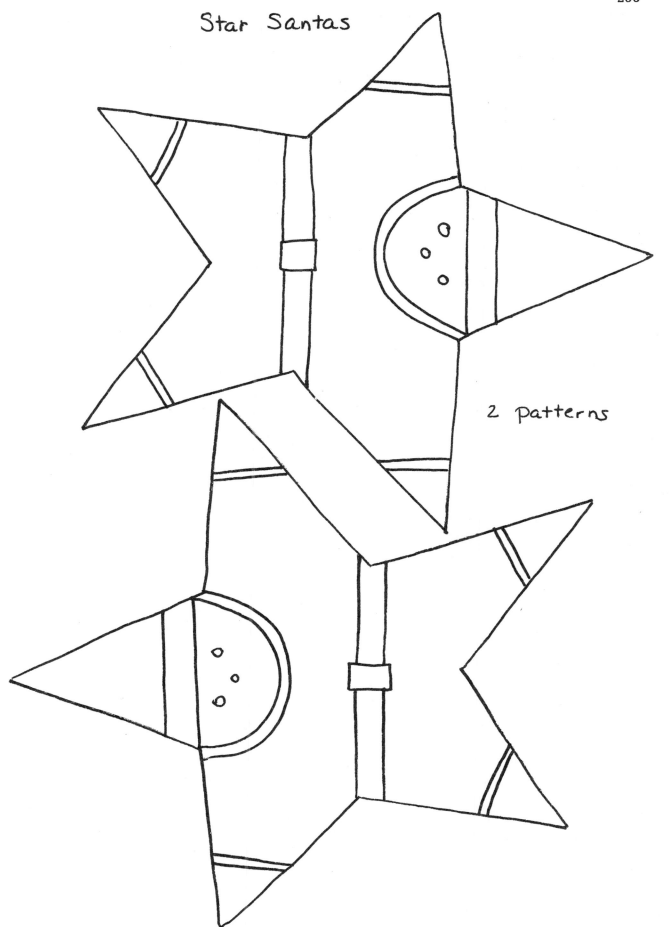

Star Santas

2 patterns

Elf Hats

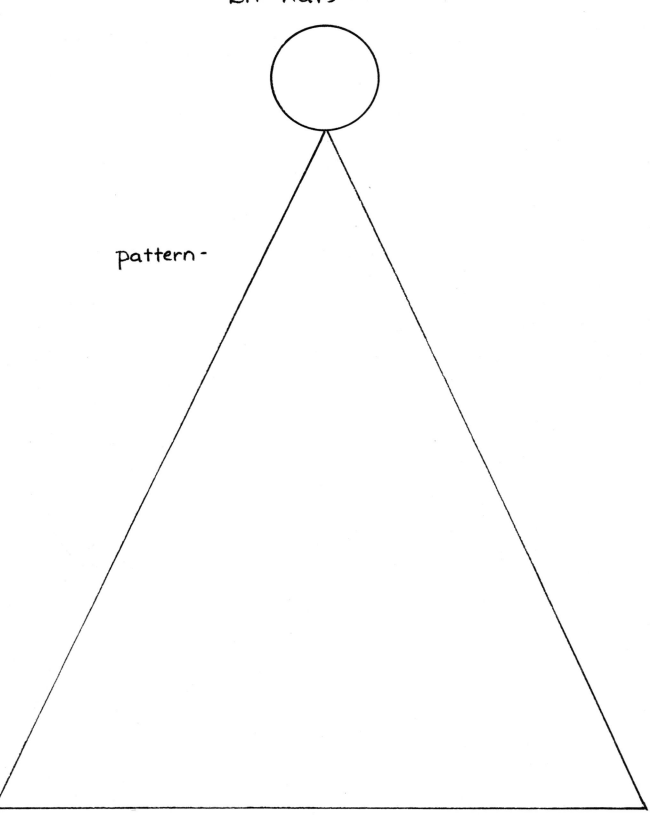

pattern -

Cookies For Santa

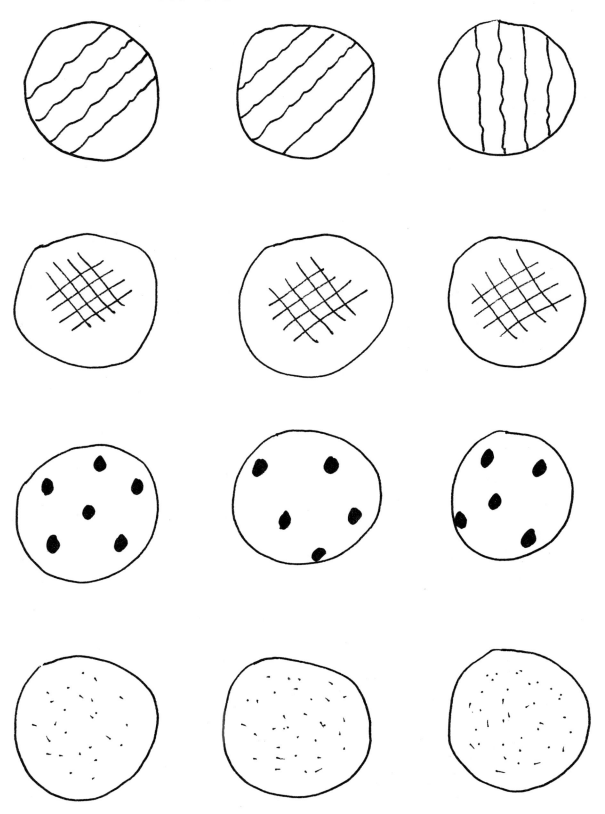

NEW YEAR'S

PROPOSED TIME: 1 day

UNIT OBJECTIVES

To develop understanding of the origins of New Year's celebrations
To develop understanding of our current New Year's celebrations

ROOM ENVIRONMENT - BULLETIN BOARDS

"Hats Off to 19--"

Cover the bulletin board, trim with border, and add the title. Enlarge the New Year Baby pattern (see Patterns, Pictures, Etc., page 244). Outline with markers and mount in the center of the bulletin board. On black construction paper, trace one top hat for the baby and one for each class member. Cut out and staple the hat on the baby's head. The students cut out their hats and turn them upside down. Using a white paint marker, write each child's name and New Year's resolution on the hat. Staple the hats on the bulletin board. Tuck paper streamers or pieces of curling ribbon behind the hats, baby, and letters of the title.

DAY 1 - NEW YEAR'S

CONCEPT INFORMATION

On January 1st of each year, we <u>welcome</u> the <u>new year</u> with parties, parades, and fireworks. The first people to <u>celebrate</u> New Year's were the Romans during the <u>first century B.C.</u> The emperor or king of Rome made up a new <u>calendar</u> and named the first month January after the <u>Roman god</u>, Janus. The Romans believed Janus had two faces. One face looked back at the old year and one looked forward to the new. The Romans began holding <u>festivals</u> on January 1st in honor of Janus.

In our country, we celebrate the <u>arrival</u> of the new year in different ways. On New Year's Eve, parties are held in homes, <u>restaurants</u> and <u>hotels</u>, and in <u>city squares</u>. At midnight, you can hear fireworks and people shouting "Happy New Year!"

On New Year's Day, parties and parades are held. One of the oldest parades is the Tournament of Roses in Pasadena, California. The beautiful <u>floats</u> in the parade are made of fresh flowers, mostly roses. Football <u>tournaments</u> or <u>"bowls"</u> have become a popular part of New Year's Day. Some of them are the Rose Bowl in California, the Orange Bowl in Florida, and the Sugar Bowl in Louisiana.

New Year's Day also has special food. We eat pork or baked ham for <u>good health</u>, black-eyed peas for <u>good luck</u>, and cabbage for <u>wealth</u> in the new year. Some people make "New Year's Resolutions," which is a list of things they wish to do better in the coming year.

LANGUAGE ARTS - SOCIAL STUDIES - SCIENCE

Discussion

Relate the concept information and define the vocabulary words.

Calendar Activity

Obtain a large calendar. Beginning with January, show and name each month of the year. Tear off the pages and give one to each child (or two). Teach the following chant. Stand the students in a line side by side in the correct order of months. The children march in place during the chant. Each child (or group) holds up his or her calendar page at the appropriate time.

<u>Choral Chant</u> - "The Twelve Months of the Year"

All Say:	January!
January Group:	January, the first month of the new year.
All Say:	February!

February Group:	February means Valentine's Day is near.
All Say:	March!
March Group:	March, here comes spring.
All Say:	April!
April Group:	April, and the rainy days it brings.
All Say:	May!
May Group:	May, the pretty flowers everywhere.
All Say:	June!
June Group:	June, summer is in the air.
All Say:	July!
July Group:	July, fun on the Fourth again.
All Say:	August!
August Group:	August, time for school to begin.
All Say:	September!
September Group:	September, Labor Day comes and autumn too.
All Say:	October!
October Group:	October, Halloween's here; taste the Witch's Brew.
All Say:	November!
November Group:	November, Thanksgiving Day is here.
All Say:	December!
December Group:	December, Christmas, winter, and the end of the year.

New Year Puzzle

Preparation - Sketch each numeral of the new year (e.g., 1-9-8-8) on a different colored sheet of large construction paper or poster paper. Cut into puzzle pieces and insert in separate envelopes. Divide the class into four groups and seat on the floor.

Procedure - Each group pieces together the numerals to spell out the new year. Numerals may be glued to mural paper and displayed. (See example, page 245.)

Note: Draw and cut fewer pieces for simpler puzzles.

Old Year - New Year

Tape two sheets of experience chart paper side by side on the chalkboard. Label one with the old year and one with the new year. Brainstorm for past and upcoming events and list on each sheet. Let the children illustrate the events of the Old Year. For the rest of the year, display the New Year sheet on a wall or bulletin board. The children illustrate each event after it has occurred.

Examples: **Old Year** - started school, Halloween Party, Thanksgiving Feast, Christmas Play. **New Year** - field trip to fire station, Valentine's Day, spring play, Easter Egg Hunt.

ART

Janus Mask

<u>Preparation</u> - Duplicate the mask (see Patterns, Pictures, Etc., page 246) on heavy white construction paper. Provide gummed reinforcements, crayons, elastic cord, and hole punchers. Demonstrate the procedure for cutting out the eyes of the mask.

<u>Procedure</u> - Cut out the masks. Color and then punch a hole in each side. Stick on reinforcements and tie on elastic cord. (See example, page 245.)

New Year's Sash

<u>Preparation</u> - For each child, cut a strip of white butcher paper 3" x 48". Provide pencils, glue, glitter, and staplers. Write the year on the board.

<u>Procedure</u> - Fold the sash in half and crease. This crease will be worn on the shoulder. Write the year on each side, cover with glue, and sprinkle with glitter. Decorate the remainder of the sash as desired. Staple the two ends together. (See example, page 245.)

New Year's Hat

<u>Preparation</u> - Make several hat patterns (see Patterns, Pictures, Etc., page 247). Distribute sheets of white construction paper, glue, glitter, and star stickers. Provide scissors, hole punchers, staplers, and elastic cord or yarn.

<u>Procedure</u> - Trace the pattern on the construction paper and cut out. Curve the hat to form a cone with the straight edges overlapping. Staple. Decorate. Punch a hole in each side and insert cord or yarn. (See example, page 245.)

MATH

New Year's Baby Top Hat

Duplicate and distribute the sheet (see Patterns, Pictures, Etc., page 248). The children fill in the missing numeral on each line.

MUSIC - MOVEMENT - GAMES

Song - "Happy New Year"

Tune: "Frère Jacques"

Happy New Year,

Happy New Year,

One and all,

One and all,

The old year is ending,

The new year's beginning,

Give a cheer

For the new year.

Game - Chinese New Year

Preparation - Explain that the Chinese recognize a different animal for each year. The twelve animals of the cycle are the rat, ox, tiger, rabbit, dragon, snake, horse, sheep, monkey, chicken, dog, and pig. (1988 is the Year of the Dragon, and so on.) Use animal cards or collect two pictures of each animal in the cycle and glue to cards. Seat the students in a circle with one child, "It," in the center. Distribute the pairs of animal cards.

Procedure - When the teacher calls out the name of one of the animals, the two children with that card must exchange seats. "It" tries to beat one of the players to his or her new seat. If successful, the player who loses his or her seat is the new "It." Occasionally, the teacher calls out "Chinese New Year!" Then all the children scramble to exchange seats. The child without a seat is the new "It."

STORY TIME

Book - Little Bear's New Year's Party - Janice

KINDERGARTEN KITCHEN

Ham Sandwiches (single serving)

1 slice of ham
2 slices of bread
Mayonnaise
Mustard

Use scissors to cut the crusts from the bread. Assemble sandwich. Cut into fourths.

New Year's Black-Eyed Peas

1 lb. dried black-eyed peas
Diced ham or bacon
1 large onion, chopped
Garlic powder
Salt
Pepper

Wash peas and soak overnight. Cook as directed on the package, along with ham or bacon, chopped onion, and spices. Season to taste. You may wish to use canned peas instead of dried.

Cabbage

Cut cabbage and boil in salted water until tender. Bits of ham may be added. Season with salt, pepper, garlic powder, and butter.

EXTRAS

New Year's Party

Throw your own New Year's Party. Wear the New Year's hats and sashes (see Art). Purchase balloons, confetti, and horns. Serve the "good luck recipes" (see Kindergarten Kitchen). Turn the hands of a clock to "midnight" to begin the New Year's celebration.

CONCEPT EVALUATION

Dear Parents,

On _____, our class will learn about New Year's. We will learn about the origins of the holiday and ways we celebrate it. Below are ways you can help.

Things To Send: _____
_____
_____

Volunteers Needed To: _____
_____
_____

Follow-Up: At the end of the unit, ask your child to share the following information:

_____
_____
_____

Thank you for your cooperation.

Sincerely,

Bulletin Board

New Year's Baby. Pattern

Examples

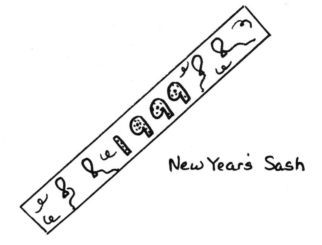

New Year Puzzle

New Year's Sash

Janus Mask

New Year's Hat

Janus Mask

New Year's Hat

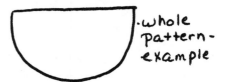

Half Pattern. Flip at center line and trace other half

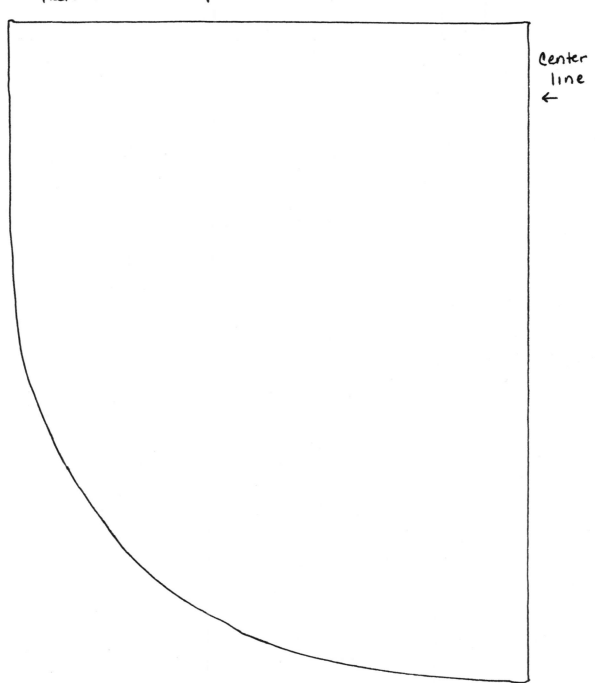

Center
line
←

New Year's Baby Top Hat - Math

1 __ __ 4 __

6   7   __

__ 10   11

12   __   14

__ 16   __

18   19   __

Name :

WINTER

PROPOSED TIME: 5 days

UNIT OBJECTIVES

To review the four seasons
To present the unique qualities of the Winter season
To develop understanding of weather, activities, and animals in winter

ROOM ENVIRONMENT - BULLETIN BOARDS

"Through a Winter Window"

Cover the bulletin board with light blue or gray paper and a black border. Mount the title at the top. Use black strips of paper to divide the bulletin board into window panes. Fill the panes with unit art projects such as snowflakes, snowmen, winter pictures, etc. Be sure to include the work of each child.

"Winter"

Cover the bulletin board as desired. Put the title at the top. Place a large calendar and a snowman in the middle. Make the snowman by cutting circles of tagboard. The children fill in the circles with styrofoam packing "squiggles." Glue on a hat, scarf, facial features, and buttons. Use the remaining space to display unit art work.

ROOM ENVIRONMENT - DISPLAYS

"Ready for Winter" - Wall Display

Trace the outline of each child on kraft paper. The students cut out and paint facial features and winter clothes on the figures. Names should be added. Tape the figures in the hall. Write the title on a piece of tagboard and mount above the display. (See example, page 276.)

"Winter Science Center"

Set up a science center on a table. Cover three sides of a box with burlap and label "Winter." Place at the back of the table. Mount pictures of winter scenes and activities on this stand-up display board. On the table, place a thermometer, magnifying glass, and other materials for experiments. Display books on winter, Eskimos, animals in winter, and winter clothing, tools, and sports equipment. Encourage the children to contribute to the center. (See example, page 277.)

"Classroom Tree"

A classroom tree is useful as well as decorative. Draw and cut out a tree from burlap or felt and staple to a wall or bulletin board (see example, page 277).   If you have the space, a classroom tree can be made by inserting a tree branch in a coffee can of plaster of paris.   Display symbols of each month and art projects on your tree.   For the winter unit, tie fishing line to paper snowflakes and hang from the tree's branches.   Hang some of the snowflakes from the ceiling.   Turn on a fan to make them swirl.

DAY 1 - INTRODUCTION

CONCEPT INFORMATION

Winter is the coldest of the <u>four seasons</u>. After winter comes the season <u>spring</u> when the flowers <u>bloom</u>, then <u>summer</u> when the weather is usually very hot, and <u>fall</u> or <u>autumn</u> when the leaves of the trees turn colors and fall to the ground. In winter, the <u>weather</u> is cold, and in some places there is <u>snow</u>. The trees have no leaves, and animals such as bears and <u>woodchucks</u> hibernate. At this time of the year we play basketball and play in the snow; or if the weather is very bad, we stay inside and play.

LANGUAGE ARTS - SOCIAL STUDIES - SCIENCE

Discussion

Display a poster or picture which depicts the four seasons. A simple version can be made by dividing a poster into four blocks. In each block, draw the same tree as it is in each season. At the base of each tree, add a seasonal object such as a snowman, flowers, a child's swimming pool, and a rake. Refer to the poster as you share the concept information and define the vocabulary words.

Book Activity - A Book of Seasons by Alice and Martin Provensen

Give each student an object or a picture of an object representative of one of the seasons such as a winter cap, an umbrella, a baseball, and a toy rake. Read the book. When each season is mentioned, the children hold up the corresponding object.

Film

Show a winter film such as "Children in Winter." Show the film again. Ask the children to point out the signs and activities of winter.

The Class Tree

Choose a tree to observe all year. Visit the tree and observe its appearance in winter.

Winter-Summer Sheet

Duplicate and distribute the sheet (page 278). Circle winter objects in red. Underline summer objects in green. Color.

Fingerplay - "Tree in Winter"

Outside the door the bare tree stands,   (Palms together high overhead)

And catches snowflakes in its hands,   (Hold above position but open palms to catch snowflakes)

And holds them well and holds them high,

Until a puffing wind comes by.   (Resume first position)

ART

Winter Scene

Preparation - Collect white materials such as styrofoam packing "squiggles," cotton balls, cotton swabs, batting, kleenex, white yarn, material scraps and fake fur scraps, and buttons. Hand out sheets of blue or gray construction paper, scissors, and glue.

Procedure - The children use the materials to create a winter scene. (See example, page 279.)

Winter Tree

Preparation - Mix black tempera to a thin consistency. Give each student a sheet of white construction paper and a straw. Provide silver glitter and glue.

Procedure - Apply a few drops of black tempera to the bottom of each child's construction paper. The children use the straw to blow the tempera toward the top of the sheet to form a tree and branches. When this has dried, dab glue and sprinkle glitter on the branches and ground area to represent snow. (See example, page 279.)

Snowflakes

Preparation - Cut a 5" square of white paper for each child. Provide scissors. Cut different lengths of fishing line or thread to suspend snowflakes from the ceiling.

Procedure - Fold the square in half. Tear off each corner. Fold in half and tear off the two remaining corners. Fold in half once again and cut a small triangle from the middle of the fold. Unfold and hang from the ceiling with fishing line or thread. (See example, page 279.)

Variation: For easier snowflake, cut paper doilies into different shapes.

MATH

Smaller-Larger Sheet

Duplicate and distribute the sheet (page 280). The students draw a circle around the smaller and an "X" on the larger figure in each column. Color.

A Snowball and a Winter Tree - Positions

Draw a bare tree on the chalkboard. Use colored chalk to color it brown. Provide white chalk for the children. Call on volunteers to draw a snowball "on the tree," "above the tree," "below the tree," "beside the tree," "on a branch of the tree," "between two branches of the tree," and so forth.

MUSIC - MOVEMENT - GAMES

Song - "A Song of Winter"

Tune: "Sing a Song of Sixpence"

Sing a song of winter

A pocketful of snow,

Mittens, boots, and jackets

Off to play we go.

When it gets too chilly

We all run back inside

To warm our frozen toes

By the cozy fireside.

Game - Do You Have the Snowball?

The students stand in a circle. Two children stand in the middle. One child is the "passer" and one child is the "guesser." Give the "passer" a cotton ball. The "passer" holds his or her hands together in a "praying position" with the cotton ball concealed between both palms. The children in the circle hold their hands in the same position. The "passer" goes from child to child, slipping his or her hands between theirs and secretly passes the "snowball" to one of them.

After the "passer" goes around the whole circle, the "guesser" tries to guess who has the snowball by asking three children, "Do you have the snowball?" If he or she guesses correctly, the "guesser" becomes the "passer" for the next round. If not, the child with the snowball becomes the "passer." In either case, another "guesser" is chosen from the group.

STORY TIME

Book - When Winter Comes - Russell Freedman
Book - The Great Snowball Contest - William McCay
Book - Winter Is Here - Jane Belk Moncure

KINDERGARTEN KITCHEN

Winter Snow Cones

Instant vanilla pudding
Milk
Flat-bottomed ice cream cones
Shredded coconut

Mix the pudding and milk as directed. Pour into the cones. Allow to
"set." Cover each with coconut.

DAY 2 - WINTER WEATHER

CONCEPT INFORMATION

In winter, our part of the Earth is tipped away from the sun, and so we have cold weather. Sometimes it sleets or snows. Sleet begins as a drop of water which falls from a cloud. It freezes as it falls through the cold air. Snow comes from clouds which are full of tiny drops of water. The drops freeze around bits of dust or sand and turn into ice crystals or snowflakes. Every snowflake is different, but all snowflakes have six sides. Snowflakes fall to the ground to form piles of snow.

Some winter days are cold; some are colder; and some are very cold. We know how cold it is by using thermometers. A thermometer is an instrument used to measure temperature, or how hot or cold something is. Most thermometers are glass tubes holding a special kind of liquid called mercury. There are numbered marks or degrees on the thermometer. When the weather is warm, the liquid in the thermometer rises. When the weather is cold, the liquid falls. The mark next to the top of the liquid tells us what the temperature is.

LANGUAGE ARTS - SOCIAL STUDIES - SCIENCE

Discussion

Relate the concept information and define the vocabulary words. Use a globe and flashlight to demonstrate the earth tipped away from the sun. As a follow-up, perform the following experiments. Explain each process and how it occurs in relation to our weather.

Ice Experiments

Place ice cubes in several different bowls. Let the students touch and describe them. Place one bowl in a sunny window, one near a heater, one on a table, one on the floor, and so forth. Observe which one melts the fastest. When the ice in one bowl has melted, pour it into a pot or pan. Heat on a hot plate until the water boils and starts to evaporate. Then hold an aluminum pie pan over the pot and observe the vapor changing into water again. Place the pie pan and water in the freezer. Observe again after the water has frozen.

Thermometer Experiments

Show the children a variety of thermometers, such as an outdoor, an indoor, and a mouth thermometer. Draw a thermometer on the board to explain how thermometers work. Place one thermometer outside and one in the room; use the other to measure the temperature of a bowl of snow or ice and a bowl of hot water. Record each temperature by using red chalk to fill in the thermometer on the board. Discuss the findings.

Home Follow-Up

Explain television weather reports. Send home the letter sheet concerning the thermometer—temperature lesson (see Patterns, Pictures, Etc., pages 281-282). The children find out the high and low temperatures and forecast for the next day by watching the television weather report. Share in class.

Class Thermometer

Cut a slit, 1½" wide, a few inches from the top—and another slit a few inches from the bottom of a piece of poster paper or a large sheet of cardboard. Measure between the two slits. Purchase one piece of 1" red ribbon an inch longer than this measurement—and one piece of 1" white ribbon an inch longer than this measurement. Sew together one end of the white and one end of the red ribbons. Insert each loose end through a slit and safety-pin together in back.

On the right side of the ribbon, mark the degrees of a thermometer. On the left side, glue or draw pictures to illustrate the different temperatures, such as: a snowman for very cold; a coat for cold; a sweater for cool, and so on, ending with a sun for hot (see Patterns, Pictures, Etc., page 283). Each day check the real thermometer and move the ribbon so that the red shows the temperature.

Fingerplay - "Jack Frost"

Jack Frost is a fairy small.   (Show smallness with thumb and pointer)

I'm sure he is out today.

He nipped my nose   (Point to nose)

And pinched my toes   (Point to toes)

When I went out to play.   (Run in place)

Snow - Book and Activity

Read Snow Is Falling by Franklyn M. Branley. Ask the children to think of words to describe snow. (Examples: crunchy, cold, smooth, powdery.) Then draw a line to divide the chalkboard in half. Label one column "Good" and the other "Bad." Brainstorm for the good and bad aspects of snow. (Examples: **Good** - pretty, fun, keeps crops from freezing, melted snow fills rivers, clean air. **Bad** - stops traffic, uncomfortable, causes accidents, costs money to plow away, costs money for damages.)

Call on students to act out various snow activities such as building a snowman, shoveling snow, and a snowball fight.

Poem - "Merry Little Snowflakes"

Merry little snowflakes falling through the air,

Resting on the steeple and the tall trees everywhere,

Covering roofs and fences, capping every post,

Covering the hillside where we like to coast.

Merry little snowflakes do their very best

To make a soft, white blanket so buds and flowers may rest,

But when the bright spring sunshine says it has come to stay,

Then those little snowflakes quickly run away!

ART

Paper Plate Snowmen

Preparation - Purchase large and small paper plates. Give each child one of each and a sheet of black and a sheet of red construction paper. Provide pencils, scissors, glue, and scrap paper. On the board, demonstrate drawing a hat and scarf.

Procedure - Glue the two plates together for the head and body. Draw the hat, facial features, scarf, etc., on the paper. Cut out and glue on the snowman. (See example, page 283.)

Note: Encourage the students to use their imaginations to create unique snowmen. Decorating possibilities include: sunglasses, ear muffs, tennis shoes, overalls, etc.

Ivory Snow Paintings

Preparation - Mix one cup water and two cups of Ivory Snow detergent. Beat with an electric mixer until thick and fluffy. Spoon into aluminum pie plates and place on the tables. Give each child a sheet of blue or gray construction paper.

Procedure - Create a winter scene with the Ivory Snow paint. Allow to dry thoroughly. (See example, page 283.)

Variation: Make Ivory Snowmen by molding the mixture into balls. Use buttons or beads for facial features. Stack and allow to dry. If necessary, insert toothpicks between the parts to hold them in place. Gently tie yarn around the neck for a scarf.

Fingerpainting With Shaving Cream

Preparation - Purchase shaving cream and aluminum foil. Set out shaving cream in pans. Give each student a 7" piece of aluminum foil.

Procedure - Use the shaving cream to fingerpaint on the foil. (See example, page 283.)

MATH

Snowballs Sheet

Preparation - Duplicate the sheet on construction paper (page 284). Prepare a large batch of popcorn. Distribute the sheets. Set out the popcorn and glue.

Procedure - The children read the numeral and glue that many snowballs (popcorn) in each block. (Eat the remaining popcorn!)

Note: The children should make a "puddle of glue" to properly hold each snowball.

Whole/Half Snowball Sheet

Preparation - Duplicate and distribute the sheet (page 285). Provide scissors and crayons.

Procedure - Read and follow the directions on the sheet.

MUSIC - MOVEMENT - GAMES

Song - "Frosty the Snowman"

Source: Children's Christmas Party (LP), Halo Records

Game - Freeze Snowflakes

Choose one student to be "It." Play music as the children pretend to be snowflakes dancing, falling, twirling, and tumbling. When "It" shouts, "Freeze Snowflakes!" the children must freeze in their positions. "It" tries to make them laugh or move, without touching. The first player to move is the next "It."

Game - Snowball Relay

Preparation - Divide the class into two even teams. Mark a starting and finish line. The two teams line up behind the starting line. Give each of the first players a tennis ball.

Procedure - The players hold the "snowball" under their chins, run to the finish line and back, and hand the snowball (with either their chin or hand) to the next player. If the snowball is dropped, the player retrieves it and starts again from that point. The team that finishes first wins.

Variation: If you have snow, use real snowballs with the students holding them in their hands. The team whose snowball melts first loses. If the snowballs do not melt, the team that finishes first wins.

STORY TIME

Book - Katy and the Big Snow - Virginia Burton
Book - The Snowman - Hans Christian Anderson
Book - The Big Snow - Berta and Elmer Hader
Book - Josie and the Snow - Helen E. Buckley
Book - White Snow, Bright Snow - Alvin Tresselt

EXTRAS

Winter White Meal

Include parents in planning and preparing a meal or snack time of things that are white such as mashed potatoes with sour cream, chicken, cauliflower, grits, cream-of-wheat, bread, milk, and ice cream.

Field Trip

Plan a field trip to a local weather bureau or the weather department of a local television station.

DAY 3 - WINTER CLOTHES AND ACTIVITIES

CONCEPT INFORMATION

Because the weather is cold in winter, we wear clothes that keep our bodies warm. We wear clothes that are made of <u>heavier material</u>, shirts with long <u>sleeves</u>, long pants, <u>thick</u> socks, warm shoes, sweaters, caps, mittens or gloves, and coats. We warm our houses and cars with <u>heaters</u> so we only put on sweaters, mittens or gloves, coats, and boots when we go outside.

When the weather is very cold, we need to be careful to avoid <u>frostbite</u>. Frostbite occurs when the skin gets so cold that it freezes. To keep from getting frostbite, it is <u>important</u> to wear <u>layers</u> of warm clothing. You should wear a <u>stocking cap</u> or a hood on your head and a <u>scarf</u> or <u>muffler</u> to cover your mouth. Mittens keep your hands warmer than gloves. Change wet <u>clothing</u> as quickly as possible if you get wet; when you get too cold, go inside.

There are many winter <u>activities</u> that we enjoy such as <u>snow skiing</u>, <u>snow sledding</u>, <u>ice hockey</u>, <u>ice skating</u>, and <u>basketball</u>. When the weather is bad, it is also fun to stay inside and read, play games, and make warm <u>snacks</u> to eat.

LANGUAGE ARTS - SOCIAL STUDIES - SCIENCE

Discussion

Place a set of winter clothes in a large paper bag and a set of summer clothes in another. Share the concept information, defining vocabulary words. Let each student take an article of clothing out of the bags and determine whether it is worn in summer or winter. Compare the differences of the two groups.

Dressing Sequence Sheet

<u>Preparation</u> - Duplicate and distribute the sheets (page 286). Provide winter clothing catalogs, scissors, and glue. Discuss the sequence of everyday dressing.

<u>Procedure</u> - From the catalogs cut pictures of three different articles of winter clothing such as socks, a shirt, and a coat. If you were dressing, which would you put on first, second, and third? Starting at the arrow, and proceeding from left to right, glue the clothing pictures in the proper order. One picture will be in each block.

Downhill Sled Race

At the top of the chalkboard, write "Downhill Sled Race." Draw two large slopes with a simple sled at the top and a finish line at the bottom of each. Below the line of each slope, draw a mark every few inches (see Patterns, Pictures, Etc., page 287). Divide the class into two teams. Ask questions, alternating teams. These may be questions involving the unit, identifying flashcards of the alphabet or shapes, and so forth. For each correct answer, the sled of that team is moved one mark (erase and draw again). The first team to reach the finish line wins.

Too Many Mittens - Book and Matching Activity

Preparation - Use the mitten pattern (see Patterns, Pictures, Etc., page 288) to trace and cut out a pair of mittens for each student in the class. Use wallpaper sample books, wrapping paper scraps, and different colors of construction paper so that each pair of mittens is different. Construct a clothesline (see Signs of Christmas, Math, Day 2) and provide clothespins.

Procedure - Read the book Too Many Mittens by Florence and Louis Slobodkin. Give each child a pair of paper mittens. Direct him or her to look closely at the mittens; then hang each one in a different place on the clothesline. After all the mittens are hung on the line, call on each child to find his or her pair and clothespin them side by side on the line.

Fingerplay - "Brrr-rr-rr"

Today I wore my snow suit

That goes from heels to throat. (Point to feet, then neck)

It shuts up with a zip, (Pretend to zip up front)

And is much warmer than a coat. (Hug yourself)

I wore a sweater under that,

And a wooly cap, bright red. (Make cap on head)

It fitted snug upon my ears (Hand on ears)

And covered my whole head! (Circular motion about head)

I wore overshoes with buckles (Point to shoes)

And mittens lined with fur, (Hand out, fingers together)

But it was so very cold,

I still shivered and said, "Brrr-rr-rr." (Shiver, arms close to body)

Going Ice Skating - Action story

Divide the students into groups and assign a group for each word. Practice the key words, responses, and motions until everyone understands. Each group should stand when responding; then sit back down.

WORD	RESPONSE	MOTIONS
Saturday	"School's Out"	Shake fists
Ice Skating	"Shoosh-shoosh"	Skate in place
Ice Skates	"Crunch, crunch"	(none)
Baby	"Waa-Waa"	Thumb in mouth
Run	"Stomp-stomp"	Run in place
Mother	"John-ny!"	Hands on hips
Mailman	"The mail must go through"	March in place
Wave	"Wave-wave"	Wave hand
Train	"Choo-choo"	Pump arms
Mary Jane	"Hi Johnny, let's kiss"	Kissing motion

It's SATURDAY, and I'm going ICE SKATING! Would you like to come along? First we have to get our ICE SKATES, and we're ready to go. Walk softly so we don't wake the BABY. Oh no, let's RUN before MOTHER sees us! Now we are on our way. There's Mr. Allen, our MAILMAN. WAVE to Mr. Allen.

Soon we have to cross the TRAIN tracks. Stop! Here comes a TRAIN! It's a long one! Let's WAVE at the man in the caboose.

Now we are at the pond and we have put on our ICE SKATES. It's time for ICE SKATING. Isn't it fun? Oh no, it's MARY JANE! Take off your ICE SKATES and RUN! No more ICE SKATING today.

ART

Lace-Up Ice Skates

Preparation - Duplicate the skate (see Patterns, Pictures, Etc., page 289) on white construction paper. Give each student a skate and a 36" piece of yarn. Provide scissors, crayons, and hole punchers.

Procedure - Cut out the skate on the dotted line. Color. Use the hole puncher to make the shoelace holes. Lace the yarn through the holes, crisscross between pairs, and finish with a bow. (See example, page 288.)

Note: Dip the ends of the yarn in glue, and dry; or use tape to prevent raveling.

Paper Mittens

Preparation - Reproduce the mittens (see Patterns, Pictures, Etc., page 290) on various colors of construction paper. Cut 12" pieces of yarn. Provide scissors, crayons, and hole punchers.

Procedure - Cut out the mittens and decorate as desired. Punch a hole on the X of each mitten. Tie each end of the yarn through a hole.

Paper Weave Caps

<u>Preparation</u> - Duplicate the cap pattern (see Patterns, Pictures, Etc., page 291) on colored construction paper. Give each child a pattern and another sheet of construction paper of a different color. Provide scissors and glue.

<u>Procedure</u> - Cut out the cap. Fold so that the top meets the bottom and the lines show. With scissors, make a small cut at each line on the fold. Unfold, insert scissors in the small cut, and cut on the lines in each direction. Do not cut beyond the lines. Cut strips 9" in length from the sheet of construction paper. The width of the strips may vary. Weave the first strip over and under, over and under the strips of the cap. If the first strip started over the edge of the cap, the second strip starts under the edge of the cap (or vice versa), and so on. When the cap is completely woven, cut the strips to match the outline of the cap and glue in place. (See example, page 288.)

MATH

Pairs Activity

Explain the concept of pairs. Display pairs of shoes, socks, mittens, and gloves. Mix them up and let the children find the matching pairs. Duplicate and distribute the sheet (see Patterns, Pictures, Etc., pages 292). The students draw lines to match the two items of a pair and color the objects.

Mitten Dot-to-Dot

Duplicate and distribute the sheet (page 293). The children draw a mitten by following the numbered dots. Color as desired.

MUSIC - MOVEMENT - GAMES

<u>Song</u> - "On a Snowy Winter Morning"

Tune: "Here We Go 'Round the Mulberry Bush"

Form a circle. Sing and act out the song.

This is the way I dress to play,

Dress to play,

Dress to play.

This is the way I dress to play

On a snowy winter morning.

Verses:

2. This is the way I put on my shirt . . .
3. This is the way I put on my pants . . .
4. This is the way I put on my socks . . .
5. This is the way I put on my boots . . .
6. This is the way I put on my coat . . .
7. This is the way I put on my cap . . .
8. This is the way I put on my mittens . . .
9. This is the way I go out to play . . . (Skip in a circle.)

Game - The Eyes Have It

This game should be played on a cold day when the children have warm caps, coats, mittens, boots, etc., at school. Divide the class into two teams. Choose two members from each team to stand in front of the class and place a grocery sack behind them. One child puts on his cap, coat, mittens, and boots; the next puts on his cap, mittens, and boots; the next puts on his coat and mittens; the last puts on his cap and coat.

Direct the two teams to observe the children's clothing; then cover and close their eyes. Quickly remove one article of clothing from one of the children and place it in the bag. Everyone opens their eyes. Give a volunteer of the first team a chance to guess what is missing. If that team can't guess, ask a volunteer of the next team. A correct response scores one point. If no one can guess, the child whose clothing it is takes it from the bag and puts it back on.

Repeat the procedure varying the article of clothing and the child. You may wish to replace the four students with others so that no one gets overheated. The team with the most points wins.

STORY TIME

Book - <u>The Snowy Day</u> - Ezra Jack Keats
Book - <u>Red Mittens</u> - Laura Bannon
Book - <u>Old Turtle's Winter Games</u> - Leonard Kessler
Book - <u>First Snow</u> - Emily Arnold McCully

KINDERGARTEN KITCHEN

Spiced Tea (Instant)

3/4 cup instant tea
2 cups Tang
1 teaspoon ground cloves
1 teaspoon ground cinnamon
1 package presweetened lemon Kool-Aid

Mix all ingredients together. Store in a jar. For each drink, mix 2 teaspoons of spiced tea with 1 cup of hot water. Stir well.

DAY 4 - ANIMALS AND BIRDS IN WINTER

CONCEPT INFORMATION

Before winter comes, animals grow thicker fur to prepare for the cold. Some animals such as the bear, the raccoon, and the woodchuck hibernate during the winter. Others like the squirrel, the beaver, and the fox do not hibernate. They store food in fall to last throughout the winter. Rabbits and deer do not hibernate or store food. They must spend the winter searching for food.

Some birds migrate to warmer places before winter comes. Other birds like robins, cardinals, and blue jays stay where they are during the winter. They too must search for food.

LANGUAGE ARTS - SOCIAL STUDIES - SCIENCE

Discussion

Share the concept information and define the vocabulary words. Show pictures of hibernating animals, animals that do not hibernate, migrating birds, and birds that do not migrate from reference books such as Childcraft - How and Why Library.

Film

Show the film "Animals in Winter." Show the film again without the sound. Call on different students to narrate the scenes.

Book and Action Story - Animals in Winter by Henrietta Bancroft

Read the book. Direct the students to place their sweaters or jackets nearby and act out the following:

We are animals searching in the forest for food. (search on all fours) Our fur has become thick (put on sweaters or jackets) to protect us from the cold. (hug yourself) Winter is here, and it is time for our long winter sleep. (close eyes and lay head against hands) But before we hibernate, we eat and eat. (pretend to eat) Now we must find a place to sleep (look for a place) Here is a cave! (cup hands) It is warm and safe. We will curl up here and (yawn) go to sleep. (pretend to sleep)

Flannel Board Story - "Why the Bear Has a Stumpy Tail"

Trace the patterns (see Patterns, Pictures, Etc., pages 294-295) on pellon and color with permanent markers. Place the figures on the flannel board as you tell the story.

One day Brown Bear was walking in the forest searching for food. He needed food before his long winter nap. Soon he met Sly Fox. Sly Fox was holding a string of beautiful fish.

"Hello Sly Fox," said Brown Bear, "Where did you catch those beautiful fish?"

"I caught them at Frozen Pond," said Sly Fox.

"I am very hungry, and I would like to catch some fish myself," said Brown Bear.

Now the Sly Fox had stolen the fish, but he didn't want to tell Brown Bear. He loved to play tricks, so he said, "Oh, they are easy to catch, Brown Bear. Just cut a hole in the ice and stick your long tail in the hole. Sit there a long time. It will sting a little when the fish bite; but if you wait, you can catch as many as I did."

Brown Bear thanked Sly Fox and hurried to Frozen Pond. He did just as Sly Fox had told him. His tail began to sting, but he sat and sat.

While he waited, he thought of the delicious supper he would have that night.

After a long time, Brown Bear thought, "I think I have enough fish now." He tried to stand up but found his tail was frozen in the ice. "That Sly Fox has tricked me again, and he will be sorry!" shouted Brown Bear. And this time he jumped up so fast that his tail came apart. The long part stayed in the ice, and that's why bears have stumpy tails—and foxes stay away from them!

Fingerplay - "Five Little Birds"

Five little birds sitting in a tree,   (Hold up 5 fingers)

One flew away saying, "It's too cold for me!" (Put down pinky)

The second said, "I'm flying south too." (Put down ring finger)

The third said, "Brrr," and away he flew. (Put down middle finger)

The fourth one said, "I'm staying here." (Wiggle pointer finger)

The fifth one said, "There's a bird feeder near." (Wiggle thumb)

So the two little birds enjoyed their dinner   (Continue to hold up two
    fingers)

And stayed at home throughout the winter.

"Where the Bear Hibernates" Sheet

Duplicate and distribute the sheets (page 296). The students color the pictures and then cut on the dotted line to separate sections. The bear is cut out and glued in the correct place for hibernation.

Listening Activity

Play "Peter and the Wolf" from Walt Disney Presents "Peter and the Wolf" (LP), narrated by Sterling Holloway.

ART

Pine Cone Birdfeeders

Preparation - Collect a pine cone and cut a 12" piece of yarn for each child. Set out peanut butter and wild birdseed.

Procedure - Stick dabs of peanut butter on the scales of the pine cone. Sprinkle birdseed on the peanut butter. Tie the string to the top of the pine cone. Hang on a tree. (See example, page 297.)

Smudge Print Rabbits

Preparation - Duplicate the rabbit (see Patterns, Pictures, Etc., page 298 on white construction paper. Give each child a copy and a sheet of white drawing paper. Provide scissors, brown crayons, pencils with erasers, and staplers. You will also need a staple remover.

Procedure - Cut out and color a border on the rabbit, using the brown color. Apply so that it is "thick." Place in the center of the drawing paper and staple. Anchor the rabbit with one hand. Place the eraser tip on the border and push outward onto the drawing paper, "smudging" the outline onto the drawing paper. Continue this all around the border. The result will be a smudge print outline of a rabbit. Remove the staple and discard the rabbit. (See example, page 297.)

Mosaics

Preparation - Provide scrap construction paper, glue, and drawing paper.

Procedure - Tear the paper into small pieces. Place the pieces on the drawing paper to form the bird, animal, or scene of your choice. Glue in place. (See example, page 297.)

MATH

"Feed the Hungry Rabbits" Sheet

Purchase breakfast cereal. Reproduce the sheet (page 299). Direct the students to feed the rabbits by gluing in each rabbit's mouth the number of cereal pieces indicated.

Book and Math Activity

Duplicate the sheet (page 300). Read the book <u>Big Tracks, Little Tracks</u> by Franklyn M. Branley. Pass out the sheets and crayons. Direct the children to draw an X on the big footprints and a circle around the little footprints in each block. Color.

MUSIC - MOVEMENT - GAMES

<u>Song</u> - "Little Bunny Foo-Foo"

Tune: "Down by the Station"

Little Bunny Foo-Foo,

Hopping through the forest

Scooping up the field mice and boppin' 'em on the head.

Down came the good fairy—and she said,

(Spoken:) "Little Bunny Foo-Foo, I don't want to see you scooping up the field mice and boppin' 'em on the head.

I'll give you three chances, and if you don't behave—
I'll turn you into a goon! The next day:

2. Same as verse 1 except on line 6,

"I'll give you two more chances . . ."

3. "I'll give you one more chance . . ."

4. "I gave you three chances and you didn't behave. Now you're a goon! POOF!

(The moral of the story: "Hare" today, "goon" tomorrow.)

<u>Game and Song</u> - "Bluebird"

Source: <u>Folk Song Carnival</u> (LP) by Hap Palmer

The children sing the song and play the game as directed.

STORY TIME

Book - <u>Buzzy Bear's Winter Party</u> - Dorothy Marino
Book - <u>The Fox Went out on a Chilly Night</u> - old song illustrated by Peter Spier
Book - <u>Winter Hut</u> - Cynthia Jameson

DAY 5 - ESKIMOS

CONCEPT INFORMATION

For <u>thousands</u> of years, <u>Eskimos</u> have been living in the <u>arctic region</u> of the earth. There, the winters are very long and cold; the summers are short and dry. Most of the year there is ice and snow.

Today some Eskimos live as we do; but some, as we will learn in this unit, still follow the old <u>traditions</u>. Most Eskimos are <u>stocky</u>, of <u>medium height</u> with <u>broad</u> faces and <u>narrow</u> eyes. Their skin is brownish-yellow in color. Eskimos have their own <u>language</u>. They live in small <u>settlements</u> and move from place to place.

Eskimos <u>invented</u> the <u>igloo</u> which is a <u>dwelling</u> made of <u>blocks</u> cut from hard snow. Eskimos live in igloos or in houses of <u>driftwood</u> or <u>stones</u> and <u>sod</u>. Eskimo women make the family's clothes from <u>animal skins</u> and fur. They make stockings of deerskin, <u>slippers</u> of bird skin, sealskin <u>boots</u> with walrus <u>soles</u>, fur pants and shirts, and coats of heavy fur.

Eskimos are <u>skilled</u> hunters. In spring and winter, they hunt <u>seal</u>, <u>walrus</u>, and <u>whale</u>. In summer and fall, they hunt <u>caribou</u> and <u>fish</u>. Eskimos hunt <u>polar bears</u> all year long. Like the American Indians, the Eskimos use animals and fish for their food, their clothes, their <u>tools</u>, and their <u>weapons</u>. The Eskimo's <u>kayak</u>, which is a one-man canoe, is covered with sealskin. The Eskimo's <u>sled</u>, which is pulled by dogs, is made of driftwood; and animal skin, bones, and <u>antlers</u>.

LANGUAGE ARTS - SOCIAL STUDIES - SCIENCE

Discussion

Display pictures of Eskimos. Relate the concept information and define the vocabulary words. Point out the arctic region on a globe.

Book

Read and discuss <u>The Little Igloo</u> by Lorraine and Jerrold Beim.

Eskimo Transparency Activity

Trace the pictures (see Patterns, Pictures, Etc., page 301) on transparencies. Label each. Place on the overhead projector. Name and explain each object. Review by pointing to the objects and asking for volunteers to name and define them.

Ice Fishing Game

Preparation - Make a fishing pole by tying and then taping string to a dowel. Tie a magnet to the end of the string. The pond can be a simple bucket or a large cardboard ice cream carton from an ice cream store. Cut a piece of poster paper small enough to cover and also balance on top of the bucket. In the center of the poster paper, cut a hole a few inches smaller than the top of the bucket.

Duplicate the "Ice Fishing Fish" (see Patterns, Pictures, Etc., page 302) on different colors of construction paper. Cut out and label each with an alphabet letter. Clip a paper clip to the mouth of each fish. Place the fish in the bucket. Lay the hole of the poster paper over the opening to resemble a hole cut in the ice.

Procedure - The students take turns dropping the fishing line into the pond. Once a fish is caught, the child identifies the alphabet letter and sets the fish aside. When all fish have been caught, they are returned to the pond. (See example, page 302.)

Fingerplay - "Two Little Eskimos"

Two little Eskimos on one fine day (Hold up pointer and middle fingers)

Ran from their igloo and began to play. (Cup one hand, fingers run out)

They fished in the ice and rode on a sled. (Fingers up and down in a
    sledding motion)

Then they rubbed noses and went home to bed. (Rub fingers together,
    then make fingers run to cupped hand)

ART

Stand-Up Walrus

Preparation - Duplicate the walrus (see Patterns Pictures, Etc., page 303) on white construction paper. Give each child a copy, a small paper plate, a piece of aluminum foil large enough to cover the plate, and 10-15 sugar cubes. Provide scissors and crayons or markers.

Procedure - Cut out the walrus on the dotted line only. Color both sides. Fold the bottom strip on the solid line. Cover the plate with the foil. Spread glue on the bottom of the strip and mount in the middle of the paper plate. Glue sugar cubes around the walrus.

Chalk-Colored Igloos

Preparation - On the chalkboard, demonstrate drawing an igloo. Pass out blue or gray paper and chalk.

Procedure - Draw an igloo. Color the igloo and surrounding snow by using the side of the chalk. (See example, page 302.)

Eskimo

Preparation - Duplicate the Eskimo (see Patterns, Pictures, Etc., page 304) on light brown construction paper. Set out cotton balls, glue, and crayons.

Procedure - Outline the Eskimo's facial features in black. Cut out. Glue the cotton balls on the circle to represent the hood. (See example, page 302).

MATH

Igloo Math

Duplicate and distribute the igloos (see Patterns, Pictures, Etc., page 305). Direct the students to count the dots and write the correct number in each block.

Ice Fishing Sheet

Purchase small crackers that are shaped like fish. Reproduce and distribute the sheet (page 306). Set out the crackers and glue. The children follow the directions on the sheet by gluing the correct number of fish on each hook.

MUSIC - MOVEMENT - GAMES

Song - "Eskimo Joe"

Tune: "Ole Dan Tucker"

Eskimo Joe was no ordinary soul;

He liked to fish barefoot, even in the snow;

He got so many fish on his line,

He had to eat them two at a time.

Chorus:

Get out of the way for Eskimo Joe;

He's got frostbite on every toe;

Old piece of rope holds up his pants,

Too fat to fly, too old to dance.

Verse 2:

"Oh me, oh my," old Joe sighed,

"There's twenty-five fish a-swimming inside."

They flipped and flopped and so did Joe.

He's flip, flip-flopping still, so the story goes.

ESKIMO GAMES

Follow the Leader

The students line up behind the leader, preferably in the snow. The leader takes different kinds of steps, changes directions, and performs various actions which the followers must imitate.

Eskimo Catch

The children form a circle and toss a beanbag back and forth to each other. Anyone who drops the beanbag leaves the circle. The last person in the circle is the winner.

KINDERGARTEN KITCHEN

Snack

Provide Eskimo pies for an afternoon snack.

Eskimo Faces

Rye bread
Cream Cheese
Raisins

Bring cream cheese to room temperature. Beat until soft. Use cookie cutters to cut round pieces of rye bread. Make the fur around the Eskimo face by applying cream cheese around the edge of the circle with a wooden popsicle stick. Make eyes, nose, and mouth with raisins.

CONCEPT EVALUATION

Dear Parents,

On _____, our class will begin our unit on Winter. The daily topics for the unit are "Introduction," "Winter Weather," "Winter Clothing and Activities," "Animals and Birds in Winter," and "Eskimos." The discussions, films, books, fingerplays, songs, and other activities will center around these topics.   Please read below to see how you can find out ways you can help.

Things To Send: _____

_____

_____

Volunteers Needed To: _____

_____

_____

Follow-Up: At the end of the unit, ask your child to share the following songs, fingerplays, or stories we have learned:

_____

_____

_____

Thank you for your cooperation.

Sincerely,

Through   A   Winter   Window

WINTER

JANUARY

SUN	MON	TUE	WED	THU	FRI	SAT
		1	2	3	4	5	6
7	8	9	10	11	12	13
14	15	16	17	18	19	20
21	22	23	24	25	26	27
28	29	30	31			

Wall Display - Ready For Winter

Displays

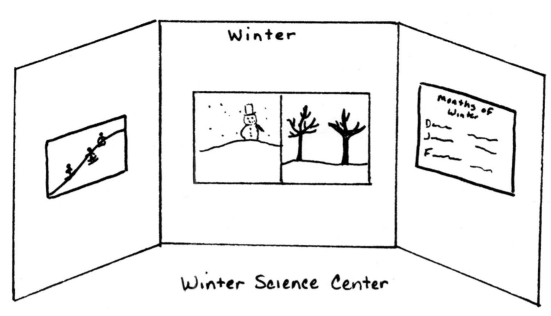

Winter Science Center

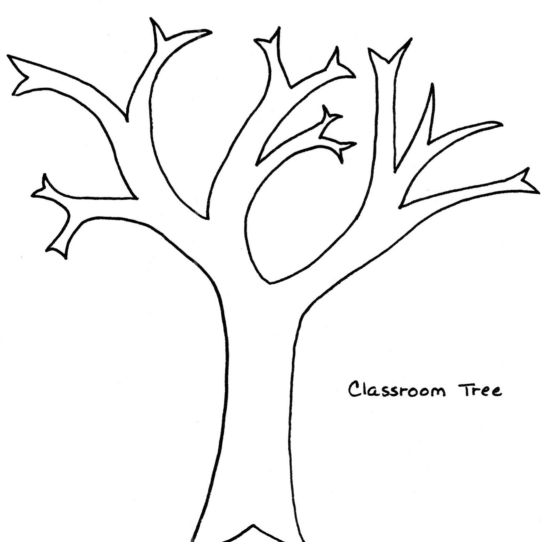

Classroom Tree

Winter. Summer Sheet

Name _____

Examples

Winter Scene

Winter Tree

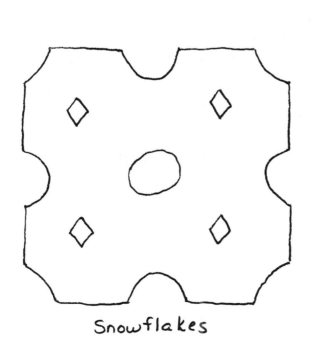

Snowflakes

Smaller - Larger Sheet

Dear Parents,

Today our class learned about thermometers and temperatures. We conducted several thermometer experiments and recorded the results on a large thermometer drawn on the chalkboard.

Please assist your child in completing the attached "Thermometer-Temperature Sheet." You and your child will need to view a television weather report and obtain the high and low temperatures and weather forecast for tomorrow.

Please send the completed sheet to school with your child tomorrow. Thank you for your cooperation.

Sincerely,

Thermometer - Temperature Sheet
Home Follow-up

Please watch the television weather forecast and complete the following:

1. Tomorrow's low temperature is forecasted to be _____°F.

2. Tomorrow's high temperature is forecasted to be _____°F.

3. Tomorrow's weather is forecasted to be : (circle)

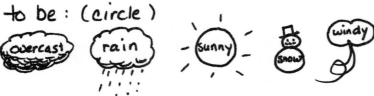

4. Record tomorrow's high temperature by "coloring in" the big thermometer.

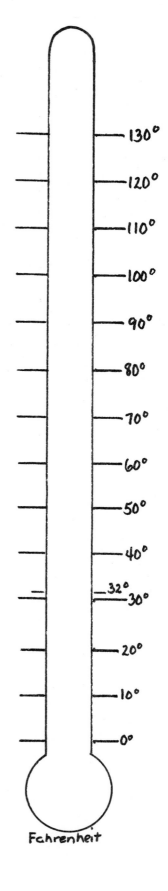

Example

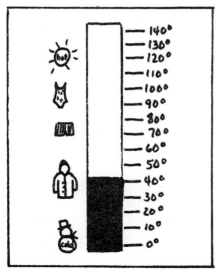

Class Thermometer

Paper Plate Snowmen

Ivory Snow Painting

Finger painting
With Shaving Cream

Snowballs Sheet

5	7
6	4

Glue the correct number of snowballs (popcorn) in each block.

Name _____

Whole / Half Snowball Sheet

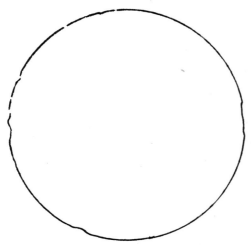

A Whole Snowball

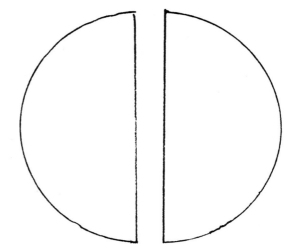

A Snowball Cut In Half
Each part is ½ .

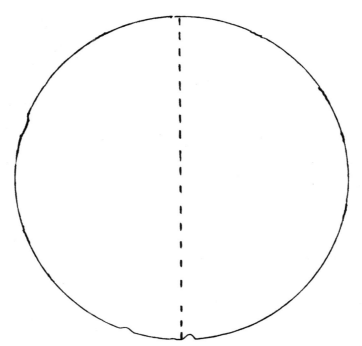

Divide the snowball in half by tracing over
the dotted line. Write ½ on each part.

Name: _____

Dressing Sequence Sheet

1st

2nd

Last

Downhill Sled Race
Example

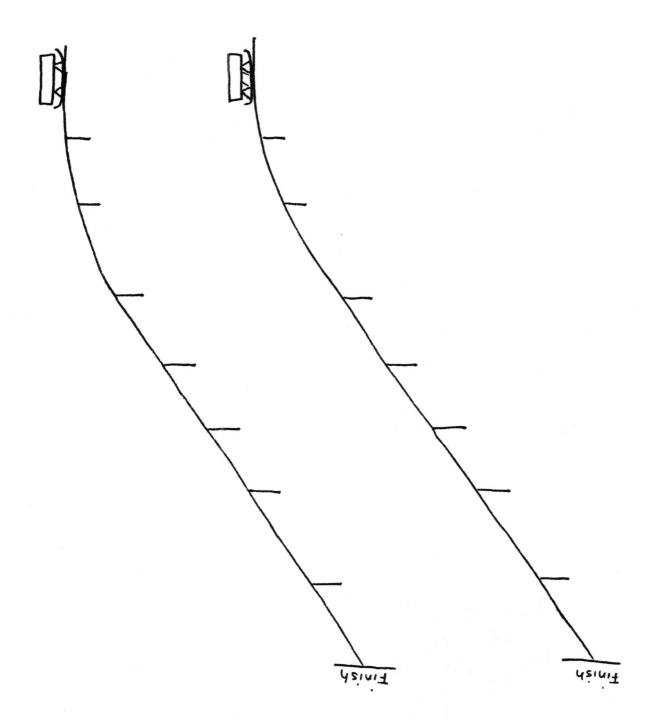

Finish

Finish

Pattern Examples

Lace-Up Ice Skates
Example

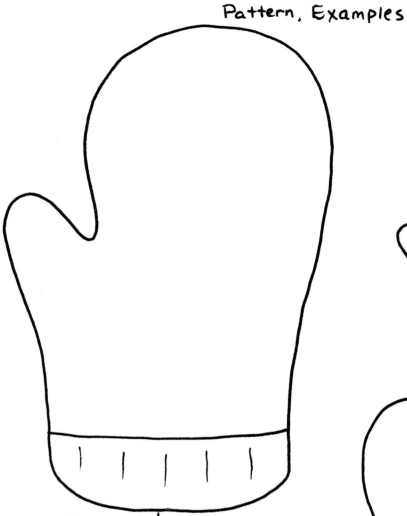

Too Many Mittens-
Mitten Pattern

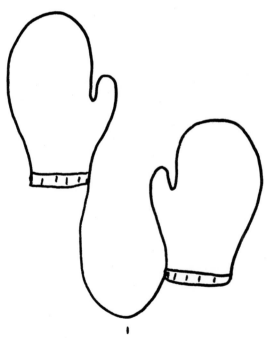

Paper Mittens
Example

Paper Weave Caps
Example

Lace-Up Ice Skates

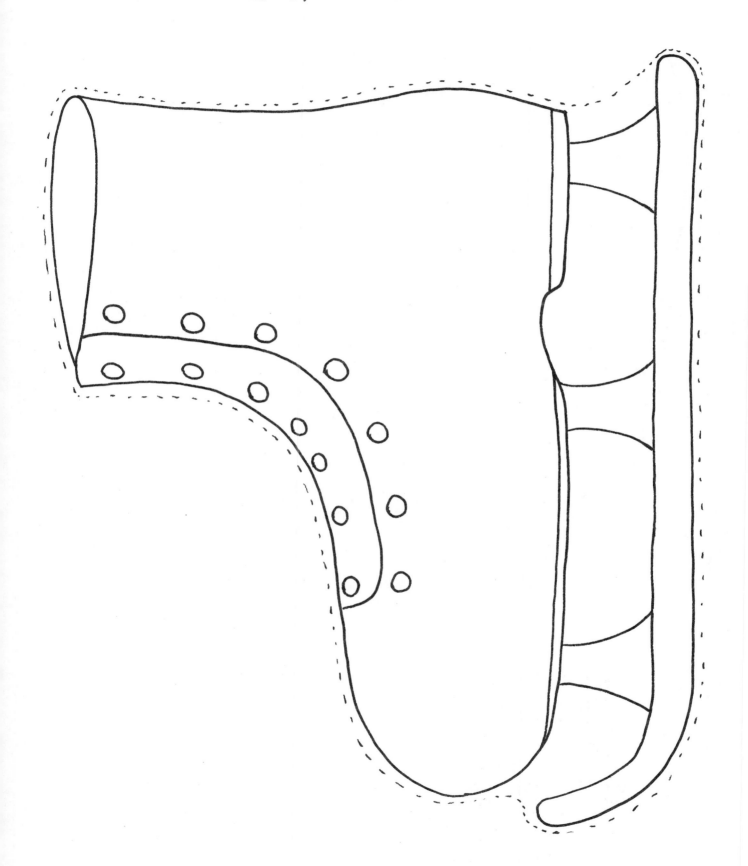

Paper Mittens

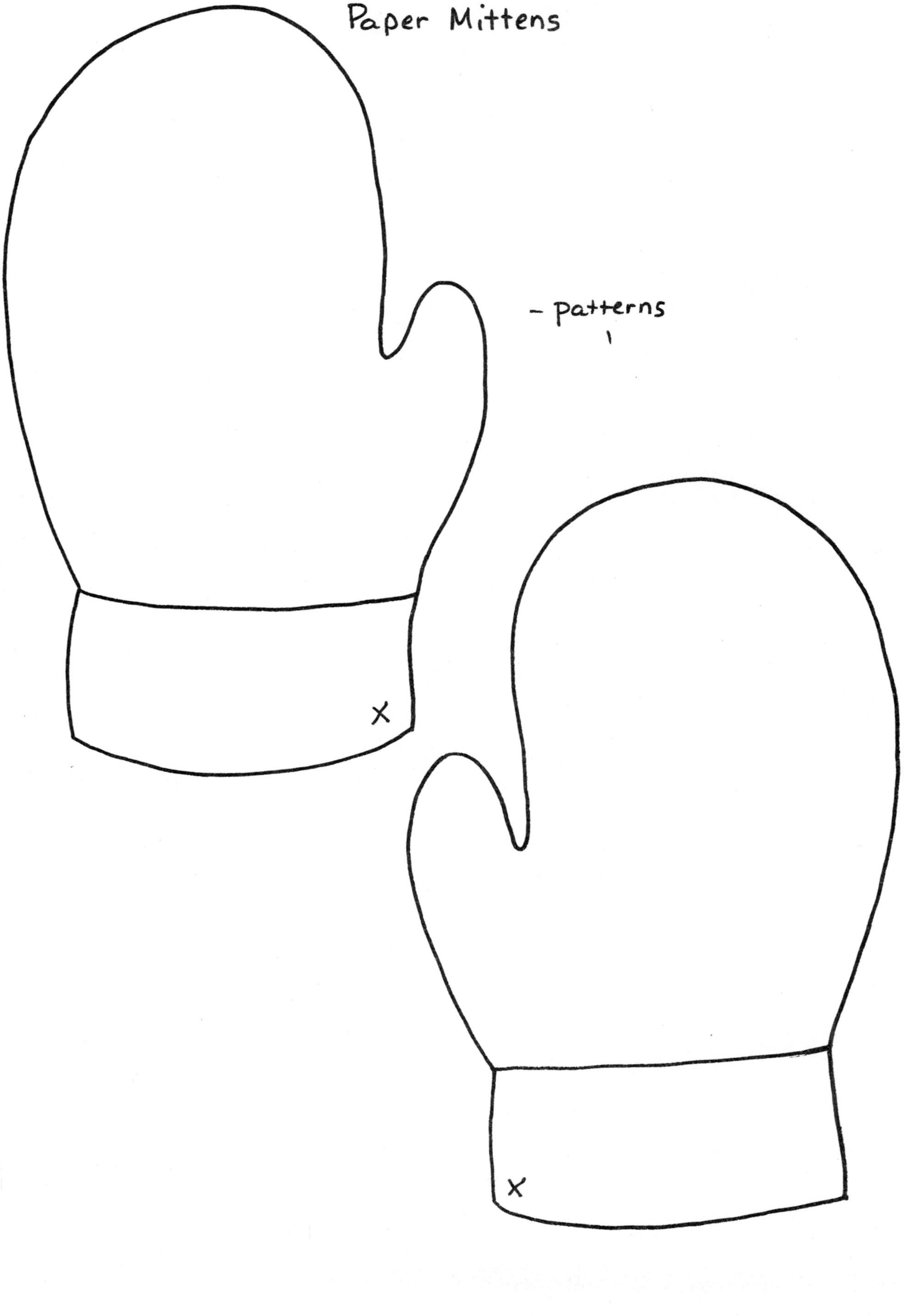

— patterns
ı

X

X

Paper Weave Caps

pattern —

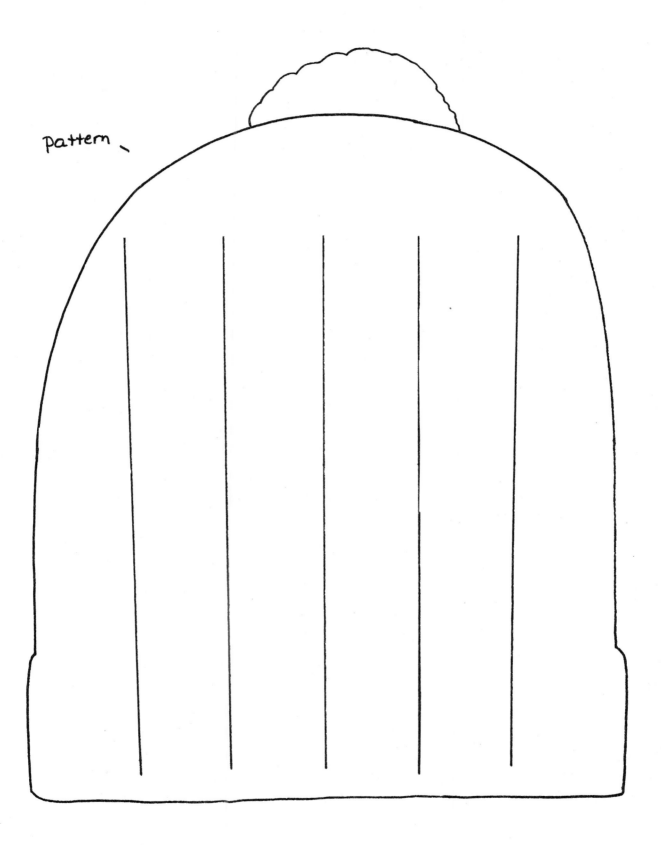

Pairs Sheet

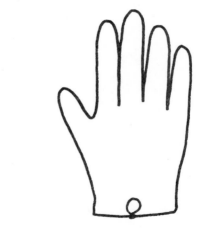

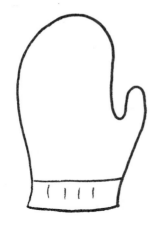

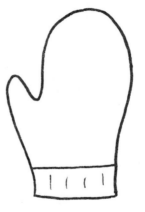

Name: _____

Mitten Dot-to-Dot

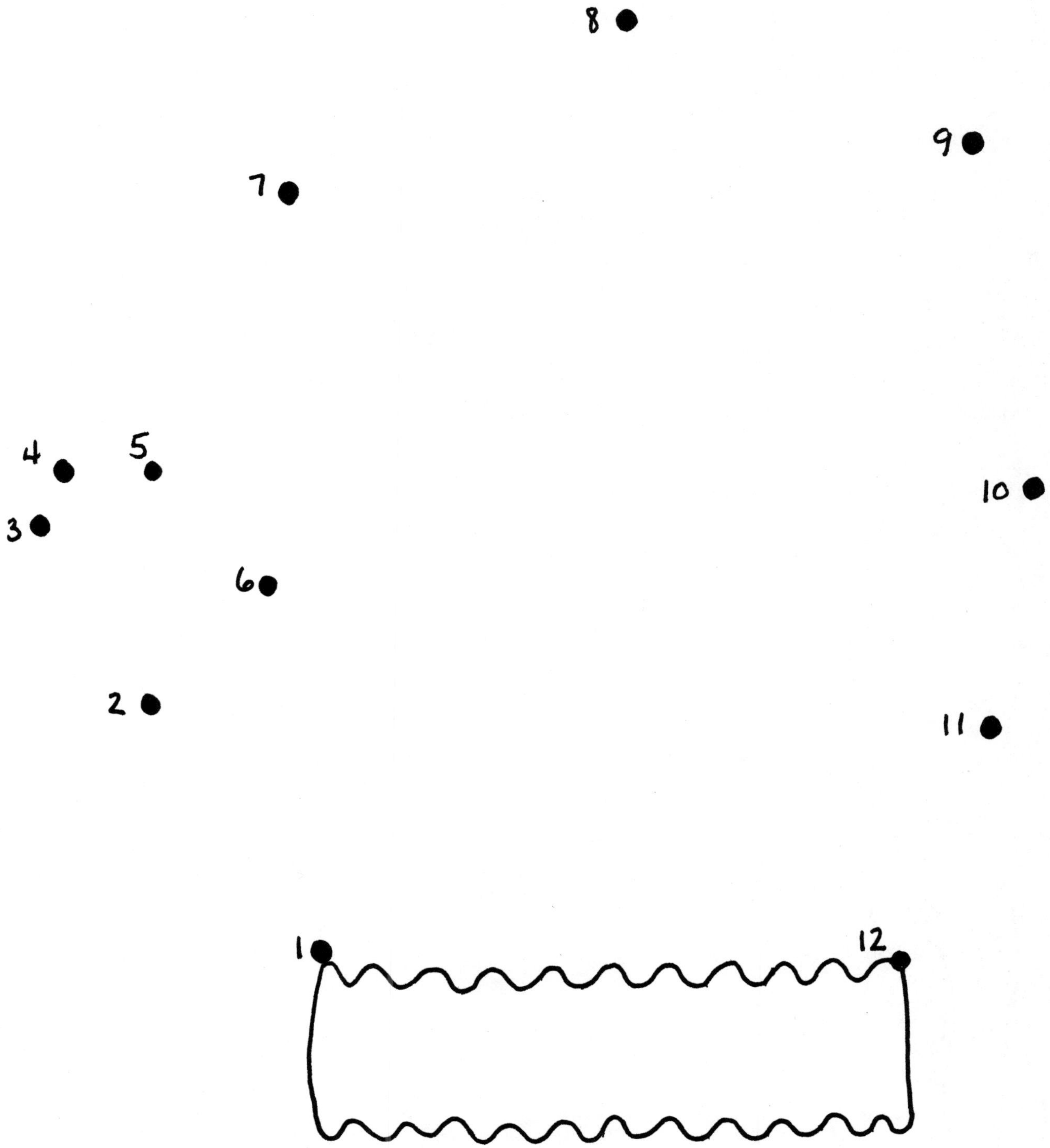

8 ●

9 ●

7 ●

4 ● 5 ●

3 ●

10 ●

6 ●

2 ●

11 ●

1 ●──────────────────── 12 ●

Why The Bear Has a Stumpy Tail

Pattern-

↑
cut
here
(overlap
on flannel
board until
bear loses
his tail)

Why The Bear Has a Stumpy Tail

Pattern -

Pattern

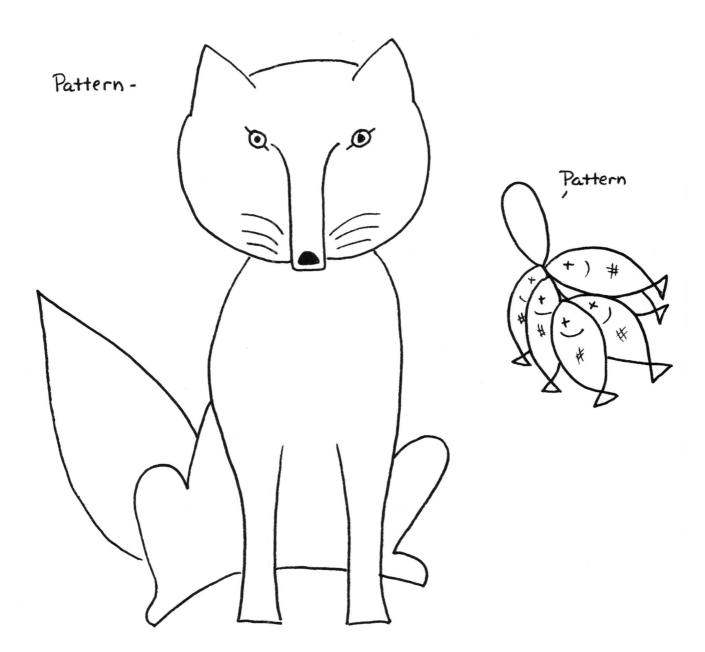

Where The Bear
Hibernates

Examples

Pine Cone Birdfeeders

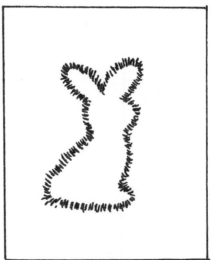

Smudge Print Rabbits

Mosaics

Smudge Print Rabbits

Feed the Hungry Rabbits

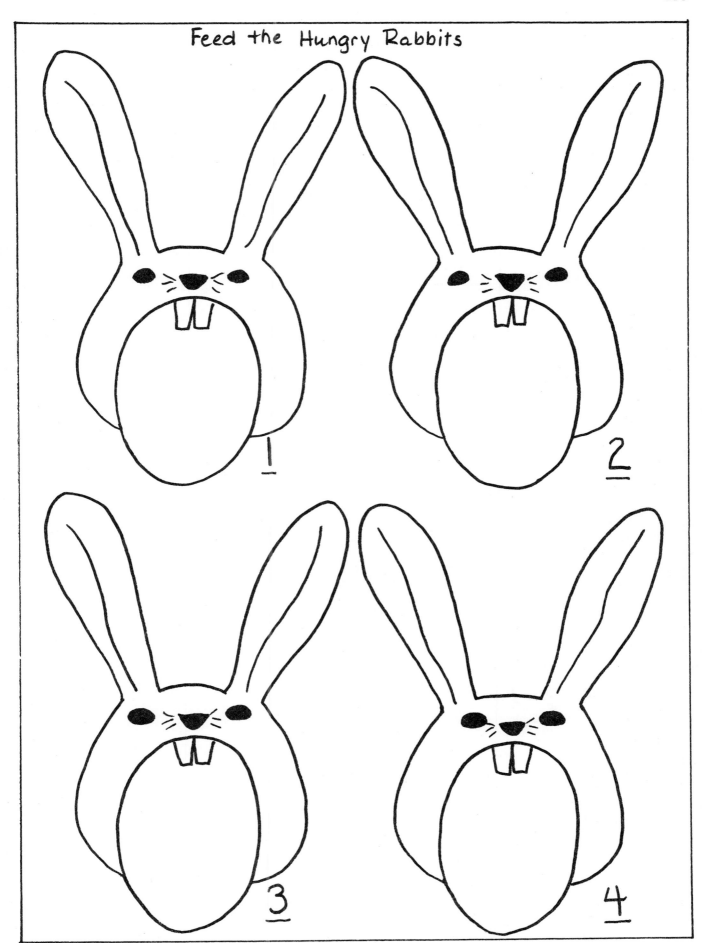

Big Tracks, Little Tracks

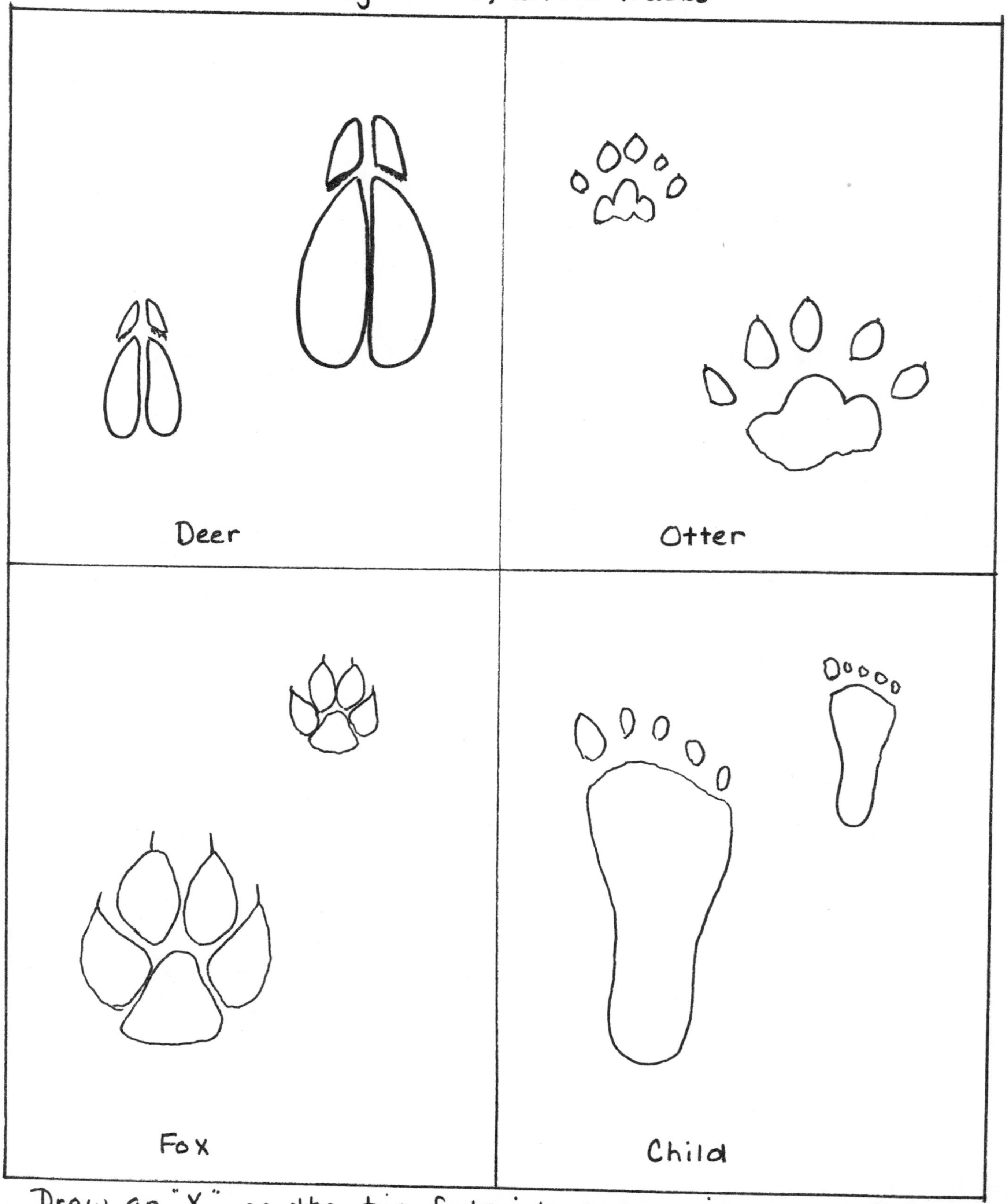

Deer

Otter

Fox

Child

Draw an "X" on the big footprints and a circle around the little footprints in each block. Color.

Name _____

Eskimo Transparency Pictures

igloo

harpoon

Eskimo

seal

Parka

whale

walrus

kayak

Examples, Pattern

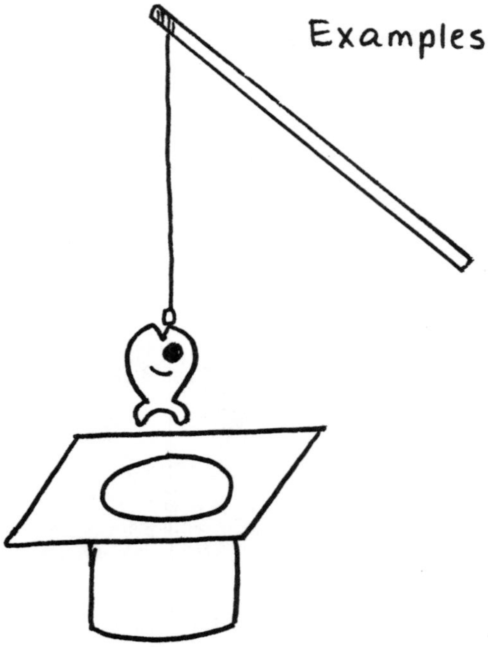

Ice Fishing Game
Example

- pattern

Ice Fishing
Fish

Stand-Up Walrus

Chalk-Colored Igloo

Eskimo

Stand-Up Walrus

Eskimo - Pattern

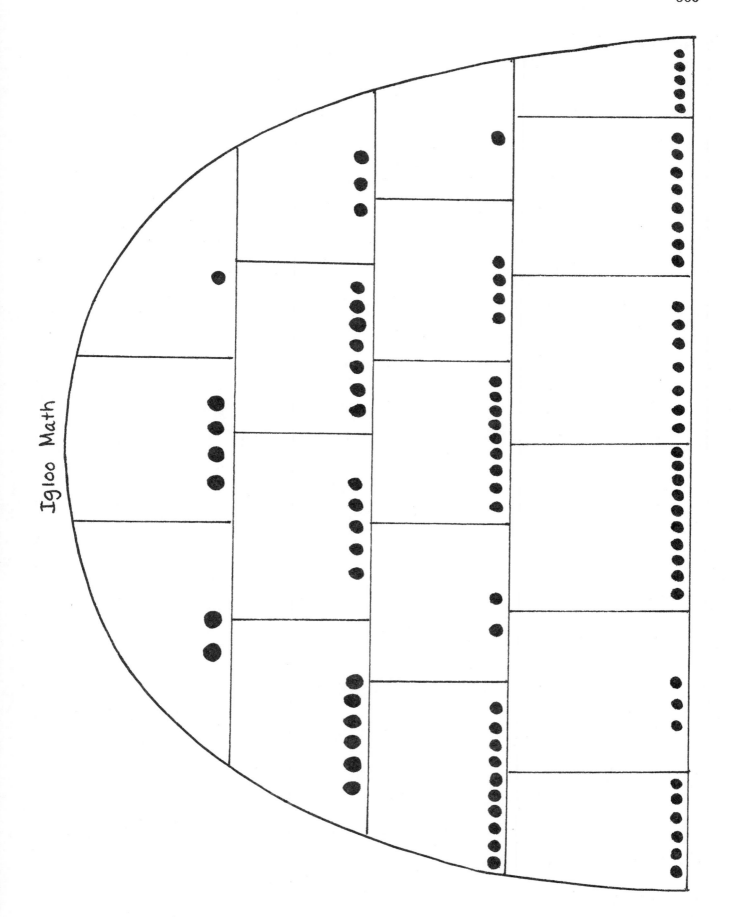

Igloo Math

Ice Fishing Sheet

How many fish are biting on the Eskimos' fishing lines? Read the numbers in each block. Glue that many fish on the hook.

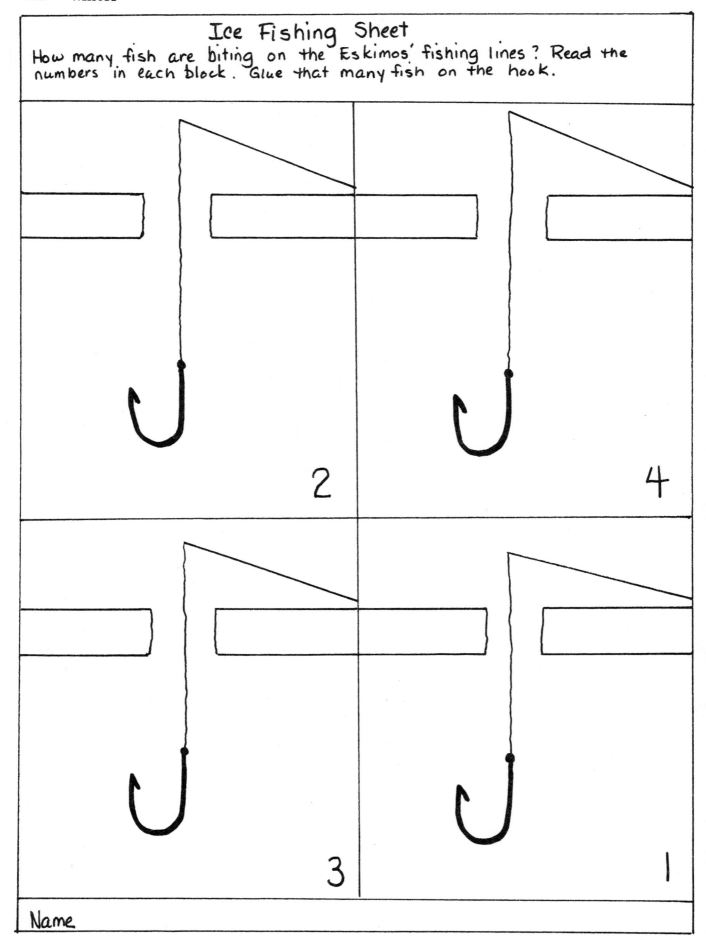

2

4

3

1

Name

MARTIN LUTHER KING, JR.

PROPOSED TIME: 1 day

UNIT OBJECTIVES

To develop understanding of Martin Luther King, Jr.'s life
To present the unique qualities of Martin Luther King, Jr.
To emphasize Martin Luther King, Jr.'s philosophy of nonviolence and his role in the Civil Rights Movement

ROOM ENVIRONMENT - BULLETIN BOARDS

"I Have A Dream"

Cover the bulletin board as desired, mounting the title at the top. On a piece of poster paper, write excerpts from Martin Luther King, Jr.'s "I Have a Dream" speech. Mount the speech in the center of the bulletin board. On strips of poster paper, write memorable quotes from Martin Luther King, Jr., (see below) and staple in various places on the bulletin board. Explain each quote; then assign various children to illustrate each one. Staple the pictures above the quotes. Martin Luther King, Jr., silhouettes may be added to the bulletin board. (See example, page 316.)

Quotes from Martin Luther King, Jr. -

From Civil Rights March on Washington, D.C.:

"I have a dream that one day on the red hills of Georgia the sons of former slaves and the sons of former slave-owners will be able to sit down together at the table of brotherhood."

". . . I have a dream that one day this nation will rise up and live out the meaning of its Creed: 'We hold these truths to be self-evident; that all men are created equal.' I have a dream!"

Other quotes:

"We must meet the forces of hate with the power of love; we must meet physical force with soul force."

"Love your enemies, bless them that curse you, and pray for them that despitefully use you."

"I will never be in front of a violent march."

"Injustice anywhere is a threat to justice everywhere."

"If a man hasn't discovered something that he will die for, he isn't fit to live."

"Don't lose faith."

"Freedom has a price . . . a very high price."

"We still have a long, long way to go in this nation before we achieve . . . brotherhood."

MARTIN LUTHER KING, JR.

CONCEPT INFORMATION

In January, we <u>celebrate</u> the birthday of Martin Luther King, Jr. Martin Luther King, Jr., was a <u>civil rights leader</u> who <u>dedicated</u> his life to helping blacks <u>attain</u> their <u>basic rights</u> as Americans.

Martin Luther King, Jr., was born on January 15, 1929, in Atlanta, Georgia. His father, Reverend Martin Luther King, Sr., was pastor of Ebenezer Baptist Church. His mother, Alberta Williams King, was the daughter of Reverend Alfred Williams. Reverend Williams and Reverend King were both active in obtaining civil rights, the rights <u>guaranteed</u> to <u>individuals</u> by the Constitution of the United States, for blacks. Both men were <u>religious</u>, hard-working, <u>self-made</u> men who loved their families.

Martin Luther King, Jr., was called "M.L." as a child. He had an older sister, Willie Christine, and a younger brother, Alfred Daniel, known as "A.D." His whole family lived with his grandparents, Reverend and Mrs. Williams, in a big house on Auburn Street. When M.L. was small, his first friends were two white boys who lived in the neighborhood. When they all started school, M.L. went to a school for blacks, and his two friends went to a school for whites. This is the way it had always been, so M.L. was not <u>concerned</u>. But when he went to play with his friends after school, their parents said, "Don't come around here anymore. You are colored and they are white, so you can't play with them anymore."

This was M.L.'s first <u>experience</u> with <u>segregation</u>. His mother <u>explained</u> that some white people could not <u>accept</u> black people as <u>equals</u>. She told him not to let it make him sad and to always remember he was as good as anyone. M.L. always remembered what she said.

Like every child, Martin Luther King, Jr., loved to run and play. He loved sports, but he also loved books and <u>studying</u>. He <u>graduated</u> from high school and went to Morehouse College in Atlanta when he was only fifteen years old. He first thought he would study <u>medicine</u>, but then decided to study <u>sociology</u>. Sociology is the <u>science</u> that explains how people live and work together. During his junior year, Martin decided he wanted to be a <u>minister</u>. He was <u>ordained</u> as a minister when he was only nineteen years old. Still he <u>wanted</u> to know more, so he went to Crozer Theological Seminary and graduated when he was twenty-two. He then earned his <u>Doctor of Philosophy degree</u> at Boston University.

In Boston he met and fell in love with Coretta Scott, a young music student. They were married in 1953 and moved to Montgomery, Alabama, where Martin became the <u>pastor</u> of Dexter Avenue Church. They eventually had four children—Yolanda, Martin Luther III, Dexter Scott, and Bernice Albertine.

On December 1, 1955, a black <u>seamstress</u> named Rosa Parks <u>boarded</u> a city bus and sat in the fifth row. She was tired and glad to be off her feet. The <u>law</u> in Montgomery <u>required</u> that, when a bus filled up, black people had to give up their seats to white people. After the bus was full, two white people boarded. Mrs. Parks was told by the driver to give up her seat, but she <u>refused</u>. She was <u>arrested</u> and put in jail. A leader in the black community heard about it and called other black leaders including Martin Luther King, Jr. They organized a black <u>boycott</u> of the buses; that is, blacks refused to ride on the buses. Blacks were <u>threatened</u> and arrested. Martin Luther King, Jr., received <u>phone threats</u>, and one day a bomb was thrown on his porch. Luckily, no one was hurt. The case against segregation went to court and finally the Supreme Court ruled segregation on buses to be <u>unconstitutional</u>. This was a great victory for blacks, but it was largely <u>ignored</u> by many whites.

Martin Luther King, Jr., spent the rest of his life trying to make <u>desegregation</u> a <u>reality</u>. He was greatly <u>influenced</u> by a man named Mahatma Gandhi, an <u>Indian leader</u> who had helped free India from <u>British rule</u>. Gandhi's <u>philosophy</u> was one of brotherly love. He felt that if people who did <u>evil</u> were met with love, they would give up their evil ways. Martin used this philosophy of <u>nonviolence</u> in his speeches for civil rights for blacks. He traveled all over the United States helping people who were working to change <u>unfair</u> laws.

The Civil Rights Movement grew. When the President proposed a civil rights bill to Congress, a <u>march</u> on Washington, D.C., was <u>organized</u> to show <u>support</u> for the bill. On August 28, 1963, more than 200,000 people gathered in Washington, D.C. There were many speeches and songs, but the most <u>memorable</u> was Dr. Martin Luther King, Jr.'s, "I Have a Dream" speech. The Civil Rights Act of 1964 was passed and signed by President Lyndon B. Johnson on July 2, 1964.

In 1964, Martin Luther King, Jr., was awarded the <u>Nobel Peace Prize</u> for his work to build peace among all Americans.

On April 4, 1968, Martin Luther King, Jr., was <u>assassinated</u> while he stood on the balcony of a hotel in Memphis, Tennessee. The assassin, James Earl Ray, <u>claimed</u> that he was <u>hired</u> to kill Martin Luther King, Jr., but this has never been <u>proven</u>. Ray was <u>convicted</u> of <u>first degree murder</u>. On April 9, King was buried in Atlanta, Georgia. On his tombstone are the words from an old Negro <u>spiritual</u> that he used in his Washington speech, "Free At Last!"

Martin Luther King, Jr., will always be remembered. His words, <u>achievements</u>, and ideas, which have changed America, live on.

LANGUAGE ARTS - SOCIAL STUDIES - SCIENCE

<u>Discussion</u>

Relate the concept information and define the vocabulary words. For a simple version of Martin Luther King, Jr.'s life, read <u>Martin Luther King, Jr. - A Picture Story</u> by Margaret Boone-Jones. For pictures of Martin Luther King, Jr., use references such as <u>Martin Luther King, Jr., A Man to Remember</u> by Patrick McKissack, <u>Martin Luther King, Jr.</u> by

Jacqueline L. Harris, or <u>Martin Luther King, Jr.,...To the Mountaintop</u> by William Roger Witherspoon. Point out Atlanta, Georgia, and Montgomery, Alabama, on a map.

Film

Show a film on the life of Martin Luther King, Jr. Review the highlights of the film.

Family Tree

Duplicate and distribute the Family Tree sheet (page 317). Explain to the class that Americans have always realized the value of their families. Martin Luther King, Jr., was always aware of his family's wonderful influence on his life. He, along with Alex Haley, the author of the book <u>Roots</u>, renewed an interest in our origins.

Direct the children to write their names on the tree trunks; then lightly color the tree. The trees are taken home to be filled in and returned as directed.

Poem - "Little Martin Luther King"

Little Martin Luther King,

Sat in church one day,

Listening to his daddy preach,

And listening to him pray.

"One day I'll talk like that," he said,

"And use those big words, too.

I'll make folks feel good inside."

Little Martin's words came true.

Ebenezer Baptist Church - Alphabet Dot-to-Dot

Duplicate and distribute the sheet (page 318). Following the alphabet letters, draw a line from dot-to-dot to complete the church. Color.

Sandwich Men

A sandwich man is a man who walks on sidewalks and streets displaying advertising on signs hung from his shoulders. One sign hangs in front and one in back. Let the children be "sandwich men" by making and wearing similar signs. Cut two pieces of poster paper for each child. Punch holes in the top and tie the signs together with nylon cord. There should be a few inches of cord between the signs to rest on the shoulders. Provide markers. The children write "Happy Birthday, Martin Luther King, Jr." on the front (or a similar message); then decorate. On the back, the children may choose to draw and color a picture of Martin Luther King, Jr., copy some of his quotes, or list facts about his life. The "sandwich men" can visit other classrooms and display their signs. (See example, page 320.)

Poem

Read "No Difference" from Where the Sidewalk Ends by Shel Silverstein.

ART

Martin Luther King, Jr., Silhouette

Preparation - Duplicate the Silhouette sheet (page 319) and staple each to a piece of black construction paper. Give each child the two sheets, a sheet of white construction paper, scissors, and glue.

Procedure - Cut out the silhouette. Cut through both thicknesses. Remove the staples and discard the white copy. Glue the black copy in the center of the white construction paper.

Freedom Pins

Preparation - Purchase safety pins; and red, white, and blue (tiny) glass beads which fit on the safety pins. Pass out the pins. Set out the beads in bowls. Tell the children, "Today we will make Freedom pins. Freedom pins show our gratitude for the many freedoms we enjoy in the United States today."

Procedure - Being very careful, open the safety pins. Slide the beads on the safety pin in any color arrangement you desire. Fill the pin up halfway, leaving room (about 1/8") for the safety pin to be pinned on your shirt and for the end to be closed. Pin on your shirt and wear in honor of Martin Luther King, Jr.'s birthday. (See example, page 320.)

Peace Doves

Preparation - Make cardboard patterns of the dove (page 321). Set out the patterns, pencils, sheets of white construction paper, 24" pieces of string, paper clips, and hole punchers.

Procedure - Fold the sheet of white construction paper in half to measure 6" x 9". Place the pattern on the sheet so that the top of the dove's head and the top of the wing are on the fold. Trace. Be sure to mark the dot on the dove's wing. Cut out. Punch a hole at the dot. Tie one end of the string through the hole and the other on the paper clip.

MATH

Birthday Cakes - Counting Sheet

Duplicate and distribute the sheet (page 322). Read the number in each block. Draw that many candles on the cake. Color all of the cakes.

MUSIC - MOVEMENT - GAMES

Song - "There's Nobody Just Like Me" from There's Nobody Just Like Me (LP) by Jamie, Hy, and Lynn Glaser

Song - "He's Got the Whole World in His Hands"

Source: Folk Song Carnival (LP) by Hap Palmer.

Martin Luther King, Jr., Birthday Picnic

Plan a picnic in celebration of Martin Luther King, Jr.'s birthday. If the weather is unsuitable, obtain permission to use the gym or auditorium. Invite parents. Ask for volunteers to prepare Martin Luther King, Jr.'s favorite foods—fried chicken, sweet potatoes, black-eyed peas, corn bread, and peach cobbler. Ask a parent (or two) to prepare cupcakes.

Suggested Picnic Activities -

Play a game of baseball (using plastic balls and bats), badminton, horseshoes, or kickball.

Supply ropes for rope-jumping and beanbags for tossing.

Play a game of Bingo.

Have a burlap sack race and a three-legged race.

Sing-along - Lead a sing-along of favorite folk and nursery songs.

(**Book**) - Tell the class, "In 1957, Martin Luther King, Jr., accepted an invitation to attend the Independence Day celebrations in Ghana, Africa. This country had just gained its independence from Great Britain. The following is a traditional story of the Ashanti people in Ghana." Then read Anasi the Spider by Gerald McDermott. Be sure to first read the prologue.

Song - "Happy Birthday"

Put one birthday candle in each cupcake. Light the candles and sing "Happy Birthday" to Martin Luther King, Jr. Each child blows out his or her candle and makes a wish. Since it is Martin Luther King, Jr.'s birthday, make an exception to the "keep the wish a secret" rule. Encourage the children to share their wishes.

CONCEPT EVALUATION

Dear Parents,

On _____, we will learn about Martin Luther King, Jr. We will begin with his childhood and cover the many achievements of his life and his work in the civil rights movement. Please read below to find out ways you can help.

Things To Send: _____

_____

_____

Volunteers Needed To:_____

_____

_____

Follow-Up: At the end of the unit, ask your child the following questions:

_____

_____

_____

Thank you for your cooperation.

Sincerely,

Bulletin Board

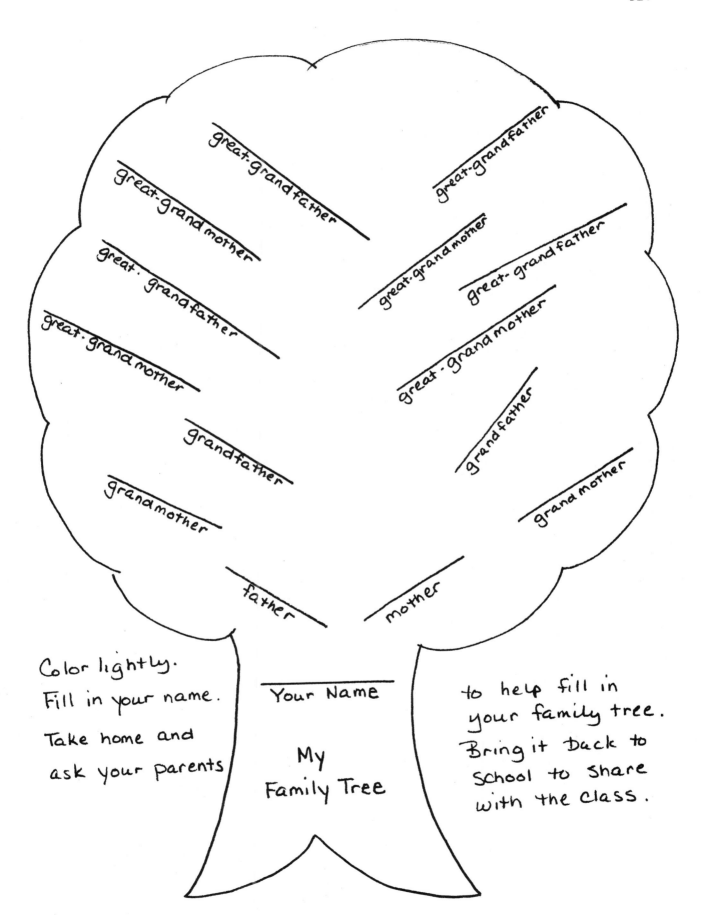

great-grandfather

great-grandmother

great-grandfather

great-grandmother

great-grandfather

great-grandmother

great-grandfather

great-grandmother

grandfather

grandmother

grandfather

grandmother

father

mother

Color lightly.
Fill in your name.
Take home and
ask your parents

Your Name

My
Family Tree

to help fill in
your family tree.
Bring it back to
school to share
with the class.

Ebenezer Baptist Church - Dot-to-Dot

Name _____

Martin Luther King, Jr. - Silhouette

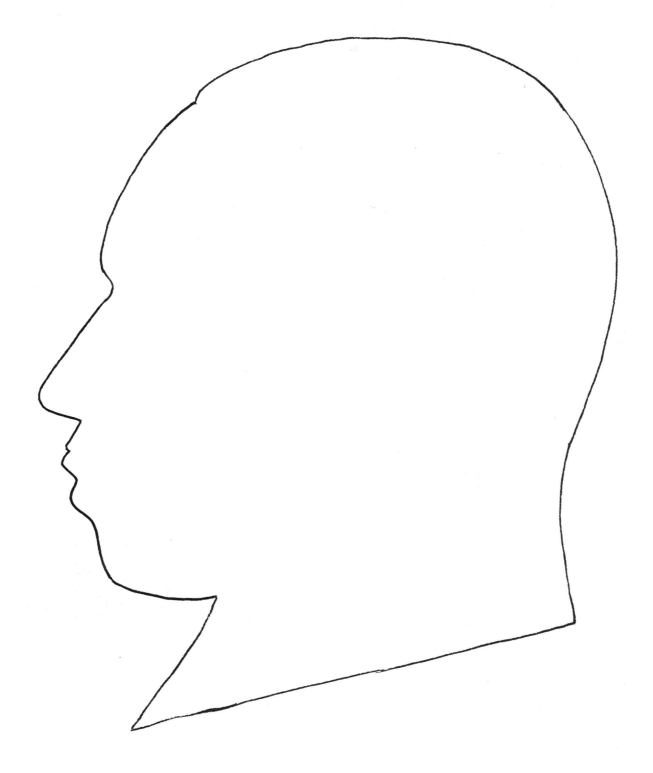

Examples

Sandwich Men Signs

Freedom Pins

Peace Doves

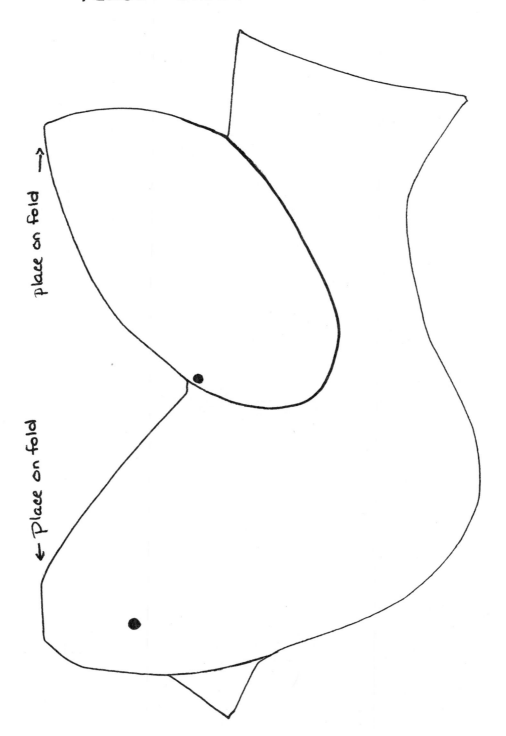

Place on fold →

← Place on fold

Birthday Cakes

5

7

4

3

Name _____

GROUNDHOG DAY

PROPOSED TIME: 1 day

Note: The ideal time to teach this teach this unit is the day before Groundhog Day. Use the follow-up activity on Groundhog Day after the groundhog's "forecast" is known.

UNIT OBJECTIVES

To develop understanding of Groundhog Day and shadows
To develop awareness of the weather

ROOM ENVIRONMENT - BULLETIN BOARDS

"February"

Cover and border the bulletin board as desired. Staple the title at the top. Make a calendar of February and write the following poem above it:

> February, February
>
> My favorite time of year
>
> Groundhog Day, Valentine's Day,
>
> And the Presidents Days are here!

Mount the poem and calendar in the middle of the bulletin board. Glue symbols on special days. Draw and color two groundhogs wearing three-cornered hats. Place on either side of the calendar. On the remainder of the bulletin board, staple silhouettes of Lincoln (see Abraham Lincoln Unit - Art, Day 3), and Washington (see George Washington Unit - Art, Day 4), and hearts and Cupids, or reserve this space for displaying art work from the February units. (See example, page 332.)

GROUNDHOG DAY

CONCEPT INFORMATION

February 2nd is Groundhog Day. Groundhogs, also called woodchucks or marmots, are small furry animals that live in holes in the ground. They are approximately eighteen inches long and weigh about eight pounds. During the winter, groundhogs <u>hibernate</u>. Some people believe that if the groundhog comes out of his home on February 2nd and sees his <u>shadow</u>, he is <u>frightened</u> and crawls back in his hole. Then there will be six more weeks of winter. If the groundhog crawls out of his home and does not see his shadow, spring will come soon. Many people believe our Groundhog Day came from a <u>similar German legend</u> about a <u>badger</u>.

Since the late <u>nineteenth century</u>, Punxsutawney, Pennsylvania, has <u>celebrated</u> Groundhog Day. On that day, the <u>townspeople</u> <u>gather</u> to watch their "official groundhog" come out of his home. The <u>outcome</u> is <u>reported</u> all over the world.

LANGUAGE ARTS - SOCIAL STUDIES - SCIENCE

Discussion

Relate the concept information and define the vocabulary words. Show pictures of groundhogs. Locate Punxsutawney, Pennsylvania on a map. Define a superstition. Ask the children to think of superstitions—black cats, ladders, mirrors, etc. Is the groundhog's "weather prediction" a superstition, or is it based on fact? If it is a superstition, then why do we celebrate Groundhog Day? (for fun)

SHADOWS - EXPLANATION AND ACTIVITIES

<u>Explanation</u> - What is a shadow? A shadow is an area of darkness caused by something cutting off or blocking out rays of light.

<u>Activities</u>:

Shadow Sketches - At around noon on a sunny day, take the children outside. Bring a box of white chalk. Observe the sun and the shadows caused by the children and by trees, buildings, etc. Spread half of the children out on a paved area. Direct them to write their names with chalk on one spot, and then stand on their names while a classmate outlines their shadows. Repeat with the other half of the class. Later in the day, repeat the procedure using a different color of chalk to outline the shadows. Compare the shadows. What caused the difference?

Shadow Animals - Turn off the lights and turn on a projector. Use your hands to make shadow animals. For a variety of shadow animals, see

"Animal Wall Shadows," <u>Childcraft How and Why Library</u>, Volume II. Let the children take turns making animals.

Shadow Play - "It's Not Nice to Fool Mother Nature"

Place a lamp or clamp-on light on a stool in a corner of the classroom. A few feet in front of this, turn a table on its side. For the curtain, hang a sheet from wall-to-wall concealing the table. Make cardboard patterns (see Patterns, Pictures, Etc., pages 333-335) and attach them to tongue depressors or plastic straws. Put a small piece of stick-on velcro on the owl's wing at the X. Put another piece on one edge of the book.
Choose children to kneel behind the table and manipulate the puppets along the edge of the table. Teach the parts to the children or read the play using different voices for each character. Turn off the classroom lights and turn on the lamp in the corner.

IT'S NOT NICE TO FOOL MOTHER NATURE

Tree:	I can't wait for spring!
Flower:	Me neither, I'm ready to bloom!
Rabbit:	Spring is my season to shine, you know—Easter and all that. People really like rabbits around that time!
Worm:	Farmers like me all the time. I help dig up the soil, and I'm ready to wiggle and diggle!
Ant:	Well, it won't be spring for six weeks if Groundhog sees his shadow.
Tree:	And today is the day!
Flower:	Oh my, it looks like it's going to be a sunny day—and you know what that means!
All Others:	SHADOWS!
Worm:	There goes spring! I'm going back underground!
Ant:	Me, too.
Tree:	Wait a minute! If Groundhog sees his shadow, what happens?
All Others:	He gets scared, runs back in his hole, and then—six more weeks of winter.
Tree:	Well, we know that today he'll see his shadow, right?
All Others:	Right—it looks like it's going to be nice and sunny.
Tree:	Okay, here's my idea. We teach Groundhog not to be afraid of his shadow.
Worm:	So what?
Tree:	So then he won't run back in his hole and . . .
All others:	Spring will be here! But . . . how do we teach him?
Tree:	Just a minute . . . (calls) Wise Owl, Wise Owl!

Owl:	Why do you wake me at this horrible hour! You <u>are</u> aware that I work at night? I was just getting to sleep . . .
Tree:	Sorry, Owl, but we need your help. We have to teach Groundhog not to be afraid of his shadow so he won't run back into his hole, and we won't have six more weeks of winter. We have to act fast!
Owl:	Certainly . . . let me get my book on phobias. Ah, here it is. Shadowphobia—fear of shadows. Let's go! (All move to the groundhog's hole.)
Tree:	Groundhog, oh Groundhog!
Groundhog:	Yes?
Tree:	Don't come out! Stay where you are! You know today's the day, don't you?
Groundhog:	Y-y-yes, and I'm already s-scared!
Tree:	Well, all your friends are here, and we want to help you. Here's Owl . . .
Owl:	Now, my dear Groundhog, the first thing you need to know is that shadows are nothing to be afraid of. The sun shines down on you and your body blocks out light. Therefore, a shadow is formed.
Groundhog:	But it moves!
Owl:	Yes, my dear fellow, but it only moves when you do—it is not alive, it is your shadow! I'm quite attached to my shadow actually. When the day is overcast, I really miss it.
Groundhog:	You do?
Owl:	Certainly!
Groundhog:	Then it's nothing to be afraid of, huh?
Owl:	Take my word for it!
Groundhog:	Okay, I'm coming out then.
All Others:	Yea! Yea!
Groundhog:	Oh, what a nice day—a-a-t-there's my shadow, but I'm not afraid!
Tree:	We're glad, Groundhog!
Groundhog:	Thank you all!
Tree:	You know everyone here, Groundhog, don't you? Here's Owl, Ant, Rabbit, Flower, and Worm.
Groundhog:	WORM?—aaaah - worms! I hate worms—aaaah! (runs back in hole).
Tree:	Wait, Groundhog, wait!
Owl:	That does it, good people—he's gone back in his hole.
Flower:	Does this mean . . . ?
Tree:	Six more weeks of winter.

Owl:	The way he ran, it may be six months.
All others:	Ohhhhh, nooooo!
Owl:	I guess it's true, then.
All Others:	What?
Owl:	It's not nice to fool Mother Nature!

Shadow Guess Who - Direct the students to cover their eyes. Tap one student. He or she stands behind the shadow play curtain. By looking at the shadow, the rest try to guess who it is.

Shadow Guess What? - Turn off the lights and direct the students to keep their eyes on the wall or screen. Hold objects such as a pencil, a ruler, a book, etc., in front of the projector. The students guess the identity of each object.

Shadow Picture - Show the optical illusion picture, "People?" and read the explanation in Childcraft How and Why Library, Volume 12.

Shadow Poem - Read "My Shadow" from A Child's Garden of Verses by Robert Louis Stevenson.

Weather Prediction - Sheet and Activity

Four or five days before Groundhog Day, duplicate and distribute the sheet (page 336). The children write the name and number of the days in the squares, ending with Groundhog Day. Each day, the proper weather symbol is cut out and glued in the square.

The day before Groundhog Day, direct the class to look at the weather for the preceding days and make predictions for Groundhog Day. Make three columns on the board. Label "Sunny," "Overcast," "Raining." As each child calls out his or her prediction, write his or her name in the proper column. On Groundhog Day, see who made the correct prediction.

Tongue Twister

Teach the following tongue twister. Let the children take turns reciting it.

"How much wood would a woodchuck chuck if a woodchuck could chuck wood? A woodchuck would chuck as much as a woodchuck could chuck if a woodchuck could chuck wood."

Note: For younger children, teach the first line only.

Fingerplay - "The Groundhog and the Shadow"

The groundhog crawled out of his hole (Form hole with thumb and fingers of left hand; groundhog is index finger of right hand—move this finger out of hole)

And took a look around. (Wiggle index finger, still in the "hole")

He saw his shadow standing there (Bring thumb out, hold at right angle to finger)

And ran back underground. (Lower finger and thumb into "hole")

ART

Groundhog Puppet

Preparation - Purchase plastic drinking straws. Collect oatmeal boxes (18-oz.). Discard the top and cut away the upper 1½". Cut pieces of brown bulletin board paper or brown construction paper to measure 5-5/8" x 14". Duplicate the groundhog on white or manilla construction paper (page 337). Give each child: an oatmeal box, the brown paper to cover the box, a straw, the groundhog sheet, a pencil, crayons, and glue. Have a stapler available.

Procedure - Glue the brown paper to the oatmeal box to cover. Turn the box upside down and punch a hole in the middle with the pencil. The hole should be big enough for the straw to fit snugly. Cut out and color the groundhog. Staple the top of the straw to the bottom of the groundhog. Put the groundhog inside the oatmeal box, guiding the straw through the hole. Manipulate the puppet by holding the box with one hand and pushing the straw up and down with the other.

Groundhog and Shadow Picture

Preparation - Duplicate the groundhog on brown construction paper (page 338). Staple each copy to a sheet of black construction paper. Cut inch-long strips of tagboard. Hand out the sheets, the strips, white construction paper, scissors, and glue. Have a staple remover available.

Procedure - Cut out the groundhog, cutting through both thicknesses. Remove the staple. Glue the black copy (shadow) in the center of the white construction paper. Fold the inch-long strip accordion style. Glue one end a little to the left of the center of the shadow. Dab glue on the top end of the strip. Center the groundhog on top of this and press to stick. On the right side, approximately ½" of the shadow should show.

MATH

February Calendar

Duplicate and distribute the calendar (page 339). Pass out red construction paper, scissors, glue, and markers. Direct the students to cut out the calendar, cut out the symbols on the dotted lines, and then glue the calendar on the red construction paper. Assist the students in numbering the days of the month. The symbols are colored and glued on the proper days.

Leap Year Poem

Explain that every four years, February has twenty-nine rather than twenty-eight days. This is called leap year. Teach the following traditional poem:

> Thirty days hath September,
>
> April, June, and November.
>
> All the rest have thirty-one;
>
> February twenty-eight alone
>
> Except in leap year, at which time
>
> February's days are twenty-nine.

MUSIC - MOVEMENT - GAMES

Song - "Groundhog, Groundhog"

Tune: "Twinkle, Twinkle, Little Star"

Groundhog, groundhog, come and play.

It's a warm and sunny day.

It's too nice to stay inside;

Wake up now and come outside.

If your shadow comes with you,

He can do the things we do!

Outside (Sunny Day) Game - Groundhog Shadow Tag

Choose one child to be "Winter." The rest of the children are "groundhogs." Designate an area to be the "Groundhog's Home." "Winter" chases the "groundhogs" and tags them by stepping on their shadows. Those tagged sit in the "Groundhog's Home." The last "groundhog" tagged is the new "Winter" for the next round.

STORY TIME

Book - <u>A Garden for Groundhog</u> - Lorna Balian
Book - <u>Shadow</u> - translated and illustrated by Marcia Brown

Follow-Up Sheets

Duplicate the Groundhog sheet on white paper (page 340). Duplicate the Groundhog Day sheet on extra long white paper (page 341). The students color and cut out both groundhogs and glue them in the correct spaces of the Groundhog Day sheet. After the groundhog's "verdict" is in, the students circle the correct "prediction."

CONCEPT EVALUATION

Dear Parents,

On _____, we will have our unit on Groundhog Day. We will learn about the groundhog, his role as a weather "predictor," about shadows, leap year, and the month of February. See below for ways you can help.

Things To Send: _____

_____

_____

Volunteers Needed To:_____

_____

_____

Follow-Up: At the end of the unit, ask your child to share the following information.

_____

_____

_____

Thank you for your cooperation.

Sincerely,

Shadow Play - Patterns

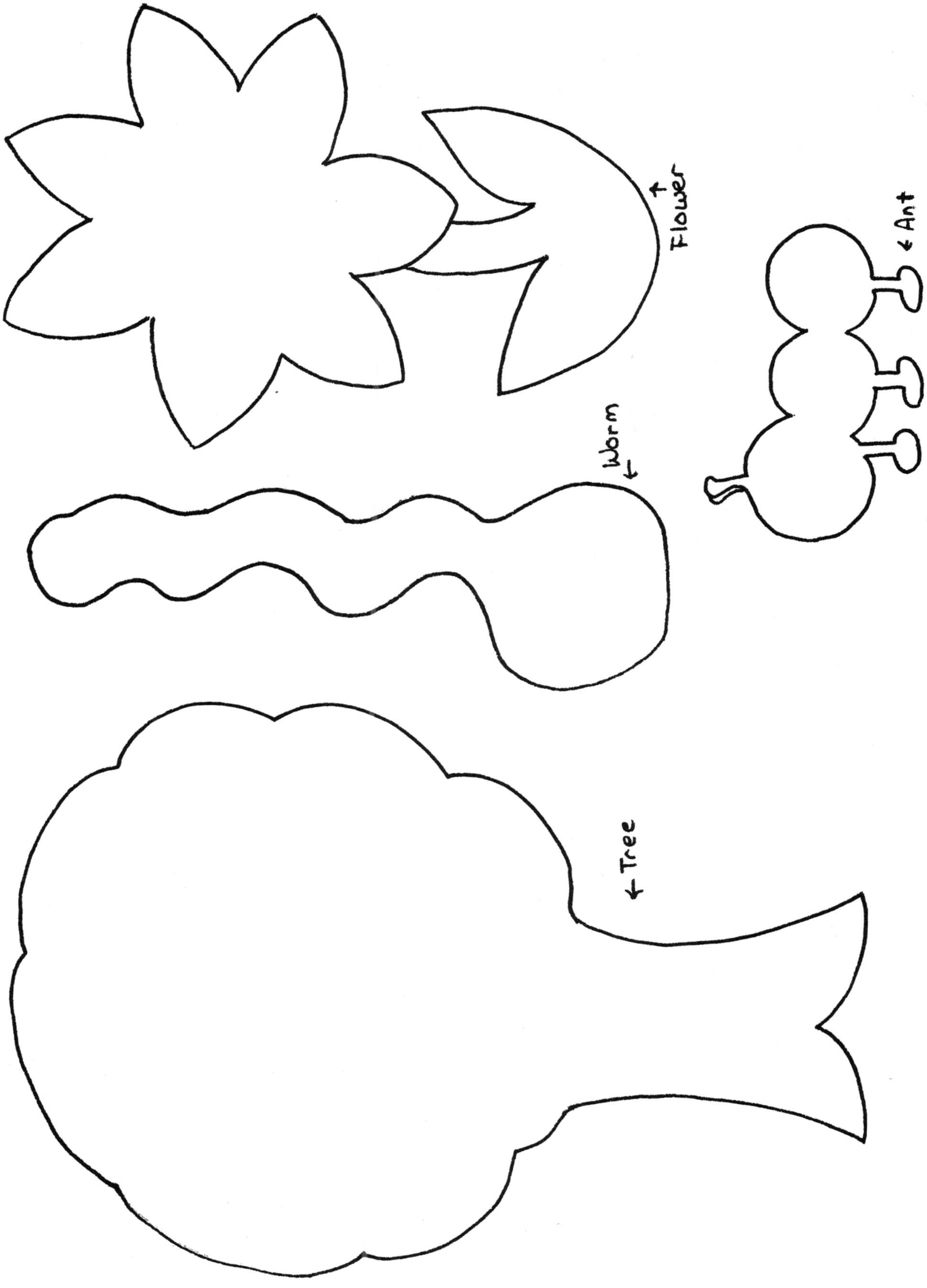

Flower

Ant

Worm

Tree

Shadow Play - Patterns

Owl

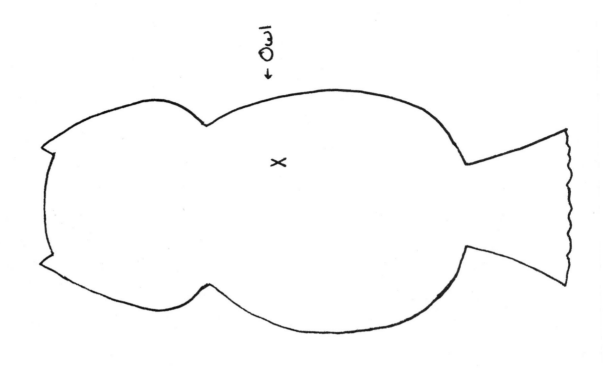

Rabbit

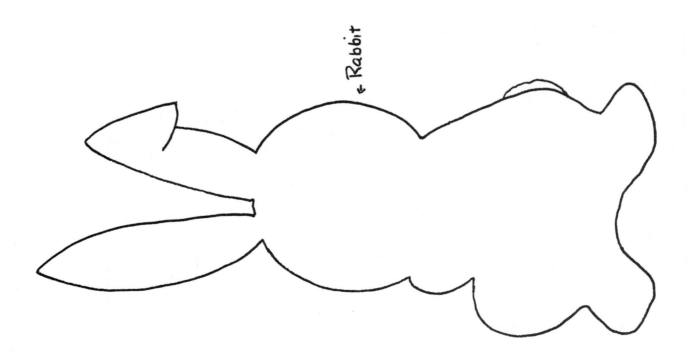

Shadow Play - Patterns

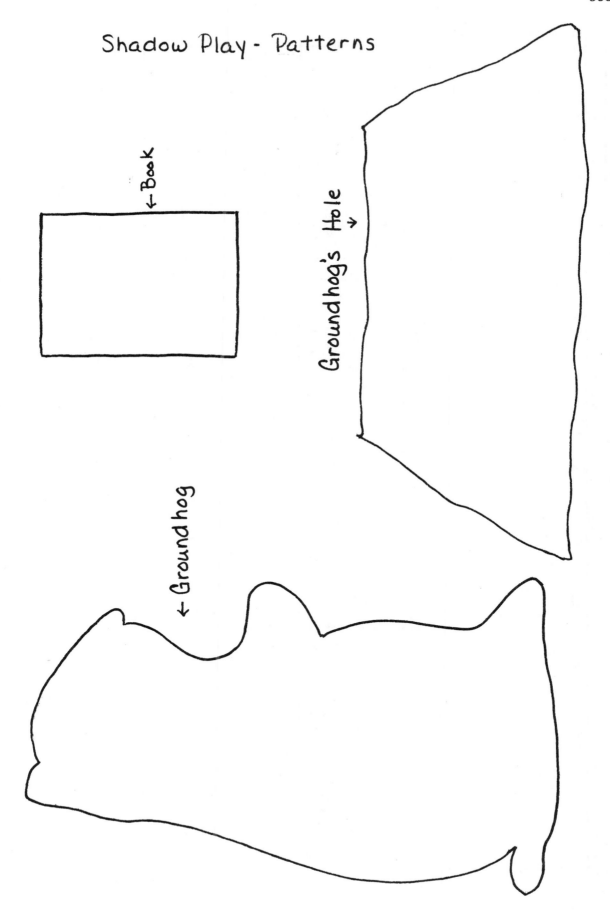

← Book

Groundhog's Hole →

← Groundhog

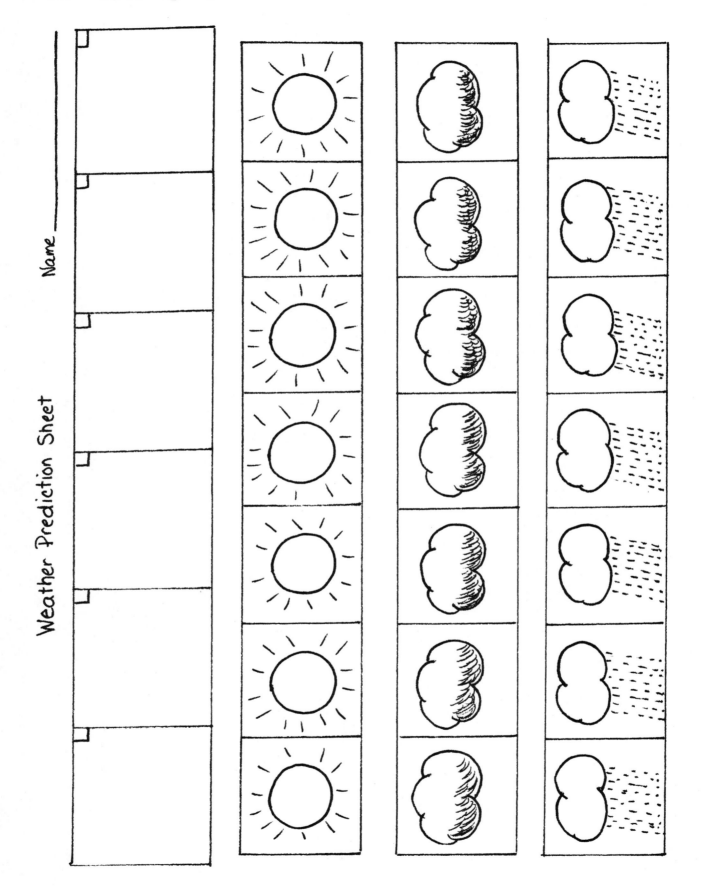

Groundhog Puppet

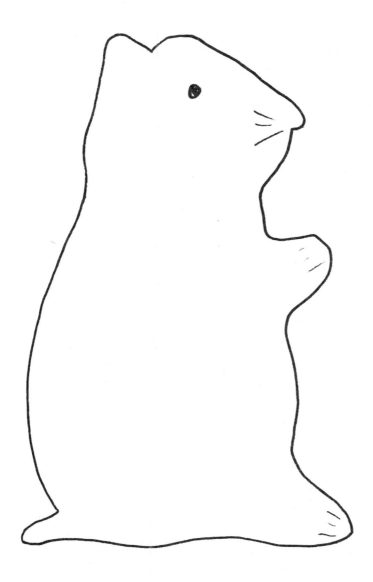

Example –

Groundhog and Shadow
Picture

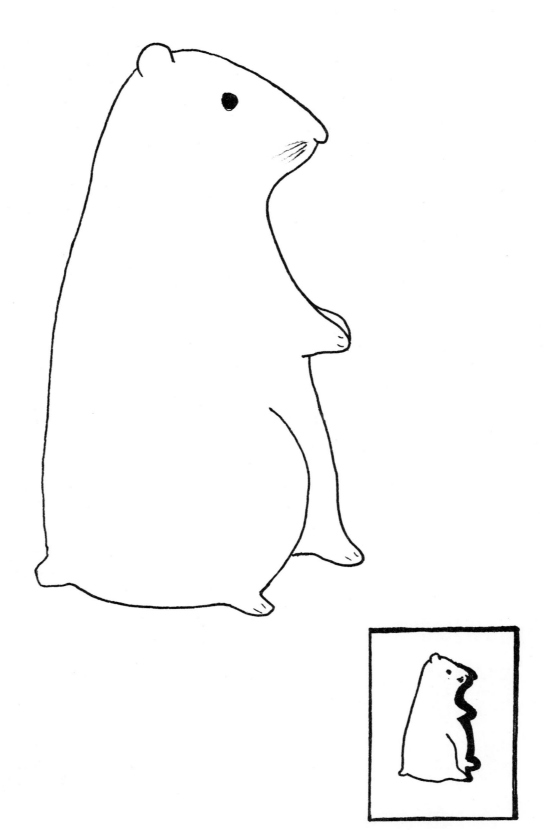

339

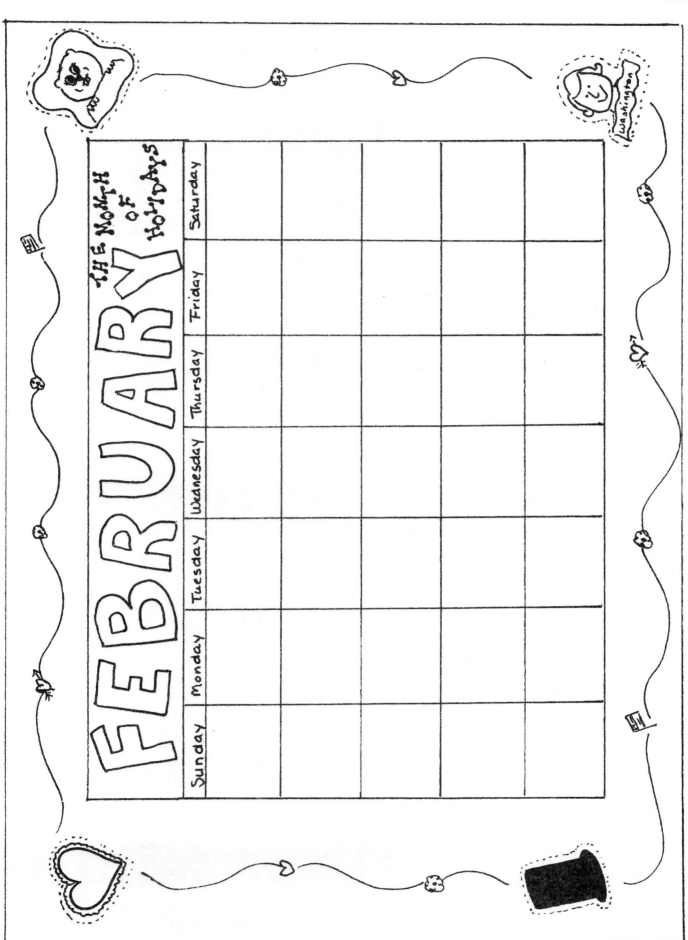

Groundhog Day Sheet- Follow-Up

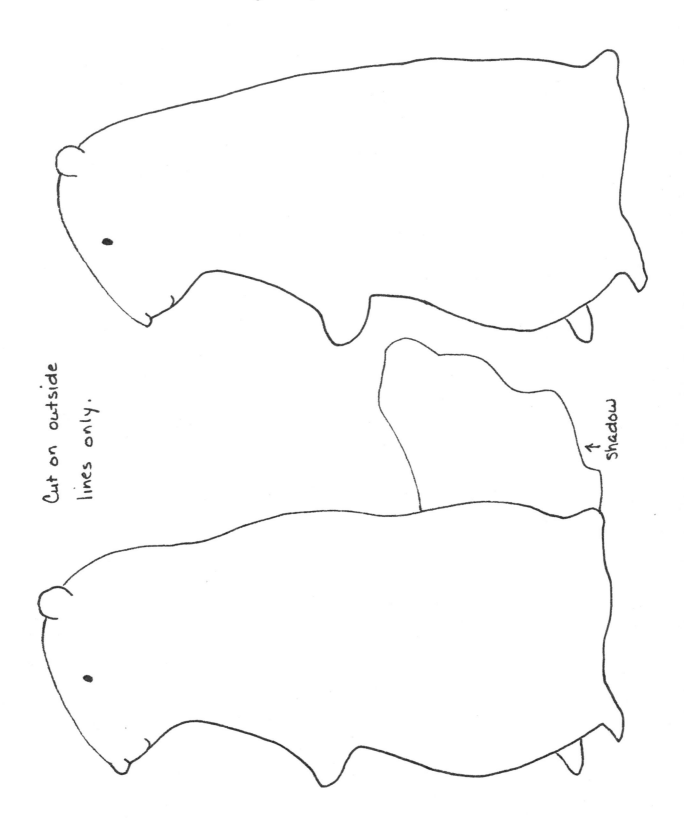

Cut on outside lines only.

Shadow

Name _____

Groundhog Day Sheet

Long Winter ?

Early Spring ?

ABRAHAM LINCOLN

PROPOSED TIME: 5 days

UNIT OBJECTIVES:

To develop understanding of Abraham Lincoln's life
To present the unique qualities of Abraham Lincoln
To promote understanding of Abraham Lincoln's role and contributions as
   President during the Civil War

ROOM ENVIRONMENT - BULLETIN BOARDS

"Happy Birthday Abe Lincoln"

Cover the bulletin board as desired. Enlarge or copy the pictures of
Abraham Lincoln, the table, and the flag cake (see Patterns, Pictures, Etc.,
page 376). Color. Staple the title at the top of the bulletin board.
Mount Abraham Lincoln in the middle, the table in front of him, and the
cake on the table. Have the children draw, color, and cut out self-
portraits (heads and upper torsos only). Slip the self-portraits behind the
table on either side of Mr. Lincoln. Staple.

ROOM ENVIRONMENT - DISPLAYS

"Abraham Lincoln Learning Center"

Use three sides of a corrugated cardboard box as a learning center. Cover
with white bulletin board paper. Label "Abraham Lincoln." At the top of
the left section, staple a paper log cabin; at the top of the center section,
staple a paper stovepipe hat; and at the top of the right section, staple an
outline of the capitol dome. On the left side, mount paper versions of the
American flag at the end of Lincoln's presidency (36 stars), the
Confederate flag, and the American flag of today. In the center, display
pictures of Lincoln's life. On the right side, staple a picture of Abraham
Lincoln telling stories and label "Laugh With Abe."

On the table in front of the learning center, place books on flags, books
on Lincoln's life, The Abraham Lincoln Joke Book by Beatrice Schenk de
Regniers, and other joke and prank books. "Fun Sheets," dittos of
crossword puzzles, word games, etc., may also be placed on the table for
individual seatwork. (See example, page 377.)

Lincoln Penny Center

Designate a table for the center. Write the center's name on a piece of
tagboard. Mount on the wall behind the table or suspend with string from

the ceiling above the table. Fold a rectangle of poster paper in half so that it will stand. (See example, page 377.) Write the following poem on the poster paper; then place it at the back of the table:

A penny's not just a penny,

It's a picture too,

Look closely at a penny.

Abe Lincoln will look at you!

In the center, place:

1. a large penny made of construction paper with the parts (front and back) labeled.

2. a box of pennies and a stack of paper. The students list the dates of the pennies on the paper. Penny rubbings can be made by placing the pennies under the paper and rubbing the side of a pencil lead on the paper. (The pennies can be arranged in different designs.)

3. ten baby food jars with slots in the tops. (Use a screwdriver and hammer to make the slots.) Cut out ten pink pigs and glue to the fronts of the jars and label 1 through 10. The students put the designated number of pennies into each "piggy bank."

4. quarters, nickels, and pennies in a plastic bowl. On each of the three smaller bowls, tape a penny, a nickel, and a quarter. The children sort coins into the proper bowls.

5. (for older students) ten or more construction paper penny shapes. On the back of each penny, write a question. Number the questions and provide answer sheets with numbers and blanks. The students write the answer for each question on the blank beside the correct number.

Sample Questions:

a. What building is on the back of the penny?

b. In what year was your penny made?

c. List all the words on a penny.

d. 5 pennies = ____ nickel (s)

e. 10 pennies = ____ nickels

f. What does liberty mean?

Wall and Ceiling Display - "Footprints"

On the wall hang a sign reading "How Did the Footprints Get on the Ceiling?" and an arrow pointing to the footprints. Tape paper footprints on the ceiling extending across the room. (See example, page 378.) The answer will be disclosed in the concept information of Day 2.

Helper Assignments - "Circuit Riders"

Before Abraham Lincoln became President, he was a lawyer who "rode the circuit." This meant that to represent the people, he had to travel on horseback to different courthouses. For any unit activity requiring helpers, choose several children to be "circuit riders." Each of the circuit riders will hand out and take up papers, etc., for certain rows or tables.

Lincoln Logs

Set out Lincoln Logs. At activity time, encourage the children to build a log cabin resembling the one in which Lincoln was born.

DAY 1 - ABRAHAM LINCOLN - EARLY YEARS

CONCEPT INFORMATION

February has two special birthdays. Abraham Lincoln's birthday is February 12, and George Washington's birthday is February 22. This week we will be learning about Abraham Lincoln.

Abraham Lincoln was one of our greatest <u>Presidents</u>. He was the sixteenth person to become President, and he changed many things for our country.

Abe Lincoln was born in a <u>log cabin</u> in the Kentucky <u>wilderness</u> (near Hodgenville) on February 12, 1809. His parents were Tom and Nancy Lincoln. His older sister's name was Sarah.

When Abraham was two years old, his parents moved to Knob Creek, Kentucky, and built another log cabin. There Abe learned to help on the farm. Even though he was very young, he held the <u>tools</u> and sat on the horse as his father <u>plowed</u>. When planting time came, he would drop the seeds into the ground.

Few children got to go to school back then, but Abe's mother was very <u>stubborn</u>. Finally she <u>convinced</u> Tom Lincoln to let Abe and Sarah go to school. The school was a log cabin with one room and no windows. It was called a "blab school" because the students shouted their lessons. The louder a student shouted, the better the teacher liked it. Once Abe learned to read and write, he didn't go back to school. In his whole life, he only had about <u>twelve months</u> of <u>schooling</u>, but every day he practiced reading and writing. After everyone was asleep, he would read by the light of the <u>fireplace</u>.

Tom Lincoln decided that Indiana would be a better place to live and to farm. So the Lincolns <u>traveled</u> over a hundred miles to Hurricane Township, Indiana. They built their log cabin home in the woods at a place called Little Pigeon Creek.

Abe worked hard on the farm and grew big and strong. He could outrun and <u>outwrestle</u> all the other boys of his age. He also had a quick <u>wit</u> and loved to hear and tell stories.

When he was nine, Abe's mother died of a <u>dangerous sickness</u>. A year or so later, Tom Lincoln married Sally Johnston who was a <u>widow</u> with three children.

Sally loved Abraham and <u>encouraged</u> him to <u>improve</u> his reading and writing. She boxed his ears when he was <u>sassy</u>. Abe grew to love his stepmother. When he was twelve, he made his own arithmetic book and in the front wrote:

> "Abraham Lincoln
>
> his hand and pen
>
> he will be good but
>
> God knows when"

Sally kept this book among her most <u>treasured possessions</u> as long as she lived.

LANGUAGE ARTS - SOCIAL STUDIES - SCIENCE

Discussion

Relate the concept information and define the vocabulary words. Ask a child to locate February 12 on the calendar. Show pictures from reference books such as <u>America's Abraham Lincoln</u> by May McNeer, <u>Lincoln - A Picture Story of His Life</u> by Stefen Lorant, and/or <u>Abraham Lincoln</u> by Ingri and Edgar Parin d'Aulaire. Point out Kentucky and Indiana on a map of the United States.

Note: For lengthy concept information, tape record or use a puppet to present the information. Stop periodically for questions and comments.

Abraham Lincoln Time Line

Extend thick yarn or rope across a bulletin board or wall. Use small plastic clothespins to mark the dates and events. On tagboard squares, draw or trace pictures from reference books for each event. Write the date and information below each picture. Each day clothespin the tagboard squares mentioned in the concept information on the time line. (See example, page 379.)

Abraham Lincoln's Life - Events

1. February 12, 1809 - born in Hodgenville, Kentucky
2. 1811 - moved to Knob Creek, Kentucky
3. 1816 - moved to Hurricane Township, Indiana
4. 1818 - mother, Nancy, died
5. 1819 - father remarried
6. 1824 - helped father farm; read every chance he got
7. 1826 - made money ferrying people
8. 1830 - moved to Decatur, Illinois
9. 1830 - took cargo to New Orleans, Louisiana on flatboat; saw slaves
10. 1831 - worked at store in New Salem, Illinois; wrestled Jack Armstrong
11. 1832 - opened his own store with a friend
12. 1834 - lost election for state representative
13. 1837 - began practicing law in Springfield, Illinois
14. 1842 - married Mary Todd

15.   1847 - won election for United States Congress

16.   1850 - circuit lawyer

17.   1861 - elected President of the United States; Civil War broke out

18.   1863 - issued Emancipation Proclamation

19.   1864 - reelected President of the United States

20.   1865 - Civil War ended

21.   April 14, 1865 - assassinated

22.   April 15, 1865 - died, buried in Springfield, Illinois

Plowing the Fields - Demonstration

Show pictures of the plows used when Abraham Lincoln was a boy. To demonstrate this sort of plowing, fill a shallow plastic box (an old dishpan would be perfect) with soil. For the plow, tape together two small dowels or toothpicks, use the wishbone of a chicken or turkey or a pair of tweezers (inverted). A small plastic horse and man are an added plus. Place the plow behind the horse and the man behind the plow.

Ask a child to assist in guiding the man as you manipulate the horse and plow. Plow one row, turn, then plow the next row. Remind the class that, as a small child, Abraham Lincoln rode on the horse while his father plowed. He also dropped seeds in the furrows. Once you've completed the "plowing," allow the children to plant radish seeds in the furrows. Show pictures of the modern methods of plowing. Compare the methods.

Choral Reading - "Abraham Lincoln" - (Booklet)

Divide the class into four groups. Read the poem; then explain the procedure. (Each group recites two lines.) Practice the lines; then perform the choral reading. Duplicate and distribute the sheet (see Patterns, Pictures, Etc., page 380) for inclusion in the Abraham Lincoln Booklet (see Art).

Teacher: Long ago on a misty morn
           A healthy baby boy was born;
           His mother named him Abraham

Group 1:   And knew that he would love the land.
           And knew that he would love the land.

Teacher: Even as a tiny lad
           He worked the farm beside his dad.
           Dusk to dawn, boy and man

Group 2:   Side by side, they worked the land.
           Side by side, they worked the land.

Teacher: The boy grew strong, the boy grew fit,
            Strong of will and quick of wit,
            A need to think, a need to know

Group 3:   Reading by the fire's glow.
            Reading by the fire's glow.

Teacher: To Washington the tall man went
            And became our sixteenth President.
            He refused to let the Union perish

Group 4:   And bravely saved the land he cherished.
            And bravely saved the land he cherished.

Abraham Lincoln Alphabet Activity and Blab School Demonstration

Write each letter of Abraham Lincoln's name on a separate sheet of white paper. Assign a letter sheet to one or two students. Hand out old magazines, scissors, and glue. The students find and cut out pictures beginning with their assigned letters, and then glue them around the letters on the sheets. Assist when necessary. (Examples: **A** - picture of an apple, ax, acorn; **B** - picture of a ball, bottle, blanket, etc.)

Just for fun, use this activity to dramatize the meaning of a Blab School like Abraham Lincoln attended. Stand the students side by side with their letter sheets. On cue, the students yell the names of the pictures on their sheets. Then demonstrate today's method by having each student identify their pictures in a normal tone of voice. Compare the two methods. Afterwards, mount the sheets in order on a classroom wall.

ART

Note: For "Lincoln's Head," Art, Day 4, the first steps should be done three or four days ahead of time. You may wish to start that project at this time.

Abraham Lincoln Booklet - Cover

Preparation - Duplicate the sheet (page 381). Place each sheet on a piece of black construction paper and staple on the X's. Give each child the two sheets, a sheet of white construction paper, scissors, glue, and crayons. Have a staple remover available.

Procedure - Cut out the figures, cutting through both layers. Remove the staples and discard the white copies. For the cover, glue the black figures to the white construction paper. Write "Abraham Lincoln" at the top and your name at the bottom of the cover.

Note: Suggested sheets to be included in the booklet will be indicated with the word "Booklet" in parenthesis (see Choral Reading - "Abraham Lincoln" — Language Arts - Social Studies - Science).

Pretzel Log Cabins - (Booklet)

Preparation - Purchase pretzels (sticks). Transfer the log cabin pattern to a ditto master and duplicate on heavy manilla paper (page 382). Give each child a sheet and glue. Set out the pretzels.

Procedure - Outline the door and window by gluing pretzels on the lines. To form the front of the house, glue the pretzels horizontally with edges extending slightly over the lines. When necessary, break the pretzels to fit. Use an ample amount of glue throughout the project. Dry thoroughly.

Note: Grape-Nuts cereal or sand may be used to make a ground area. Spread glue on the area and sprinkle on the cereal or sand. Shake off the excess.

MATH

Planting Seeds - Sets

Preparation - Purchase dried beans, popcorn, and pumpkin seeds (or collect seeds from fruits, etc.). Duplicate and distribute the sheet (page 383). Set out crayons, glue, and seeds.

Procedure - Color the field brown. Color lightly to avoid covering the lines. The straight lines are the rows. On the first row, "plant" pumpkin seeds by gluing the first seed on the X and proceeding from left to right. In the same manner, "plant" the corn seeds on the second row and the beans on the third row. Count the seeds on each row and write the total in the circle.

MUSIC - MOVEMENT - GAMES

Action Song - "Paw Paw Patch" ("Where, Oh Where Is Pretty Little Susie?") - (Booklet)

Sing the song, which was one of Abraham Lincoln's favorites, and perform the actions. Duplicate (see Patterns, Pictures, Etc., page 384) to include the booklet.

Where, oh, where is pretty little Susie? (Shade eyes, look from
    side to side)

Where, oh, where is pretty little Susie? (Repeat same actions)

Where, oh, where is pretty little Susie? (Repeat same actions)

Way down yonder in the paw-paw patch. (Pointing motion)

Chorus:

Picking up paw-paws; put 'em in your pocket,   (Bend down, pick up
    paw-paws, put in pocket)
Picking up paw-paws; put 'em in your pocket,   (Repeat same actions)
Picking up paw-paws; put 'em in your pocket,   (Repeat same actions)
Way down yonder in the paw-paw patch. (Pointing motion)

Come on, boys, let's go find her, (Wave "come on")
Come on, boys, let's go find her, (Repeat same actions)
Come on, boys, let's go find her, (Repeat same actions)
Way down yonder in the paw-paw patch. (Pointing motion)

(Repeat Chorus)

Come on, boys, bring her back again, (Join hands with a partner, skip)
Come on, boys, bring her back again, (Repeat same actions)
Come on, boys, bring her back again, (Repeat same actions)
Way down yonder in the paw-paw patch. (Drop hands, pointing motion)

(Repeat Chorus)

Game - Cross the Creek

Use masking tape to form two parallel lines for the creek. Place a walking board across the creek. Have beanbags and a towel available. The children remove their shoes and socks and take turns performing the walking board activities below. Anyone who "falls in the creek" "swims to the shore" (swimming motion), "dries off" with the towel, and gets back in line.

1. Walk forward slowly.

2. Walk forward with hands on hips.

3. Walk forward to the center of the board, balance on one foot to the count of three, then walk forward again.

4. (The teacher places one beanbag in the center of the walking board.) Walk forward, step over the beanbag without looking at your feet.

5. (The teacher places three beanbags at intervals on the walking board.) Walk forward, step over each beanbag without looking at your feet.

6. (The teacher removes the beanbags.) Walk sideways.

7. Hop on one foot.

8. Place a beanbag on your head, and walk forward.

9. Place a beanbag on your head. Walk to the center, squat down, then stand up, and walk forward.

10. Place a beanbag on your head. Walk forward to the center, turn, and walk back.

STORY TIME

At story time each day, read a fable from Aesop's Fables, a book Lincoln read and enjoyed. Those listed are in picture book form.

Book - The Lion and the Mouse - Aesop - (Troll Associates)

Each day read excerpts from The Abraham Lincoln Joke Book by Beatrice Schenk de Regniers.

KINDERGARTEN KITCHEN

Abe's Favorite Apple Pandowdy

1 can pie-sliced apples (pie filling)
1/4 cup brown sugar
1 package spice cake mix
3/4 cup chopped pecans
2 sticks butter, melted

Preheat oven to 325°. Grease a 2-quart casserole dish. Place sliced apples in the dish and sprinkle with brown sugar. Spread the cake mix over the apples. Sprinkle with chopped nuts and cover with the melted butter. Bake until top is "set" (1-1½ hours). Cool.

DAY 2 - ABRAHAM LINCOLN - 12-21 YEARS OLD

CONCEPT INFORMATION

At the age of twelve, Abraham Lincoln was almost as large and as strong as a full grown man. He walked sixteen miles and got a job in Troy, Indiana, helping the owner of a ferryboat. At nineteen, Abe did carpentry work to earn money. After his sister, Sarah, died in childbirth, his friend James Gentry, a trader, knew Abe needed something to take his mind off of his grief. So he hired Abe to take a flatboat of merchandise to New Orleans, Louisiana, 1,200 miles away.

The journey was full of dangers. Seven slaves tried to kill Abe and his friend, Allen, while they slept. But Abe and Allen fought them off. Abe was fascinated by New Orleans. He had never seen such a mixture of people—French, Mexican, Spanish, Creole, Indian, and Negro. He had also never seen slaves being sold at slave markets. Abe thought it was wrong and said he would never want to own a slave.

Abe enjoyed the adventure but was glad to be home again. One day after Sally had whitewashed the inside of the cabin, he decided to pull a prank. He picked up Sally's younger son and dipped his feet in mud. Then Abe held the boy and had him walk up the wall and on the ceiling, leaving muddy tracks. His stepmother thought it was a wonderful joke, but she made Abe scrub the walls and ceiling.

After fourteen years in Indiana, Tom Lincoln was still poor. When relatives sent a letter telling of the good land in Illinois, he decided to move again. The family sold their farm and traveled to Decatur, Illinois. Abe worked as a rail-splitter for awhile, then decided to set out on his own.

LANGUAGE ARTS - SOCIAL STUDIES - SCIENCE

Discussion

Share the concept information. Define the vocabulary words. Ask a child to display pictures from the various references (see Discussion, Day 1.)

WATER AND FLOAT OR SINK EXPERIMENTS

Abraham Lincoln's first job was on a ferryboat. He later worked on a flatboat. Show pictures of both. Discuss the purpose of a ferryboat and the purpose of a flatboat. Display pictures of other kinds of boats. Ask, "How does a boat float?" A boat (or any object) floats because it is lighter than water of the same size. If the boat is heavier or weighs more than the same amount of water, it sinks.

Water Has Weight Experiment - Show that water has weight by allowing a child to hold two identical cups. Fill one with water. Which is heavier? Let all the children hold the two cups.

Float or Sink Experiment - Fill two baby food jars three-fourths full of water. In one, place a marble and label "sink"; in the other, place a small piece of sponge and label "float." Screw on the tops. Set a glass bowl three-fourths full of water on a table. Around it, lay a variety of objects that will float or sink—a clothespin, a wooden bead, a toothpick, a sponge, a cotton swab, a rubber band, a spool, a cork, etc. Review the terms "float" and "sink." Show the students the two baby food jars. Ask, "Did the marble float or sink?" and "Did the sponge float or sink?"

After discussing this, put the two jars on either side of the bowl. Have a volunteer test one of the objects in the glass bowl of water. If it sinks, place it by the "sink" baby food jar containing the marble. If it floats, place it by the "float" baby food jar containing the sponge. Repeat the procedure until all objects are classified.

Name Fun

Purchase or borrow from the library a book which lists names and their meanings. Divide one sheet of an experience chart into squares, one for each student in your class. Write each student's first name at the top of the square. Tape the sheet to the chalkboard. Write "Abraham - father of the multitudes" on the chalkboard next to the sheet. Explain that our names have meanings. Abraham Lincoln was named after his grandfather. His first name means "father of the multitudes" (large numbers). Ask, "Why was Abraham a good name for President Lincoln?"

Now use the name book to find and read the meaning of each child's name. Write the meanings in the "name squares." When the activity is completed, cut out the squares and safety pin to the children's shirts.

Name Search

On scratch paper, create a word search puzzle using the names of the students in the class (see example in Patterns, Pictures, Etc., page 385). Write the children's names as shown; then fill in the blank areas with various letters. Write the puzzle on the board low enough for the children to reach. Ask the children to search the puzzle for their names. Let each child circle his or her name with colored chalk.

Rail-Splitting Demonstration

To find a rail-splitter, contact a logging company or a person who sells firewood. Invite the rail-splitter to demonstrate for the class.

Jokes and Pranks and Tricks

Tell the class, "Abe Lincoln had a wonderful sense of humor. He loved tricks, jokes, and pranks (such as his "footprints on the ceiling" prank). Have you ever played a joke, prank, or trick on someone? Has someone played one on you?" Encourage the students to relate any experiences. Remind them that tricks, etc., should be funny to everyone involved and should never be dangerous. Share some of the jokes, pranks, and tricks below with your class.

1. "Broken Nose" Trick - Place your hands in a "praying position" with your nose in between. Slightly open your mouth and put both thumbnails behind your front teeth. Tell the "victim" that you can break your nose. Move both palms (with the nose in between) to one side—and at the same time click your thumbnails on your teeth. Move both palms to the other side and click your thumbnails again. It will sound like your nose is breaking.

2. "Pillow Hat" Prank - Slightly open a door. Balance a pillow on top of it. The next person who comes through the door gets a "pillow hat."

3. Joke - Customer to Waiter: What's that fly doing in my soup?" Waiter to Customer: "The back stroke!"

4. Nickel Trick - Tell the victim, "I bet you I can put this nickel where everyone can see it except you." Then place the nickel on his or her head.

5. "Sneaky Note" Prank - Write "kiss me" on a piece of paper. Attach a piece of tape to the top. Pretend you are patting the victim on the back and stick the sneaky note to his or her back.

6. "Make a Wienie" Trick - (Don't overdo this one!) Make your hands into fists. Now extend your pointer or index fingers to make them touch. Stare at the place where both fingers meet while bringing them closer and closer to your eyes. Soon you will see a wienie in between the two fingers. Or follow the same procedure but move the fingers away from your eyes while looking right above them.

7. Elephant Joke - Question: How do you stop an elephant from charging? Answer: Take away his charge cards!

8. "I Yawn, You Yawn, Everybody Yawn Yawn" Prank - When you're sitting in your classroom, the library, or with your family, pretend to yawn. Don't yawn too loudly. Make it seem real. Wait a minute and then yawn again. Pretty soon someone else will yawn, then someone else. It's contagious!

9. "Stick Out Your Tongue" Trick - Ask the "victim," "Can you stick out your tongue and touch your nose?" After the victim tries unsuccessfully to touch his nose with his tongue, show him how. Stick out your tongue, and touch your nose with your finger.

10. "Grab the Money" Pranks - Use strong glue to glue a dime or quarter to the pavement. Hide and watch people try to pick it up. Or, tape a long piece of thread to a dollar bill. Put the dollar on the floor or sidewalk with the tape side down. Hide, holding the other end of the thread in your hand. When someone tries to pick up the dollar, yank the thread.

ART

Log Cabin - Fingerpainting

Preparation - Set out paper and fingerpaints.

Procedure - Fingerpaint a picture of Abraham Lincoln's log cabin.

Footprints On the Ceiling - (Booklet)

Preparation - Mix brown tempera and pour thin layers in aluminum pie pans. Hand out white construction paper. Demonstrate the procedure.

Procedure - Form a fist with your right hand and dip the side of your palm (including the pinky finger) in the tempera. Print at the bottom of the paper to form the foot. Now dip a finger in the paint and print above the foot to make five toes. Vary the sizes of the toes just like a real footprint. A little higher on the sheet, repeat the procedure with your left hand. Continue alternating hands to make footprints to the top of the sheet.

MATH

Hidden Numerals Picture

Duplicate and distribute the sheet (page 386). Direct the class to find the hidden numerals, 1-10, and trace over each one with a crayon. Color the picture.

MUSIC - MOVEMENT - GAMES

Action Song - "Skip to My Lou" - (another Lincoln favorite)

Sing the song and perform the appropriate actions. For complete verses, actions, and directions for improvisation, see American Folk Songs for Children by Ruth Crawford Seeger.

Game - Huckle Buckle Beanstalk

The players cover their eyes and count in unison to twenty while the teacher hides a designated object. Everyone searches for the object. When a player locates the object, he or she says, "Huckle Buckle Beanstalk," being very careful not to give away the hiding place. He or she then sits down. As each player spots the object, the same procedure is followed. After everyone is seated, the object is produced. The first player who located the object gets to hide it in the next round.

Variation: Divide the class into two teams. In each round, the first player to locate the object scores a point for his or her team.

STORY TIME

Book - The Hare and the Tortoise - Aesop - (Troll Associates)
Book - The Abraham Lincoln Joke Book - Beatrice Schenk de Regniers

DAY 3 - ABRAHAM LINCOLN - ON HIS OWN

CONCEPT INFORMATION

Abraham Lincoln worked for a man named Denton Offut. First, Abe took a <u>flatboat</u> to New Orleans, Louisiana, for him; then he became a <u>clerk</u> in Mr. Offut's store in New Salem, Illinois.

Offut <u>bragged</u> that his new clerk could <u>outsmart</u>, <u>outrun</u>, and <u>outfight</u> any man in the county. Others said that a big man named Jack Armstrong could beat Lincoln any day. So Abe <u>wrestled</u> Jack Armstrong and won. From then on, Jack and Abe were good friends.

People thought Abe was <u>peculiar</u> because he read so much, but they liked him anyway. Folks would gather around to hear Abe's funny stories and jokes.

Abraham Lincoln and a friend, William Berry, opened their own store. One day Abe bought a <u>barrel</u> full of old <u>junk</u> from a man and found a <u>law book</u> in the barrel. He began reading the book and studying the <u>law</u>. He then moved to Springfield, Illinois to become a <u>lawyer</u>. He bought himself store clothes and began wearing a <u>stovepipe hat</u> on his head.

In Springfield, he met and later married Mary Todd. They bought a house and in a few years had three <u>noisy</u> little boys. Although Mrs. Lincoln didn't <u>approve</u>, Abe would roll and play on the floor with his sons, milk his cow, tend his horse, and was a friend to all the children in town. He was an important lawyer, but he was still the same Abe Lincoln who had <u>split</u> <u>rails</u> and pulled pranks. Instead of using a bag to hold <u>important</u> papers as others lawyers did, he put them in his stovepipe hat. One day some of the children in town tied a string across the street so high that everyone in town could pass under it except Abe Lincoln with his stovepipe hat. Off flew the hat and the papers <u>scattered</u> in all <u>directions</u>! Abe laughed and laughed at their fine prank.

Lincoln spent much of his time as a lawyer "riding the circuit" or riding his horse from <u>courthouse</u> to courthouse.

In 1847, Abraham Lincoln was <u>elected</u> to <u>Congress</u>. He and his family then moved to Washington, D.C. When his <u>term</u> was over, they returned to Springfield where he practiced law for fifteen years.

LANGUAGE ARTS - SOCIAL STUDIES - SCIENCE

Discussion

Relate the concept information and define the vocabulary words. Point out Illinois on the map. Show pictures from references (see Discussion, Day 1).

Over Your Head Drill Game

Preparation - Write the drill questions on slips of paper. To make a stovepipe hat container, cover a coffee can with black construction paper. Cut a circle of black construction paper four inches larger than the diameter of the can. Glue the bottom of the can in the middle of the circle. (See example, page 387.) Place the drill questions in the "Stovepipe Hat." Write the stunts (below) on slips of paper and place them in a shoebox labeled "Over Your Head."

Procedure - Divide the class into four groups. The circuit rider draws questions from the hat and gives one to each group. The groups decide the correct answer and choose one member to answer for the group. If the answer is correct, the groups stands and bows as the class applauds. If the answer is incorrect, the circuit rider draws a stunt from the "Over Your Head" box. The group then performs the stunt. Proceed in this manner, allowing each group to participate and all questions to be answered.

Sample Questions:

1. What was Abe Lincoln's first job after leaving home? (store clerk)

2. Abraham studied hard and became a _____. (lawyer)

3. Who did Abraham Lincoln marry? (Mary Todd)

4. How many children did Abraham and Mary Lincoln have? (3)

5. Where did Abraham Lincoln carry his important papers? (in his hat)

6. Why was Abraham Lincoln called a rail-splitter? (because of his ability to split logs into rails)

7. Identify February 12, 1809. (Abraham Lincoln's birthdate)

8. What is Aesop's fables? (one of the books Abraham Lincoln read as a child; short stories that teach lessons)

Sample Stunts:

1. Walk like Frankenstein.

2. Hop like a rabbit.

3. Waddle like a duck.

4. Moo like a cow.

5. Make a vampire face.

6. Roar like a lion.

7. Make a fish face.

8. Gobble like a turkey.

Letters to Abraham Lincoln - (Booklet)

Tell the students, "Today you are each going to write (or dictate) a short letter to young Abe Lincoln telling him about yourself." On the chalkboard write the following content ideas:

1. Information on your family, your friends, your home, pets, and chores

2. Where you live

3. How you dress

4. What you do for fun

5. Information on your school and what you study there; how you get to school each day

Poem - "Abraham Lincoln Wrestles Jack Armstrong"

Read the poem. If you wish to use the poem as a fingerplay, demonstrate the actions which are in parenthesis. Reread the poem. The class performs the actions.

Variation: Skit. Choose children to act out the parts as you read the poem.

Said Denton Offut, owner of the store,   (Wiggle left thumb as if talking, keep rest of hand in fist)

My clerk, Abe, is the best for sure,

He can outthink, outlift, outthrow,

Outrun, and outwrestle anyone I know."

"Except Jack Armstrong," the customer said.   (Wiggle right thumb as if talking, keep rest of hand in fist)

Up against Jack, your clerk is dead!

Big Jack can easily wrestle down

Any man alive for miles around."

Spectators came from near and far   (Raise and "walk" last 3 fingers of left and right hands)

To see Big Jack and Abraham spar.

A spot was cleared near Denton's place

For the men to meet face to face.   (Raise both pointer fingers)

Armstrong was the first to attack   (Right pointer "jumps on" left pointer)

But, fast and hard, Abe struck back.   (Left pointer "jumps on" right pointer)

Jack went down, but Abe stood tall.   (Hold left pointer vertically and right pointer horizontally)

Then Jack's gang joined in the brawl. (Raise last 3 fingers of right hand, "walk" them toward left pointer finger)

The gang closed in around the man,   (3 fingers near left pointer)

But Jack jumped and lent a hand. (Raise right pointer)

"Abe won the match, boys, fair and square. (Wiggle right pointer as if talking)

He's the strongest, anywhere."   (Repeat same action)

The match was over; the match was done,

The crowd yelled, "Yea! Yea, Abe Lincoln!" (Wiggle last 3 fingers of each hand as if talking)

He's honest, he's fair, he's brave and true!"   (Repeat same action)

Abe had won the match and new friends too.   (Make left pointer bow)

ART

Stovepipe Hat - Pencil Can

Preparation - Collect empty orange juice cans. Distribute the cans, black construction paper, scissors, glue, and cardboard circle patterns (2" larger than the diameter of the cans).

Procedure - Glue the black construction paper on the can to fit. Trace the circle pattern on black construction paper for the "brim" of the hat. Cut out. Glue the can to the center of the circle. (See example, page 387.)

Lincoln Silhouette - (Booklet)

Preparation - Trace and cut out several silhouette patterns on cardboard. Give each child one sheet of black construction paper and one sheet of white drawing paper. Set out scissors, glue, patterns; and white, yellow and/or orange crayons.

Procedure - Use the crayons to trace the pattern (page 388) on the black construction paper. Cut out and glue in the center of the white paper.

MATH

Working On a Flatboat

Duplicate and distribute the sheet (page 389).   Read the directions and sentences.   The children fill in the blanks as directed.

MUSIC - MOVEMENT - GAMES

Song - "The Blue-Tail Fly" - ("Jimmy Crack Corn")

Lincoln especially enjoyed singing "The Blue-Tail Fly."

Sources: <u>American Folk Songs for Children</u> (Book) by Ruth Crawford Seeger, and <u>Disney's Children's Favorites</u>, Volume I (LP)

Game - Wrestling Contest

Hold your own wrestling matches, but use leg wrestling in place of "the real thing."   You may divide the class into teams with winners scoring points for their teams; or have single or double elimination matches.

To leg wrestle, two players lie on the floor. They should be side by side and on their backs (heads in opposite positions).   "Inside" elbows are hooked.   On cue, they raise their "inside" legs, hook them at the knees, and try to turn each other over.   The player who is forced to turn over backwards loses the match.

STORY TIME

Book - <u>The Ant and the Grasshopper</u> - Aesop - (Book and Record, Walt Disney Productions)
Book - <u>The Abraham Lincoln Joke Book</u> - Beatrice Schenk de Regniers

DAY 4 - ABRAHAM LINCOLN - THE PRESIDENT

CONCEPT INFORMATION

While Abraham Lincoln was <u>busy</u> being a <u>lawyer</u> in Springfield, Illinois, there was a <u>quarrel</u> going on between the <u>states</u> of the <u>South</u> and the states of the <u>North</u>. The <u>North</u> thought it was wrong to own <u>slaves</u>, but the South thought it was right.

A <u>senator</u> from Illinois, Stephen Douglas, made <u>speeches</u> saying that each state should decide for itself whether or not it wanted slavery. Abraham Lincoln did not feel this way. He felt that slavery was wrong and thought all men were <u>created equal</u>. He had <u>debates</u> with Senator Douglas who was called the "Little Giant." Lincoln said that all people in the United States should be free and that "A house divided against itself could not stand." This meant that the North and the South had to work out their <u>differences</u> and stay together to <u>preserve</u> the United States as a <u>country</u>.

People liked what Abe said and asked him to run for President. They called him "Honest Abe," "The Rail Candidate," or "The Rail-Splitter." Abraham Lincoln won the election and was <u>inaugurated</u> in 1861. He and his family moved to the White House.

But the North and South still argued, and the South decided to form its own country—the Confederate States of America. Lincoln spent many long hours deciding how to save the United States. Finally he sent soldiers from the North to force the <u>Southerners</u> back into the Union. The Civil War had begun.

Lincoln was a friend to all soldiers. In <u>memory</u> of those men who died at Gettysburg, Pennsylvania, Lincoln made his most famous speech—the Gettysburg Address. On January 1, 1863, Lincoln signed a paper that <u>freed</u> slaves forever. It was called the Emancipation Proclamation. In 1865, the South surrendered and the war was over. The Union was saved. Many people thought that Lincoln should <u>punish</u> the South, but Lincoln said they should be welcomed back into the Union "with <u>malice towards none</u>, with <u>charity for all</u>."

In April, 1865, President and Mrs. Lincoln went to see a <u>play</u> at Ford's Theatre. There, an actor named John Wilkes Booth, drew a pistol and shot Abraham Lincoln. The President died the next day and was buried in Springfield, Illinois.

Many people had <u>criticized</u> Lincoln when he was President. His job as President during the Civil War had been one of the most <u>difficult</u> of any President. But soon people understood that Lincoln had been right.

LANGUAGE ARTS - SOCIAL STUDIES - SCIENCE

Discussion

Share the concept information and define vocabulary words. Use additional references, such as <u>The Civil War in Pictures</u> by Fletcher Pratt and <u>An Album of the Civil War</u> by William Loren Katz, to display pictures of the Civil War.

Why Lincoln Grew a Beard - Explanation and Book

Abraham Lincoln did not grow a beard until after he was elected President. Many people think he grew a beard because of a letter he received from a little girl named Grace Bedell. Show a picture of the letter from <u>Lincoln, His Words and His World</u> by the Editors of Country Beautiful Magazine. Read the letter and Lincoln's response which is pictured in <u>Lincoln</u> by Stefan Lorant. Then read <u>Abe Lincoln's Beard</u> by Jan Wahl.

The Presidency - "Puppet" Discussion

<u>Preparation</u> - Make a fist (thumb inside) with your left hand. Use tempera to paint a face on the thumb and first finger section (see Patterns, Pictures, Etc., page 390). Do the same with your right hand. Use these "puppets" to relate the following information on the presidency. Hand #1 is a school-aged child. Hand #2 is younger.

Hand #1: We've been learning about Abraham Lincoln in school.

Hand #2: Who is he?

Hand #1: He was the sixteenth President of the United States.

Hand #2: The sixteenth what?

Hand #1: The sixteenth President of the United States—you know, the President.

Hand #2: What's that?

Hand #1: The President? Well, good grief! He's the Chief Executive, the leader of our land.

Hand #2: Oh, like a king, huh?

Hand #1: A king! No, no, no! Don't you know anything?

Hand #2: I know my name!

Hand #1: Remember the Pilgrims? They sailed across the ocean to a new land, America, to get away from that mean ole king in England.

Hand #2: I always wanted to be a king . . .

Hand #1: He made them go to his church and follow his rules. They were oppressed.

Hand #2: Momma says that I make her oppressed.

Hand #1: No, that's "depressed." Anyway, they came to America, but still that ole king wanted to boss them around.

Hand #2: My sister bosses me—it makes me so mad!

Hand #1: Well, the king sent soldiers but the colonists fought back and they won. So then America was independent.

Hand #2: What's that? It sounds funny.

Hand #1: It means America was a country. It was free of the ole king.

Hand #2: I always wanted to be a king—wear a crown and boss my sister. Then what happened?

Hand #1: The Americans decided they wanted a new kind of government—or way to run the country—called a democracy.

Hand #2: A democrazy?

Hand #1: A "democracy"—where every man has a part in running the government.

Hand #2: Can I, can I?

Hand #1: When you're old enough, you can. You will vote for people to be Senators and Representatives—people who make our laws—and you'll vote for the person that you want to be President.

Hand #2: I want me to be President!

Hand #1: That's possible, too!

Hand #2: Will I wear a crown?

Hand #1: No, no, the President isn't a king. He's the Chief Executive. He makes sure the laws are carried out. He is also Commander-in-Chief of the Armed Forces. It's all in the Constitution.

Hand #2: Isn't that a game show?

Hand #1: No!   America was a new country with a new kind of government, so a group of men—George Washington, James Madison, Ben Franklin . . .

Hand #2: Did Ben bring his kite?

Hand #1: No, silly—he brought his brain! All these smart men knew we had to have the rules for our new government written down. So they wrote the Constitution. The Constitution makes sure Americans are free and that no one acts like that ole king.

Hand #2: I always wanted to be a king, but now I think I'll be the President!

Hand #1: It's a hard job! When Lincoln was President, some of the states in the South wanted to form their own union—where they could still have their slaves. Lincoln had to send the army, and then there was a war!

Hand #2: Oooh—did anyone get shot?

Hand #1: Many people died before the South surrendered.

Hand #2: Lincoln was mean to send the army.

Hand #1: No, Abraham Lincoln was a kind man. It was a hard decision for him. It hurt him to see men die. But he loved our country and knew it had to be saved.

Hand #2: And was it?

Hand #1: We're here, aren't we?

Hand #2: What happened to the slaves?

Hand #1: President Lincoln made it against the law to own another person, a slave. So there is no more slavery.

Hand #2: He was a good President, huh?

Hand #1: Yes, he was.

Hand #2: It's too hard to be a President. When I grow up, I'm gonna be a clown.

Hand #1: Good idea!

Letters From Abe Lincoln - (Booklet)

Direct the circuit riders to pass out the letters written (or dictated) to Abe Lincoln (see Language Arts - Social Studies - Science, Day 3). Each student should get a letter written by a classmate. Tell the students, "Today you will pretend to be young Abe Lincoln and answer your classmate's letter." The students read (or listen to) the letters and write (dictate) the responses. On the chalkboard, write the following content ideas: (Information on:)

1. Abraham Lincoln's family, home, and friends
2. Where Abraham Lincoln lives
3. The way he spends his days—chores and fun
4. What he likes to read
5. How he looks and dresses
6. What he wants to be when he grows up

Staple together the letters and responses; then direct the circuit riders to take them up.

Poem - "Nancy Hanks" - Rosemary and Stephen Vincent Benet, from
A Book of Americans (Also found in collections of favorite poems.) Read the poem; then encourage the children to answer the questions.

ART

Flags - American and Confederate - (Booklet)

Preparation - Duplicate and distribute the two sheets (pages 391-390). Set out crayons or markers. Show pictures of United States flags from an encyclopedia or a reference such as <u>Flags of the U.S.A.</u> by David Eggenberger.

<u>Procedure</u> - Color the two flags.   One is the American flag at the end of Lincoln's presidency (36 states).   The other is the Confederate flag.

Variation: Cut squares of red, white, and blue tissue paper. Crumple the squares. Apply glue to the flags and fill in with the crumpled tissue paper squares.

Lincoln's Head - Dried Apple

<u>Preparation</u> - For this project, you will need the following: apples, peeled and cored (ask cafeteria workers or parents to assist); for the beard and hair, black fabric fringe cut into short lengths (depending on apple size); wire coat hangers, pulled into diamond shapes; toilet tissue rolls; $3\frac{1}{2}$" circles of black construction paper; black tempera paint and brushes; white glue; plastic knives; wooden manicure sticks; nail files; nails; large containers of salt water for soaking apples.

<u>Procedure</u> - Paint the toilet tissue roll black and set it aside to dry. Carve Lincoln's face in the apple using the various tools. "Draw" the eyes, nose, ears, and mouth with a nail. Then "dig out" the eye areas, and scrape off flat areas on either side of the nose and ears, and so forth. Soak the apples in the salt water for twenty minutes to prevent discoloration.

Holding the coat hanger upside down, insert the hook part through the core of the apple. (You may have to bend the hook to hold the apple properly.) Hang in a warm, well-ventilated room for three or four days. Glue the toilet tissue roll to the black construction paper circle to make the stovepipe hat. (If it is too tall, cut away a portion from the top of the roll.)

When the apples are dry, they will feel spongelike and resemble an old person's face. Remove them from the coat hangers. Glue on the beard and hair fringe. Leave the top of the head bare since it will be covered with the hat. Glue on the stovepipe hat. (See example, page 393.)

Note: When the apple dries, the face "shrivels forward," so place the ears farther back than usual.

MATH

Dot-to-Dot Stovepipe Hat

Duplicate and distribute the sheet (page 394). The children draw the hat by connecting the numbered dots.

Old Hat, New Hat - Tall and Short Activity

Read Old Hat, New Hat by Stan and Jan Berenstain. Show the pictures.
Hand out sheets of unlined paper. Direct the students to fold the sheet in
half, and in half once again. Unfold the sheet and use a crayon to draw
lines on the folds. Number the four blocks. Give the following directions:
"Draw a tall stovepipe hat in the first block. Color it black. In the
second block, draw a short cowboy hat and color it brown. Draw the tall
hat of your choice in the third block, and the short hat of your choice in
the fourth block. Color as desired."

MUSIC - MOVEMENT - GAMES

Song - "When Johnny Comes Marching Home" - Patrick Gilmore - 1863

When Johnny comes marching home again, Hurrah, hurrah,

We'll give him a hearty welcome then, Hurrah, hurrah;

The men will cheer, and the boys will shout,

The ladies they will all turn out,

And we'll all be there when Johnny comes marching home!

Game - Rope Jumping

Assist the children in learning and/or practicing rope jumping. Teach and
use the following rope-jumping chants:

Down in the meadow

Where the green grass grows,

There sat _____ (name) sweet as a rose.

She (he) sang, she (he) sang, she (he) sang so sweet,

All the boys (girls) came and kissed her (him) on the cheek.

How many kisses did she (he) get? (count)

One, two, buckle my shoe;

Three, four, close the door;

Five, six, pick up sticks;

Seven, eight, lay them straight;

Nine, ten, count again.

Not last night but the night before,

Twenty-four robbers came knocking at my door,

I asked them what they wanted, and

This is what they said,

"Spanish dancer, jump the rope,

Spanish dancer, jump and shout,

Spanish dancer, turn around,

Spanish dancer, you jump out."

I like coffee,

I like tea,

I want _____ (friend's name)

To jump in with me.

Cinderella dressed in yellow

Went downstairs to kiss her fellow.

How many kisses did she get?

1, 2, 3, ...

Game - Tug of War

Divide the class into two teams—the blue and the gray. Provide a long rope. Draw a line on the ground. The two teams line up on either side of the line and hold the rope. At the signal, each teams pulls the rope. The team that succeeds in pulling the other over the line wins the war.

STORY TIME

Book - The Abraham Lincoln Joke Book - Beatrice Schenk de Regniers
Book - The Country Mouse and the Town Mouse - Aesop - edited by
        Denise W. Guyne.

Read other Aesop's fables but stop mid-story and let the children make up their own endings. Read the rest of the story and compare the endings.

DAY 5 - HAPPY BIRTHDAY ABRAHAM LINCOLN

CONCEPT INFORMATION

In February of each year we celebrate Abraham Lincoln's birthday with a national holiday to remember this great man and all that he did for our country. Lincoln is remembered in other ways too. There are streets, parks, and towns named for him. His face appears on the penny and the five-dollar bill. The building on the back of the penny and the five-dollar bill is the Lincoln Memorial. It is a huge building in Washington, D.C., built to remember Abraham Lincoln. Inside the Lincoln Memorial is a big statue of Lincoln.

In 1911, an architect named Henry Bacon was chosen to design the Lincoln Memorial. He decided that the building would be a Greek temple of white marble with thirty-six columns, one for each state in the Union during Lincoln's time. The names of the states were carved above the columns.

The twenty-nine-foot statue was sculpted out of clay by Daniel Chester French and then cut from marble by the Piccirilli brothers in New York. It was placed on the chamber of the Lincoln Memorial. General Electric Company designed special lights to shine on the statue. On one side wall, Lincoln's Gettysburg Address was carved, and on another, his Second Inaugural Address. An artist, Jules Guerin, painted murals which were attached to the walls.

The Memorial was finished and dedicated on May 30, 1922. Since then, thousands of people have visited the beautiful memorial and have read the words above the statue,

> "IN THIS TEMPLE
>
> AS IN THE HEARTS OF THE PEOPLE
>
> FOR WHOM HE SAVED THE UNION
>
> THE MEMORY OF ABRAHAM LINCOLN
>
> IS ENSHRINED FOREVER."

LANGUAGE ARTS - SOCIAL STUDIES - SCIENCE

Discussion

Share the concept information and define vocabulary words. Show pictures of the Lincoln Memorial. Give the children shiny new pennies and a five-dollar bill to examine. Read and show the pictures of "The Pictures On a Penny," Childcraft How and Why Library, Volume 8.

Note: Save the pennies for art.

Film

Show a film on Abraham Lincoln's life.

Time Line

Complete the time line.   Review the events of Abraham Lincoln's life by pointing to each picture and calling on volunteers for identification.

Abe Letters and Booklets

Hand out the letters written to and from Abe Lincoln.   Read or allow the students to read each letter and response.   Unstaple and distribute both letters to the correct "authors." Hand out the other sheets from each day to be included in the booklets.   Distribute the front cover and a piece of construction paper for the back cover.   Assemble the booklets, stapling on the left side.

Abraham Lincoln Review - True or False?

Make several patterns of the "True or False Stovepipe Hat" (see Patterns, Pictures, Etc., page 395).   The children trace the patterns on black construction paper, cut out the hats, and glue on tongue depressors for handles.

Read the following series of statements.   The children hold up the hat when the statement is true.

1. Abraham Lincoln was born in a log cabin in Louisiana.

   Abraham Lincoln was born in a log cabin in Kentucky.

   Abraham Lincoln was born in a log cabin in Illinois.

2 Abraham Lincoln was born in December.

   Abraham Lincoln was born in January.

   Abraham Lincoln was born in February.

3. Abraham Lincoln's father was named Abraham, Senior.

   Abraham Lincoln's father was named Tom.

   Abraham Lincoln's father was named Sherman.

4. Abraham Lincoln went to school every day.

   Abraham Lincoln went to school for five years.

   Abraham Lincoln went to school for about twelve months.

5. Whenever he could, Lincoln played baseball.

   Whenever he could, Lincoln painted houses.

   Whenever he could, Lincoln read books.

6. Abraham Lincoln took cargo on a flatboat to New Orleans.

   Abraham Lincoln took cargo on a flatboat to St. Louis.

   Abraham Lincoln took cargo on a flatboat to Washington, D.C.

7. Abraham Lincoln wrestled Jack Denton.

   Abraham Lincoln wrestled Hulk Hogan.

   Abraham Lincoln wrestled Jack Armstrong.

8. Abraham Lincoln studied and became an architect.

   Abraham Lincoln studied and became a lawyer.

   Abraham Lincoln studied and became a doctor.

9. Abraham Lincoln carried his papers in his purse.

   Abraham Lincoln carried his papers in his briefcase.

   Abraham Lincoln carried his papers in his hat.

10. Abraham Lincoln was a circus lawyer.

    Abraham Lincoln was a circuit lawyer.

    Abraham Lincoln was a circle lawyer.

11. Abraham Lincoln was a United States Congressman.

    Abraham Lincoln was a United States Judge.

    Abraham Lincoln was a United States Clerk of Court.

12. Abraham Lincoln married Mary Tyler Moore.

    Abraham Lincoln married Mary Douglas.

    Abraham Lincoln married Mary Todd.

13. Abraham Lincoln was elected President and went to Washington, D.C.

    Abraham Lincoln was elected President and went to New York City.

    Abraham Lincoln was elected President and went to Mexico City.

14. While Lincoln was President, World War II began.

    While Lincoln was President, the Civil War began.

    While Lincoln was President, the French and Indian War began.

15. Abraham Lincoln thought slavery was bad.

Abraham Lincoln thought slavery was good.

Abraham Lincoln thought slavery was none of his business.

16. Lincoln's famous speech was called the Spaghetti Burger Address.

Lincoln's famous speech was called the Gettysburg Address.

Lincoln's famous speech was called the Jitterbug Express.

17. Abraham Lincoln's Emancipation Proclamation freed the slaves.

Abraham Lincoln's Slavery Document, Part I, freed the slaves.

Abraham Lincoln's Constitution freed the slaves.

18. The South won the war.

The North won the war.

The English won the war.

19. Abraham Lincoln died of typhoid fever.

Abraham Lincoln died of a heart attack.

Abraham Lincoln died of a bullet wound.

20. In memory of Abraham Lincoln, the Washington Monument was built.

In memory of Abraham Lincoln, the White House was built.

In memory of Abraham Lincoln, the Lincoln Memorial was built.

Poem - "A Reply to Nancy Hanks" by Julius Siliberger, from <u>A Time for Poetry</u> by May Hill Arbuthnot

Reread "Nancy Hanks" by Rosemary and Stephen Vincent Benet (see Language Arts - Social Studies - Science, Day 4), then read the reply by Julius Siliberger. Compare this reply to the children's answers to "Nancy Hanks."

ART

Penny Necklaces

<u>Preparation</u> - Purchase blue sticker stars. Make several of the circle patterns from cardboard (page 395). Cut blue yarn into 25"-30" pieces. Give each student: a shiny penny, white construction paper, a piece of yarn, and several stars. Set out pencils, scissors, red markers, glue, hole punchers, and the circle patterns.

Procedure - Trace the circle pattern on the white construction paper. Cut out. Color red stripes on the white circle. Punch a hole at the top. Glue the penny (Lincoln side up) in the center of the circle. Stick stars around it. Insert the yarn through the hole and tie the two ends together. (See example, page 395.)

Murals

Preparation - Provide a long sheet of mural paper, markers, and crayons or tempera paint.

Procedure - Divide the class into four groups. Each group is assigned a different part of Abraham Lincoln's life to illustrate on the mural paper. A quick review of events for each group is helpful.

MATH

How Many Pennies?

Put different amounts of pennies in four or five small jars. Write the correct totals on pieces of masking tape and stick to the bottoms of the jars. The children try to guess the correct number of pennies in each jar. After the guesses have been written on the chalkboard, the children count the pennies in each jar. The winners receive a shiny penny.

Variation: For older children, fill one big jar with pennies.

MUSIC - MOVEMENT - GAMES

Birthday Party for Abraham Lincoln

Celebrate Abraham Lincoln's birthday with a birthday party. The following are suggested activities:

Story - Read "Lincoln's Birthday," Chapter 2, Patriots' Days by John Parlin.

Patriotic Cupcakes

Preparation - Purchase cake mix, ready-to-spread white frosting, cans of red and blue decorator frosting, cupcake liners, birthday candles, decorating sprinkles, sugar crystals, small candies, tiny paper American flags, and punch. Provide plastic knives or tongue depressors or wooden popsicle sticks.

Procedure - Mix and bake the cupcakes. Set out the frosting and other items for decorating. Give each child a cupcake, one candle; and a tongue depressor, plastic knife or popsicle stick. The children frost and then decorate the patriotic cupcakes as desired. Stick a small flag in the best decorated cupcakes (each one!).

Song - "Happy Birthday to Abe Lincoln"

Group the cupcakes together on a platter or tray. Light the candles and sing "Happy Birthday" to Abe Lincoln. Serve the cupcakes and punch.

Sing-Along - Sing the songs learned in the unit.

Game - Lincoln Charades

Each child or group pantomimes an activity or event from Abraham Lincoln's life. The others try to guess the activity or event. Examples: Abe at school, Abe splitting rails, Abe plowing, Abe wrestling Jack Armstrong, Abe campaigning, Abe getting married, Abe playing with his sons.

Game - Penny Toss

Arrange 5-10 clear plastic tumblers in a small circle on the floor. Write numbers on masking tape and stick on each tumbler to indicate points. Draw or tape a line 6' away from the tumblers. (The distance depends on the age and abilities of the class.) The players sit behind the line and attempt to toss pennies into the tumblers. Scores may be tallied for individuals or teams.

STORY TIME

Book - The Abraham Lincoln Joke Book - Beatrice Schenk de Regniers

CONCEPT EVALUATION

Dear Parents,

On _____, our class will begin the unit on Abraham Lincoln. The daily topics will be "Abraham Lincoln, Early Childhood," "Ages 12-21," "On His Own," "The President," and "Happy Birthday Abraham Lincoln." Most of our activities will center around these topics. Please see below for ways you can help.

Things To Send: _____

_____

_____

Volunteers Needed To:_____

_____

_____

Follow-Up: At the end of the unit, ask your child to share the following stories, songs, or fingerplays we have learned:

_____

_____

_____

Thank you for your cooperation.

Sincerely,

Bulletin Board

Abraham Lincoln Learning Center

Wall & Ceiling Display

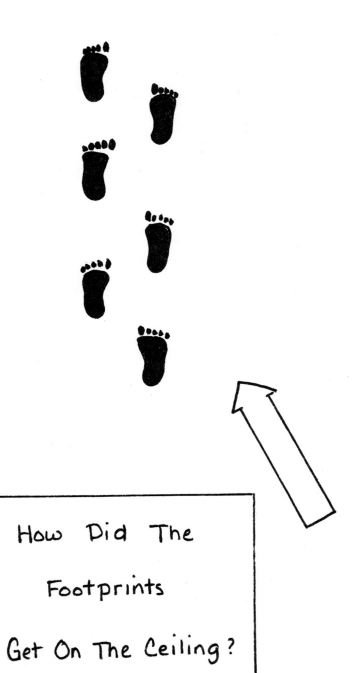

How Did The Footprints Get On The Ceiling?

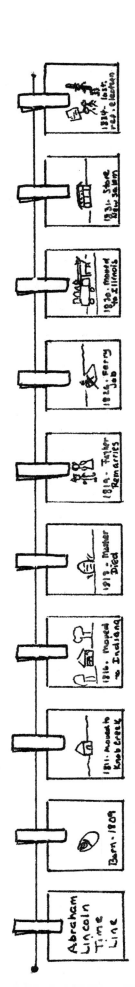

CHORAL READING - ABRAHAM LINCOLN

Teacher: Long ago on a misty morn
                A healthy baby boy was born;
                His mother named him Abraham

Group 1:   And knew that he would love the land.
                And knew that he would love the land.

Teacher: Even as a tiny lad
                He worked the farm beside his dad;
                Dusk to dawn boy and man

Group 2:   Side by side they worked the land.
                Side by side they worked the land.

Teacher: The boy grew strong, the boy grew fit,
                Strong of will, quick of wit,
                A need to think, a need to know

Group 3:   Reading by the fire's glow.
                Reading by the fire's glow.

Teacher: To Washington the tall man went
                And became our sixteenth President,
                Refused to let the Union perish

Group 4:   And bravely saved the land he cherished.
                And bravely saved the land he cherished.

Abraham Lincoln Booklet Cover

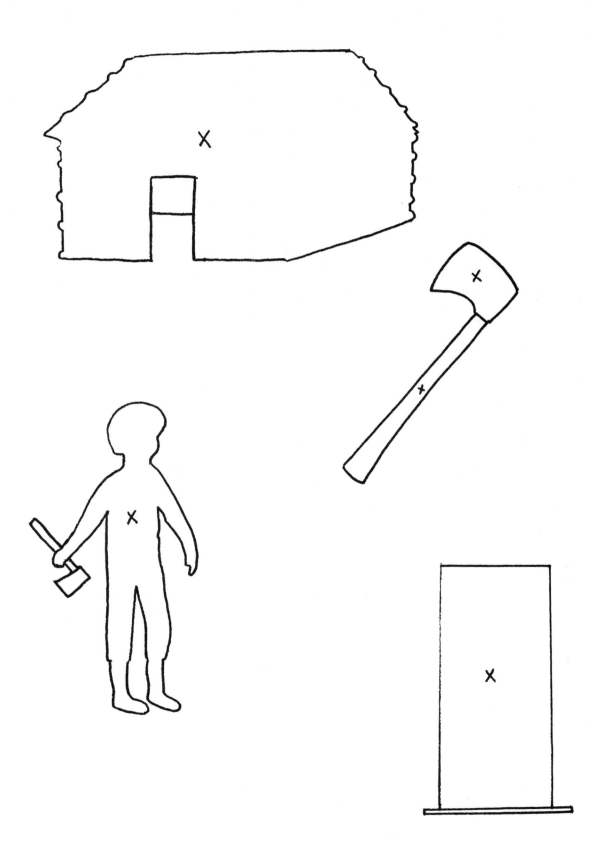

Pretzel Log Cabins

– example

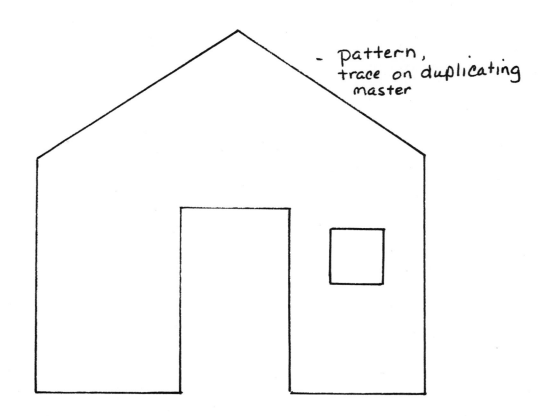

– pattern,
trace on duplicating
master

Planting Seeds - Sets

Name : _____

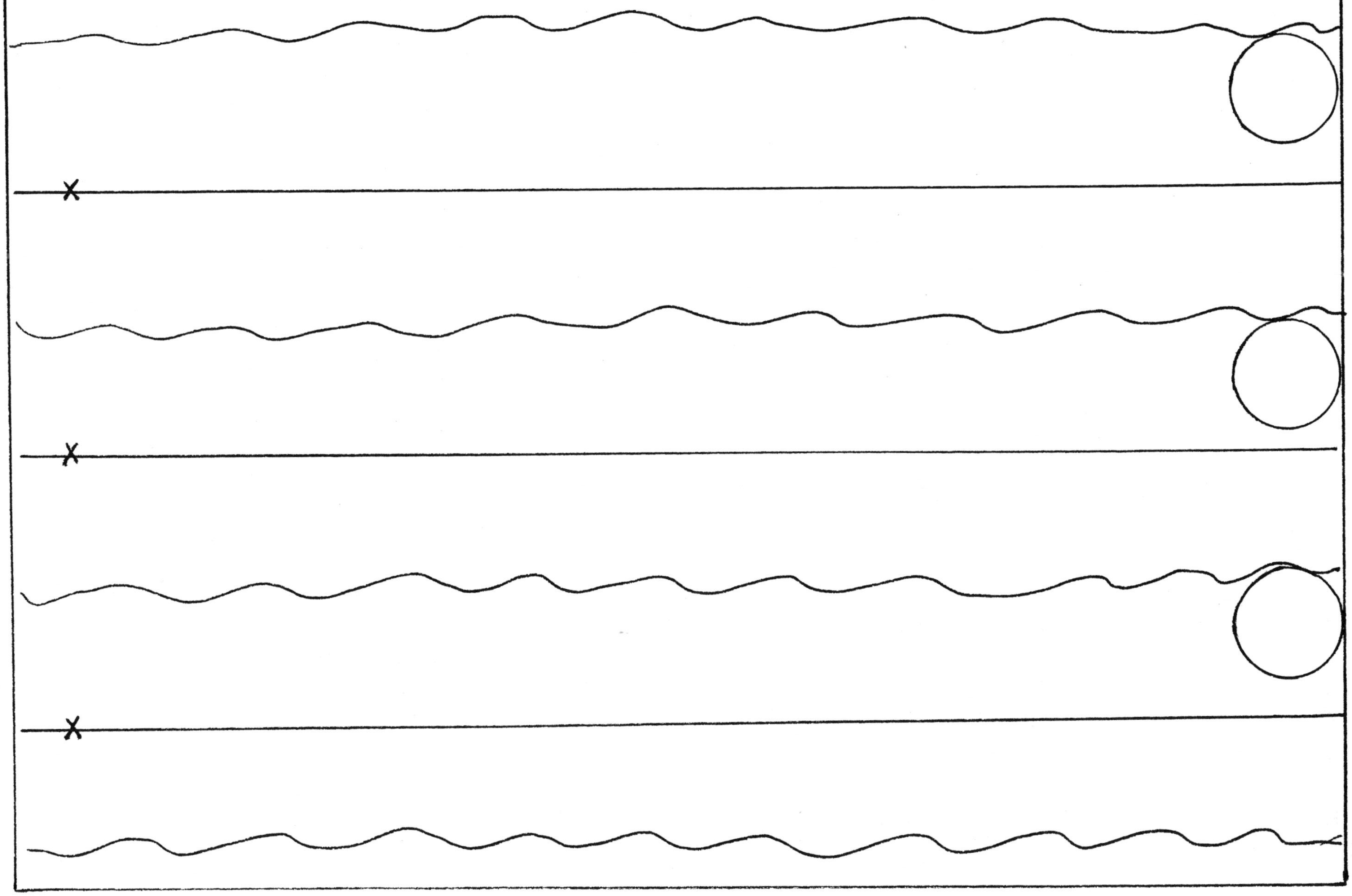

"PAW-PAW PATCH"

(Where, Oh, Where Is Pretty Little Susie?")
(One of Abraham Lincoln's favorite songs)

Where, oh, where is pretty little Susie?   (Shade eyes, look from
    side to side)
Where, oh, where is pretty little Susie?   (Repeat same actions)
Where, oh, where is pretty little Susie?   (Repeat same actions)
Way down yonder in the paw-paw patch.   (Pointing motion)

Chorus:
Picking up paw-paws; put 'em in your pocket,   (Bend down, pick up
    paw-paws, put in pocket)
Picking up paw-paws; put 'em in your pocket,   (Repeat same actions)
Picking up paw-paws; put 'em in your pocket,   (Repeat same actions)
Way down yonder in the paw-paw patch.   (Pointing motion)

Come on, boys, let's go find her,   (Wave "come on")
Come on, boys, let's go find her,   (Repeat same actions)
Come on, boys, let's go find her,   (Repeat same actions)
Way down yonder in the paw-paw patch.   (Pointing motion)

Repeat Chorus:

Come on, boys, bring her back again,   (Join hands with a partner, skip)
Come on, boys, bring her back again,   (Repeat same actions)
Come on, boys, bring her back again,   (Repeat same actions)
Way down yonder in the paw-paw patch.   (Drop hands, pointing motion)

Repeat Chorus

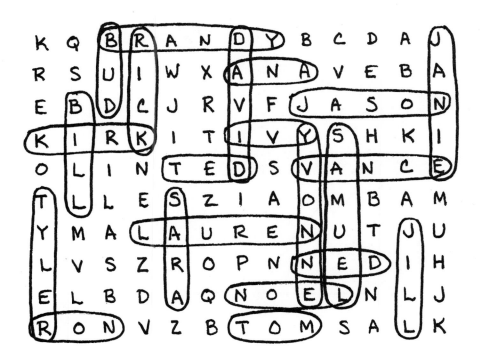

Name Search

Example

Hidden Numerals Picture

Examples

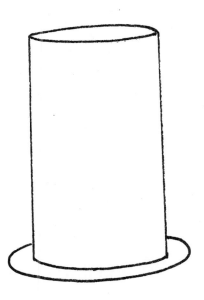

Stovepipe Hat Container
Over Your Head Drill Game

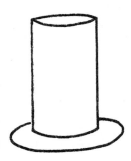

Stovepipe Hat - Pencil Can

Lincoln Silhouette

Working On a Flatboat

Abe worked hard to load these flatboats. Look at each row. Put a check above the flatboat that has more barrels. Then count the barrels on each flatboat and put the number in the blank below. Color.

1.

Abe loaded ___ barrel.

Abe loaded ___ barrels.

2.

Abe loaded ___ barrels.

Abe loaded ___ barrels.

3.

Abe loaded ___ barrels.

Abe loaded ___ barrels.

The Presidency - - Puppet Discussion

- hand

Example

American Flag - 36 States

Confederate Flag

Example

Lincoln's Head - Dried Apple

Dot-to-Dot Stovepipe Hat

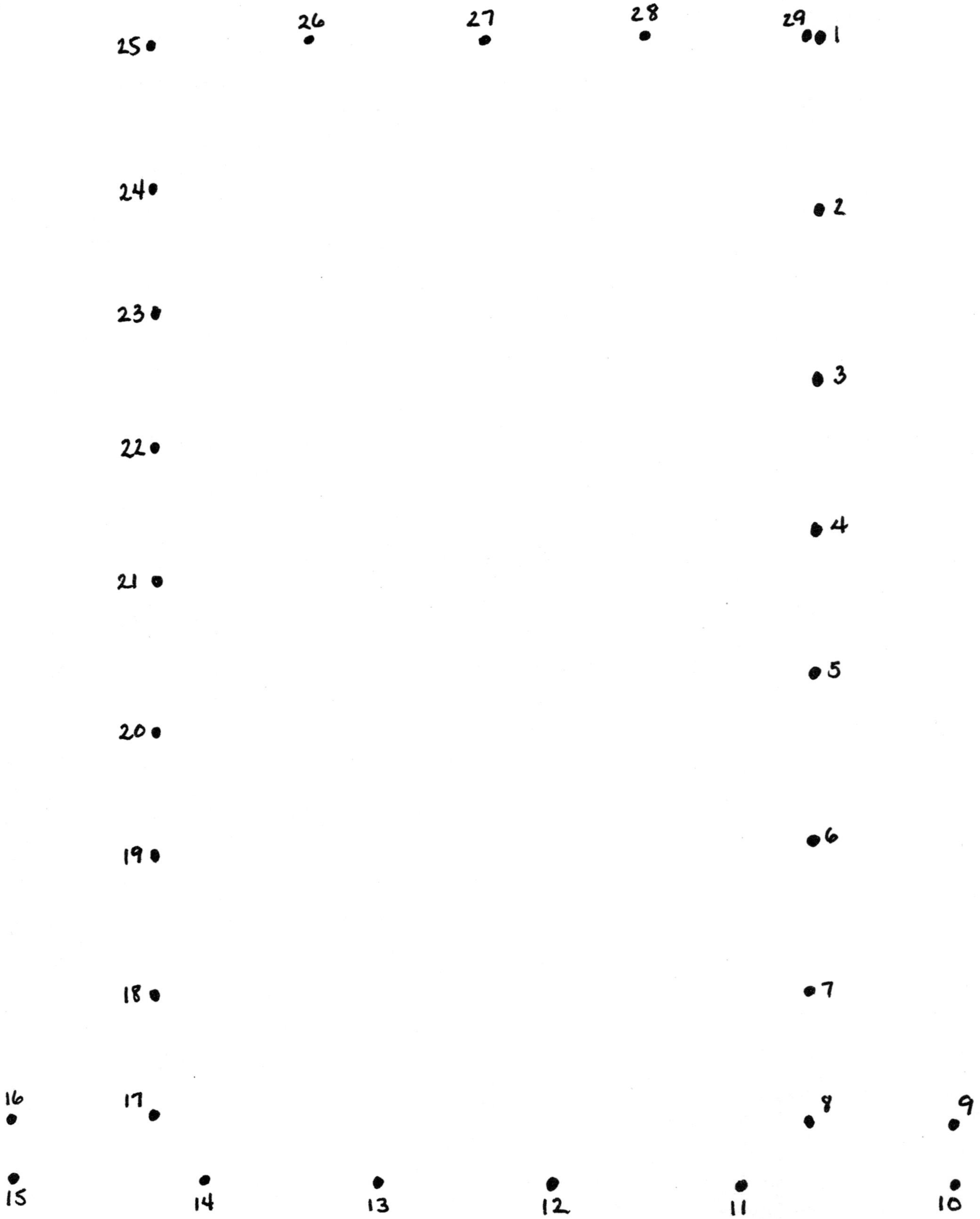

25•

26
•

27
•

28
•

29
•• 1

24•

•2

23•

•3

22•

•4

21 •

•5

20•

19•

•6

18•

•7

16
•

17
•

8
•

9
•

15
•

14
•

13
•

12
•

11
•

10
•

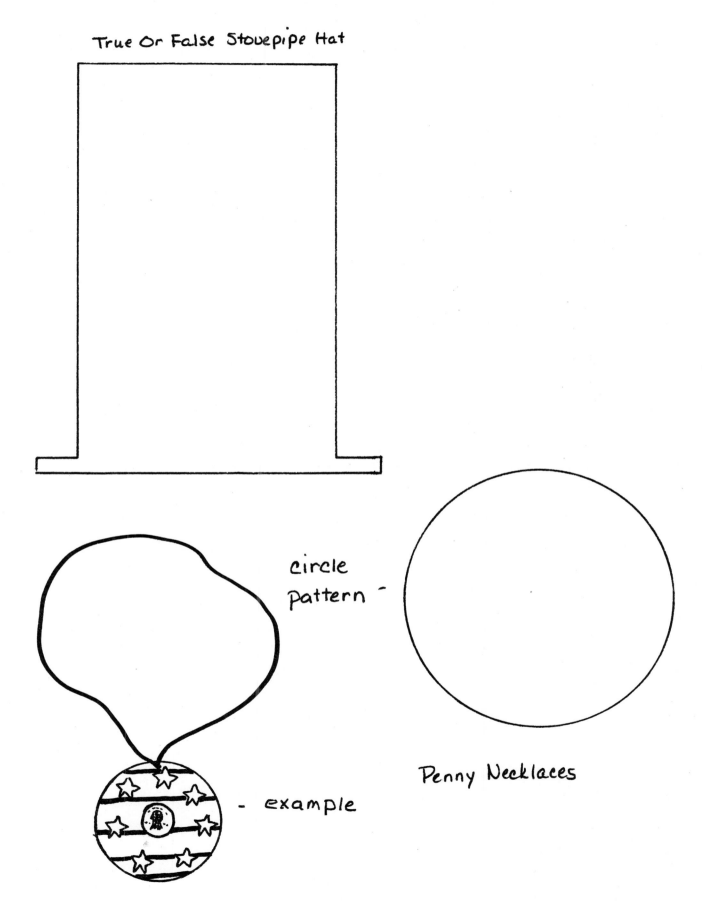

True Or False Stovepipe Hat

circle Pattern -

Penny Necklaces

- example

VALENTINE'S DAY

PROPOSED TIME: 5 days

UNIT OBJECTIVES

To develop understanding and appreciation for Valentine's Day
To present the origins of Valentine's Day
To promote understanding of Valentine symbols
To encourage enjoyment of Valentine's Day

ROOM ENVIRONMENT - BULLETIN BOARDS

"Have a Heart"

Cover the bulletin board with light blue or white paper and frame with red border trim. Make red letters for the title and staple in the middle of the bulletin board. Staple the children's "Heart People" (see Art, Day 1) in the remaining space. (See example, page 424.)

"My Favorite Things"

Cover the bulletin board as desired. Mount the title at the top. Make several heart patterns (see "Heart People," Patterns, Pictures, Etc.). Give each child a piece of red and a piece of white or pink construction paper, an old magazine, a 10" piece of red yarn, scissors, crayons, and glue. Set out the patterns to be shared. Have a hole puncher available.

Direct the children to trace the heart pattern on the red and the white or pink construction paper. Cut out both hearts. Look through the magazines and find a large or several smaller pictures of "your favorite things." Glue those on the white or pink heart. Write your name on the red heart. Punch a hole on the right side of the red heart and on the left side of the white or pink heart. Insert the yarn through both holes and tie a bow. The hearts are arranged and stapled on the bulletin board. (See example, page 424.)

ROOM ENVIRONMENT - DISPLAYS

Learning Center - "Smart Hearts"

Make a learning center from two or three sides of a corrugated cardboard box. Cover with white paper or burlap. Staple the title at the top and place on a table. (See example, page 424.) Put the following activities in the center:

1. <u>How Many Candies in the Jar</u> - Fill a small jar with sugar motto hearts or cinnamon red hots. Place in a box top along with slips of paper, a pencil, and a clothespin. The children write their names and how many candies they think are in the jar on the slips of paper. The clothespin holds the children's responses.

2. <u>Math Heart Puzzles</u> - Cut out ten to twenty-five red construction paper hearts. Use a marker to make a straight, zigzag, curved, or wavy line to divide the hearts in half. On one side, write a numeral. On the other side, draw the corresponding number of dots. Cut on the dividing lines and store in a Ziploc bag. The children count the dots, find the correct numeral, and put the heart puzzles together.

3. <u>Heart Rubbings</u> - Place five to ten cardboard hearts, paper, and pencils in a shallow box. The children arrange the hearts as desired, lay the paper on top, and use the side of the pencil lead to cover the paper and make heart rubbings.

4. <u>Cupid's Arrows Math Game</u> - Cut ten 3" hearts from styrofoam which is at least $1\frac{1}{2}$" thick. Glue each heart to a 5" square of poster paper. Number each card 1-10. Put toothpicks ("arrows") in a small jar or box. The children read the number on the card and insert that many arrows in the heart.

5. <u>Various Valentine Activity Sheets</u> - Purchase an inexpensive Valentine activity book (found in the coloring book section of stores) containing dot-to-dot sheets and mazes. Glue the sheets to construction paper, laminate, and place in the center. Include wipe-off markers and wiping cloths.

Room Decorations

Make three-sided valentines to hang from the ceiling. The children trace the heart patterns (see page 427) on three sheets of construction paper. Fold each in the center. Glue together the sides of the three hearts so that the three folds meet in the center. Dry. Punch a hole at the top. Insert string, yarn, or fishing line; knot and tie the other end to a paper clip. Hang or tack to the ceiling. (See example, page 425.)

Wall Decoration

On mural paper, write "Happy Valentine's Day from the _____ (your grade) Class" in block letters. Direct the children to paint with tempera paint. Let each child make and write his or her name on a paper heart. Glue the hearts around the words. Display in a hallway or the cafeteria. (See example, page 426.)

DAY 1 - ORIGINS

CONCEPT INFORMATION

St. Valentine's Day <u>originated</u> from several <u>events</u> and <u>customs</u>. It is named after St. Valentine who has a <u>Christian priest</u>. There were two (or maybe more) St. Valentines, so no one really knows which one is <u>honored</u> on our <u>holiday</u>. Both were priests and were put to death by the cruel <u>Roman Emperor</u>, Claudius. The first St. Valentine's story is as follows:

Claudius was badly in need of men for his <u>army</u> so he passed a law <u>forbidding</u> men to <u>marry</u>. He thought that married men would not be good soldiers but instead would want to stay home with their wives and children. St. Valentine knew that this was wrong. So he <u>disobeyed</u> the law and <u>performed</u> <u>secret marriages</u>. He was put in prison and <u>beheaded</u> on February 14th.

The second story tells of a priest named St. Valentine who was put in prison for <u>refusing</u> to <u>worship</u> the <u>Roman gods</u>. He had always been a friend to children, so they threw <u>bouquets</u> of flowers and love notes to him through the bars of the prison. While he was in prison, he prayed for a <u>miracle</u> for the <u>blind</u> daughter of the <u>jailer</u>, and one day she could see. Before he was <u>beheaded</u> on February 14th, he sent her a good-bye note which read "From your Valentine." Some people say we send valentines or love notes on February 14th in his <u>memory</u>.

A Roman custom also <u>contributed</u> to the holiday we have today. The Romans held a <u>festival</u> called the Festival of Lupercalia at the same time of the year as Valentine's Day. Because the city of Rome had problems with hungry wolves killing sheep and people, they prayed to the <u>Roman god</u>, Lupercus, whom they believed watched over the sheep and <u>shepherds</u>. The <u>holiday</u> was held in <u>honor</u> of Lupercus. Later the holiday changed into a holiday for the <u>Roman goddess</u>, Juno, whom the Romans believed ruled over <u>marriages</u>. It became a holiday of love. When the <u>Christian church</u> became powerful, the <u>Pope</u> changed the holiday to honor St. Valentine.

Whatever the origins, today St. Valentine's Day is a happy holiday. We send cards, candy, flowers, and other small gifts to friends and family to show that we care.

LANGUAGE ARTS - SOCIAL STUDIES - SCIENCE

Discussion

Share the concept information and define the vocabulary words. Locate February 14th on the calendar. Show pictures from <u>Valentine's Day</u> by Joyce K. Kessel.

Book

Read <u>Best Valentine Book</u> by Pat Whitehead, emphasizing the word for each alphabet letter. Go back through the book, reading the sentences on each page and calling on volunteers to supply the alphabet letter and word.

Valentine's Day Crossword Puzzle

Duplicate and distribute the crossword puzzle (page 426). Draw one on the chalkboard. Read each clue and call on volunteers for the answers. Write the words in the puzzle on the board. The children then fill in their puzzle sheets.

Poem and Stand-Up Collage

Read the poem "Love" by Shel Silverstein from the book <u>Where the Sidewalk Ends</u>. Write each letter of the word "Love" on a large square of stiff cardboard. Organize a group for each letter. Provide old magazines or workbooks, scissors, and glue. Each group cuts out pictures beginning with their assigned letter and glues them around the letter to make a collage. The card should be completely covered except for the letter. Punch holes at the inside edges of the squares and tie with yarn to connect. Arrange the cards so the collage will stand.

Making Sentences - Candy Activity

Pour several boxes of candy hearts with printed mottoes into a bowl. Each student draws a heart and then makes a sentence including the motto. At the end of the activity, reward the students with the sugar hearts.

ART

Heart People

Preparation - For each child, duplicate the two hearts (page 427) on red construction paper and the nine smaller hearts (page 428) on white paper. Provide scissors, glue, and white scrap paper.

Procedure - Cut out all of the hearts. Glue together the two points of the red hearts to form the body. Glue the white hearts on the body as shown in the example. Use the scrap paper for added features such as hats, hair, eyeglasses, clothes, etc. (See example, page 424.)

Sponge Heart Prints

<u>Preparation</u> - Cut sponges into heart shapes. Mix red tempera and pour a thin layer into aluminum pie plates. Provide white paper.

<u>Procedure</u> - Pinch the top of the sponge and dip into the paint. Allow excess paint to drip off. Print on the paper as desired. (See example, page 429.)

Note: Sponge "sheets" used in packing and shipping are the easiest to cut into shapes.

MATH

Sets of Valentine Symbols

Duplicate and distribute the sheet (page 430). As directed, the students fill in the number of objects in each set.

MUSIC - MOVEMENT - GAMES

Song - "I'm a Little Valentine"

Tune: "I"m a Little Teapot"

I'm a little valentine,

Made for you,

Of paper, lace, and a dab of glue.

I'm signed and sealed and on my way,

To say "I love you" on Valentine's Day.

Game - Musical Hearts

Place the chairs in a row. There should be one chair less than the number of children. Make a paper heart to lay in the seat of each chair. Play music. The children march around the chairs until the music stops. Then they rush to get a chair, picking up the heart before sitting down. The child without a chair sits in an area designated the "Love Nest," and one more chair is removed. If you prefer no eliminations, leave the same number of chairs for each round. The child without a chair remains in the game and attempts to get a chair in the next round.

STORY TIME

Book - <u>The Valentine Cat</u> - Clyde Robert Bulla
Book - <u>Sparky's Valentine Victory</u> - Marilyn J. Walton

KINDERGARTEN KITCHEN

Gelatin Hearts

2 packages unflavored gelatin
1 package strawberry or cherry-flavored gelatin (6-oz. size)
2 1/2 cups water
1/2 cup sugar

In one cup of cold water, dissolve the unflavored gelatin and set aside.

Boil one cup of water. Mix in flavored gelatin and sugar and bring back to a boil. Remove from heat. Stir in unflavored gelatin mixture and 1/2 cup cold water.

Pour into two 9" square nonstick greased pans which have been sprayed with nonstick cooking spray. Refrigerate until firm. Cut with heart-shaped cookie cutters. Eat with fingers. Yield: 18 to 24

Note: Use sugar-free gelatin if desired.

DAY 2 - CUPID

CONCEPT INFORMATION

One of the symbols of Valentine's Day is a little child with wings holding a <u>bow</u> and a <u>quiver</u> of <u>arrows</u>. The child's name is Cupid, and he is a <u>character</u> from <u>Greek and Roman mythology</u>. To explain things which they did not understand, the Greek and Roman people made up <u>myths</u> or stories. One such story is about Cupid. Cupid was known as the <u>god</u> of love. His mother, Venus, was the <u>goddess</u> of love and beauty. Cupid used his arrows to shoot love into people's hearts. The person he shot would fall <u>deeply</u> in love. He is a perfect symbol for the holiday of love, Valentine's Day.

LANGUAGE ARTS - SOCIAL STUDIES - SCIENCE

Discussion

Relate the concept information, defining the vocabulary words. Show pictures of Cupid from references (see Discussion, Day 1) and Valentine cards.

Cupid Stories

Have the children make up stories about Cupid. Use a tape recorder to record each story. Play for the class. If desired, write story starters on the board such as:

> I was playing in the park when I saw . . .
>
> Cupid was flying in the woods when . . .
>
> I was eating lunch when I looked out my window and saw . . .
>
> Cupid was so tired! "What a day!" he said . . .
>
> Today I saw Cupid shooting an arrow at . . .

Cupid's Arrows - Linetracer

Duplicate and distribute the sheet (page 431). The children use crayons to trace the path of Cupid's arrows and color the hearts.

"Looking for Mr. Cupid" - Puppet Skit

Use hand puppets of any kind to portray the detectives and other characters. To make a police line-up, draw lines across a sheet of paper. Cut different people from magazines and a picture of Cupid from a Valentine card. Glue in a row across the sheet.

Narrator: Dum, de, dum, dum (from "Dragnet" theme). The following story is true. Some of the names have been changed to protect the innocent. For the guilty, we show no such mercy! Du, du, du—du, du, du, duh . . . (theme continued).

(Two detectives walk on stage.)

Moe: I tell you Pill, this job is getting to me. Day after day, crime after crime. It's tough always being right.

Pill: Is it time for lunch yet?

Moe: It's 9:00 a.m., Pill—we just had breakfast.

Pill: Well, I just happen to have a tuna sandwich in my pocket from yesterday. . . .

(Lady runs on stage.)

Lady: Detectives, detectives, you must help poor little ole me!

Moe: Yes, Ma'am?

Lady: You could never imagine that such a thing would happen in our quaint little ole community. . . .

Pill: Excuse me, do you happen to have some salt on you?

Lady: Yes, well, as a matter of fact, I do. I never go anywhere without the proper seasonings!

Moe: Ma'am—this problem?

Lady: Oh yes, well, I was picking roses in my perfectly picturesque garden when, suddenly it happened. . . .

Moe: Just the facts, Ma'am, what actually occurred?

Lady: Why, an arrow, an invisible arrow—smack into my heart!

Moe: Now let me get this straight—an invisible arrow . . .

Lady: Yes.

Moe: Was shot . . .

Lady: Yes.

Moe: Into your heart.

Lady: Why yes, you are the smart one!

Moe: Did you see any suspicious-looking characters?

Lady: Only a child with wings and a bow and arrow.

Moe: A child with wings . . .

Lady: And a bow and arrow.

Moe: Right. We'll look into it, ma'am.

Lady: Oh, thank you detectives!

(Lady leaves.)

Moe: Obviously an unbalanced person.

Pill: Pretty good salt shaker, though!

(Man runs on stage.)

Man: Detectives, detectives!

Moe: Yes, sir?

Man: I've been shot. . . .

Pill: Don't see any blood. . . .

Man: In the heart, with an invisible arrow. Yesterday—and now I feel wonderful, but . . .

Moe: Can't have people being shot, no matter what.

Man: Right.

Moe: Would you recognize the perpetrator if you saw him?

Man: I think so.

Moe: Pill, catch that wacko, um, excuse me, lady, before she leaves. (Pill leaves and returns with lady.) Okay people, we have some suspects just brought in by our top-notch police force. We got 'em in a line-up. (Hold up line-up.) Do you see him?

Lady: Yes!

Man: There he is, the short one with the wings and bow.

Moe: Okay, we'll book him—ouch, he got me!

Pill: Ouch, he got me, too! (Use different voices to say five or six "ouches.")

Man: He's shooting those arrows in everyone's hearts!

Lady: Do something, detective —aren't you going to book him?

(Moe and Pill dance and skip around.)

Moe: Book him? I'm going to buy my wife some roses—maybe we'll take a stroll in the park . . .

Pill: I'm buying my wife a box of candy—make that two—I'll eat one on the way home . . .

Lady: They're right, you know—what's a little ole invisible arrow or two—I feel marvelously grand!

Man: Me, too! Would you like to join me for dinner?

Lady: I'd love to!

(They gaze into each other's eyes.)

Pill: Can I go too? I know a great tuna fish sandwich place. . . .

Moe: Pill, remember your wife, the candy? . . . Come on . . .

(They all skip happily off the stage.)

Narrator: Dum, de, dum, dum—dum, de, dum, dum, dah . . .

Arrow Hunt

Make twenty-seven arrows by cutting the arrowheads and feathers from construction paper. Staple to plastic or paper drinking straws. Label one arrowhead with the word "Cupid" and the rest with letters of the alphabet. Hide the arrows in the room.

Divide the class into two even teams. Make two columns on the chalkboard for scorekeeping. The teams search for the arrows. When all arrows are found, the players return to their seats. The player with the "Cupid" arrow scores five points for his or her team.

Alternate teams and call on each player to identify the letters on his or her arrows. If the letter is identified correctly, the player scores two points for his or her team. If the player cannot identify the letter, he or she scores one (finder) point for the team. One more point can be earned if a teammate can identify the letter. The team with the most points wins the game.

Note: If some players find no arrows, ask players with several arrows to share. If your class is extra large, make two sets of arrows.

ART

Peppermint Arrows

Preparation - Purchase peppermint sticks covered with cellophane. Make several cardboard patterns of the two hearts (page 432). Hand out half-sheets of red construction paper, pencils, scissors, and the peppermint sticks. Set out glue, the heart patterns, and a stapler.

Procedure - Trace two of each heart on the red construction paper and cut out. Staple together the two smaller hearts for the arrowhead and the two remaining hearts for the feathers of the arrow. Put two staples on each curved side of the hearts (see example in Patterns, Pictures, Etc., page 432). Spread glue on the cellophane at both ends of the peppermint stick. Insert one end of the stick between the layers of the arrowhead (heart) and one end between the layers of the feather (heart). Dry.

Heart Crowns

Preparation - Make several cardboard patterns of the small, medium, and large hearts (page 432). From (large) red construction paper, cut strips 3" x 18". Pass out sheets of white, pink, and red construction paper; the 18" strips; and pencils. Set out the patterns, glue, and a stapler. Show a finished crown.

Procedure - Trace the different sized hearts on the three colors of construction paper and cut out. Hearts may be glued in any arrangement on the crown. If you wish to have three-layered hearts (as shown in the example), trace and cut out two large, two medium, and two small hearts of each color.   You will have a total of eighteen hearts.   Using three different colors, glue a medium heart within a large heart and a small heart within the medium heart.   Repeat for six hearts.   Spread glue on the back tips of the heart and glue at the top of the 18" strip, varying the angles of the hearts.   Staple the crown to fit.

Wet Chalk Cupid

Preparation - Hand out drawing paper.   Set out bowls of water and colored chalk.

Procedure - Dip the chalk in water.   Draw and color a picture of Cupid. Continue to dip the chalk in water throughout the project.

MATH

Target Practice - Game and Sheet

Duplicate and distribute the Target Practice sheet (page 433).   Explain the directions.   Draw a heart-shaped target on the chalkboard low enough for the children to reach.   Draw three heart-shaped sections within the target. Number the center heart (bullseye) 10, the next section 7, the next section 5, and the last section 1.

One child at a time stands a few feet from the target, covers his eyes with one hand, and then walks to the chalkboard.   With chalk, the child marks an X on the chalkboard, attempting to hit the bullseye.   He then uncovers his eyes, returns to his place, and fills in the first blank on the sheet with his score.   Erase the X and repeat the procedure until each child has had three turns.   Assist the children in adding their totals.

Dot-to-Dot Cupid

Duplicate and distribute the sheet (page 434).   The children draw Cupid's bow by connecting the numbered dots.

MUSIC - MOVEMENT - GAMES

Song - "Cupid Went A-Flying"

Tune: "Frog Went A-Courting"

Verse 1:   Cupid went a-flying and he did go, M-hm,
Cupid went a-flying and he did go, M-hm,
Cupid went a-flying and he did go,
Shot an arrow from his bow, M-hm, m-hm, m-hm.

Verse 2:   His arrow hit Miss Lily Mae, M-hm,

His arrow hit Miss Lily Mae, M-hm,

His arrow hit Miss Lily Mae,

She fell in love that very day, M-hm, m-hm, m-hm.

Verse 3:   Miss Lily married Dapper Dan, M-hm,

Miss Lily married Dapper Dan, M-hm,

Miss Lily married Dapper Dan,

And Cupid came as his best man, M-hm, m-hm, m-hm.

Verse 4:   They had three kids, Max, Sam, and Sue, M-hm,

They had three kids, Max, Sam, and Sue, M-hm,

They had three kids, Max, Sam, and Sue,

The babysitter was you-know-who, M-hm, m-hm, m-hm.

Verse 5:   Now when Cupid wants to roam, M-hm,

Now when Cupid wants to roam, M-hm

Now when Cupid wants to roam,

He leaves his bow and arrows home, M-hm, m-hm, m-hm.

Game - Walking Hearts

Safety pin a sheet of drawing paper on the back of the students' shirts. Pin one on yourself too, but somewhat lower. Give everyone a crayon. Direct the students to form a line behind you. Play follow the leader. As the children are following you, they try to draw a heart on the paper pinned on the child in front of them. After the activity is completed, direct the students to remain in the line. Unpin the sheets and give them to their owners to display to the class.

STORY TIME

Book - The Great Valentine's Day Balloon Race - Adrienne Adams
Book - A Sweetheart for Valentine - Lorna Balian

KINDERGARTEN KITCHEN

Toasted Hearts

Cut bread into heart shapes with cookie cutters. Spread with butter, toast; then top with strawberry jelly or preserves.

DAY 3 - HEARTS

CONCEPT INFORMATION

The heart is the most important <u>organ</u> in the human body. Today because of modern science, we have been <u>educated</u> about the heart; we know what it does, how it looks, and how to keep it healthy. The people of long ago did not know much about the heart. Some thought that the heart <u>processed thoughts</u> like the brain, and some thought that the heart <u>contained</u> the <u>soul</u>. Many people thought that the heart was the <u>source</u> of <u>emotions</u> or feelings. Due to this <u>belief</u>, the heart became the symbol for love. Even now we speak of the heart as if it holds our feelings. We say "I love you with all my heart" or "He broke my heart."

Hearts appear on greeting cards, in flower arrangements, in needlework designs, and on clothes. It is a favorite symbol throughout the year; but on Valentine's Day, it is used more than any other symbol.

LANGUAGE ARTS - SOCIAL STUDIES - SCIENCE

Discussion

Share the concept information. Define the vocabulary words. Show a valentine heart and a picture of a human heart. Cut a heart, square, rectangle, circle, triangle, and ellipse out of sponges. Cut a hole in the top of a box. Place the shapes inside. The children take turns putting one hand in the box and finding the heart shape.

The Real Thing - The Human Heart

Duplicate and distribute the sheet (page 435). Relate the following information on the heart:

Your heart is a muscle in the middle of your chest between your lungs. It works all of the time pumping blood through your body—through your lungs and your blood vessels. In your heart are valves which open and close like doors to let blood in and out. The opening and closing of these valves causes the beating sound that you hear or feel. Your heart beats about 100,000 times a day!

Direct the students' attention to the sheet. Point out the heart, the arteries, and the veins. The students color the heart as directed. Borrow a stethoscope and let the students listen to their heartbeats. On the chalkboard, list the ways we keep our hearts healthy: correct diet, regular exercise, proper rest and relaxation, no smoking. Discuss each.

Heart Words

List the following words on the board. For each student, write one of the words on a sheet of drawing paper. Read the list and discuss the meanings of the words. The students illustrate the word on their sheets and show it to the class.

Words - heartburn, heartstrings, heart-to-heart, hearty, heartfelt, heartless, heartbeat, heartsick, heartwarming

Mother Goose Rhyme - "The Queen of Hearts"

Read and teach the rhyme to the class. Show the queen, king, and jack (knave) of hearts from a deck of playing cards. Choose three children to play the parts of the Queen, Knave, and King of Hearts. Use paper hearts on a paper plate for the tarts. The class recites the rhyme as the three children act it out. Repeat several times using different children to play the parts.

> The Queen of Hearts,
>
> She made some tarts
>
> All on a sunny day;
>
> The Knave of Hearts,
>
> He stole those tarts,
>
> And took them clean away.
>
> The King of Hearts
>
> Called for the tarts,
>
> And beat the Knave full sore;
>
> The Knave of Hearts
>
> Brought back the tarts,
>
> And vowed he'd steal no more.

Palm Reading

Enlarge the diagram of the palm (page 436). Show the diagram to the class and explain as follows: "The line patterns on your palms are different from anyone else's. Palm readers think that the lines on your palm can be used to predict many things about your life. Most people don't really believe these predictions; nonetheless, it is an enjoyable activity." Have the children look at their left palms and the diagram as you identify and explain the lines.

Heart Line — No heart line means you are a logical rather than an emotional person.

— Curved - You are an affectionate person.

— Straight - You are emotionally strong.

— Long - You are a romantic person.

— Short - You are not openly affectionate.

— Deep - You are loyal to the ones you love.

— Faint - You are shy about your feelings.

Head Line — Curved - You are creative and have a good memory.

— Straight - You have a logical mind.

— Long - You have a good memory.

— Short - You would rather act than think.

— Deep - You are a realistic person.

— Faint - You have trouble concentrating.

Life Line — Curved - You will be very active in your old age.

— Straight - You will lead a careful life.

— Long - You will have an average life span.

— Short - Your life is controlled by other people.

— Deep - You have the ability to overcome health problems.

— Faint - you will have changes in life.

ART

Lacy Valentines

Preparation - Purchase gummed reinforcements. Each child will need approximately 20. Hand out the large heart patterns from Heart Crowns (see Art, Day 2), red construction paper, scissors, glue, crayons, and reinforcments.

Procedure - Trace and cut out two hearts of identical size. Stick the reinforcements around the edges of one heart. Half of each reinforcement will extend past the edge of the heart. Spread glue on the back of the second heart. Lay it on top of the first heart and press to stick. Dry. Write a message on the heart. (See example, page 437.)

Heart Hats

Preparation - Use the Heart Hat pattern (page 438) to make several cardboard patterns. Mix white tempera paint or provide white paint markers. Give each student two sheets of red construction paper. Set out the paint or markers, the patterns, pencils, scissors, and staplers.

Procedure - Trace the heart on both sheets of red construction paper and cut out. Position the hearts in front of you with the points at the top. Use the markers or tempera to decorate one side of both hearts. Dry.

With the decorated sides out, staple the hearts together beginning at the point and ending at the sides. Place the hat on your head with the point at the top.

Torn Hearts

Preparation - Purchase paper doilies. Distribute doilies, half-sheets of red or pink construction paper, pencils, glue, and markers. If necessary, demonstrate tearing on a line.

Procedure - Draw a heart on the construction paper and tear it out. Use the markers to decorate or write a message on the heart. Glue to the center of the doilies. (See example, page 437.)

MATH

Heart Number Puzzle

Duplicate and distribute the Puzzle sheets (pages 439-440). The children color the objects and cut out the puzzle parts on the first sheet, and then glue them in place on the outline sheet.

Flannel Board Hearts - Sets

Cut 10-15 hearts (page 437) from red pellon. Use a long piece of yarn to form a large heart on the flannel board. Call on children to make a set of 5 hearts, to make a set of 10 hearts, to make a set of 2 hearts, and so on. Hold up a flashcard of each number if desired.

MUSIC - MOVEMENT - GAMES

Game - Cutting Contest

Set out scissors and stacks of paper. Let the children practice cutting one paper heart. At the cue, the children cut as many hearts as they can in five minutes (or whatever time you wish to allot). The child who cuts the most hearts wins the game. Suggested prize: a box of sugar "motto" hearts.

Game - Tearing Hearts

The children stand holding a piece of paper behind their backs. At the cue, they attempt to tear a heart from the paper.

Note: If this is too difficult for your class, you can:

a. let the children tear out the hearts in the normal fashion (hands in front) and see who finishes first, or

b. cut out the top part of the heart on each sheet of paper. The children tear the bottom part (point area) only.

Game - Stepping on My Heart - Relay Race

Cut four 16" hearts from red poster paper. Divide the class into two even teams. Designate a starting and finish line. The two teams line up behind the starting line. The first two players are each given two hearts and race to the finish line by stepping from one heart to the other. Once they reach the finish line, the players run back and give the hearts to the next players in line. The team finishing first wins the game.

STORY TIME

Book - A Valentine for Cousin Archie - Barbara Williams
Book - One Zillion Valentines - Frank Modell

KINDERGARTEN KITCHEN

Queen of Hearts' Tarts

2 1/4 cups all-purpose flour
2 teaspoons baking powder
1/4 teaspoon salt
1/2 cup shortening
1 cup sugar
2 eggs, beaten
1/2 teaspoon vanilla
1 tablespoon milk
Strawberry preserves

Sift together flour, baking powder, and salt. Set aside. Cream together shortening and sugar. Add eggs, vanilla, milk, and sifted ingredients. Mix well.

Roll out on a floured surface. Cut with heart-shaped cookie cutters. Bake at 375° for 8-10 minutes. Cool.

With plastic knives or wooden popsicle sticks, spread strawberry preserves on each cookie and top with another cookie. Yield: 25 "double" cookies

DAY 4 - FLOWERS AND GOODIES

CONCEPT INFORMATION

From long ago until today, flowers have been symbols of love and friendship. Before there were Valentine cards, flowers were given as gifts on Valentine's Day. In the early 1600's, the wealthy people in France gave Valentine parties. The men drew names and gave flower bouquets to their partners. In England, children went from house to house singing Valentine's Day songs and were rewarded with flowers. The rose, in particular, has always been a symbol of love.

In the 1700's, meanings were assigned to different flowers. The rose meant "I love you sincerely"; the violet meant "I love you too"; the lily of the valley meant "I'm sorry"; and the gardenia meant "I secretly love you." Today, flowers are still given on Valentine's Day to say "I love you." Pictures of flowers decorate Valentine cards, and flowers are many times referred to in the verses of the cards. One of these verses is "Roses are red, Violets are blue, Honeysuckle is sweet, and so are you!" Flowers are an important part of Valentine's Day. Most holidays have special foods or goodies. For Valentine's Day, the goodies are chocolate candy in heart-shaped boxes, hard candy hearts printed with mottoes, and heart-shaped cookies and cakes. Many of these are decorated in the colors of Valentine's day—red which stands for warmth, white which stands for faith, and pink which is a mixture of both.

LANGUAGE ARTS - SOCIAL STUDIES - SCIENCE

Discussion

Share the concept information, defining the vocabulary words. Show the flowers or pictures of the flowers mentioned and, if possible, a variety of Valentine goodies.

The Big Flower - Making Complete Sentences Activity

Make a large flower from poster paper. (See page 442.) Explain the activity; then announce to the class, "I am giving this Big Flower to Danny (chosen pupil's name)." Danny takes the Big Flower and says, "I have the Big Flower. I am going to give it to Susan." Continue the activity until all of the children have had a turn. Then ask the class to make additional complete sentences about the Big Flower.

Fingerplay - "A Day for Love"

Pretty red hearts   (Trace outline of heart in the air with index fingers)

And two-by-two.   (Hold up two fingers of both hands)

Holding hands   (Clasp hands together)

And "I love you." (Clasp hands to heart)

Scented flowers, (Hand "holds" flower to nose, sniff)

From garden vines.

A day for love; St. Valentine's. (Trace outline of heart in the air with index finger)

Valentine's Day Sequence Sheet

Duplicate the sheet (page 441). The students cut out the pictures in each story strip. Beginning at the arrows, glue them in the correct order in the spaces below.

Drying Flowers

Pick wildflowers or flowers from a "volunteered" garden. Include ferns, ivy, and other greenery. Dry, using either of the following methods:

Pressing - Put several thicknesses of newspaper on a table. Lay the flowers and plants on the newspaper so that they do not touch. Cover with several more thicknesses of newspaper. Lay boards, books, bricks, or any flat heavy objects on top of the newspapers. The drying process should take about two weeks. Change the newspapers every day for two or three days, then once or twice within the two-week period.

Drying with Sand - Pour about 2" of sand in shoeboxes. Cut the stems of the flowers short enough to stand in the sand with the blossoms resting on top. Arrange the sand so that the flower is well anchored in this position. Gently trickle another 2" of sand over the blossoms. The drying process takes a week to a week and a half.

Dried flowers can be glued to poster paper to form pictures or wreaths, or displayed in vases filled with sand. Handle gently.

ART

Hearts and Flowers

Preparation - Collect large wooden (thread) spools and styrofoam egg cartons of different colors. Purchase green pipe cleaners. Cut apart the individual egg cups of the cartons. Cut the egg carton tops in half. Give each child a spoon, two egg cups, four pipe cleaners, and an egg carton top (half). Set out patterns of 2" hearts, pencils, scissors, glue, and scrap pieces of green paper.

Procedure - Trace two hearts on the egg carton top and cut out. Use the scissors to scallop or "zigzag" the tops of the egg cups to resemble flowers. Punch a hole in the center of each cup and heart with the pencil. Insert the ends of the pipe cleaners through the holes and bend. Cut leaves from the green paper and glue to the stems. Dry. Insert the other ends of the pipe cleaners in the hole of the spool. Curve or bend the stems to arrange and balance the hearts and flowers. (See example, page 442.)

Note: Spools can be spray-painted before the activity and trimmed with a piece of ribbon tied in a bow. If spools are not available, paint or cover with paper a half-pint milk carton. Cut styrofoam and fit inside the milk carton to anchor the hearts and flowers.

Flowers and Hearts Mosaics

Preparation - Duplicate the sheet (page 443). Set out construction paper of different colors and glue.

Procedure - Tear the construction paper into small pieces. Fill in the hearts, flowers, and background by spreading glue on each area and applying the paper pieces to cover.

MATH

Candy Numerals

For each child, write a different numeral on a piece of paper. Set out small cinnamon candies or sugar hearts and glue. The children spread glue and then place the candies on the number, following the lines.

Note: Buy enough candy so the children can have a treat when they have finished. (See example, page 442.)

MUSIC - MOVEMENT - GAMES

Song - "Lavender's Blue"

Lavender's blue, dilly dilly,

Rosemary's green,

When you are king, dilly dilly,

I shall be queen.

Who told you so, dilly dilly,

Who told you so,

'Twas my own heart, dilly dilly,

That told me so.

Note: Sources for tune - Jim Along Josie (book) compiled by Nancy and John Langstaff, and "Read and Hear Nursery Songs" - Golden Press

Game - Pass the Flower

Cut two small tissue paper flowers. Purchase drinking straws. Divide the class into two even teams. Pass out the straws. The two teams stand in two lines. The players in each line stand side by side.

Place the tissue flowers in the palms of the first player in each line. The players suck on the straws to lift the flowers from their palms and pass it to the next players' palms. The flowers are passed from player to player down each line in this manner. If a flower is dropped, the player picks it up and resumes the game at the point where the flower was dropped. The team that finishes first wins the game.

STORY TIME

Book - A Valentine for Fuzzboom - True Kelley
Book - Valentine's Day Grump - Rose Greydanus

DAY 5 - VALENTINE CARDS

CONCEPT INFORMATION

Some people think that the first valentine was sent by St. Valentine. Others think that the first one was sent in 1415 by Charles, the Duke of Orleans. Imprisoned in the Tower of London, he sent love poems to his wife. By the 1600's, people were sending homemade valentines decorated with hearts, flowers, ribbons, and lace. Ribbons went back to the days when ladies gave ribbons to their favorite soldiers. The soldiers kept the ribbons with them when they went to war. The word "lace" comes from a Latin word meaning "to catch." Ladies thought that lace would "catch the hearts" of the men they loved.

In the 1700's, English companies began making beautiful paper valentines. When a man named Joseph Addenbrooke found a way to make paper lace, it was used to decorate the valentines. In 1840, manufacturers started using machines to print Valentine cards. This made them less expensive and more popular. Now a wide variety of pretty, inexpensive Valentine cards are available. Thousands are sent each year on this special holiday.

LANGUAGE ARTS - SOCIAL STUDIES - SCIENCE

Discussion

Relate the concept information and define the vocabulary words. Show pictures of past and present Valentine cards from references, such as Valentine's Day by Joyce K. Kessel and Valentine's Day by Fern G. Brown. Show examples of today's Valentine cards. Read the messages.

Rebus Valentines

Copy the rebus valentines (see Patterns, Pictures, Etc., page 444) on transparencies or on the chalkboard. If using transparencies, place them on an overhead projector. Call on volunteers to solve different parts of the rebus messages.

The C Bag - C Sounds Activity

Write an upper and lower-case "C" on a paper bag. Stand the bag on a table. In front of the bag, place a cut-out picture of Cupid, several Valentine cards, a small box of Valentine candy, a stuffed cat, a toy car, a small candy cane, scissors, a pencil, a flower, a ruler, an eraser, a book, and so forth. The students take turns finding objects that begin with the "C" sound and putting them in the bag.

Fingerplay - "Five Happy Valentines"

Five happy valentines   (Hold up 5 fingers)

From the ten cent store,

I sent one to Mother,   (Bend down thumb)

Now there are four.

Four happy valentines   (Hold up 4 fingers)

Pretty ones to see,

I gave one to Brother,   (Bend down index finger)

Now there are three.

Three happy valentines,   (Hold up 3 fingers)

Yellow, red, and blue.

I gave one to Sister,   (Bend down middle finger)

Now there are two.

Two happy valentines,   (Hold up 2 fingers)

My, this is fun,

I gave one to Daddy,   (Bend down ring finger)

Now there is one.

One happy valentine,   (Hold up 1 finger)

The story is almost done;

I gave it to Baby,   (Bend down pinky)

Now there are none.

Note: This fingerplay lends itself well to further elaboration for presentation in a school or class play.   For this purpose, make five Valentine cards from poster paper,   Draw an object in the middle of each such as a heart, a flower, and an animal.   Cut out an oval so that the child's face "becomes" the face of the object.   Let the children paint the objects and decorate the remaining areas of the cards.

Five children stand in a row holding the cards with their faces in the "holes."   One child stands beside each "card" to point at it and lead it off stage as the lines pertaining to that card are recited.

Tatting Demonstration

Question parents and friends to locate someone who knows how to tat. Tatting is a method of making lace by looping and knotting thread.   Invite the person to demonstrate this skill for the class.

ART

Pop-Up Valentine Cards

<u>Preparation</u> - Duplicate and distribute the card (page 445). Set out markers or crayons, and scissors.

<u>Procedure</u> - Cut out the card, following the solid lines. Make a fold on each dotted line of the heart. Then use your fingers to pull the center top of the heart down as you fold the card in half on the center dotted line. Crease. Use the markers or crayons to decorate the card and color the pop-up heart.

Valentine Card Holders

<u>Preparation</u> - Give each student 1½ paper plates and a piece of red yarn 3' long. Provide staplers, hole punchers, and valentine stickers.

<u>Procedure</u> - Staple the two plates together, curved sides out, as shown in the example (page 446). Punch holes at 2" intervals around the plates. Insert the yarn in a hole at the top and tie a knot, leaving a 5" "tail." Using the other end, sew in and out of the holes. Tie both ends in a bow. Decorate with stickers and label with your name. Clothespin to the class art line, tack to a bulletin board, or lay on each child's desk.

Variation: Other card holders are Valentine bags made of decorated white bags, or Valentine boxes made of covered and decorated shoeboxes. Cut slots in the tops of the Valentine boxes.

Card Mobiles

<u>Preparation</u> - A good collection of old Valentine cards is needed for this project. Also collect white clothes hangers, those made of thinner wire being the best. Bend each hanger into a large circle; then pull the hook section forward so that it "sits" in the center of the circle as shown. Cut five lengths of yarn from 10" to 18" for each mobile. Provide each child with a hanger, the yarn pieces, and five or ten valentine cards depending on your supply. Set out glue. (Provide crayons or markers if using the five-card method.)

<u>Procedure</u> - Tie one end of each yarn piece at intervals around the hanger circle. Dab with glue to prevent sliding. If using five cards, decorate the backs with crayons or markers. Punch a hole at the top of each card and tie to the yarn pieces. If using ten cards, cut out the front "pages" and glue two together back-to-back. Punch a hole in the top and tie to the yarn pieces. An extra piece of yarn can be tied in a bow at the "neck" of the hanger. (See example, page 446.)

MATH

Mailing Valentine Cards

Purchase a package of children's Valentine cards. Let the children put the cards in the envelopes and "address." Make a mailbox out of a shoebox. Place the mailbox on a table. Hold up a numeral flashcard and ask a child to "mail" that many valentines. The child counts the valentines and places them in the mailbox. Take the valentines out of the mailbox and let the class count them aloud. Compare the total with the flashcard. Repeat, using different numerals and volunteers.

MUSIC - MOVEMENT - GAMES

Song - "I Am Making Valentines"

Tune: "Mary Had a Little Lamb"

I am making valentines,

Valentines, valentines,

I am making valentines,

For the ones I love.

Watch me as I cut and paste,

Cut and paste, cut and paste,

Watch me as I cut and paste,

My special valentines.

See me mail my valentines,

Valentines, valentines,

See me mail my valentines,

To the ones I love.

Game - Queen of Hearts

Place chairs in two rows back-to-back. Choose one child to be the Queen of Hearts. (Remove this child's chair.) Assign two children to be paper, two to be glue, two to be scissors, two to be lace, two to be ribbon, two to be crayons, and so forth. The Queen of Hearts walks around the rows and says, "It's time to make my valentines. Come paper, come lace, come crayons . . ." and so forth. When the Queen of Hearts has all the supplies she desires, she says, "Finished!" Then the players scramble for a chair. The player left without a chair is the new Queen of Hearts.

Note: Decrease or increase the number of children in each category (glue, lace, etc.) as needed.

STORY TIME

Book - <u>Arthur's Valentine</u> - Marc Brown
Book - <u>The Best Valentine in the World</u> - Marjorie W. Sharmat

KINDERGARTEN KITCHEN

Heart Cake

Chocolate cake mix
Vanilla ready-to-spread frosting
Red food coloring
Small cinnamon candies

Prepare the cake mix as directed. Pour the batter in one 9" square pan and one 9" round pan. Bake as directed. Cool.

Cut the round cake layer in half and freeze for about 30 minutes. Use icing to stick together the parts as shown. Mix a few drops of red food coloring with the frosting to color it pink. The children use plastic knives or wooden popsicle sticks to frost the cake. Decorate with cinnamon candies.

Note: Freezing prevents the cut parts of the cake from crumbling when applying the frosting.

EXTRAS

Valentine's Day Party

At least a week ahead of time, send a note to parents with information about the Valentine's Day party. Include a list of each child's name for the cards. Encourage the children to address their own cards. Have extras on hand for those who forget. Exchange cards and enjoy refreshments. Play any of the unit games. Sing Valentine's Day songs.

CONCEPT REVIEW

Divide the class into two teams. On the chalkboard, draw a heart for each team. Make squares within each heart by drawing horizontal and vertical lines. Alternating teams, ask a player one question concerning the unit. If the response is correct, color in a square of that team's heart. Repeat until all players have been asked a question and one team's heart is completely colored in. That team wins the game.

CONCEPT EVALUATION

Dear Parents,

On _____, our class will begin a unit on Valentine's Day. Through discussions, poems, fingerplays, games, and other activities, we will learn the origins of Valentine's Day, the symbols of Valentine's Day, the custom of sending Valentine cards, and about the human heart. Please read below to see how you can help.

Things To Send: _____

_____

_____

Volunteers Needed To:_____

_____

_____

Follow-Up: At the end of the unit, ask your child to share the following songs, fingerplays, or stories we have learned:

_____

_____

_____

Thank you for your cooperation.

Sincerely,

Bulletin Boards

Have a Heart

My Favorite Things

Learning Center

Room Decoration

Wall Decoration

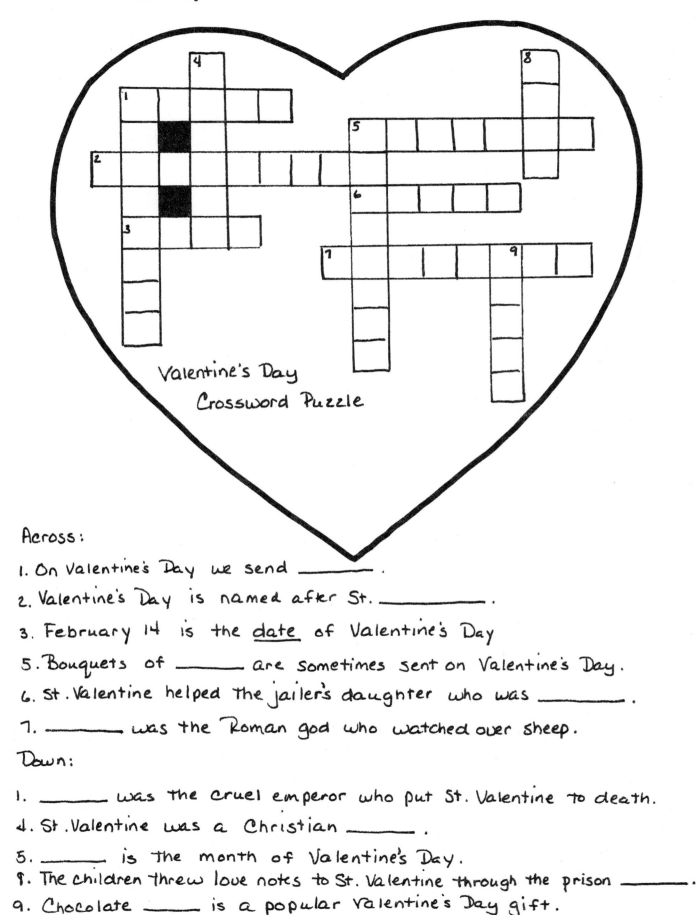

Valentine's Day
Crossword Puzzle

Across:

1. On Valentine's Day we send _____.

2. Valentine's Day is named after St. _____.

3. February 14 is the <u>date</u> of Valentine's Day

5. Bouquets of _____ are sometimes sent on Valentine's Day.

6. St. Valentine helped the jailer's daughter who was _____.

7. _____ was the Roman god who watched over sheep.

Down:

1. _____ was the cruel emperor who put St. Valentine to death.

4. St. Valentine was a Christian _____.

5. _____ is the month of Valentine's Day.

8. The children threw love notes to St. Valentine through the prison _____.

9. Chocolate _____ is a popular Valentine's Day gift.

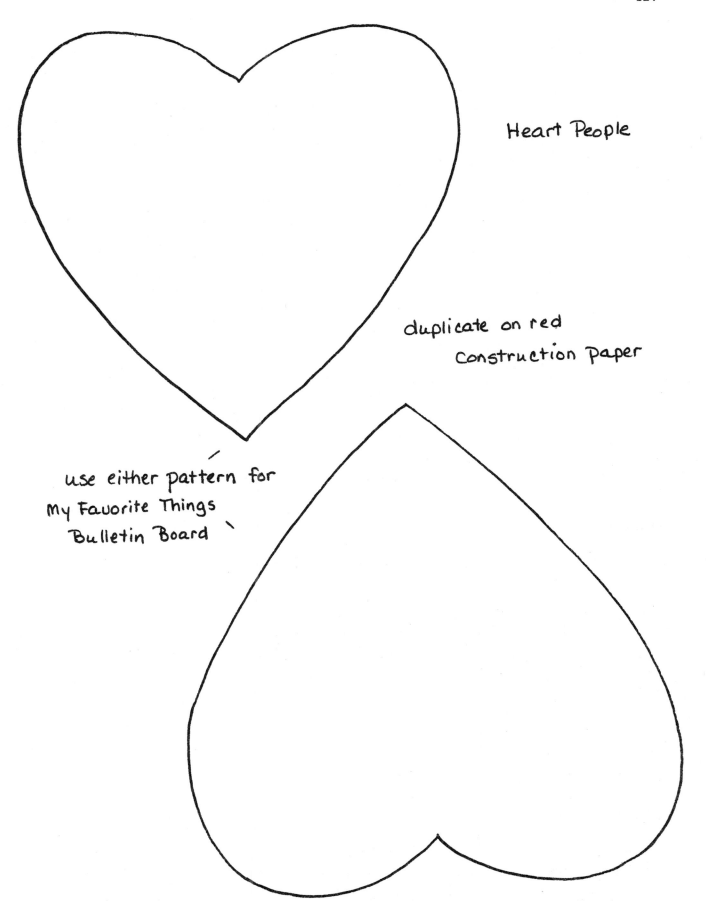

Heart People

duplicate on red
Construction Paper

use either pattern for
My Favorite Things
Bulletin Board

Heart People

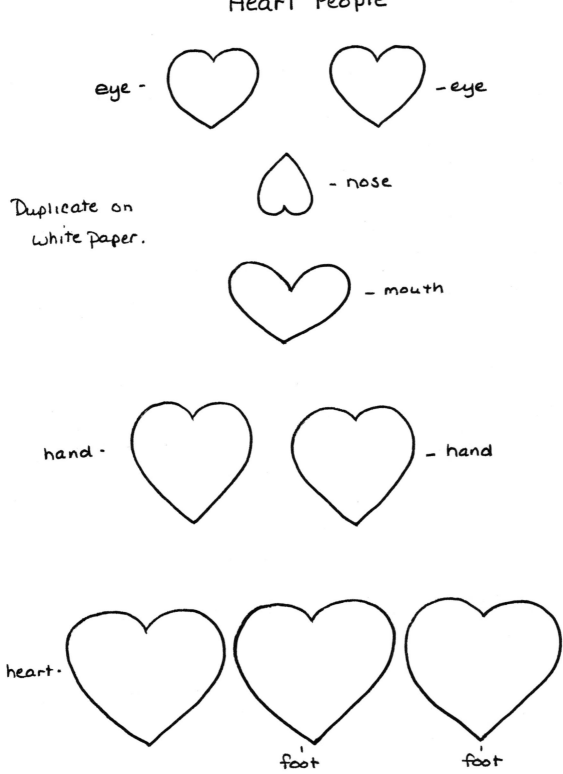

eye -   - eye

- nose

Duplicate on white paper.

- mouth

hand -   - hand

heart -

foot   foot

Examples

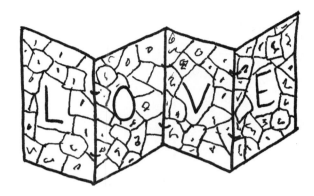

Poem·"Love"· Stand-Up Collage

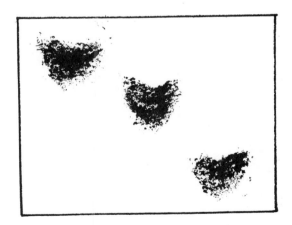

Sponge Heart Prints

Sets of Valentine Symbols

Count the symbols in each block. Fill in the blank. Color.

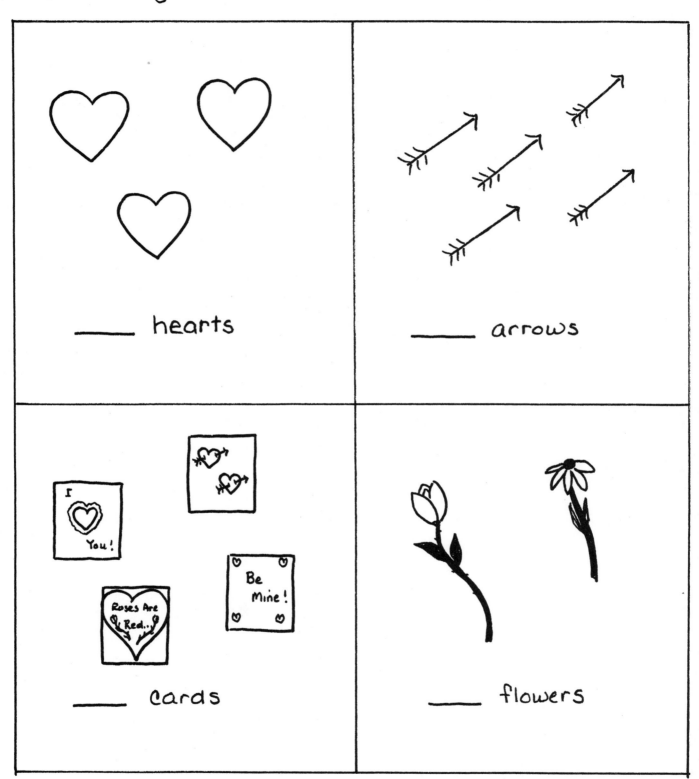

_____ hearts

_____ arrows

_____ cards

_____ flowers

Name _____

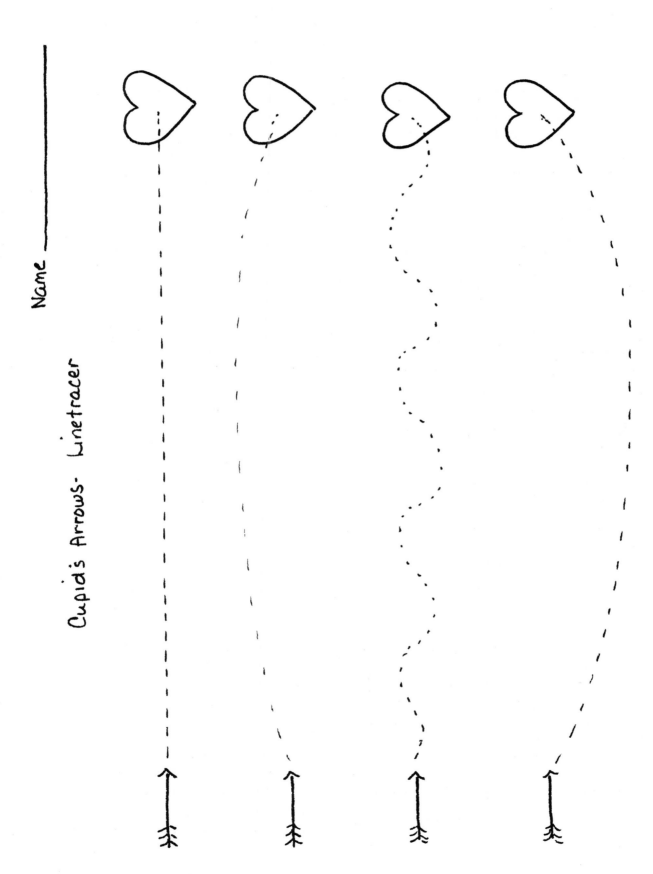

Name

Cupid's Arrows- Linetracer

Patterns, Examples

arrowhead

feather

example

Peppermint Arrows

Heart Crowns

example

Target Practice

Play Target Practice. After each turn, fill in the blanks below. Add the total points scored.

I scored ___ points on the target.

I scored ___ points on the target.

I scored ___ points on the target.

My total points scored are _____ .

Name _____

Dot-to-Dot Cupid

Follow the numerals and draw a line to connect the dots.

The Human Heart

Name: _____

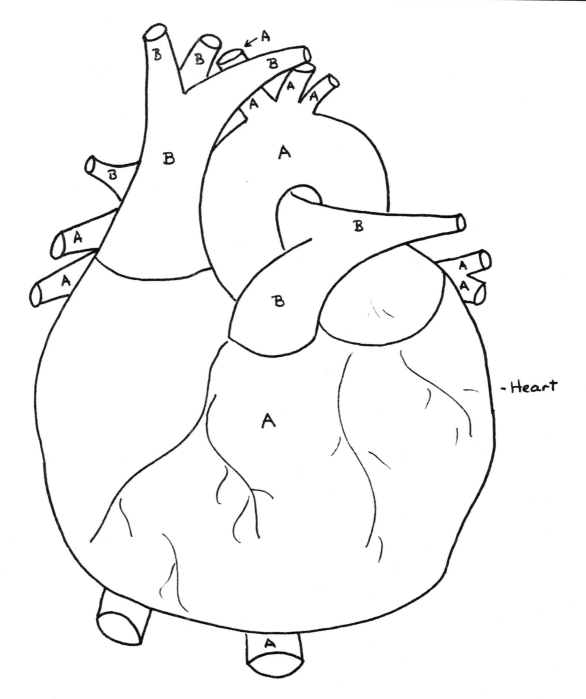

A. **Arteries** - The large tubes which carry blood from the heart. Color them red.

B. **veins** - the blood vessels which carry blood to the heart. Color them blue.

Palm Reading

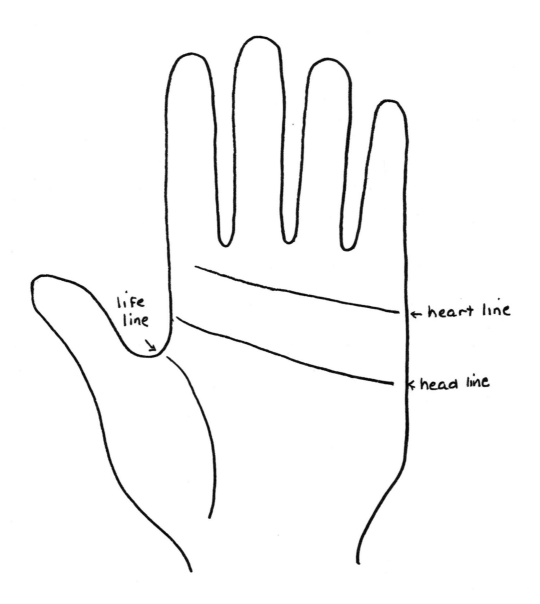

Examples- Patterns

Lacy Valentines
Example

Torn Hearts
Example

Flannel Board Hearts
Pattern

Heart Hat · Pattern, Example

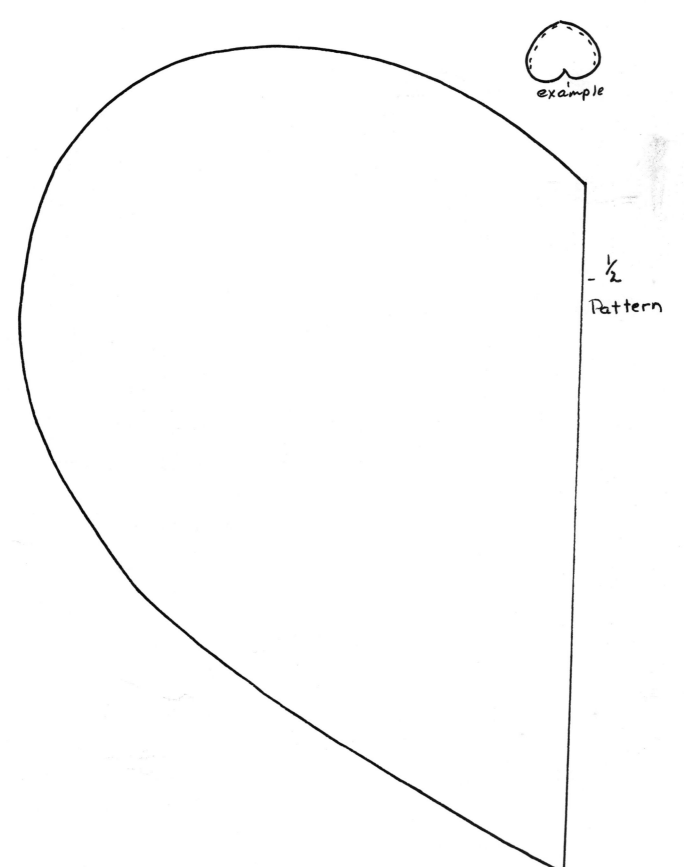

example

- ½
Pattern

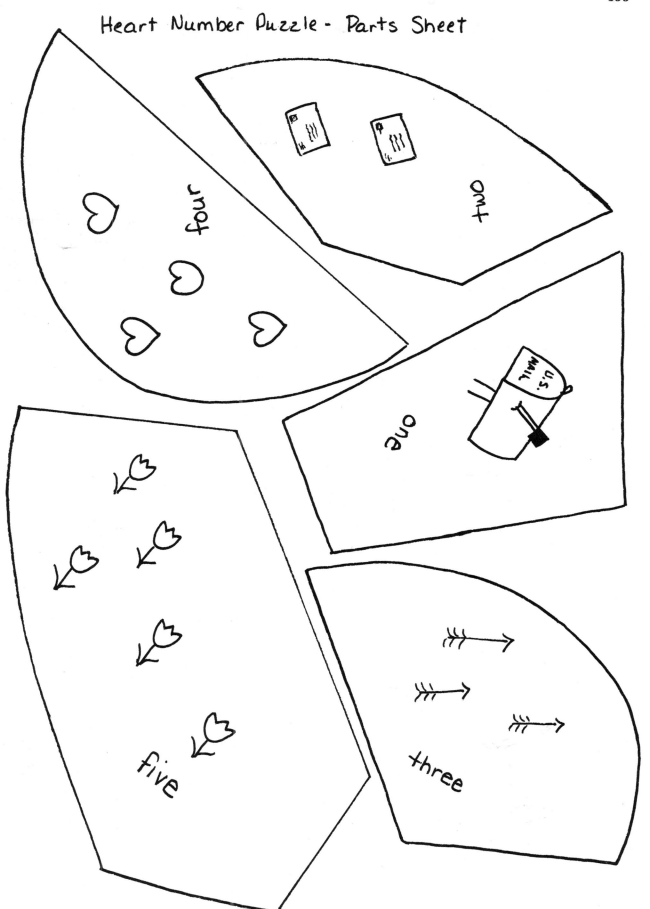

Heart Number Puzzle - Parts Sheet

Heart Number Puzzle- Outline Sheet

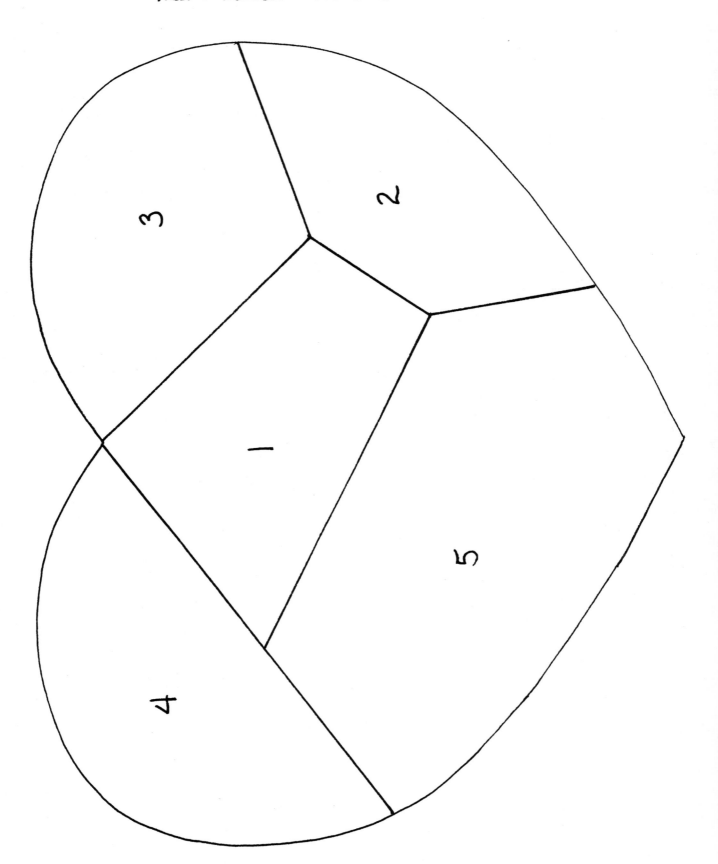

Valentine Day Sequence Sheet

Name _____

Examples

- The Big Flower
  (enlarge)

Hearts &
Flowers

- Candy Numerals

Flowers and Hearts Mosaics

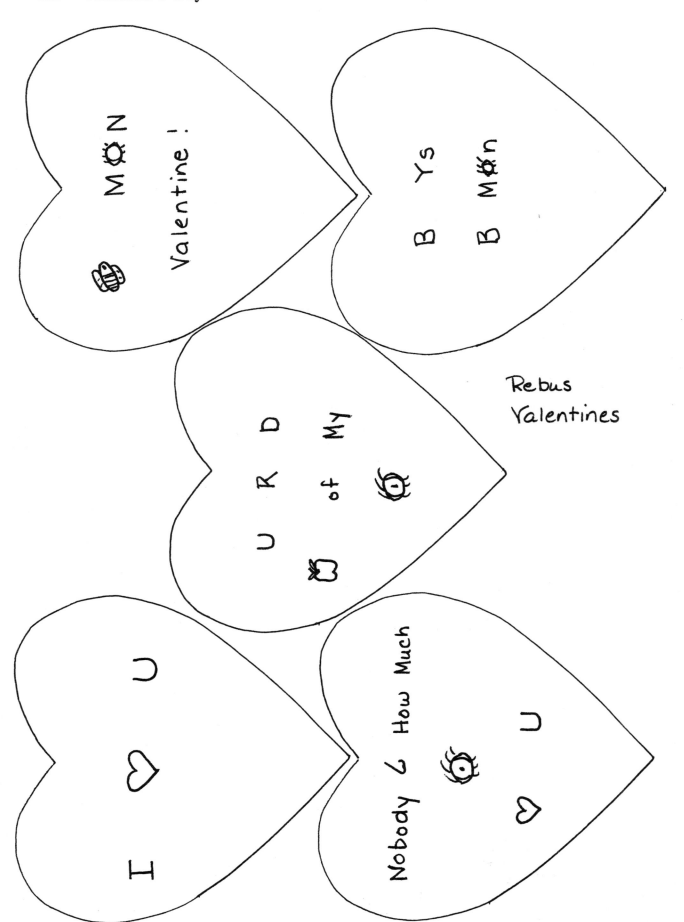

Rebus Valentines

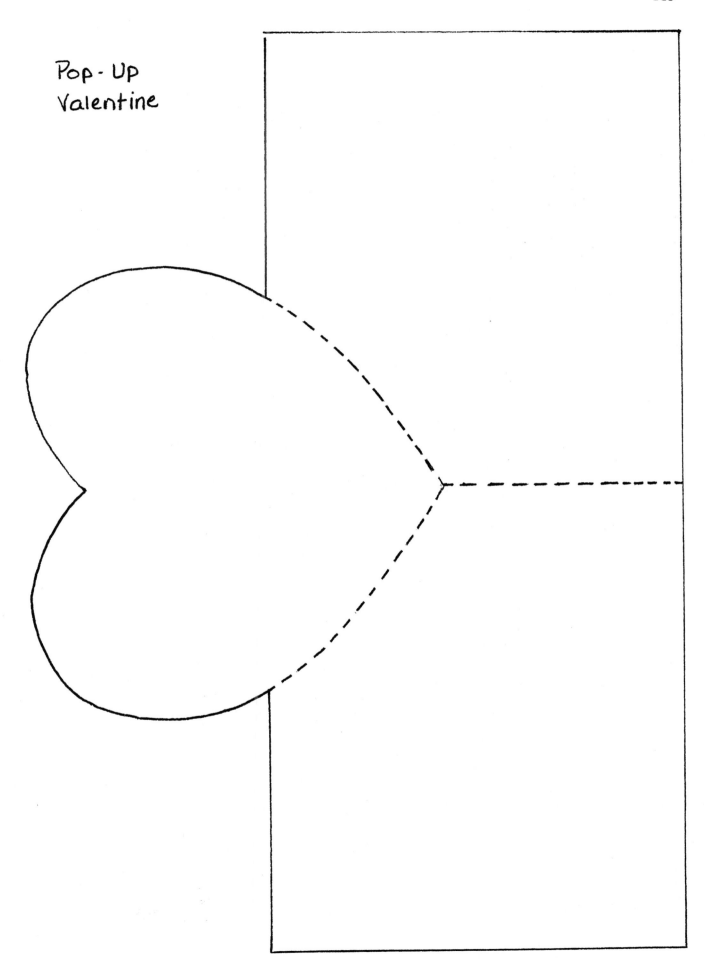

Pop - Up
Valentine

Examples

Valentine Card Holders

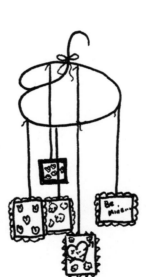

Card Mobiles

GEORGE WASHINGTON

PROPOSED TIME: 5 days

UNIT OBJECTIVES:

To help the children understand and relate to George Washington's life
To develop understanding of George Washington's role in the French and
    Indian War and the American Revolution
To develop appreciation for George Washington's role as first President of
    the United States and his many contributions to our country

ROOM ENVIRONMENT - BULLETIN BOARDS

"George Washington at School"

Cover the bulletin board as desired. Make larger versions of the horn
slates, quill pens, three-cornered hats, and young George Washington's
head as shown in the example in Patterns, Pictures, Etc. (page 478). Make
a large sheet of paper from tagboard and copy the "Rules of Conduct" (see
below) which were found in George Washington's copybook. Place the title
at the top, the "Rules of Conduct" in the center, and the remaining
objects around the sides and bottom of the bulletin board.

Rules -

Sleep not when others speak.

Let your voice be pleasant at all times.

Sit not when others stand.

Speak not when you should be silent.

Take nothing up from another's desk.

Speak no ill of anyone.

Walk not when others stop.

Treat all as you would yourself be treated.

ROOM ENVIRONMENT - DISPLAYS

"George Washington Learning Center"

Make a learning center from three sides of a corrugated cardboard box.
Cover with bulletin board paper or material. Staple the title at the top.
On the left side, staple paper versions of the Cambridge flag (considered
the first flag in our country), the "Betsy Ross" flag, and the flag of today.
Label each flag. Mount pictures of George Washington, Mount Vernon,
battle scenes, and so forth, on the center section. On the right side,
staple a square of tagboard which reads:

"George Washington loved to count

Everything he could,

He counted buttons, rocks, and trees

And stacks of firewood.

He counted when he was happy.

He counted when he was bored.

George loved to run and play

But counting he adored."

On the table below the center, place books on flags, books on George Washington, and counting materials—an abacus, cups of beads, seeds, coins, and anything else that might be interesting to count. Include small tablets and pencils for tallying. Fun sheets—counting problems, crossword puzzles, coloring sheets, and word games—can be put in the learning center for individual seatwork. (See example, page 479.)

Wall Display - "George Washington Readers"

Make poster paper tombstones with the epitaphs (see Language Arts-Social Studies - Science, Day 1) similar to those George Washington and his friends used to learn the alphabet, reading, and arithmetic. Tape the tombstones to a wall along with the title "George Washington Readers." (See example, page 479.)

Doorway

Make a large cardboard arrow and tape it on the door frame of the classroom door at a height of 6' 2". Purchase a pair of size 13 innersoles. Use two-sided tape to secure the innersoles to the floor in front of the door. The children can compare their heights and shoe sizes to George Washington's.

Hat Space

Make a designated place for the three-cornered hats (see Art, Day 1) which will be worn each day. Use a shelf, clothes pegs, or the art clothesline.

449

DAY 1 - GEORGE WASHINGTON - EARLY CHILDHOOD

CONCEPT INFORMATION

George Washington was born on February 22, 1732, in Virginia. At that time, children were born in the houses of their parents. George Washington's parents, Augustine and Mary Washington, were living on Wakefield <u>Plantation</u> near the Potomac River. The nearest town was called Pope's Creek.

When George Washington was six years old, the Washington family moved to "Ferry Farm" on the Rappahannock River. George had one younger sister, Betty, and three younger brothers, Samuel, John, and Charles. He had two older half-brothers, Lawrence and Austin.

On the Washington's plantation were many <u>shops</u> for making shoes, candles, and <u>barrels</u>. There were houses for <u>spinning</u>, <u>weaving</u>, cooking, and a dozen other things. George visited these every day to learn how many things were done. His father also taught him about <u>tobacco</u> farming. Once he fell asleep while hiding in a barrel to escape his "<u>tag-along</u>" brothers and sister. Being younger than George, they would <u>misbehave</u> in the shops; and the shopkeepers would ask all of them, including George, to leave. George was very serious about learning about the <u>plantation</u>.

When George Washington was seven, he began going to Master Hobby's school in a little house in a <u>churchyard</u> two miles away. Master Hobby was allowed to use the house because was the <u>janitor</u> of the church. The people had no teacher, so Master Hobby agreed to teach the children. Close to the schoolyard was the <u>graveyard</u>. Having no books, the children used these to learn the alphabet, to learn to read, and to learn arithmetic problems.

LANGUAGE ARTS - SOCIAL STUDIES - SCIENCE

Discussion

Share the concept information and define the vocabulary words. Show pictures from <u>George Washington</u> by Clara Ingram Judson, <u>George Washington</u> by Ingri and Edgar Parin d'Aulaire, or <u>A Man Named George Washington</u> by Gertrude Norman. These books may also be read to recount the highlights of George Washington's life. Ask a child to indicate George Washington's birthday on the calendar. Show a United States map and point out Virginia.

Poem - "For a Little Pupil" - Anonymous - (Booklet - Duplicate sheet, page 480, for inclusion in booklet on the following page.)

Napoleon was great, I know,

And Julius Caesar, and all the rest,

But they didn't belong to us, and so
I like George Washington the best.

George Washington Booklet

The booklet will be made up of activity sheets and art projects from the unit. Suggested materials to be included are indicated by the word "Booklet" in parenthesis.

Tombstone Activity

Direct the children's attention to the wall display "George Washington's Readers." With younger children, read the epitaphs and ask for volunteers to identify letters and numerals. With older children, let volunteers read the epitaphs and answer math problems concerning the dates.

1. **Mary Adams**

   Born 1650 - Died 1699

2. **The School Master**

   "The children always said
   I had eyes in the back of my head,
   So watch oh children, what you do
   Four sets of eyes are watching you!"

3. **The Sailor**

   "Well it's land, ho! for me
   Once that I die,
   But I hope there's an ocean
   Way up in the sky!"

4. **John Stokes**

   Born 1621 - Died 1666

5. **Martha Smithers**

   "Born a wife,
   Died a wife,
   She was a wife all her life."

6. **The Banker**

   "Five, Ten, Fifteen, Twenty,
   I spent my life counting money,
   Now my life's said and done
   Don't ask me for a refund!"

Follow-Up - (Booklet)

Duplicate and then distribute two Tombstone sheets (page 481) to each child. The children copy two of the epitaphs or write original epitaphs on their tombstones.

Rebus Cards

Copy and then cut apart the cards (pages 482-485). Explain to the class that one of the popular classroom games in George Washington's time was rebus. In rebus, pictures, letters, numbers, and symbols are used to make words. Hold up each card and call on volunteers to solve the rebus puzzles.

Demonstration

On George Washington's plantation, there were shops for carpenters, blacksmiths, tanners, and shoemakers. There were houses for spinning, weaving, knitting, and cooking. If you do not have a list of resource people in your community, question parents and friends—or call trade schools, colleges, and local organizations which exhibit or teach such skills. If possible, schedule a short demonstration for each day of the unit.

ART

Three-Cornered Hats

Preparation - Duplicate the hat pattern (page 486) on blue construction paper. Give each child three sides. Set out scissors, red glitter, and bottles of glue (partially opened to regulate the flow). Provide a stapler.

Procedure - Cut out the three sides. Use the glue bottle to write your name on each side. Sprinkle red glitter on the glue and shake off the excess. Staple together the sides to fit.

Note: Each day the students wear the hats for the George Washington lessons.

Bread Dough Hornbooks - (Nonedible!)

2 cups all-purpose flour
1 cup salt
1 cup water
Rubber printing set
Cooking oil

Mix well adding water a little at a time. Form into a ball; then knead for 7-10 minutes. Divide into eight portions, a portion for each hornbook.

With floured hands, form a rectangle and add a handle at the bottom. The hornbook should be about 1/4" thick.

Wipe individual letter stamps with a light coat of cooking oil; then press the alphabet stamps about 1/8" into the bread dough. Bake at 325° on foil-covered cookie sheets for 30 minutes or until the surface turns a light golden brown. (See example, page 487.)

Note: For a more golden finish, baste the hornbooks with whole, beaten eggs.

MATH

George Helps - Counting Sheet

Duplicate and distribute the sheet (page 488). Read the sentences. Direct the students to count the objects, fill in the blanks, and color the objects.

MUSIC - MOVEMENT - GAMES

Song - "George Washington Our First President"

Tune: "John Jacob Jingleheimer Schmidt"

George Washington, our first President

Father of our country too

When February comes each year,

We all stand up and cheer

"Hip Hip Hurray George Washington!"

Game - Drop the Handkerchief

The players form a circle. "It" walks or skips around the outside of the circle and "nonchalantly" drops the handkerchief behind one of the players. The player picks up the handkerchief and chases "It." If "It" makes it around the circle and to the player's spot before being tagged, he or she remains there. The player with the handkerchief is the new "It." If "It" is tagged by the player with the handkerchief, he or she is "It" for another round.

STORY TIME

Book - George Washington's Breakfast - Jean Fritz (Read over a period of two or three days.)

DAY 2 - GEORGE WASHINGTON - LATER CHILDHOOD

CONCEPT INFORMATION

George Washington <u>studied</u> very hard in school. He was known for <u>keeping his word</u>, and he <u>planned</u> all of the school <u>contests</u>. The most exciting one was the Boy's Raft Poling Contest. Everyone came to watch the boys <u>pole</u> their <u>rafts</u> for a mile down the river. The <u>current</u> was <u>swift</u> and rough, and many of the boys fell in the river.

When Indians began <u>attacking</u> some of the Virginia <u>settlers</u>, all of the men began <u>drilling</u> so that they could <u>protect</u> their <u>settlement</u>. George formed a <u>company</u> of boys at school. They drilled with cornstalks for guns, and George was their captain. One day they divided into two groups and had a <u>mock</u> fight. Soon the boys forgot George's orders and began hitting each other. No one paid any attention to George's cries to stop. Soon bruised and bloody boys were running home to their mothers. Captain George went home ashamed, for he felt that he had <u>failed</u>. His troops had <u>disobeyed</u> him.

When George was eleven, his father died. His half-brother, Lawrence, took over running the plantation. George now went to a very good school thirty miles away. He lived with his other half-brother, Austin, who lived near the school. When he was thirteen, George began studying <u>surveying</u> along with his other subjects. Surveying is <u>determining</u> the <u>location</u> and <u>boundaries</u> of a piece of land.

When George was fifteen, he finished his schooling and his course in surveying. When he was sixteen, he surveyed his brother's plantation, Mount Vernon. He did such a good job that others were soon asking for his services.

LANGUAGE ARTS - SOCIAL STUDIES - SCIENCE

Discussion

Relate the concept information, defining the vocabulary words. Display pictures from <u>George Washington, the Pictorial Biography</u>, by Clark Kinnaird, and other references (see Discussion, Day 1). Show pictures of surveying from <u>Surveying</u>, Boy Scouts of America (Merit Badge Series) or an encyclopedia.

A Visit From George Washington

Recruit an older student, a parent, or friend to visit the class as George Washington. Costume suggestions include a three-cornered hat (a paper one will do), blouse with full sleeves, vest, knee pants, knee socks, and buckled shoes. Buckles can be made from foil-covered cardboard or hair barrettes. Powdered hair is necessary for an older George Washington.

Give the "actor" simple references on George Washington and/or a copy of the unit concept information. Include the list of discussion topics below:

> George Washington's house
>
> George Washington's schools, teachers, and school activities
>
> George Washington's clothes
>
> George Washington's chores
>
> George Washington's games, interests.

Prepare the students for George Washington's visit. Brainstorm for topic discussions and list them on the board. After the visit, guide the students in recalling highlights of the visit. Write the information in the form of a story on an experience chart. Encourage the students to compare "George Washington's" clothes, house, chores, etc., with their own.

Cherry Tree Legend and Puppet Play

Make the three puppets (see Patterns, Pictures, Etc., page 489) from poster paper. Color with markers. Staple each to a plastic drinking straw. Set up a puppet theatre or use a table turned on its side. Choose three children to manipulate the puppets as you tell the story below. Tell the class, "Today we will learn the famous legend about 'George Washington and the Cherry Tree.' A legend is a story that may be based on the truth, but cannot be proven. Supposedly an elderly aunt of George Washington's told this story."

(George and Tree on stage.) When George was six years old, he was given a hatchet which he began "trying out" on everything that he could find. (George makes chopping motion.) On the Washington plantation grew many beautiful cherry trees. On day George tried the new sharp edge of his hatchet on a beautiful young English cherry tree. (George chops Tree. Tree falls.)

George's father (father comes on stage) asked George if he knew who had cut down the tree. George gave his famous answer, "I cannot tell a lie, Pa. I did cut it with my hatchet."

"Run to my arms, my dear son," replied George's father. "Run to my arms! By telling the truth, you have paid for the tree a thousand times over! Your honesty is worth a thousand trees of silver and gold." George Washington was taught to tell the truth at an early age. Throughout his life, people described him as being "honest and fair." The legend shows this quality of George Washington.

Note: The children love to hear this story and enjoy performing the puppet play over and over. Repeat until all of the children have participated.

Tracing Sheet - George Goes Fishing

Duplicate and distribute the sheet (page 490). The children complete the sheets as directed.

Fingerplay - "Chop, Chop, Chop" - (Booklet)

(Duplicate page 491 to include in the booklet.)

Chop, chop, chop went George's hatchet. (Chopping motion)

Crunch, crunch, plunk went the tree. (Hold arm upright, make it slowly fall)

"Who, who, who?" asked his father, (Outstretched arms, palms up)

The truth, truth, truth? - It was me! (Motion both thumbs toward chest)

Cherries on the Tree - Flannel Board Review Game

Preparation - List the questions on paper. Cut the questions apart and put them in a box. Cut two large trees from brown and green pellon and place on the flannel board. Cut numerous cherries from red pellon and place in a box or bowl. Divide the class into two teams and assigned a tree to each.

Procedure - A member of the first team draws a question from the box. If he can answer it correctly, he gets to place a cherry on the team's tree. If he cannot answer it, he can pass it to another teammate to answer, or put the question back in the box. If he passes it to a teammate and the teammate misses it, the other team gets a cherry on their tree.

Then the question is "thrown out" to the class for anyone to answer with no additional points awarded. If the teammate answers it correctly, he gets to place a cherry on the team's tree. Repeat the procedure with the second team and continue until all of the questions are answered. The team that earns the most cherries wins the game.

Sample Questions:

1. When was George Washington born? (1732)

2. Where was George Washington born? (Virginia)

3. What was George Washington's father's name? (Augustine)

4. What was George Washington's mother's name? (Mary)

5. What was the name of the plantation where George Washington moved when he was six? (Ferry Farm)

6. How many brothers and sisters did George Washington have? (one sister, three brothers, two half-brothers)

7. Who was George Washington's first teacher? (Master Hobby)

8. How did the children at George Washington's school learn their lessons? (tombstones)

9. What does the Cherry Tree Story tell us about George Washington? (that he was honest)

10. When he was thirteen, what did George Washington begin studying in school? (surveying)

ART

George and the Cherry Tree - (Booklet)

Preparation - Duplicate the sheet (page 492) on heavy white or manilla paper. Pass out the sheets, markers or crayons, scissors, and a metal paper fastener per child.

Procedure - Cut the sheet on the dotted line. Color the two parts of the tree and George Washington. Cut out the top part of the tree. Insert the fastener through the X and then through the X of the lower part of the tree. Turn over the sheet and spread apart the ends of the fastener.

George's Hatchet

Preparation - Make cardboard patterns of the hatchet blade (page 493). Duplicate the leaf clusters on green construction paper and the cherries on red construction paper (page 493). For each child provide: one leaf cluster, two cherries, one sheet of black construction paper (6" x 9"), and one half-sheet of brown construction paper (4-1/2" x 12"). Set out white or yellow crayons, scissors, glue, and staplers.

Procedure - Use a white or yellow crayon to trace two hatchet blades on the black construction paper. Cut out. Cut out the leaf cluster and cherries. For the handle, roll the brown construction paper into a long tube and mash it so that it is flat. Staple at each end. Glue the blades together with the handle in between. They should be approximately 3/4" from the top of the handle. Glue the leaf cluster on one side of the blade as shown, and the cherries on the stem of the leaf cluster.

MATH

Cherry Pies

Preparation - Duplicate the pie crust pattern (page 494) on manilla or light brown paper. Duplicate the pie (page 495) on white paper. Give each child the two sheets, a half-sheet of red construction paper, scissors, and glue.

Procedure - Cut out the pie by cutting on the dotted line. Read the numbers on each slice. Draw, cut out, and glue that many red construction paper cherries on each slice. Cut out the pie crust and make the slices by cutting on the dotted lines. Be sure to stop cutting where the dotted lines end. Apply glue to the inner circle of the pie. Lay the pie crust on top of the pie, matching the big dots. Press in the center so that the glue will stick. Once the glue has dried, the slices can be lifted to see the cherries underneath.

Variation: Instead of cutting cherries from red construction paper, color the cherries on each slice.

MUSIC - MOVEMENT - GAMES

Song - "Mr. Washington's Sad Song" - (Booklet)

Tune: "Yankee Doodle"

Teach the words; then sing the song. Duplicate and distribute for the booklet (page 496).

In the days of old, George Washington
Went out one day to play,
Chopped down his father's cherry tree.
At least that's what they say.
George was a naughty boy with his little hatchet;
And for such a naughty deed, he should really catch it!

When George's father saw the tree,
He nearly blew his top.
Said he, "We'll have no more of this,
It's simply got to stop!
Who'd destroy a lovely tree, I cannot understand it.
He'll be made to pay for this, that despicable bandit!"

When Georgie heard his father there,
It made him very sad.
Said he, "I cannot tell a lie,
I'm guilty, dear old Dad!
I cut down your cherry tree with my little hatchet,
I must tell the truth to you, even though I catch it."

But Georgie's father smiled and said,
"You've filled my life with joy.

I cannot mourn a cherry tree

When I have an honest boy."

Georgie was a good boy with his little hatchet.

He told his dad the truth and so—he really didn't catch it!

— Courtesy of the Boy Scouts of America

Game - Raft Race

Make a start and finish line approximately twenty feet apart. Divide the class into two even teams. Each team forms a raft as follows: three children stand side by side and join hands for the first row, three more children join hands and line up behind them to form the second row, and so forth.

Except for row 1, each outside child places his or her free hand on the shoulder of the person in front of him or her. The "rafts" are positioned behind the starting line. At the signal, the "rafts" must move as quickly as possible past the finish line, turn, and return. The first "raft" to cross the starting line wins. The "rafts" must stay intact during the race.

Note: Each raft can be formed with as few as four players, two rows of two players.

STORY TIME

Book - <u>George Washington's Breakfast</u> - Jean Fritz - (continued)

KINDERGARTEN KITCHEN

Georgie's Jelly Cookies

1 cup butter or margarine
1/2 cup granulated sugar
2 cups all-purpose flour
1/4 teaspoon salt
2 teaspoons vanilla
Cherry jelly

Cream together the butter or margarine and sugar. Add flour, salt, and vanilla. Mix well. Roll into small balls. Use one finger to make an indentation in the center of each ball. Spoon jelly into the indentation. Place on ungreased cookie sheet. Bake at 325° for 10-15 minutes or until golden brown.

DAY 3 - GEORGE WASHINGTON - ADULT, SOLDIER

CONCEPT INFORMATION

When George Washington was nineteen years old, his half-brother, Lawrence, died. George became <u>master</u> of Mount Vernon. He was also an <u>officer</u> in the Virginia <u>militia</u>. The militia was an army of <u>citizens</u> <u>available</u> for <u>emergencies</u>. When the <u>French traders</u> and soldiers of <u>Canada</u> began taking over land belonging to the English, George was chosen as an <u>aide</u> to General Braddock of the British Army. In the <u>thick</u> of battle his horse was killed, a bullet tore through his hat, and another ripped his coat. The British Army suffered a <u>defeat</u> but the word of Washington's <u>courage</u> spread. For three years, he <u>commanded</u> troops in the West; and the French finally <u>retreated</u> to Canada. George went home and married Martha Custis, a widow with two children named Jack and Patsy.

For almost twenty years, George Washington farmed the land Lawrence had left him. He planted tobacco, wheat, corn, and peas. He grew pear, cherry, and dogwood trees. And together with Martha, he watched Jack and Patsy grow up.

But new <u>trouble</u> was <u>in store for</u> the American <u>colonies</u>. The <u>colonists</u> had made a new home in America without help from England. They wanted to make their own <u>laws</u>. The colonists tried to make King George III of England understand this, but he refused to listen. The colonists decided that they wanted to be free or independent from England. A group of men met in Philadelphia, Pennsylvania, and wrote a <u>document</u> called the <u>Declaration of Independence</u>. After everyone agreed on the Declaration of Independence, it was read to the people on July 4, 1776. <u>The Liberty Bell</u> in the city of Philadelphia rang out the news. The colonies were now the United States of America. The American people were happy, but King George III was angry. He sent soldiers from England to fight the colonists.

The Americans saw that they would have to fight. They called for an army, and men came from all the colonies. George Washington was asked to be their <u>commander</u>. This war was called the American Revolution or the Revolutionary War.

George Washington was now a <u>general</u>, but his men were not soldiers. They were farmers, hunters, and storekeepers. They had no <u>uniforms</u>, no guns, and no <u>training</u>. Washington had to work hard to get these things for his men.

The <u>winter quarters</u> for the army was called Valley Forge, which was near Philadelphia. Many of the soldiers were sick and hungry that winter. But on one Christmas night, Washington and his men crossed the Delaware River. The British soldiers, taken by surprise, gave up. After that, the French king sent men, guns, and money to help the Americans. After eight long years, the war for <u>freedom</u> was won.

LANGUAGE ARTS - SOCIAL STUDIES - SCIENCE

Discussion

Share the concept information and define the vocabulary words. Show pictures from George Washington references (see Discussion, Day 1 and Day 2). Use additional references for pictures of the French and Indian War and the American Revolution, such as The French and Indian Wars by Francis Russell and The Golden Book of the American Revolution - American Heritage.

Stand-Sit Review Game

To review the concept information, direct the children to listen to each statement. If the statement is true, the children stand; if it is false, the children remain seated. Encourage the children to make their own decisions.

1. The winter quarters for George Washington's army was called Mount Vernon   (False)

2. George Washington became master of Mount Vernon when his half-brother, Lawrence, died. (True)

3. George Washington was only a baby when the French and Indian War began. (False)

4. George Washington grew coffee beans on his plantation. (False)

5. The Declaration of Independence was a popular song in 1776. (False)

6. The Liberty Bell is found in Philadelphia. (True)

7. The colonies became the United States of America on July 4, 1776. (True)

8. At that time, King Henry I was the King of England. (False)

9. George Washington married a widow named Martha Custis. (True)

10. George Washington's stepchildren were named Jack and Patsy. (True)

Book

Read The Story of the Liberty Bell by Natalie Miller.

United States Flags - Transparency Activity - (Flags Sheet)

Duplicate the Flags sheet (page 497).   Before the activity, draw four rectangles on transparencies.   Place the transparencies on the overhead projector.   Draw and color the flags while relating the information (below) on each.   After the transparency activity, distribute the "Flags" sheet. The children identify the flags as directed.

Cambridge or Grand Union Flag - (upper left on Flags sheet, page 497) - The Grand Union flag was the first flag of our country.   No one knows who designed this flag or when it was adopted.   Some believe that in 1775 a Congressional Committee, including Benjamin Franklin and George Washington, met to discuss army business and adopted the Grand Union flag.   However, there is no proof of this.   On January 1, 1776, the Grand Union flag was first raised at George Washington's headquarters of the Continental Army in Cambridge, Massachusetts.

Betsy Ross Flag - (lower right on Flags sheet, page 497) - The first flag of the new United States was officially designed and adopted is sometimes called the "Betsy Ross flag."   The American Revolution was still being fought when the Continental Congress met again in Philadelphia.   On June 14, 1777, they resolved that the United States flag would have thirteen stripes (white and red) and white stars on a blue field.

There are many theories about who made the first flag.   The most popular is the Betsy Ross story.   Elizabeth "Betsy" Ross was an expert seamstress in Philadelphia.   The story relates that George Washington prepared the design for the flag and took it to her home.   Mrs. Ross sewed together a flag from George Washington's sketch, changing only the number of points on each star from six to five.   When the flag was completed, it was shown to the Congress by George Washington.

The Second Stars and Stripes - (lower left on Flags sheet, page 497) - In 1794, two more states, Vermont and Kentucky, joined the Union.   To make room for two more stars and for those of future states, the stars were placed in rows on the blue background.   This new flag was the flag of the first five Presidents, George Washington, John Adams, Thomas Jefferson, James Madison, and James Monroe.   It was also the flag which inspired Francis Scott Key, a young American lawyer, to write the "Star Spangled Banner," our national anthem.

The Current Flag - (upper right on Flags sheet, page 497) - In 1958, Alaska become our forty-ninth state; and in 1960, Hawaii became our fiftieth.   Now there are fifty stars on the flag of the United States of America.

I'm Crossing the Delaware

Enlarge and draw the "I'm Crossing the Delaware" game board on a piece of poster paper (see page 498). On each side, color in the "river banks." In between the river banks, draw wavy lines of different colors extending all the way across the poster paper.

Divide the class into teams and give each team a small plastic boat (or construction paper cut into a boat shape) for a marker. All of the boats are lined up on one river bank. Shuffle a pack of alphabet cards.

To begin the game, hold up one alphabet card such as the letter "B". The first team must think of a word beginning with that letter and one player then says, "I'm crossing the Delaware with a banana." Since the response was correct, the team's "boat" is moved to the first "wave." A second card is held up for the next team and the procedure is repeated. If a response is incorrect, the team's boat does not advance. The first team to reach the opposite river bank wins the game.

Variation: The game can be used for various drills—numbers, colors, shapes, object identification, etc.

ART

George Washington Booklet Cover - Cherry Tree

Preparation - Duplicate the booklet cover (page 499) on white construction paper. Provide green and brown construction paper, and red construction paper strips $\frac{1}{2}$" x 3" long, crayons, pencils, and glue.

Procedure - Trace over the title with a crayon. Tear the green construction paper into small pieces and glue to cover the top of the tree and ground, overlapping the edges. Repeat with brown construction paper to cover the tree trunk. To make the cherries, wrap the red construction paper strips around a pencil. Remove the pencil and secure the loose end of the curl with glue. Dab generous amounts of glue on the tree. Set the "cherries" in the glue so that the inner spiral is exposed. Write your name at the bottom of the booklet cover. (See example, page 500.)

Variation: Sponge-paint tree and ground area.

Betsy Ross Flag

Preparation - Mix red tempera paint and pour shallow layers into trays. For each child, cut a piece of corrugated cardboard with one wavy side exposed into a rectangle $4\frac{1}{2}$" x 6" wide. Cut so that the corrugations, which form the stripes, are in the right direction. Cut a piece of blue construction paper 2" x $2\frac{1}{2}$" wide. In addition, provide white paint markers, glue, and a sheet of white unlined paper.

Procedure - Dip the wavy side of the corrugated cardboard into the red tempera. Gently shake off the excess. Press on the white paper. Allow the paint to dry. With the paint marker, make thirteen stars in a circle on the piece of blue construction paper. After the stars have dried, glue the blue piece in the top left corner of the flag.

Note: Corrugations vary in size. If you prefer the flags to have the correct number of stripes, count the corrugations, measure, and cut.

Tin Lanterns

Preparation - Collect tin cans (any size desired). Clean and remove the tops and any labels. Let the children use crayons to mark designs on the cans. Fill each can with water and freeze. Provide hammers, nails of different sizes, and electrical wire for the handles. You will also need wire cutters, old towels or newspapers on which to work, and candles which are shorter than the cans. Cut the wire into handles. Explain to the class that in George Washington's time, tin lanterns were used, especially when going from place to place. The tin lanterns kept the candles from going out.

Procedure - Once the water has frozen solid, holes may be punched in the tin cans. Lay the cans on the towels or newspapers, and punch the holes with the hammer and nails. Remember to punch a hole on either side at the top of the lantern for the handle. Empty the ice from the cans and dry thoroughly. Insert the handle in the holes and twist the ends. The teacher should light each candle and tilt to drip wax into the bottom of the lantern. Set the candle upright in the melted wax and allow the melted wax to harden. (See example, page 500.)

Note: Caution the children that only an adult may light the candle.

MATH

Fingerprint Cherry Trees - (Booklet)

Duplicate and distribute the sheet (page 501). Provide red ink pads or red tempera in pie pans. The students read the number in each block and make that many fingerprint cherries on the tree.

Cherry Count - Counting, Adding, Subtracting

Purchase several bags of cranberries (make-believe cherries) and paper cupcake liners. Give each child a "bowl" (liner). Put the cranberries in plastic bowls or pans and set on the tables. Tell the children, "Put two cherries in your bowl (2). Put two more cherries in your bowl (2 + 2). Now, count the cherries. How many are there? (2 + 2 = 4) Take one cherry out of your bowl (4 - 1). How many are left? (4 - 1 = 3)"

As you call out these directions, write the numerical equations shown in parentheses on the board. Also check the children's bowls for accuracy. Proceed in this manner varying the number of cherries to be counted, added, and subtracted. Call on volunteers to write the numbers and equations on the board.

Variation: Draw a circle for the bowl and small circles for the cherries on a ditto master and duplicate. Let the children color and cut out. Follow the same procedure with the paper cherries.

MUSIC - MOVEMENT - GAMES

Song - "Yankee Doodle" - (Booklet)

Yankee Doodle is a song that was sung by the soldiers in the Revolutionary War. Some people think that our soldiers sang it to make fun of the German soldiers sent by England to fight us. Wherever it came from, it was sung by Americans as they fought for freedom. Teach the words to the song (see Patterns, Pictures, Etc., page 502). The children march and play rhythm instruments as they sing the song. Duplicate the song to include in the booklet.

Outside Game - Soldier, Soldier

This game is an adaptation of "Red Rover." Divide the class into two "armies"—the colonists and the British. Appoint a captain for each army. The two armies stand about twenty feet apart. The soldiers stand side by side with arms locked. The colonists's army chants, "Soldier, soldier, march right over!" The British army captain chooses a soldier to run to the colonist's side and attempt to break through the locked arms of any two soldiers. If the British soldier is successful, he brings back a member of the colonist's army. If he cannot break through, he remains with the colonists.

Continue in this manner, alternating armies. Make sure the captains include each child. At the end of the game, the army with the most soldiers is the winner.

KINDERGARTEN KITCHEN

Four Layer Cherry Pie

Preheat oven to 350°. Spread the following layers in a 9" x 13" pan:

1st layer: 1 stick margarine, melted
                1 cup flour
                3/4 cup nuts, finely chopped

                Mix margarine and flour together. Use a spoon to press mixture in the pan. Sprinkle nuts on top. Bake for 15 minutes. Chill well.

2nd layer: 8 oz. cream cheese, softened
                1 cup confectioners sugar

                Mix well; then fold in:

                1 cup Cool Whip (from large container of Cool Whip)

                Pour and spread over first layer. Chill.

3rd layer: 1 large can cherry pie filling

                Pour and spread over second layer. Chill.

4th layer: Cool Whip (remainder of large container) Spread over third layer. Chill.

DAY 4 - GEORGE WASHINGTON - PRESIDENT

CONCEPT INFORMATION

After George Washington said goodbye to his soldiers, he went back to Mount Vernon. He was so happy to be home with Martha Washington, Jack, and Patsy. He ran his <u>plantation</u> and hoped he would never have to leave his home again.

America still had troubles. The colonies were free, but they had to find a way to work together. Washington and other wise men from the new states had a meeting and worked out a <u>plan</u> to keep the United States strong and free.

Now America needed a man to <u>govern</u> their new country. They needed a <u>President</u> but who was such a man? Everyone gave the same answer—George Washington. But Washington had left the army to live quietly in the country. He did not want to be President.

A meeting was called to vote for President, and Washington was the man chosen. When he heard this, he knew that he had to say yes for the country. George Washington became President on April 30, 1789. At that time the country only had thirteen <u>states</u> and the <u>capital</u> was New York City. In 1790, Congress voted to move the capital to Philadelphia until another capital further <u>south</u> could be found. They voted to <u>locate</u> the capital city somewhere along the Potomac River. George Washington chose the spot where our <u>nation's capital</u>, Washington, D.C., now stands. This was only a short <u>distance</u> from Mount Vernon.

George Washington was President for eight years. He worked hard to give his country a new start. This was <u>difficult</u> since there had been no government like this before. He had to make careful <u>decisions</u>. George Washington's <u>duties</u> were <u>heavy</u>, and he missed the long rides around his plantation. His health was not as good as it once was. When his time as President was nearly over, the people begged him to run again. But he and Martha decided that it was time for other good men to take his place.

In 1797, George and Martha Washington returned to Mount Vernon to live. Every day after breakfast Washington rode his horse about the plantation talking to workers. He worked on his flower garden, had tea with Martha, and visited with friends. Mount Vernon was a popular <u>gathering place</u> for nieces and nephews also. People in the government still came to George Washington for help. His <u>advice</u> was needed on many important problems.

On a December day in 1799, Washington rode about his farm as usual. A wet snow <u>dampened</u> his clothing, and he became sick. The <u>remedies</u> used then were not like they are today. His <u>illness</u> grew worse and on December 14th, George Washington died. The whole country <u>mourned</u> his death. Bells <u>tolled</u>, flags hung at <u>half-mast</u>, and people went to church to pay their <u>last respects</u> to this great leader. George Washington was buried on the <u>grounds</u> of the home he loved, Mount Vernon.

LANGUAGE ARTS - SOCIAL STUDIES - SCIENCE

Discussion

Share the concept information.   Define the vocabulary words.   Show pictures of George Washington as President and the First Lady, Martha Washington. Point out New York City, Philadelphia, and Washington, D.C., on a map.   Show pictures of all of the Presidents from the encyclopedia or other reference.   Ask a child to identify George Washington.

If I Were President - (Booklet)

Have a tape recorder and blank tape available Write "If I Were President, . . ." on the chalkboard.   Review the duties of the President of the United States.   Start the tape recorder.   Call on students to identify themselves and complete the sentence on the board.   When the activity is completed, replay the tape.   The students will enjoy hearing the voices and responses. Later, replay the tape to yourself and write each student's response on a sheet of paper to include in the booklet.   Older students can write their own responses.

Class Election

Let the children practice a simplified version of the election process by electing a president of the class.   Make a ballot box by cutting a slot in the top of a box.   Cut slips of paper for voting.   Divide the class into two "parties," the Republicans (Elephants) and the Democrats (Donkeys). One party nominates several people for president.   Write the names on the board.   Hand out the slips of paper and pencils to the members of that party.   Each child writes the name of his or her choice on the paper and puts it in the ballot box.   Tally the votes and announce the winner.

Repeat the process with the other party.   Ask the two candidates to give short speeches listing their qualifications.   Afterwards, everyone casts their votes and the winner is announced.

Note: The term of office may be for the day, week, month, or year. Other officers may be included in the election.   If you wish to extend the activity, the children can make campaign posters and buttons, etc.

Poem - "Washington" - by Nancy Byrd Turner

Read the poem which is found in many collections of popular poems, including Childcraft, Volume 2, and Favorite Poems Old and New, selected by Helen Ferris.

George Washington's Life - Stand-Up Sequence Card

Cut out and distribute pieces of tagboard, 8" tall by 28" wide.   Provide crayons or markers.   Direct the children to fold the piece in half (to measure 8" x 14"), and then in half again. Unfold. One end will be pointing in the wrong direction. Fold in the opposite direction. (When viewed from overhead, the card will resemble two joined Indian tepees!) On the four sections, proceeding from left to right, the children draw and color George Washington as a child, as a surveyor, as a soldier, and as the first President of the United States. (See example, page 503.)

ART

George Washington Silhouette - (Booklet)

Preparation - Duplicate the sheet (page 504). Staple each sheet on top of a sheet of black construction paper and distribute. Hand out sheets of white construction paper and scissors. Set out glue. Have a staple remover available.

Procedure - Cut out the silhouette following the lines on the top (white) sheet. Remove the staple and discard the white copy. Glue the black silhouette in the center of the construction paper.

George Washington's Wig

Preparation - Make several cardboard patterns of the wig as shown in Patterns, Pictures, Etc. (page 505). Provide a 12" x 18" sheet of white construction paper for each child. Set out the patterns, pencils, scissors, and staplers.

Procedure - Fold the construction paper in half to measure 12" x 9". Place the pattern on the fold as indicated. Trace. Following the lines, cut through both layers. Place the top of the wig inside your three-cornered hat. The fold will fit within the back corner. Staple all around.

MATH

Martha Washington Goes Shopping

Duplicate and distribute the sheet (page 506). The students draw lines to match each item with the proper box as directed.

MUSIC - MOVEMENT - GAMES

Song - "Would You Be the President?"

Tune: "Have You Seen the Muffin Man?"

Divide the class into two groups. Teach the song, assign parts, and sing.

All: Oh, would you be the President,
          The President, the President?
          Oh, would you be the President,
          Our leader for a day?

Group I: Yes, I'd love to be the President,
          The President, the President.
          Yes, I'd love to be the President,
          Our leader for a day.

Group 2: No, I'd never be the President,
          The President, the President.
          No, I'd never be the President,
          Our leader for a day.

(Both groups sing at once:)

Group l: Yes, yes, yes, yes, yes, yes, yes, yes,
          Yes, yes, yes, yes, yes, yes, yes, yes,
          Yes, yes, yes, yes, yes, yes, yes, yes,
          Yes, yes, yes, yes, yes, yes!

Group 2: No, no, no, no, no, no, no, no,
          No, no, no, no, no, no, no, no,
          No, no, no, no, no, no, no, no,
          No, no, no, no, no, no!

Song - "America" - Words by Reverend Samuel Francis Smith)

Recite and explain the words to the song. Teach the words and tune.

Action Game - Martha Washington Went to New York

The children stand in a semi-circle, repeat each line, and imitate the actions. All actions are continued until the end of the game.

1. Martha Washington went to New York to buy a feather fan. (Fan yourself.)

2. Martha Washington went to New York to buy a pair of scissors. (Make cutting motion with your fingers and keep fanning.)

3. Martha Washington went to New York to buy a hobbyhorse. (Bob up and down as you continue the other motions.)

4. Martha Washington went to New York to buy a cuckoo clock. (Repeat "cuckoo" while performing the other motions.)

KINDERGARTEN KITCHEN

Martha Washington's Tea Cakes

1/2 cup butter or margarine, softened
1 cup sugar
1 tablespoon milk
2 eggs, beaten
2 teaspoons baking powder
2 1/2 cups all-purpose flour
2 teaspoons vanilla

Preheat oven to 350°. Cream butter and sugar. Mix in milk and eggs. Add baking powder, flour, and vanilla. Mix well. Drop by rounded teaspoonfuls onto an ungreased cookie sheet. Bake until light golden brown. Serve with tea. Yield: 4 dozen approximately

DAY 5 - HAPPY BIRTHDAY GEORGE WASHINGTON

CONCEPT INFORMATION

In February of each year, we <u>observe</u> a <u>national holiday</u> to <u>celebrate</u> the birthday of our first President, George Washington. George Washington is called the "Father of Our Country" because he spent much of his life helping our country become strong and <u>independent</u>. George Washington is also remembered in other ways. Our nation's capital, Washington, D.C., one of our <u>states</u>, Washington, and many cities, streets, and buildings are named after this great man. His face appears on the quarter, the one-dollar bill, and on postage stamps.

Each year, over a half million people visit George Washington's home, Mount Vernon. Approximately fifty years after George Washington's death, it was offered for sale. But a lady from South Carolina, Ann Pamela Cunningham, felt that George Washington's home should not be sold; it should be <u>saved</u> for the people of America. She formed an <u>organization</u> called the "Mount Vernon Ladies' Association of the Union" which <u>raised</u> money to <u>purchase</u> and <u>preserve</u> the house and <u>property</u>.

A million people a year visit the Washington <u>Monument</u> in Washington, D.C. Pierre L'Enfant, the architect who designed the city, included a monument to George Washington in his plans. However, the monument was not begun until 1848, fifty years after Washington's death. It was opened to the <u>public</u> in 1885. The shape of the monument is an obelisk, a tall four-sided stone <u>pillar</u> which <u>tapers</u> to a point resembling a <u>pyramid</u>. The monument is 555 feet, 5-1/8 inches tall, and the outside is made of white <u>marble</u>. Inside, visitors can climb 898 steps or take an <u>elevator</u> to reach the top of the Washington Monument. At the top, there are windows for <u>viewing</u> the city.

Another <u>national memorial</u> which includes George Washington is the Mount Rushmore Memorial in the Black Hills of South Dakota. <u>Carved</u> in the side of the mountain are the heads of George Washington, Thomas Jefferson, Theodore Roosevelt, and Abraham Lincoln. The famous <u>sculptor</u>, Gutzon Borglum, <u>designed</u> and <u>supervised</u> the <u>gigantic</u> memorial which took about twelve years to <u>complete</u>.

After George Washington's death, Major General Henry Lee, who had fought with George Washington in the American Revolution, made a speech about George Washington. The words he said are still remembered because everyone in America felt the same way. He said of George Washington, "First in war, first in peace, and first in the hearts of his countrymen . . ."

LANGUAGE ARTS - SOCIAL STUDIES - SCIENCE

Discussion

Share the concept information, defining the vocabulary words. Display pictures of Mount Vernon, the Washington Monument, and Mount

Rushmore.   Pass around a quarter, a dollar bill, and a five-cent George Washington postage stamp.   Remember to let the children wear their three-cornered hats.

Book

Read <u>Let's Go to Mount Vernon</u> by Mary Jo Borreson.

Film

Show a film of George Washington's life.

George Washington Crossword Puzzle

On the chalkboard, draw the George Washington Crossword Puzzle (see Patterns, Pictures, Etc., page 507).   Read the clues below.   Call on volunteers for the answers; then write in the words.

Across

1.   George (Washington) was our first President.
4.   George's first job was as a (surveyor).
7.   George's mother was named (Mary).
8.   George Washington's home was Mount (Vernon).
9.   Washington's face is on the (quarter).
10.   Washington is called the "(Father) of Our Country."
11.   The winter headquarters of Washington's army was Valley (Forge).
12.   George's wife was named (Martha).

Down

2.   In George's time, men wore three-cornered (hats).
3.   George cut down a (cherry) tree.
5.   George had (two) stepchildren.
6.   Washington led the forces in the (Revolutionary) War.
7.   The Washington (Monument) is over 555 feet tall.
10.   (Ferry) Farm was George Washington's home as a child.
13.   George Washington was an aide in the (French) and Indian War.

"To Tell the Truth" Game

Make two copies of the "To Tell the Truth" questions and the three "Contestant" sheets (see Patterns, Pictures, Etc., pages 508-511).   Make a copy of the "Score Sheet" (page 512) for each student (optional).   If your students cannot read well, "borrow" three older students for the contestants.   Set up a table and three chairs for the contestants.   Fold three index cards in half; label with the numbers 1, 2, and 3; and set them on the table at each contestant's place.   Give each contestant a construction paper three-cornered hat (see Art, Day 1) to wear and the contestant sheets. Cut apart the questions and distribute to the students. Keep a copy of the question sheet and the contestants sheets for yourself.

Explain the game to the contestants and then to the students. The three contestants will each profess to be George Washington. When a student asks a particular question, such as #3, the contestants will each read the prepared answer for #3. For each question, Number 1 contestant will answer first; Number 2 will answer second; and Number 3 will answer last.

After the students vote for their choice, the contestants follow the directions at the bottom of their sheets. The students will be questioning the three contestants to see who is the real George Washington. When the teacher calls a question number, the student with that number reads the question. (If the students cannot read, read the questions to them beforehand to memorize. Prompt if necessary.) They may use the score sheets to put a check for correct responses and an X for incorrect responses.

At the end of the questioning, ask the students to vote (one time only) for their choice of "The Real George Washington." Tally the votes on the board; then say, "Will the real George Washington please stand up?"

George Washington Booklet

Distribute the front covers and accumulated sheets. Assemble the booklets using a piece of construction paper for the back cover. Staple together on the left side.

ART

Big Quarter

Preparation - Duplicate and distribute the sheet (page 513). Cut 8" x 11" pieces of poster paper or tagboard. Tear pieces of aluminum foil 6" x 12". Give each child the sheet, the poster paper, and the aluminum foil. Set out scissors, glue, cotton swabs, toothpicks, and pencils.

Procedure - Glue the sheet to the poster paper or tagboard. Let it dry. Cut out the circle and George Washington's face. Glue George Washington in the center of the circle under the word "liberty" and above the date. Partially open the top of the glue. Use the glue to outline the letters of the word "liberty" and the numbers of the date. Try to keep a steady flow of glue. Use a cotton swab to correct mistakes.

After the glue has dried thoroughly, cover the "quarter" with aluminum foil (shiny side out). Fold the foil in half and slip the "quarter" in between the layers; then fold the foil around and behind the edges of the "quarter." Gently smooth and mold the foil around George Washington's face. Also, use a pencil or toothpick to gently outline the lettters and numbers so that they "stand out."

George Washington's Birthday Parade Streamers and Signs

<u>Preparation</u> - For the streamers, purchase rolls of red, white, and blue crepe paper. Cut into pieces measuring 3'. Give each child three pieces of crepe paper (one of each color) and a large rubber band. Have a stapler available.

For the signs, cut tagboard into 15" squares. Give each child a square, a stick used for stirring paint, a sheet of scratch paper, and a pencil. Set out strong glue and markers.

<u>Procedure</u> - For the parade streamers, pull the ends of the streamers through the rubber band. Work the rubber band to the middle of the streamers. Gather the six halves in one hand with the rubber band on top and staple together.

For the signs, use the scratch paper to practice a design in honor of George Washington's birthday. Use the markers to write and decorate the sign on the tagboard squares. Use a generous amount of glue to attach the stick to the back of the sign. Dry. Staple crepe paper streamers in the corners of the sign if desired. (See examples, page 514.)

MATH

Coded Message

Duplicate the sheet (page 515). Tell the class, "During times of war, secret messages are sent in code so that the enemy cannot understand them. On the sheet is a make-believe secret message which George Washington sent during the war." Distribute the sheet and explain the code. The message can be decoded as a group or as an individual activity. Assist when necessary. (Correct answer - "We will soon surprise-attack the British. We will win the war.")

MUSIC - MOVEMENT - GAMES

Birthday Party for George Washington

Celebrate George Washington's birthday with a party. The following are suggested activities:

Birthday Cake

Cherry Chip cake mix
1 can cherry pie filling

Mix the cake as directed. Pour into a 9" x 12" cake pan. Pour the cherry pie filling on top. Bake at 350° for 30 minutes. Cool. Put birthday candles on the cake.

Graham Cracker Flags

Graham crackers
Ready-to-spread white frosting
Cans of decorator frosting (push-nozzle) - red, white, and blue
Plastic knives

Spread the white frosting on the graham crackers with the plastic knives. Use the decorator frosting to create any of the United States flags covered in the unit.

Song - "Happy Birthday George Washington"

Light the candles on the cake and sing "Happy Birthday" to George Washington. Serve the cake with vanilla ice cream (a favorite of George Washington's) and cherry Kool-Aid. Eat the Graham Cracker Flags too!

Game - Pin the Star on the Flag

Make an American flag (see Language Arts - Social Studies - Science, U.S. Flags - Transparency Activity, Flags Sheet, Day 3) on poster paper omitting the star of your state (see list below). Draw an X where the star should be. Tack the flag to a bulletin board or piece of corrugated cardboard. Make a paper star for each child. Have stick pins nearby. Give a star to a child, blindfold him or her, and let him or her place the star on the flag. Stick-pin the star wherever the child places it. Repeat with each child. The child closest to the X wins. A nice prize is a small American flag.

STATES IN ORDER OF ADMISSION TO THE UNION

1.	Delaware	21.	Illinois
2.	Pennsylvania	22.	Alabama
3.	New Jersey	23.	Maine
4.	Georgia	24.	Missouri
5.	Connecticut	25.	Arkansas
6.	Massachusetts	26.	Michigan
7.	Maryland	27.	Florida
8.	South Carolina	28.	Texas
9.	New Hampshire	29.	Iowa
10.	Virginia	30.	Wisconsin
11.	New York	31.	California
12.	North Carolina	32.	Minnesota
13.	Rhode Island	33.	Oregon
14.	Vermont	34.	Kansas
15.	Kentucky	35.	West Virginia
16.	Tennessee	36.	Nevada
17.	Ohio	37.	Nebraska
18.	Louisiana	38.	Colorado
19.	Indiana	*39.	North Dakota
20.	Mississippi	*40.	South Dakota

41.	Montana	46.	Oklahoma
42.	Washington	47.	New Mexico
43.	Idaho	48.	Arizona
44.	Wyoming	49.	Alaska
45.	Utah	50.	Hawaii

*Both North Dakota and South Dakota were admitted at the same time.

Cherry Drop - Purchase cranberries. Position a large wide-mouthed jar on the floor. Each child gets five chances to drop a mock cherry (cranberry) into the jar from waist level. The child who gets the most cherries in the jar wins. In case of a tie, have additional turns. A nice prize is a shiny George Washington quarter.

Sing-Along - Sing the songs learned in the unit.

STORY TIME - Read An American ABC by Maud and Miska Petersham. Go back through the book. Read the alphabet letters, show the pictures, and let the children supply the alphabet word and information.

George Washington's Birthday Parade - In honor of George Washington's birthday, obtain permission to have a parade through the school and around the grounds. The children can wear their three-cornered hats and wave their streamers. Have some children play rhythm instruments and others hold the parade signs. March and sing "Yankee Doodle" and other songs learned in the unit.

CONCEPT EVALUATION

Dear Parents,

On _____, our class will begin a unit on George Washington. We will learn about his childhood, his roles in the French and Indian War and the Revolutionary War, and his role as first President of the United States. The lessons and activities each day will center around these topics. Below are ways you can help.

Things To Send: _____

_____

_____

Volunteers Needed To: _____

_____

_____

Follow-Up: At the end of the unit, ask your child to share the following fingerplays, songs, or poems we have learned:

_____

_____

_____

Thank you for your cooperation.

Sincerely,

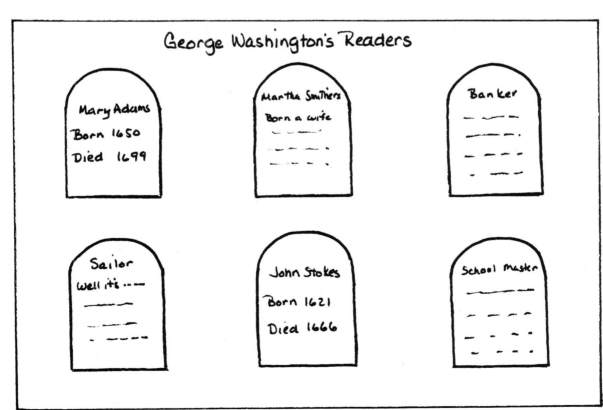

FOR A LITTLE PUPIL

Napoleon was great, I know,
And Julius Caesar, and all the rest,
But they didn't belong to us, and so
I like George Washington the best.

Tombstone Sheet

Name _____

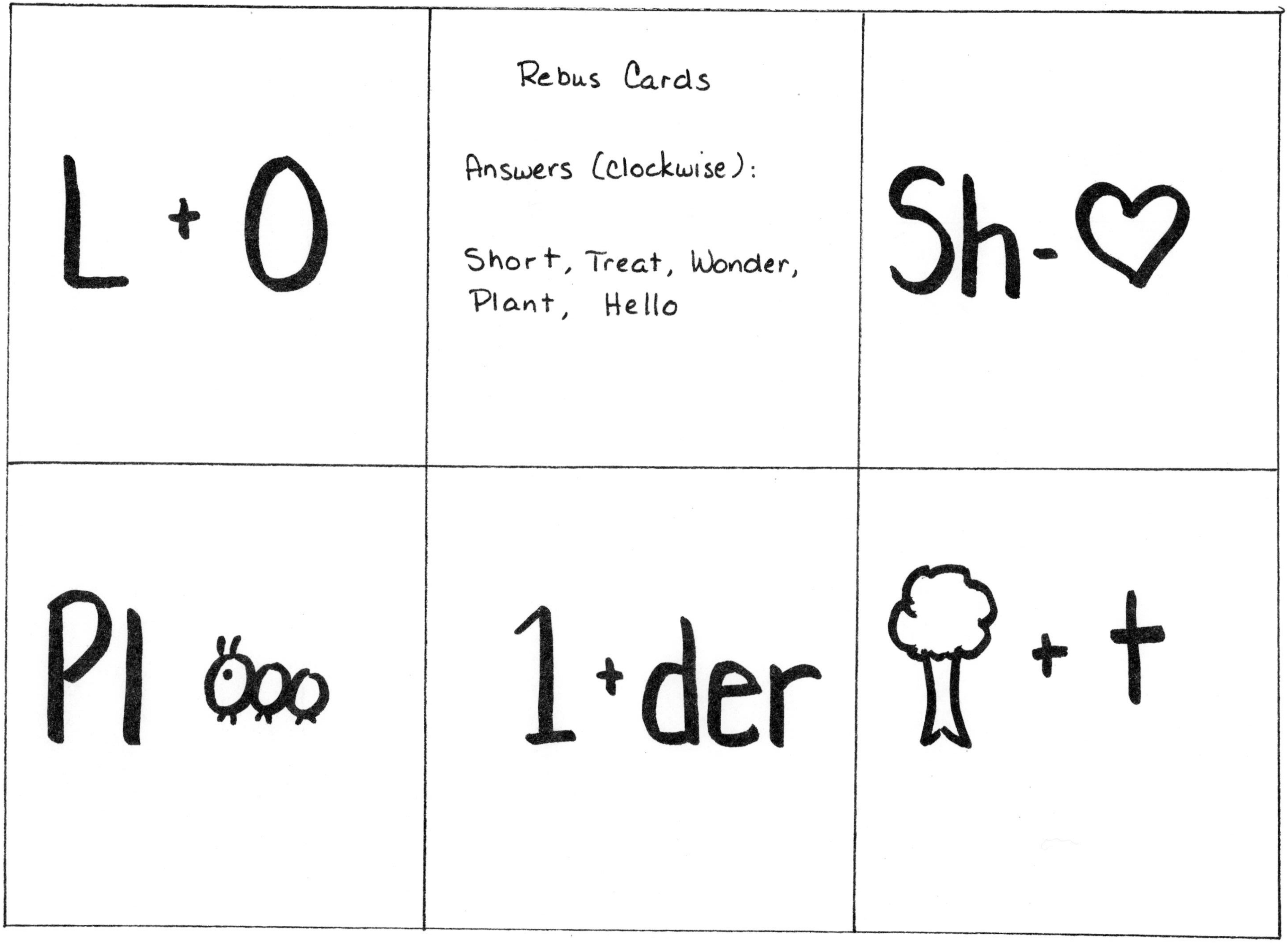

Sh-♡

+ + +

Rebus Cards

Answers (clockwise):

Short, Treat, Wonder, Plant, Hello

1 + der

L + O

Pl

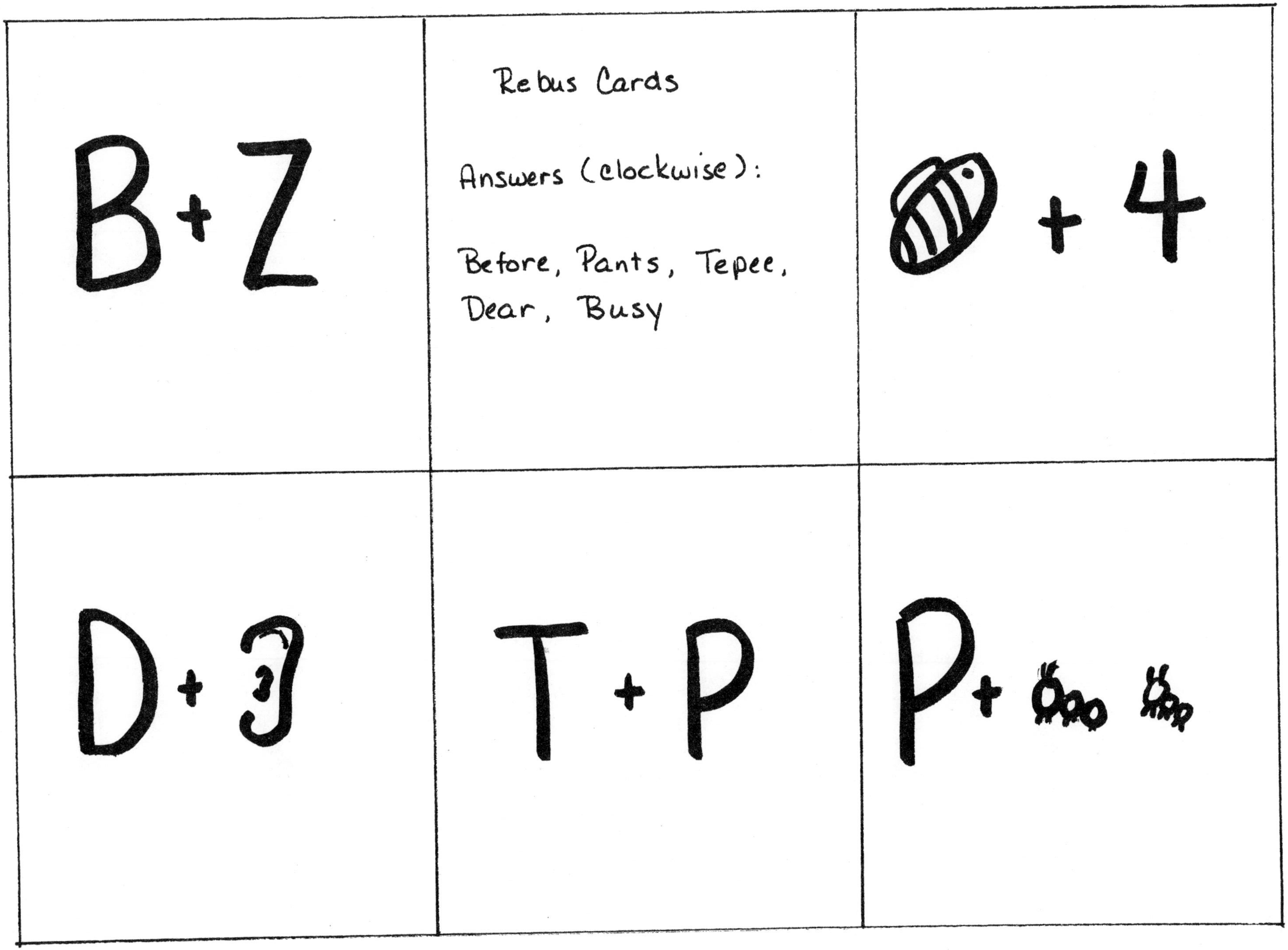

Bee + 4

P + ants

Rebus Cards

Answers (clockwise):

Before, Pants, Tepee,
Dear, Busy

T + P

B + Z

D + 3

L +

cy

Rebus Cards

Answers (clockwise):

Lie, Fancy, Stop, Beware, Dizzy

S +

D + Z

ware

E + Z

2 + L

Rebus Cards

Answers (clockwise):

Easy, Tool, Nosy, Penny, Indian

2 + 7

N+D+N

Yu + 7

3-Cornered Hats-
Pattern

Duplicate 3 for
each child.

Example

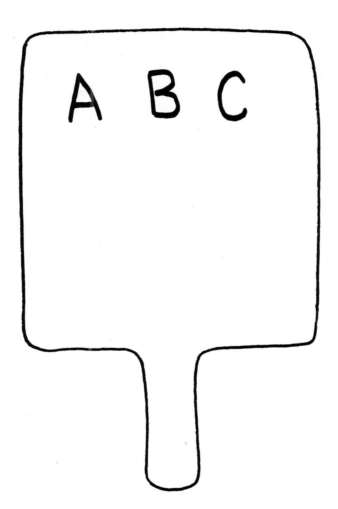

Bread Dough Hornbooks

George Helps · Counting Sheet

George helped in the shops on his father's plantation.

He made ___ horseshoes.

He made ___ barrels.

He made ___ cookies.

He made ___ candles.

Name _____

Cherry Tree
Legend. Puppets

George Goes Fishing

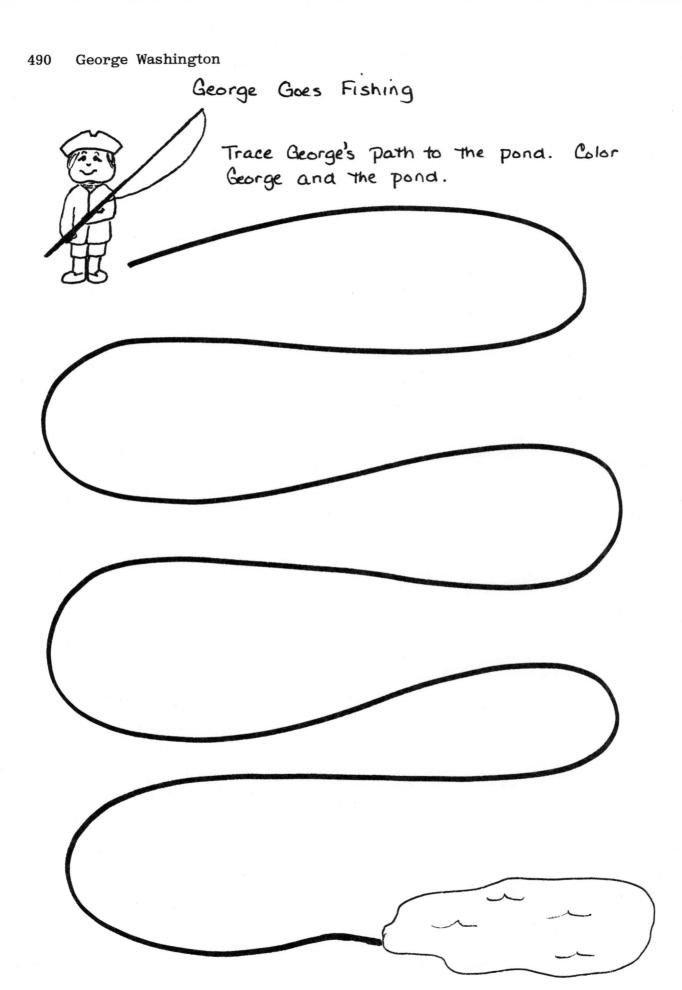

Trace George's path to the pond. Color George and the pond.

FINGERPLAY - "CHOP, CHOP, CHOP"

Chop, chop, chop went George's hatchet. (Chopping motion)

Crunch, crunch, plunk went the tree. (Hold arm upright, make it slowly fall)

"Who, who, who?" asked his father. (Outstretched arms, palms up)

The truth, truth, truth? - It was me! (Motion both thumbs toward chest)

George and the Cherry Tree

George's Hatchet

Pattern - hatchet blade

pattern - leaf cluster

pattern - Cherry

Example

Cherry Pies - Pie Crust

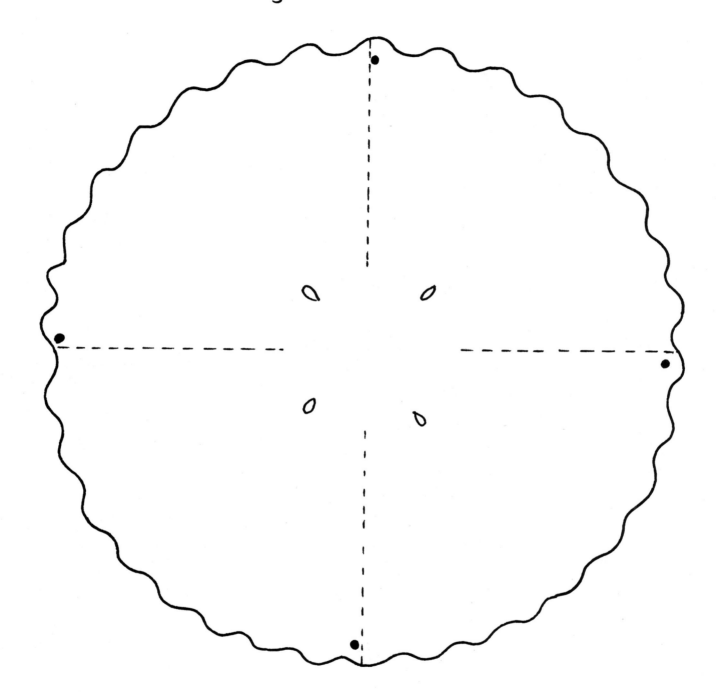

Cherry Pies - Pie

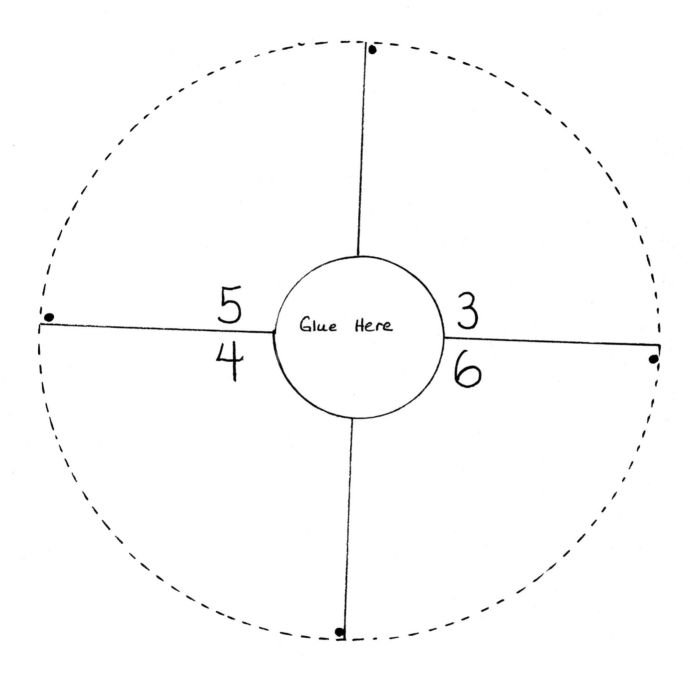

"MR. WASHINGTON'S SAD SONG"

Tune: "Yankee Doodle"

In the days of old, George Washington
Went out one day to play,
Chopped down his father's cherry tree.
At least that's what they say.
Georgie was a naughty boy with his little hatchet;
And for such a naughty deed, he should really catch it!

When George's father saw the tree,
He nearly blew his top.
Said he, "We'll have no more of this,
It's simply got to stop!
Who'd destroy a lovely tree, I cannot understand it.
He'll be made to pay for this, that despicable bandit!"

When Georgie heard his father there,
It made him very sad.
Said he, "I cannot tell a lie,
I'm guilty, dear old Dad!
I cut down your cherry tree with my little hatchet,
I must tell the truth to you, even though I catch it."

But Georgie's father smiled and said,
"You've filled my life with joy.
I cannot mourn a cherry tree
When I have an honest boy."
Georgie was a good boy with his little hatchet.
He told his dad the truth and so—he really didn't catch it!

— Courtesy of the Boy Scouts of America

Flags Sheet

Circle the Betsy Ross Flag in red. Underline the Grand Union Flag in green. Circle The Second Stars and Stripes in blue. Underline the current flag in orange. Color all of the flags.

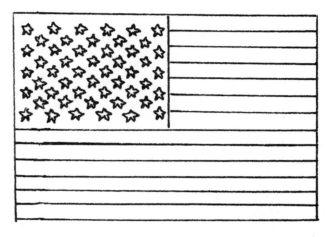

I'm Crossing the Delaware
(Gameboard)

Bank

Bank

Bank

Bank

George Washington

Examples

Cherry Tree - Booklet
Cover

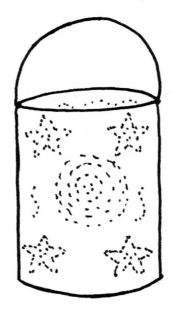

Tin Lantern

Fingerprint Cherry Trees

7

10

9

8

Name:

"YANKEE DOODLE"

Father and I went down to camp,

Along with Cap'n Gooding

And there we saw the men and boys,

As thick as hasty pudding.

Chorus:

Yankee Doodle keep it up

Yankee Doodle Dandy

Mind the music and the step

And with the girls be handy.

Verse 2:   Substitute "Da" for the
words and clap out the
rhythm.

Verse 3: Repeat first verse.

George Washington's Life
Stand-Up Sequence
Card

George Washington - Silhouette

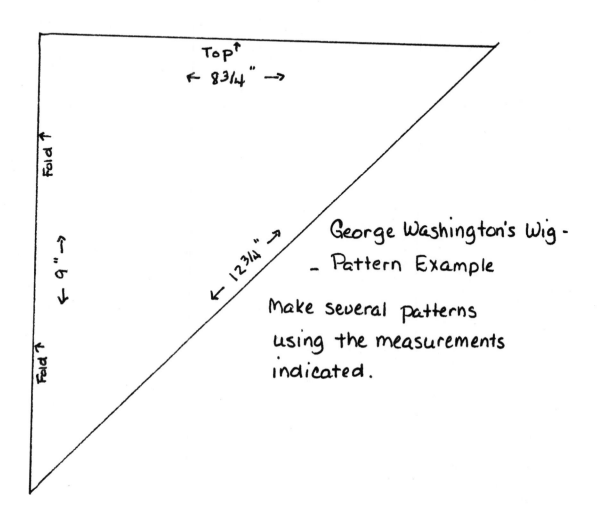

Pattern, Example

Top ↑
← 8 3/4" →

Fold ↑

← 9" →

Fold ↑

← 12 3/4" ↗

George Washington's Wig -
- Pattern Example

Make several patterns
using the measurements
indicated.

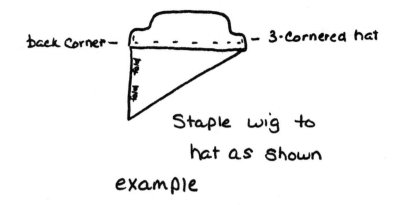

back corner — — 3-Cornered hat

Staple wig to
hat as shown

example

Martha Washington Goes Shopping name:

Martha Washington went shopping. Can you tell which item goes in which box? Draw lines to match the two.

George Washington Crossword Puzzle

"TO TELL THE TRUTH" - QUESTIONS

(MC) Contestant #1, please stand and tell us your name.
     Contestant #2, please stand and tell us your name.
     Contestant #3, please stand and tell us your name.

Now the student with Question #2 may begin questioning. Each contestant will answer the question (#1 first, then #2, and then #3)

2. George #1, #2, and #3, when were you born?

3. George #1, #2, and #3, where were you born?

4. George #1, #2, and #3, what were your parents' names?

5. George #1, #2, and #3, tell us about the first school that you attended.

6. George #1, #2, and #3, what did you do when you were 16?

7. George #1, #2, and #3, did your father build Mount Vernon?

8. George #1, #2, and #3, in the American Revolution, what did you do?

9. George #1, #2, and #3, what did you do after the war?

10. George #1, #2, and #3, did you want to become President?

11. George #1, #2, and #3, when you became President, where was the capital?

12. George #1, #2, and #3, how long were you the President of the United States?

13. George #1, #2, and #3, was your job as the first President difficult?

14. George #1, #2, and #3, how did you make decisions as President?

15. George #1, #2, and #3, what would you like people to remember about you?

GEORGE WASHINGTON #1 - CONTESTANT SHEET

Questions:

1. My name is George Washington.

2. I was born on February 22, 1732.

3. I was born in Virginia.

4. Mr. and Mrs. Washington

5. I had to go to Master Hobby's school. It was in a house by a church.

6. I learned to run my father's plantation.

7. Yes, he built it.

8. I was commander of all the armies. It was a very hard job.

9. I became the first President of the United States.

10. Yes, I thought I was the best man for the job.

11. It was in Boston—home of the Boston Tea Party.

12. I was President for four long years.

13. No, after fighting in the war, being President was easy.

14. I talked to Martha and she helped me decide what to do.

15. That I was handy with an ax.

*After the voting, I will say "Will the real George Washington please stand up?

Act like you about to stand up, but sit back down.

GEORGE WASHINGTON #2 - CONTESTANT SHEET

Questions:

1. My name is George Washington.

2. I was born in 1732 on February 22.

3. I was born in Virginia.

4. Mary and Augustine Washington

5. I went to Master Hobby's school. It was in a small house by a church. There was a graveyard next to it. We used the tombstones to do our lessons.

6. I had finished school, so I started surveying.

7. No, it was built by my brother, Lawrence.

8. I was commander of all the Virginia soldiers.

9. I went home to my family at Mount Vernon.

10. No, I wanted to live quietly at Mount Vernon.

11. It was in New York City, but it was soon moved to Philadelphia.

12. I was President for eight years.

13. Yes, it was hard because I had to decide how to make our new government work.

14. I thought a lot, talked to other people, and decided what would be best for our country.

15. I would like people to remember that I was honest and fair and tried to do my best.

*You are the real George Washington. After I ask the real George Washington to stand up, wait a minute and then stand up.

GEORGE WASHINGTON #3 - CONTESTANT SHEET

Questions:

1. My name is George Washington

2. I was born on February 22, 1732.

3. Virginia - I was born in Virginia.

4. My parents were named Mary and Augustine.

5. I went to Master Hobby's school. It was all in one room near a church. It wasn't too much fun.

6. I helped my brother run his plantation.

7. No, it was my brother Samuel's house.

8. I was commander of all the soldiers from Kentucky. It was an important job.

9. I began surveying again.

10. No, I wanted to take Martha and the kids to Paris.

11. It was in Washington - a city named for me.

12. I was President for six years. I was too tired to serve any more.

13. Yes, it was hard because Martha had to learn how to be First Lady.

14. When I really couldn't decide something, I flipped a coin.

15. I would like them to remember that Washington, D.C., is named after me.

*After I announce "Will the real George Washington please stand up?" act like you are standing up, then sit down, then rise again, then sit down.

"TO TELL THE TRUTH" - SCORE SHEET

	GEORGE 1	GEORGE 2	GEORGE 3
1.			
2.			
3.			
4.			
5.			
6.			
7.			
8.			
9.			
10.			
11.			
12.			
13.			
14.			
15.			

Big Quarter

Examples
George Washington's Birthday

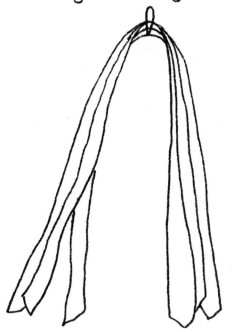

Parade Streamers· Example

Happy Birthday George!

Parade Sign - example

Coded Message

23 5   23 9 12 12   19 15 15 14   19 21 18 16 18 9 19 5

1 20 20 1 3 11   20 8 5   2 18 9 20 9 19 8 .

23 5   23 9 12 12   23 9 14   20 8 5

23 1 18 .

A - 1		N - 14
B - 2		O - 15
C - 3		P - 16
D - 4		Q - 17
E - 5		R - 18
F - 6		S - 19
G - 7		T - 20
H - 8		U - 21
I - 9		V - 22
J - 10		W - 23
K - 11		X - 24
L - 12		Y - 25
M - 13		Z - 26

BIBLIOGRAPHY

Barth, Edna, Hearts, Cupids and Red Roses, New York, Clarion Books, Ticknor & Fields: A Houghton Mifflin Co., 1974.

Barth, Edna, Holly, Reindeer, and Colored Lights, New York, Seabury Press, 1971.

Bleeker, Sonia, The Eskimo, New York, William Morrow & Co., 1959.

Blough, Glenn O., Christmas Trees and How They Grow, New York, Toronto, London, Whittlesey House, a division of McGraw Hill Book Co., 1961.

Borreson, Mary Jo, Let's Go to Mount Vernon, New York, G. P. Putnam's Sons, 1962.

Brandt, Sue R., Facts About the Fifty States, New York, London, Toronto, Franklin Watts, 1979.

Branley, Franklyn M., A Book of Stars For You, New York, Thomas Y. Crowell, 1967.

Branley, Franklyn M., Snow Is Falling, New York, Thomas Y. Crowell, 1963.

Brown, Fern G., Valentine's Day, New York, Toronto, London, Sydney, Franklin Watts, 1983.

Brown, Harriett M., and Joseph H. Guadagnolo, America Is My Country: The Heritage of a Free People, Boston, Houghton Mifflin Co., 1961.

Childcraft How and Why Library, Volumes 1-14, Chicago, Field Educational Enterprises Corp., 1976.

"Christmas," World Book Encyclopedia, Chicago, Field Educational Enterprises Corp., 1961.

Country Beautiful Magazine, Lincoln, His Word and His World, New York, Hawthorne Books, 1965.

Cuyler, Margery, The All Around Christmas Book, New York, Holt, Rinehart & Winston, 1982.

Dalgliesh, Alice, Christmas, New York, Charles Scribner's Sons, 1934.

d'Aulaire, Ingri and Edgar Parin, <u>Abraham Lincoln</u>, Garden City, New York, Doubleday & Co., Inc., 1957.

d'Aulaire, Ingri and Edgar Parin, <u>George Washington</u>, Garden City, New York, Doubleday & Co., Inc., 1936.

Debham, Betty, "Rally 'Round the Teddy," <u>The Mini Page</u>, Fairway, Kansas, Universal Press Syndicate, May 14, 1983.

Eggenberger, David, <u>Flags of the U.S.A.</u>, New York, Thomas Y. Crowell, 1959.

Harris, Jacqueline L., <u>Martin Luther King, Jr.</u>, New York, London, Toronto, Sydney, Franklin Watts, 1983.

Judson, Clara Ingram, <u>George Washington</u>, Chicago, New York, Follett Publishing Co., 1961.

Kessel, Joyce K., <u>Valentine's Day</u>, Minneapolis, Minnesota, Carolrhoda Books, 1981.

Lorant, Stefan, <u>Lincoln - A Picture Story of His Life</u>, New York, W. W. Norton & Co., 1952.

McKissack, Patrick, <u>Martin Luther King, Jr., A Man to Remember</u>, Chicago, Children's Press, 1984.

McNeer, May, <u>America's Abraham Lincoln</u>, Boston, Houghton Mifflin Co., 1957.

Meyer, Carolyn, <u>Lots and Lots of Candy</u>, New York, London, Harcourt, Brace, Jovanovich, 1976.

Miers, Earl Schenck, <u>That Lincoln Boy</u>, Cleveland and New York, The World Publishing Co., 1968.

Miller, Natalie, <u>The Story of the Lincoln Memorial</u>, Chicago, Children's Press, 1966.

Norman, Gertrude, <u>A Boy Named Washington</u>, New York, G. P. Putnam's Sons, 1960.

Patterson, Lilli, <u>Christmas in America</u>, Champaign Illinois, Garrard Publishing Co., 1969.

Patterson, Lilli, <u>Christmas Feasts and Festivals</u>, Champaign, Illinois, Garrard Publishing Co., 1968.

Rey, H. A., <u>The Stars</u>, Boston, Houghton Mifflin Co., 1952.

Rockland, Mae Shaftner, <u>The Hanukkah Book</u>, New York, Schocken Books, 1975.

518

Russel, Solveig Paulson, <u>Peanuts, Popcorn, Ice Cream, Candy & Soda Pop and How They Began</u>, Nashville, New York, Abbington Press, 1970.

Sandburg, Carl, <u>Abe Lincoln Grows Up</u>, New York, Harcourt, Brace & Co., 1956.

Sechrist, Elizabeth Hough and Janette Woolsey, <u>It's Time for Christmas</u>, Philadelphia, Macrae Smith Co., 1959.

Simon, Norma, <u>Hanukkah</u>, New York, Thomas Y. Crowell Co., 1966.

Stevenson, Augusta, <u>George Washington, Boy Leader</u>, New York, Bobbs-Merrill, Co., Inc., 1942.

Tudor, Tasha, <u>Take Joy</u>, New York, World Publishing Co., 1966.

Weems, Mason L., <u>The Life of Washington</u>, Cambridge, Massachusetts, The Belknap Press of Harvard University, 1962.

Zappler, Georg and Lisbeth, <u>Science in Winter and Spring</u>, Garden City, New York, Doubleday & Co., Inc., 1974.